PIPE FITTINGS

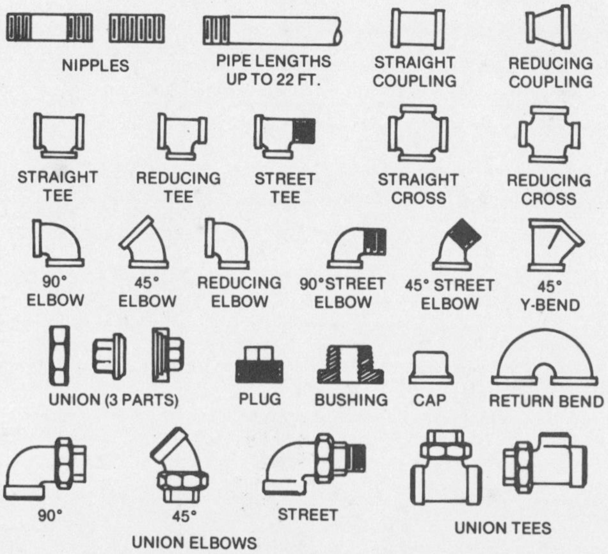

Here are the common steel pipe fittings. Nipples are simply short lengths of pipe threaded on both ends. Reducing fittings join two different sizes of pipe.

Compression fittings of the flared-tube type are the easiest for the novice to handle when working with copper tubing.

AF785014

STANDARD STEEL PIPE
(All Dimensions in Inches)

Nominal Size	Outside Diameter	Inside Diameter	Nominal Size	Outside Diameter	Inside Diameter
1/8	0.405	0.269	1	1.315	1.049
1/4	0.540	0.364	1 1/4	1.660	1.380
3/8	0.675	0.493	1 1/2	1.900	1.610
1/2	0.840	0.622	2	2.375	2.067
3/4	1.050	0.824	2 1/2	2.875	2.469

SQUARE MEASURE

144 sq in = 1 sq ft
9 sq ft = 1 sq yd
272.25 sq ft = 1 sq rod
160 sq rods = 1 acre

VOLUME MEASURE

1728 cu in = 1 cu ft
27 cu ft = 1 cu yd

MEASURES OF CAPACITY

1 cup = 8 fl oz
2 cups = 1 pint
2 pints = 1 quart
4 quarts = 1 gallon
2 gallons = 1 peck
4 pecks = 1 bushel

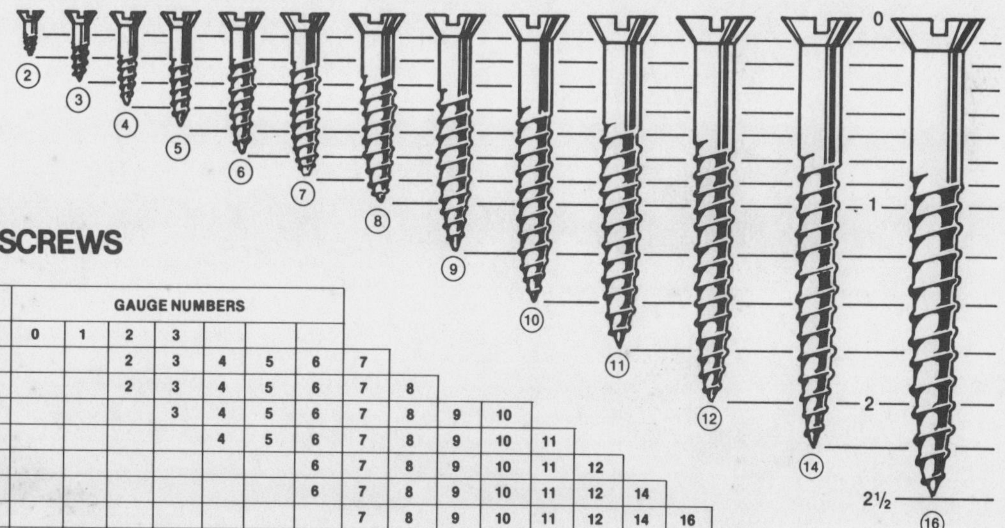

WOOD SCREWS

LENGTH	GAUGE NUMBERS																
1/4 INCH	0	1	2	3													
3/8 INCH			2	3	4	5	6	7									
1/2 INCH			2	3	4	5	6	7	8								
5/8 INCH				3	4	5	6	7	8	9	10						
3/4 INCH					4	5	6	7	8	9	10	11					
7/8 INCH							6	7	8	9	10	11	12				
1 INCH							6	7	8	9	10	11	12	14			
1 1/4 INCH								7	8	9	10	11	12	14	16		
1 1/2 INCH							6	7	8	9	10	11	12	14	16	18	
1 3/4 INCH									8	9	10	11	12	14	16	18	20
2 INCH									8	9	10	11	12	14	16	18	20
2 1/4 INCH										9	10	11	12	14	16	18	20
2 1/2 INCH													12	14	16	18	20
2 3/4 INCH														14	16	18	20
3 INCH															16	18	20
3 1/2 INCH																18	20	24
4 INCH																18	20	24

WHEN YOU BUY SCREWS, SPECIFY (1) LENGTH, (2) GAUGE NUMBER, (3) TYPE OF HEAD—FLAT, ROUND, OR OVAL, (4) MATERIAL—STEEL, BRASS, BRONZE, ETC., (5) FINISH—BRIGHT, STEEL BLUED, CADMIUM, NICKEL, OR CHROMIUM PLATED.

HOW WOULD YOU LIKE to work in this shop? It's a magnificent one, and laid out for maximum utility and convenience. You can improve your shop layout, too. See the tips on page 3142.

In this volume . . .

HERE'S ANOTHER SHOP that's a masterpiece; study it for ideas. And on page 3142 you'll find tips that will help carry out those ideas.

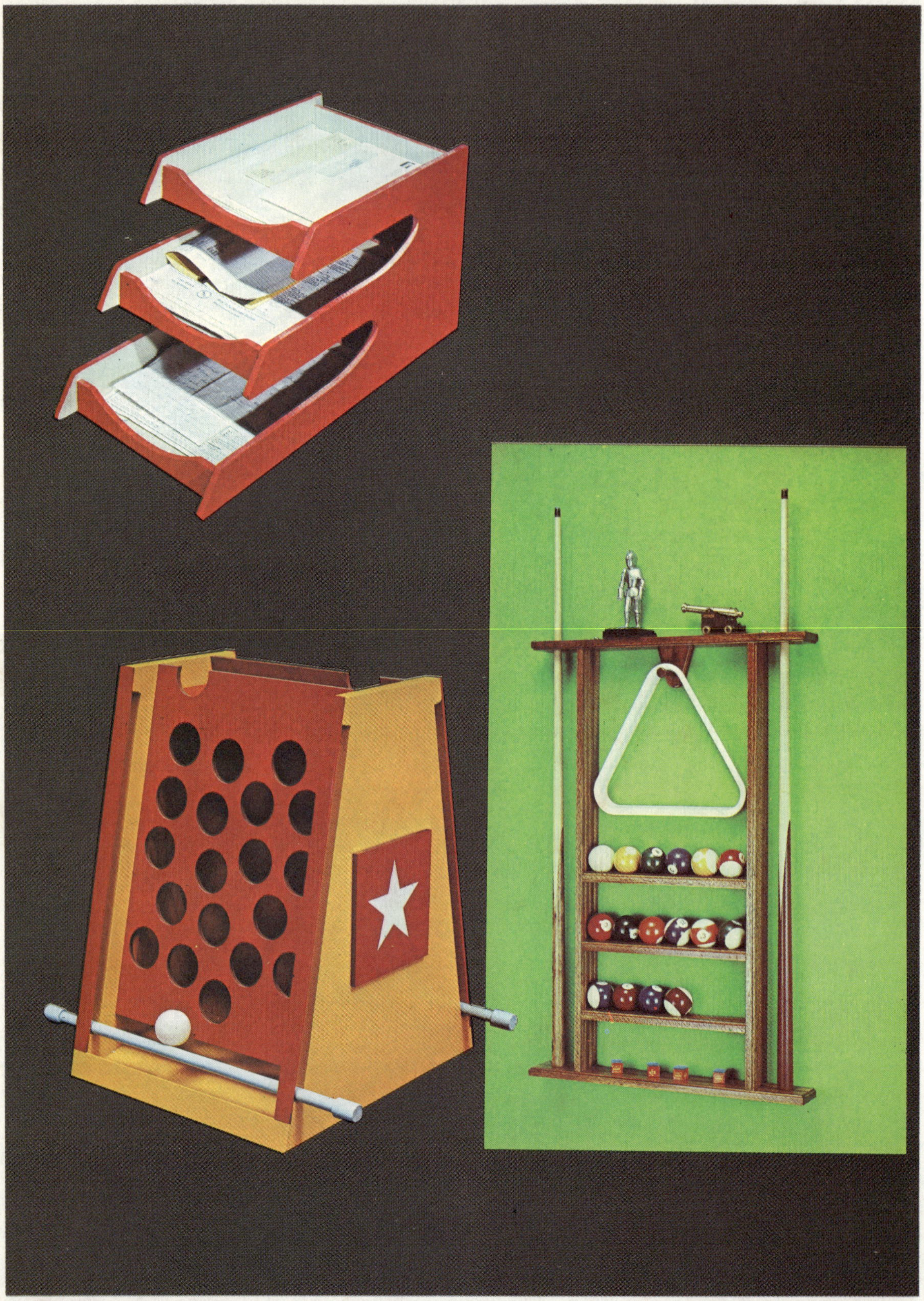

THESE THREE PROJECTS are neatly designed, fun to make, and you can finish them in a few hours—a mail organizer, a "Swiss cheese" game, and a cue-and-ball rack. For plans, see page 3062.

IT'S A GREAT YEAR for choosing wine—and also choosing a wine rack. Select from the three shown here. They're all attractive and easy to make. They include a countertop rack (above), a wall-mounted rack (left), and a plexiglas beauty. See page 3070 for the plans.

TRANSFORM YOUR YARD into a night-blooming beauty! You'll find the latest in fixtures and techniques on page 3144. Learn to spotlight special features, illuminate pools and steps.

Popular Mechanics

do-it-yourself encyclopedia

in 20 volumes

a complete how-to guide for the homeowner, the hobbyist—
and anyone who enjoys working with mind and hands!

All about:

home maintenance
home-improvement projects
wall paneling
burglary and fire protection
furniture projects
finishing and refinishing furniture
outdoor living
home remodeling
solutions to home problems
challenging woodworking projects
hobbies and handicrafts
model making
weekend projects
workshop shortcuts and techniques
hand-tool skills
power-tool know-how
shop-made tools
car repairs
car maintenance
appliance repair
boating
hunting
fishing
camping
photography projects
radio, TV and electronics know-how
clever hints and tips
projects just for fun

volume 20

ISBN 0-87851-085-0
Library of Congress Catalog Number 77 84920

© 1982 THE HEARST CORPORATION

All rights reserved. No part of this book may be reproduced or used in any form or by any means—graphic, electronic, or mechanical, including photocopying, recording, taping or information storage and retrieval systems—without written permission of the publishers.

The Hearst Corporation cannot assume responsibility for proper application of techniques, implementations or proper and safe functioning of any of the manufactured or reader-built items, products or projects resulting in whole or in part from all or any part of any plans, prints, projects or instructional materials published in this volume.

The Hearst Corporation cannot assume responsibility for the continuing availability of any special parts listed in articles in this volume.

MANUFACTURED IN THE UNITED STATES OF AMERICA

contents

VOLUME 20

VENEERING
Veneering: beautiful wood on a budget 3044

WALL TILE
Backup board for ceramic tile 3049

WALLPAPER
How to hang wallpaper 3052

WASHING MACHINES
How to fix an automatic washer 3056

WEATHER INSTRUMENTS
Build a colonial weather station 3060

WEEKEND PROJECTS
Little projects that take little time 3062
Fun projects 3066

WINDOWS
How to replace a broken window pane 3068

WINE RACKS
Take your choice—three novel wine racks 3070

WINTERIZING, AUTOS
How to protect your car against the cold 3074

WINTERIZING, HOMES
The 10 worst heat thieves in your home 3078

WIRING, ELECTRICAL
Protect your family from outdoor electric shock 3082

WOOD BENDING
How to put a bend in wood 3088

WOOD FINISHES
Fine finishes for furniture 3094

WOOD LATHES
Make a faceplate lathe from odds and ends 3100
Build a miniature tabletop lathe 3103

WOOD LATHE TECHNIQUES
How to use your wood lathe like an expert 3106

WOOD SCULPTURE
Interlocking wood sculpture—an ancient art 3118

WOODS
Working properties of common woods 3122

WORKBENCHES
The basic workbench 3124
Workbench fit for a pro 3126
Tailgate workbench 3131
Build a shop inside a bench 3132
Cabinet bench for a small shop 3138

WORKSHOPS
How to lay out your workshop 3142

YARD LIGHTING
Transform your yard with night lighting 3144
How to light a game area 3149

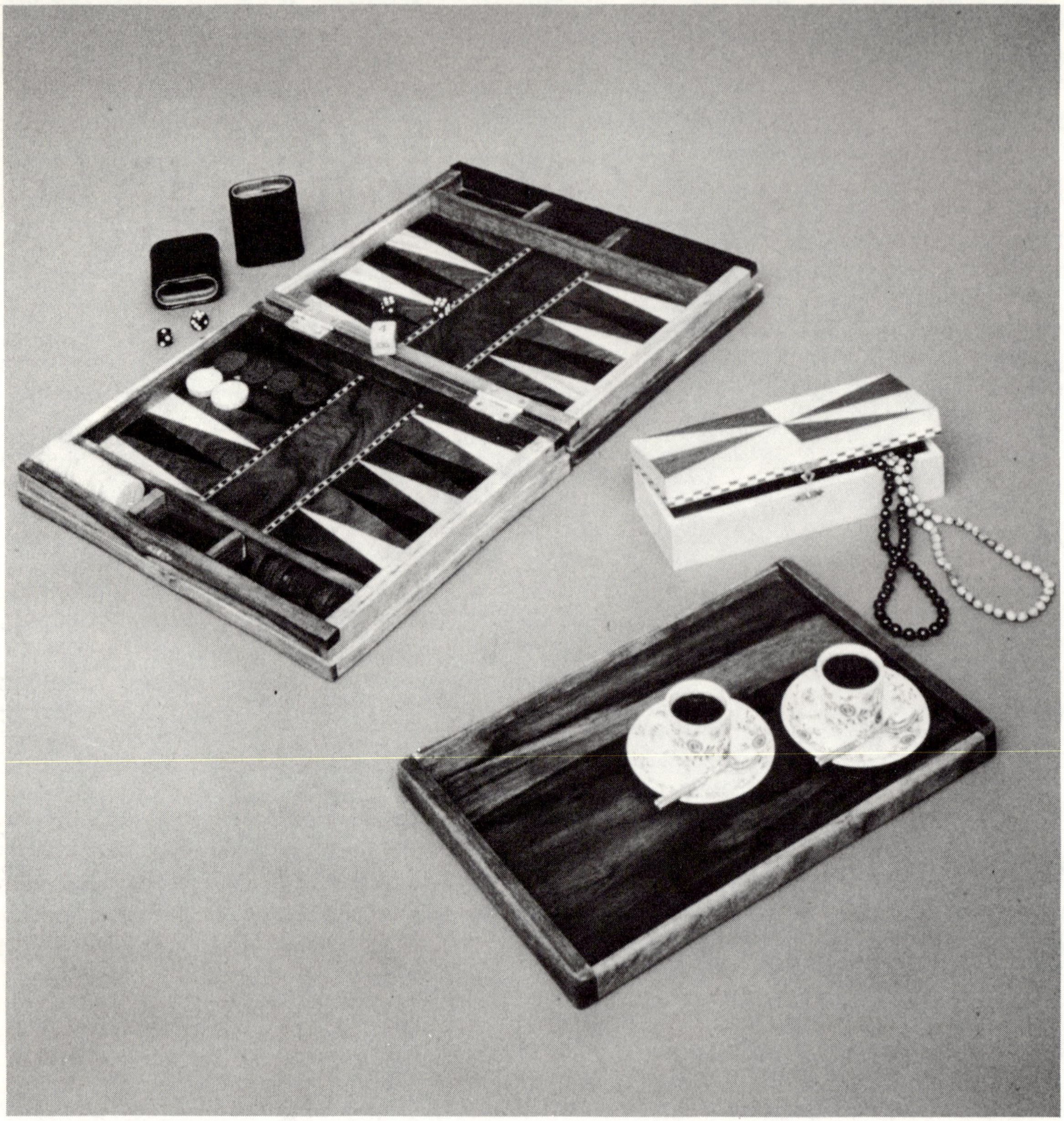

Veneering: beautiful wood on a budget

By PENELOPE ANGELL

■ YOU CAN BUILD the intriguing markings and the meandering grain patterns of exotic hardwoods into your projects once you know the secrets of veneering. These wafers of wood offer an inexpensive way to give unfinished furniture and humble surfaces the rich look of hardwood. Veneers can also counteract warpage when they're applied to both sides of a panel. Since you can select the veneer pieces that join together, you can create patterns in wood; for example, a book match design where two sides are mirror images from the center. You can also join four pieces of veneer so their grain forms a diamond shape. Veneers usually come in 1/28 to 1/36-in. thicknesses in sheets from 4 to 12-in. wide and 3 ft. or longer.

SEE ALSO

Abrasives . . . Adhesives . . . Finishes, wood . . . Jewelry boxes . . . Marquetry . . . Sanding . . . Staining, wood . . . Woods

TOP VENEER is glued to box with tape side up, using slip-sheet. Brown or wax paper between veneer and box is removed as veneer is positioned.

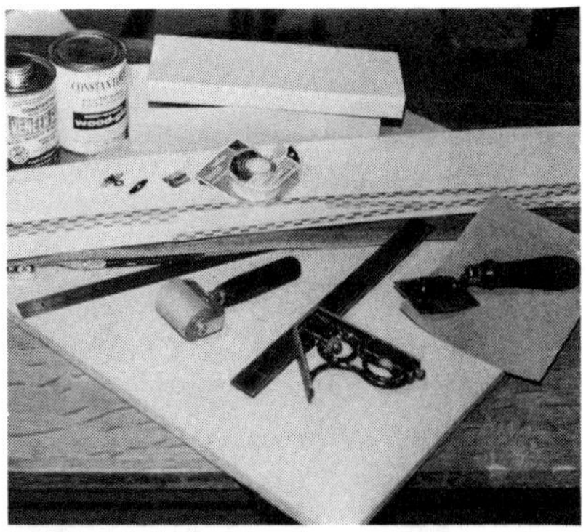

TOOLS YOU'LL need include a model knife equipped with fine blades; steel rule to cut against; a square; veneer roller; and a veneer saw.

TOP OF BOX is pressed down with a veneer roller immediately after veneer has been positioned to insure a secure bond over entire glued area.

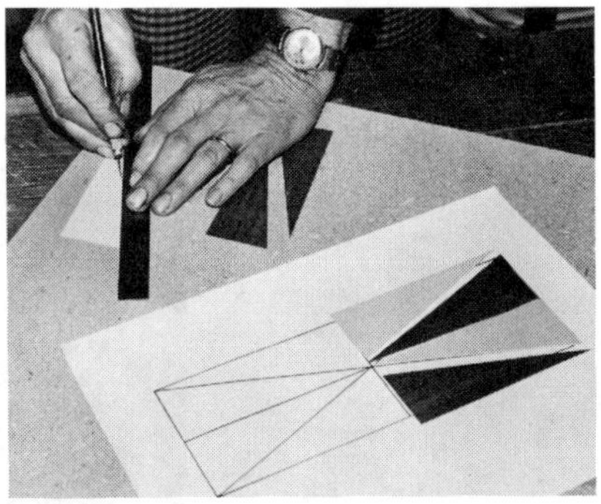

VENEERS FOR top design are cut to size with a model knife. Light veneer is aspen and dark is mahogany. Place pieces on pattern to check fit.

OVERHANGING VENEER is cut off with a veneer saw. Later it's sanded smooth. The extra overhang is added at the corners to insure a smooth edge.

■ WITH A LITTLE EFFORT and *not* much money you can turn an inexpensive basswood box from a craft shop into a unique and elegant box for jewelry or odds and ends by applying veneer. You can make the top design by cutting two light and two dark rectangles, halving them diagonally and joining the pieces together alternating wood types.

Materials include a box, light and dark veneer, fancy inlay border, hinges, lock, veneer tape, contact adhesive, No. 180 garnet paper and varnish or other finish. Begin by removing any hardware and tracing the box outline on paper—top, sides, front and back. Draw the design shown or one you've devised yourself. Cut the veneer sections for the top exactly to size with a model knife and tape them together.

Glue the assembled design (make sure joints are tight) to the box—taped side up—with contact adhesive. To assure proper veneer placement (you can't move it once it's down), put a sheet of brown wrapping paper or wax paper between the box top and the veneer, leaving a slight margin at the front. Align the front veneer and box edges, press the veneer in place, then gradually slip the sheet away. Then roll the veneer firmly and evenly.

Next mark and cut the veneer and border for the sides, lid and bottom, allowing an extra 1/16 in. to overhang at each corner. Tape the veneer and inlay together and glue them to the box using the slip-sheet method just described. Go over the veneer with a roller and trim the overhangs.

Mark, cut, tape and glue the front and back veneers in the same way, again allowing a 1/16-in. overhang that is trimmed off. To finish the box, first peel off your tape. A razor blade used carefully helps. Sand the surface smooth, then wipe it with a tack cloth and carefully apply a finish of your choice.

If you can't locate veneers or inlay borders in your area try Constantine, 2050 Eastchester Rd., Bronx, NY 10461; or Craftsman Wood Service, 1735 West Cortland Ct., Addison, IL 60101.

TRAY

JOINING VENEERS makes it possible to create patterns in the grain. Set up your patterns by joining veneer sections with short pieces of tape across the joint and add one long horizontal strip.

APPLY PLASTIC RESIN, such as Weldwood, with a thin-nap roller to be sure the glue is evenly applied over all the surface. Any area not covered may cause a bump. Work quickly after you apply the resin.

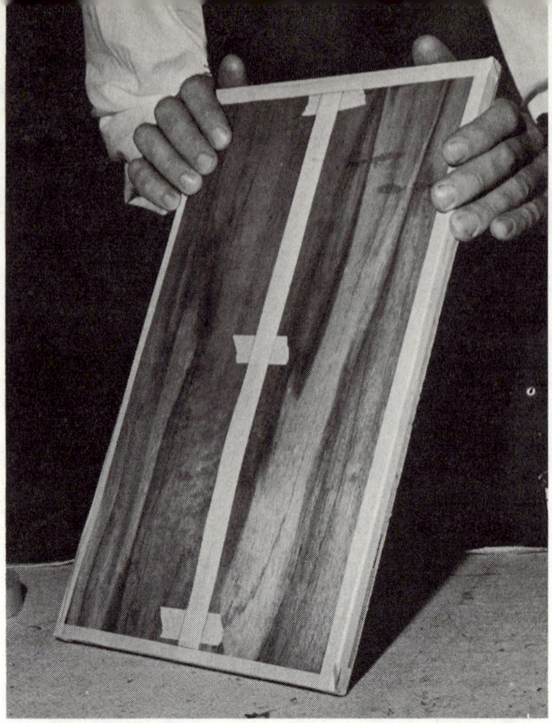

TOP AND BOTTOM veneer edges all have been taped to plywood and the tray is now ready for the press.

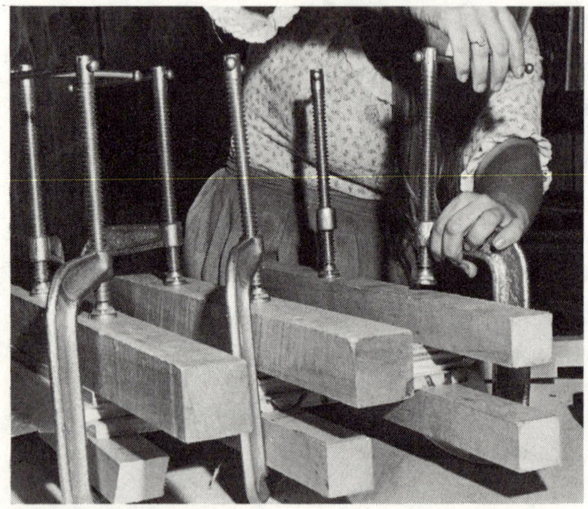

TO MAKE PRESS, use three hardwood 2x2s, birch plywood and wax paper on each side. Hold with C-clamps.

■ YOU CAN MAKE a striking grain design as on this tray top by using two pieces of veneer taped together. Materials you'll need are a piece of ½-in. plywood good on both sides for the core of the tray (10x15 in. or whatever size you wish), veneer for the tray top (we used African Bubinga) and tray bottom (a less expensive plain mahogany is fine here), ½x1¼-in. cherry or other wood edging strips to size; veneer tape and tung oil.

Tools and equipment needed include a model knife, metal straightedge, plastic resin or yellow glue, short-nap roller, file and sandpaper in grits from 60 to 400. Either glue requires a veneer press made by sandwiching the tray between wax paper, two sheets of plywood the same size as the tray and three 2x2s on either side. Six C-clamps hold the assembly together in a modified veneer press while the glue dries.

Begin by cutting the veneers for the tray top and bottom the same size as the plywood piece. Cut the veneer so its grain is at right angles to the top layer of plywood to help prevent warping. Tape veneers together with short crosspieces, then with one long vertical strip.

Next apply plastic resin evenly to the back of the veneer that goes on the tray top, facing the tape side up. Now work quickly until the tray is in the press. Place the veneer on the plywood and tape the edges. Glue and tape the tray bottom veneer.

Place the tray in the press with wax paper on each side and start applying pressure with the C-clamps, working from the middle out. After you've turned down all clamps part way, begin from the middle again and tighten them as much as possible. Wait about 12 hours; then remove the tray and peel off the tape. Align veneer and plywood edges.

Sand with the grain, clean, then rub on tung oil. Glue and press the long edging pieces to the tray with bar clamps. Then do the same to the short edgings, round the corners, sand and finish with tung oil.

BACKGAMMON BOARD

■ THIS BACKGAMMON board is made with four wood veneers and inlay banding. Materials you'll need are four pieces of ½x14x17-in. birch plywood good on two sides (two pieces each for the board and a press), wood strips to make the box and inner compartments, edging for plywood, two 3-in. butt hinges, a box catch, plastic resin or yellow glue, sandpaper from coarse to fine grit; masking tape and tung oil.

You need light and dark veneers for the playing triangles, another for the center of the board face and board back, a fourth for the inner compartments, plus inlay banding.

Tools needed are a plane, glue roller, table saw, sharp model knife, four bar clamps and a press. The veneer press, although larger, is used as it was in the preceding project. It's made of eight 2x2s, two plywood sheets, two layers of wax paper and eight C-clamps.

cutting and taping veneer

Mark the veneer layout for the face and back of the backgammon board on two pieces of plywood. Each side of the boards must be completely veneered to prevent warpage. *Be sure to set up a right and left-hand panel with alternating colored triangles.*

Make cardboard templates of the veneer triangles and draw outlines on the veneer. The latter may need trimming later, so make templates slightly larger than required. The jig shown can help you cut the veneer with a model knife. Use moderate pressure and make repeated passes over the veneer. To plane the veneer, brush it lightly with the grain across the plane's cutting edge.

Cut all veneer pieces. Inlay bands can be cut and taped now or glued later in a space cut and chipped out of the veneer after it's pressed.

You can begin taping the face pieces together with short crosspieces of tape pulled tightly. Then tape the joints lengthwise, covering the cross tapings. Tape the face veneers for both panels, then tape both back inlay and veneers.

Mix the plastic resin and smooth some on a plywood panel; then place the back veneer on the panel (tape side up) and tape edges. Place veneered side down in the press on wax paper; then glue and tape edges of the face veneer to top side of the panel. Cover with wax paper, plywood and the top 2x2s evenly spaced; then apply pressure with C-clamps.

After the proper glue-setting time has elapsed, remove the panel and repeat the process for the second panel. Remove the tape, sand the panels with the grain and oil lightly.

constructing the box

Cut the ¾x1¼-in. pieces and make lap joints. Glue them together; then clamp and glue them to faces of the panels using bar clamps and eight C-clamps as in the photo. Use wax paper and scrap wood between the board and clamps.

Cut, glue and clamp the edging to the plywood panels, make the box compartments and hinge the box parts together. Sand, chip away any excess glue and lightly oil the box.

You can get a catalog of playing pieces like those shown from Backgammon Headquarters, 669 Madison Ave., New York, NY 10021.

veneering, continued

BACKGAMMON BOARD

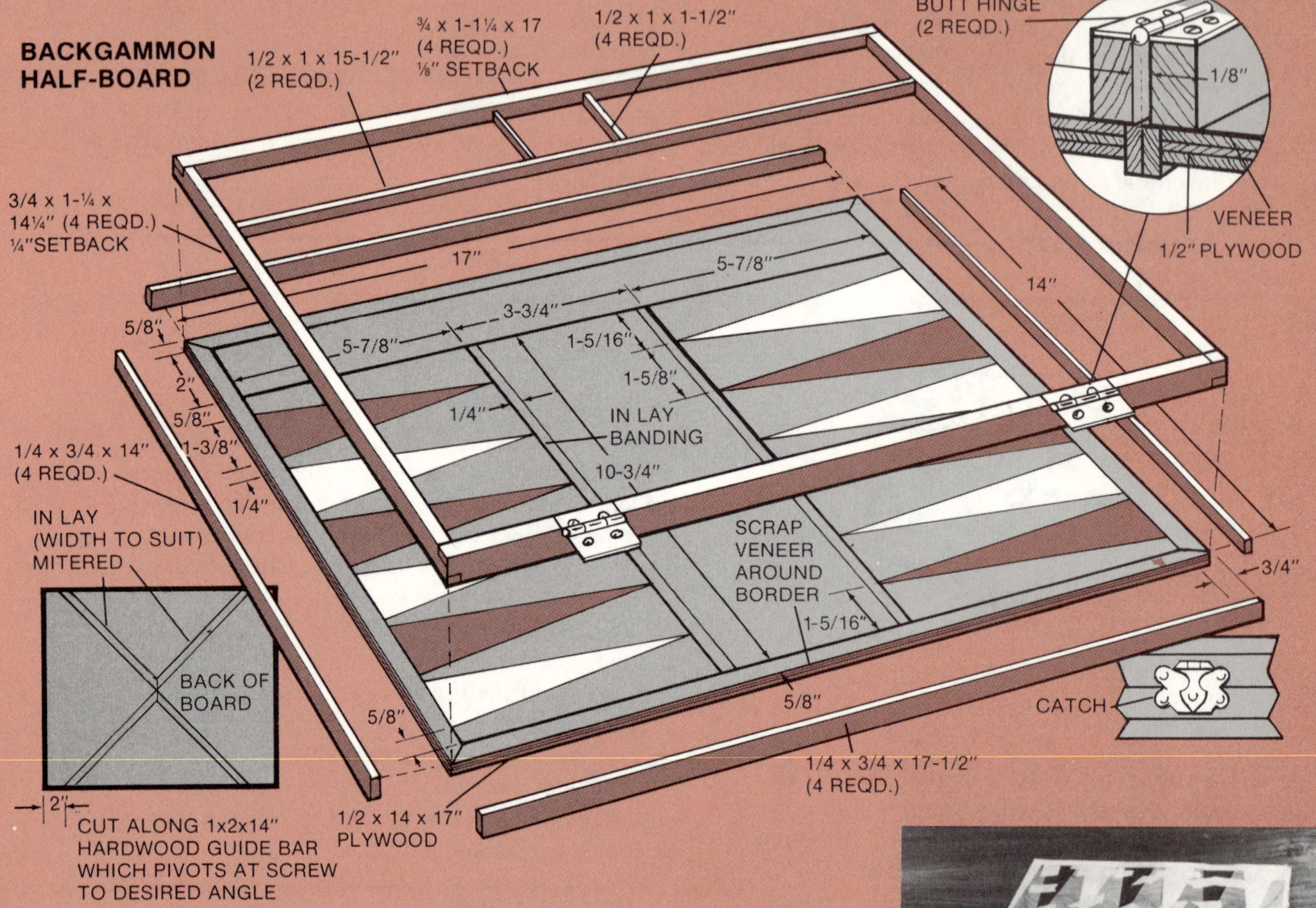

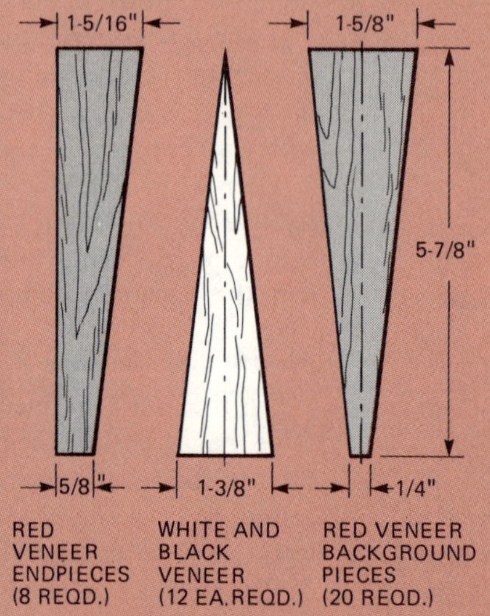

FIRST STEP of taping is shown. Tape strips are added crosswise, then longer strips placed lengthwise.

WOOD PIECES that make box are glued and clamped to the board (right). Bar clamps apply pressure sideways and C-clamps apply pressure up and down.

AFTER

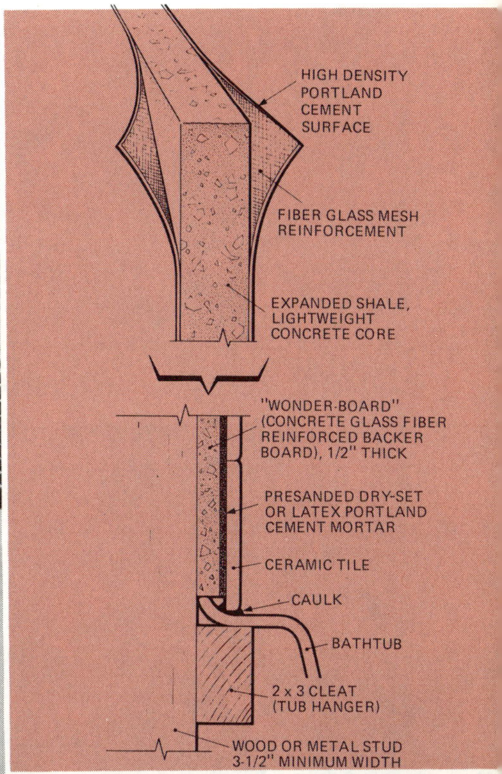

BEFORE

Backup board for ceramic tile

■ THE PROBLEM of tiles dropping off walls is common in bathrooms where ceramic tile is installed over gypsum wallboard or gypsum plaster. A new type of backup board can end all those problems, and it's easy to apply.

Wonder-Board, a panel that's claimed by its maker to be unaffected by moisture, is made of lightweight concrete reinforced with fiberglass. It won't shrink, swell, delaminate or decay.

It's now available at most American-Olean dealers. A 2-in.-wide fiberglass tape that seals joints and corners is also available.

The concrete-fiberglass panels are less than half the weight of the conventional installation of paper, metal lath and Portland cement plaster. They also eliminate the inconvenience of cutting and nailing the paper and metal lath, mixing mortar, troweling on two coats, and the messy cleanup after using wet mortar.

The board is timesaving and easy to use. You can score, snap and nail or screw it to the studs in less time than it takes to apply conventional materials. After the corners and joints are mortared and taped, you're ready to apply tile.

A quality ceramic tile properly installed with

SEE ALSO
Bathrooms . . . Bathtubs . . . Home improvement . . . Tile, wall

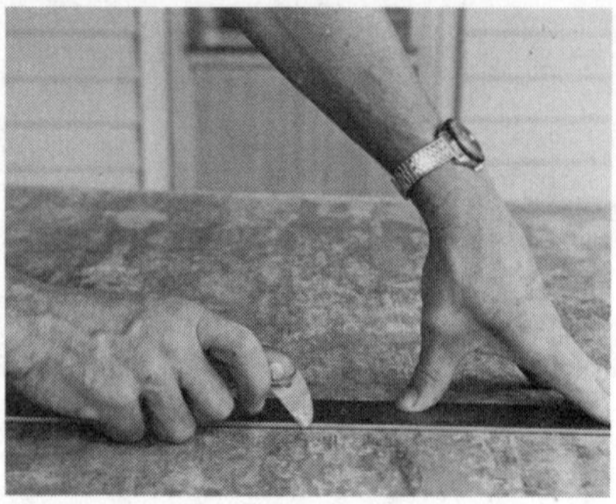

1 Score Wonder-Board with a knife. Cut through fiberglass to cement core.

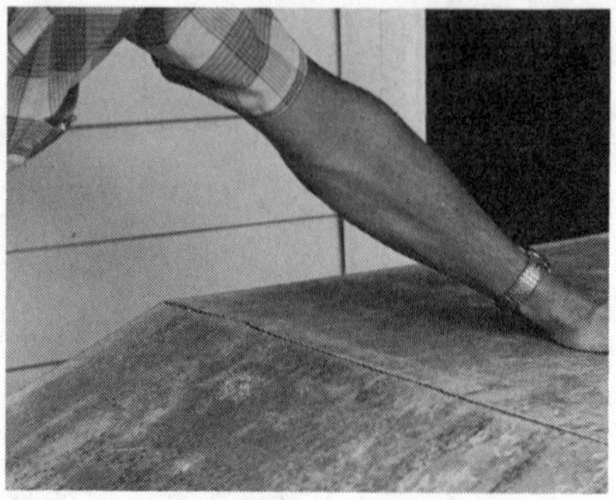

2 After the board has been scored, snap it in two parts along the line.

3 Cut through the bottom fiberglass layer from the other side.

4 Measure the wall to locate needed pipe holes on the board.

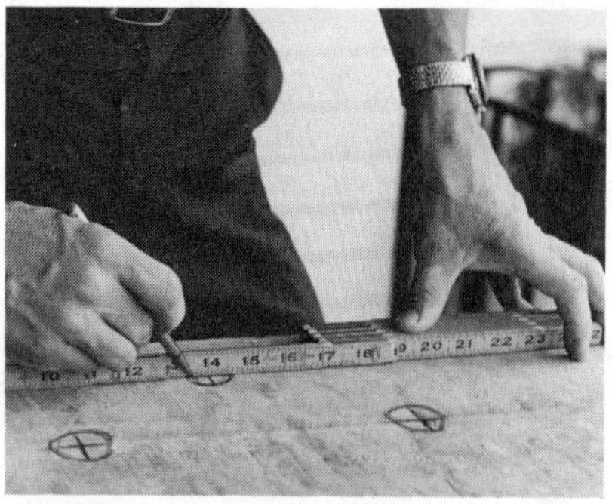

5 Using a pencil, mark the pipe holes to be bored in the Wonder-Board.

6 Bore or cut holes a bit oversize to permit shifting panel if needed.

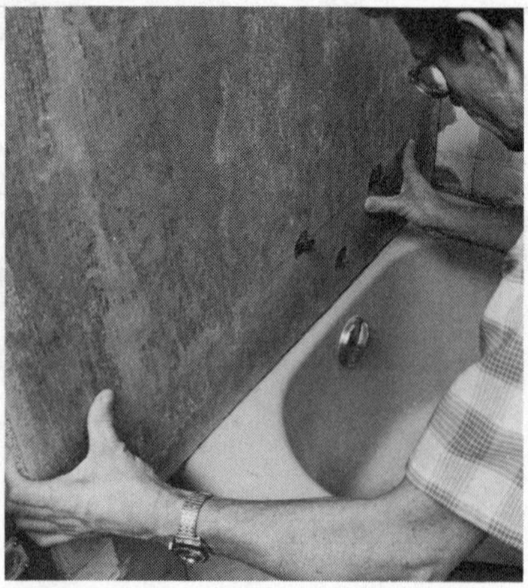

7 Before fastening board to wall, check accuracy of the hole locations.

8 Nail backup board to the studs. Position nails within ½ in. of board edges.

9 Installation is complete. Bottom edge of the board is set on the tub's lip.

10 Next, cut fiberglass tape to lengths needed for all joints and corners.

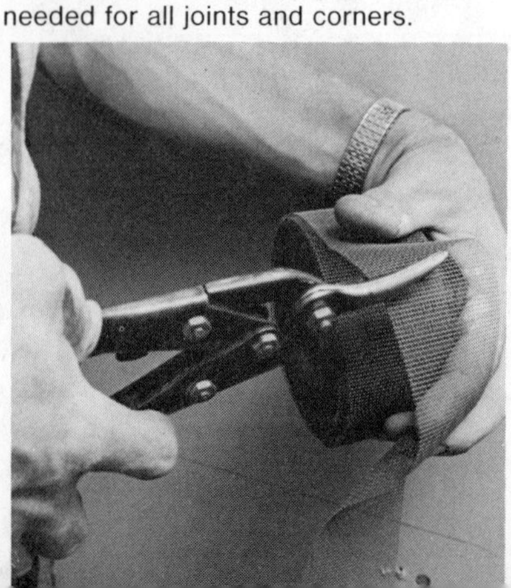

11 Embed tape in corners and on the seams using a dry-set mortar.

12 Horizontal and vertical joints are mortared, taped and dried.

13 Remove pipes. Apply thin layer of presanded dry-set or latex cement.

14 Mark pipe holes on tile. Test-fit by holding tile sheet in position.

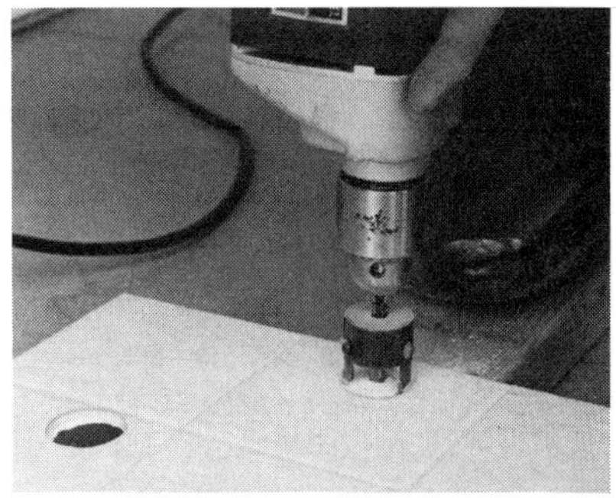

15 Drill pipe holes in tile. This one is Redi-Set pregrouted sheet tile.

16 Install pre-drilled tile on wall and then replace the water pipes.

17 For interesting pattern fit tile sheet of contrasting color diagonally to the surrounding sheets. Tile cutter cuts the surrounding sheets to fit.

18 After precut sheets of tile are in place, insert the diamond section.

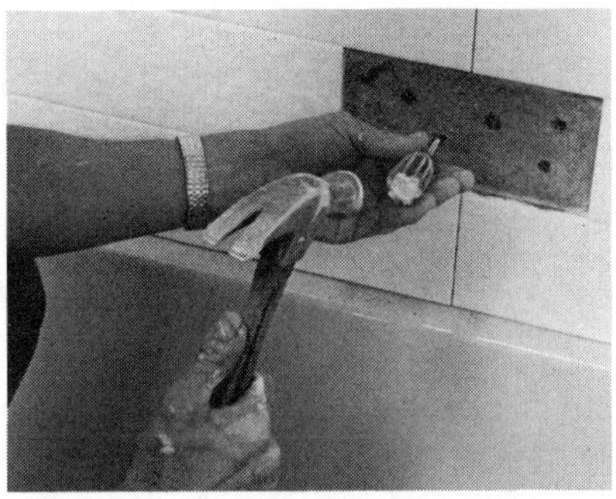

19 To install soap dish, punch holes in board with a hammer and screwdriver.

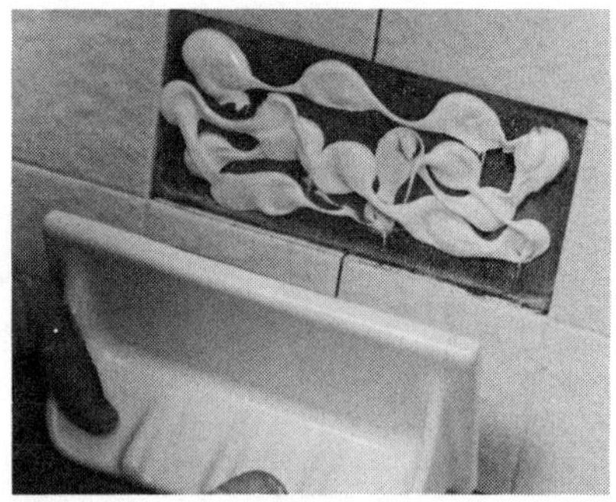

20 Apply silicone rubber liberally to Wonder-Board and install dish.

21 Grout all joints between sheets with the same silicone used in sheets.

dryset or latex Portland cement mortar over Wonder-Board is an attractive, low-maintenance and long-lasting wall covering for areas subjected to moisture, water and steam.

Boards are available in ½-in. thicknesses in 30x60-in. panels, and 36-in. widths 48, 60 and 72 in. long. The material is also available in a ⅜x36x60-in. panel for installation *only* over plaster, gypsum board, plywood or other equally solid backing. With the thinner ⅜-in. panel you must use fasteners that are long enough to pass through the backing material and anchor firmly in the wall studs. This thinner board is good for remodeling surfaces that present a bonding problem and where space is tight.

How to hang wallpaper

■ THANKS TO the many "fabric"-backed wall coverings now available, wallpapering is easier than ever. Since these newer materials come in a wide variety of attractive patterns, they are especially desirable for a first venture.

There are several good reasons. First, these wall coverings are easier to work with than ordinary wallpaper. You can correct mistakes by peeling off strips already in place, without fear of ripping the material. Ordinary wallpaper, once pasted in place, usually cannot be reused. Second, any adhesive on the surface can safely be washed off after the covering is in place.

Finally, wall coverings of the cloth type can be moved in position on the wall until they match perfectly with strips already in place. This maneuverability is extremely limited with ordinary wallpaper.

SEE ALSO
Brick, simulated . . . Drywall patching . . . Painting, interior . . . Remodeling . . . Tile, wall . . . Wall tile

Tools needed

- Carpenter's square
- Spirit level
- Cutting board, ¾ x 24 x 72-in.
- Clean sponge
- Yardstick
- Stepladder
- Plumb line and chalk
- Large scissors or shears
- Two plastic buckets (one for paste and one for washing)
- 4-in. brush for applying paste (for unpasted wall covering)
- Plastic water tray (for prepasted wall covering)
- 12-in. smoothing brush
- Wall covering trimmer, utility knife or single-edge razor blades
- Dropcloth
- Corner and seam rollers
- All tools required for wallpapering are available at well-stocked paint and wall-covering stores.

How to measure

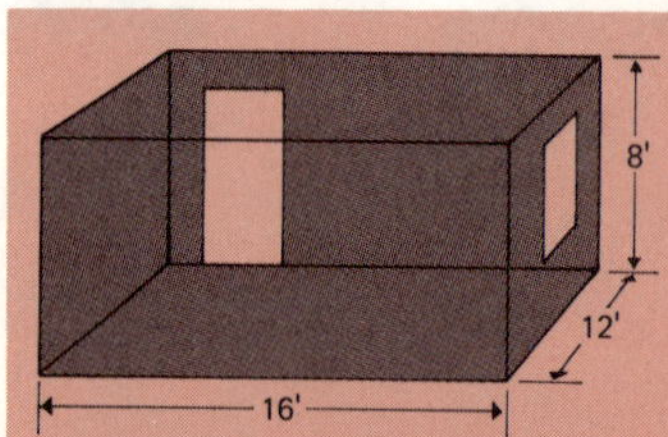

A standard wall-covering roll contains 35 sq. ft.—narrow rolls are longer than wide ones. To allow for waste and matching, figure on covering 30 sq. ft. with each roll.

1. Measure the distance around room at baseboard.
2. Measure wall height from baseboard to ceiling.
3. Find number of rolls you need in chart (right). For example, if room is 8x12x16 ft. with a door and window (as sketched above):
4. Add room dimensions around baseboard: 12+12+16+16=56 ft.
5. Find 56 in first column of chart.
6. Find number opposite 56 in applicable wall-height column (8 ft.): 14 rolls are needed.
7. Compute square feet of window-door openings and trim, deduct proportionate number of rolls; in this case, deduct one roll for door and window—13 rolls are needed to cover the walls.
8. Before you paper a ceiling, use column at far right to estimate the number of rolls needed—eight in this case.

ROOM ESTIMATING CHART

Around Room (ft.)	Rolls for Walls in Room With Height of 8′	9′	10′	Border (yds.)	Ceiling (rolls)
28	8	8	10	11	2
30	8	8	10	11	2
32	8	10	10	12	2
34	10	10	12	13	4
36	10	10	12	13	4
38	10	12	12	14	4
40	10	12	12	15	4
42	12	12	14	15	4
44	12	12	14	15	4
46	12	14	14	17	6
48	14	14	16	17	6
50	14	14	16	18	6
52	14	14	16	19	6
54	14	16	18	19	6
56	14	16	18	20	8
58	16	16	18	21	8
60	16	18	20	21	8
62	16	18	20	22	8
64	16	18	20	23	8
66	18	20	20	23	10
68	18	20	22	24	10
70	18	20	22	25	10
72	18	20	22	25	12
74	20	22	22	26	12
76	20	22	24	27	12
78	20	22	24	27	14
80	20	22	26	28	14
82	22	24	26	29	14
84	22	24	26	30	16
86	22	24	26	30	16
88	24	26	28	31	16
90	24	26	28	32	18

Types of wall coverings and adhesives

Prepasted wall coverings are popular with do-it-yourselfers because they save time and create considerably less mess. They are available in most of the same designs as unpasted wall coverings.

Unpasted wall coverings offer a slightly greater selection of patterns and finishes, including both flocked and foil coverings. Different types of unpasted wall coverings require different types of adhesive. Use the chart at the right to determine the kind you need.

It is important to mix wheat paste or stainless paste at least one hour before you use it. Allowance for this setup time makes it easier to eliminate dry lumps. Properly mixed, the paste will be lump-free and have the consistency of heavy cream.

ADHESIVES CHART

	Wheat Paste or Stainless Paste	Liquid Strippable or Wheat Paste	Vinyl Adhesive	Stainless Paste
Regular wallpaper	X			
Strippable wallpaper		X		
Vinyl wall covering			X	
Foils			X	
Burlap with backing			X	
Burlap (porous)	X			
Cork with backing			X	
Silks and fabrics				X
Flocks, murals, hand prints, borders	Use adhesive appropriate for wall covering's backing			

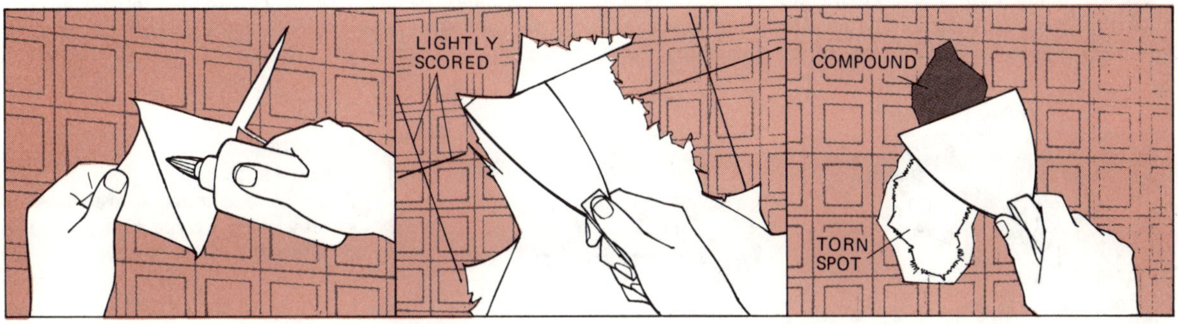

Dealing with old wallpaper

Don't underestimate the importance of properly preparing the walls to be covered. A professional generally removes an existing covering as there is always the possibility that it may work loose and ruin the new job. If you do cover existing wallpaper, make sure it's tight and smooth.

Cut an X in any air bubble and glue the paper back with white glue. Corners should be cut from floor to ceiling and reglued. Uneven spaces—where paper has pulled off the wall in spots, for example—should be filled with spackling compound and sanded. Check the joints of existing paper, fill with spackling compound and sand smooth where necessary—otherwise they may show through a new covering.

If there are two or more layers of paper on the walls, remove them. The best way is to rent a steamer. It's easy to use and you will have no trouble if you follow instructions. Another way to remove paper is by sponging the walls with hot water and using a scraper. Keep in mind that the wetter the paper is, the faster it will come off. When removing paper from drywall, take care not to get under its layer of finish by mistake.

Some extra tips to make the job easier: Before starting the soaking operation, spread many layers of newspaper on the floor—remember that the paper that comes off the wall will have softened glue on the back, which can adhere to the floor, necessitating another soaking and scraping. Lightly score crosshatch marks over the paper with a utility knife (carefully so you don't damage the wall beneath); this will break the surface so that hot water will dissolve the old paste faster.

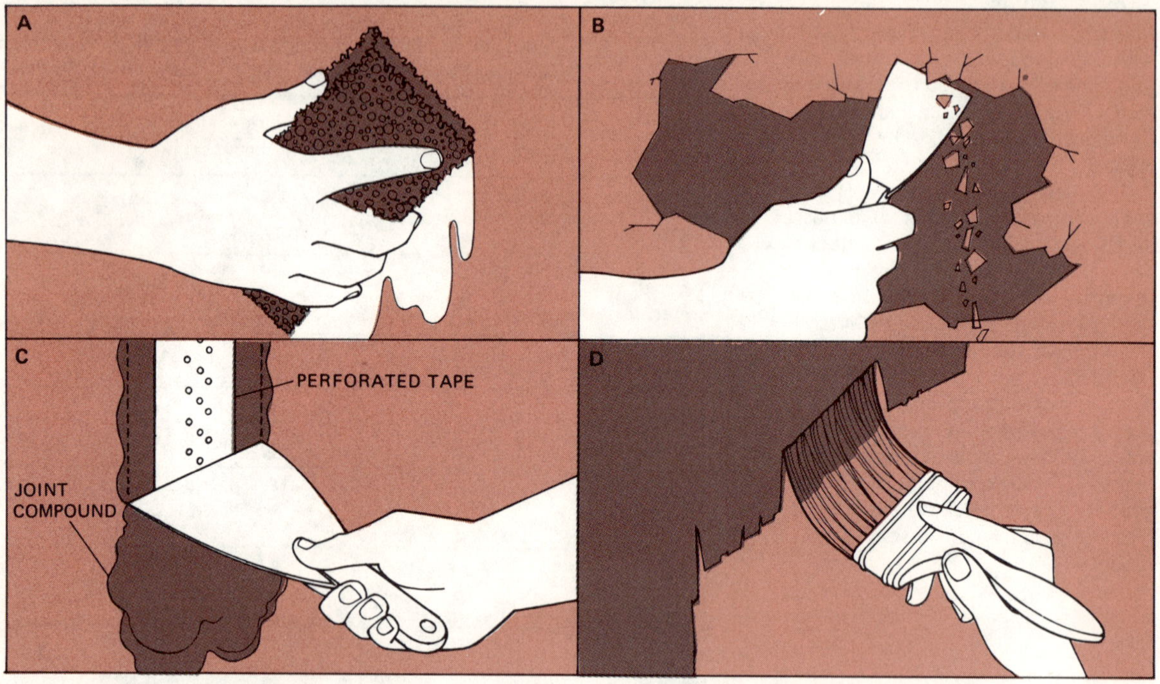

Preparing plaster and drywall surfaces

On unpainted plaster, make any needed repairs, scrape out loose cracks and fill with spackling compound (joint compound). Then apply a coat of wall size. Painted plaster should be thoroughly washed with detergent and water, rinsed with clear cold water. Make sure no soapy residue is left to dry on the surface. If necessary, remove peeling, chipped or cracked paint with a wide putty or joint knife and sand the surface smooth. Repair cracks or holes with spackling compound, sanding when dry. Dull a gloss or semigloss finish on existing paint with a strong soda solution or coarse-grit sandpaper; slick walls will not satisfactorily accept wall covering adhesives. On new plasterboard, tape seams and apply compound according to maker's directions. Set nailheads without breaking paper (dimple with hammer), cover with compound. Sand surfaces smooth when dry. Use two coats if necessary. Prime walls with oil, alkyd or latex primer-sealer; with latex, be sure to allow curing time. Sizing surfaces lets you slide covering in position, assures better adhesion.

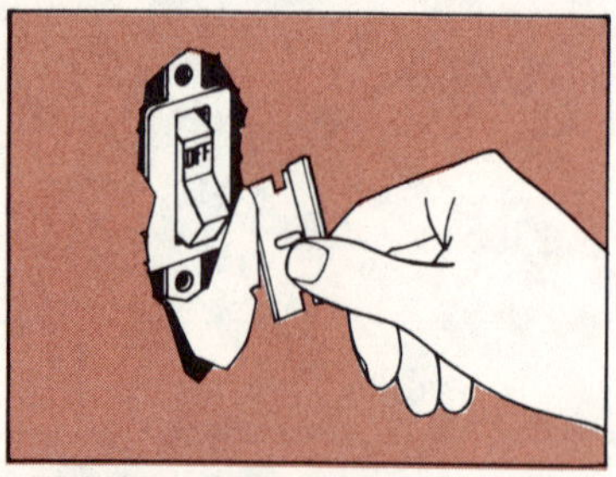

Switches, fixtures

Before wall covering is applied, all switch plates and outlet covers should be removed and wall fixtures loosened and pulled away from the wall. Remove fixture wall brackets *after turning off power at service panel* and then disconnecting wires. When the wall covering is in place, cut an area slightly smaller than wall plate so that plate covers cutout completely.

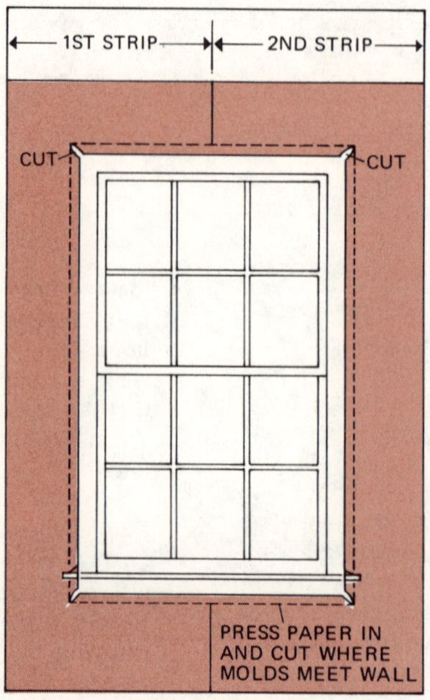

Papering around windows, doors

Doors and windows are handled exactly alike, except that a window means extra wall to be covered below it. Make a rough cutout by measuring from the last strip to the window casing and add ½ in. Measure the same way from ceiling and baseboard to trim. Remove the cutout before applying paste. Hang the strip, press in around casing and roll the joint with the seam roller, trim excess paper. Measure cutout size for the second strip as for the first and hang it, butting the first strip, in the same manner. Press and roll at joint with casing, trim. If you have taken care in cutting strips, pattern-matching at doors and windows will present no problem.

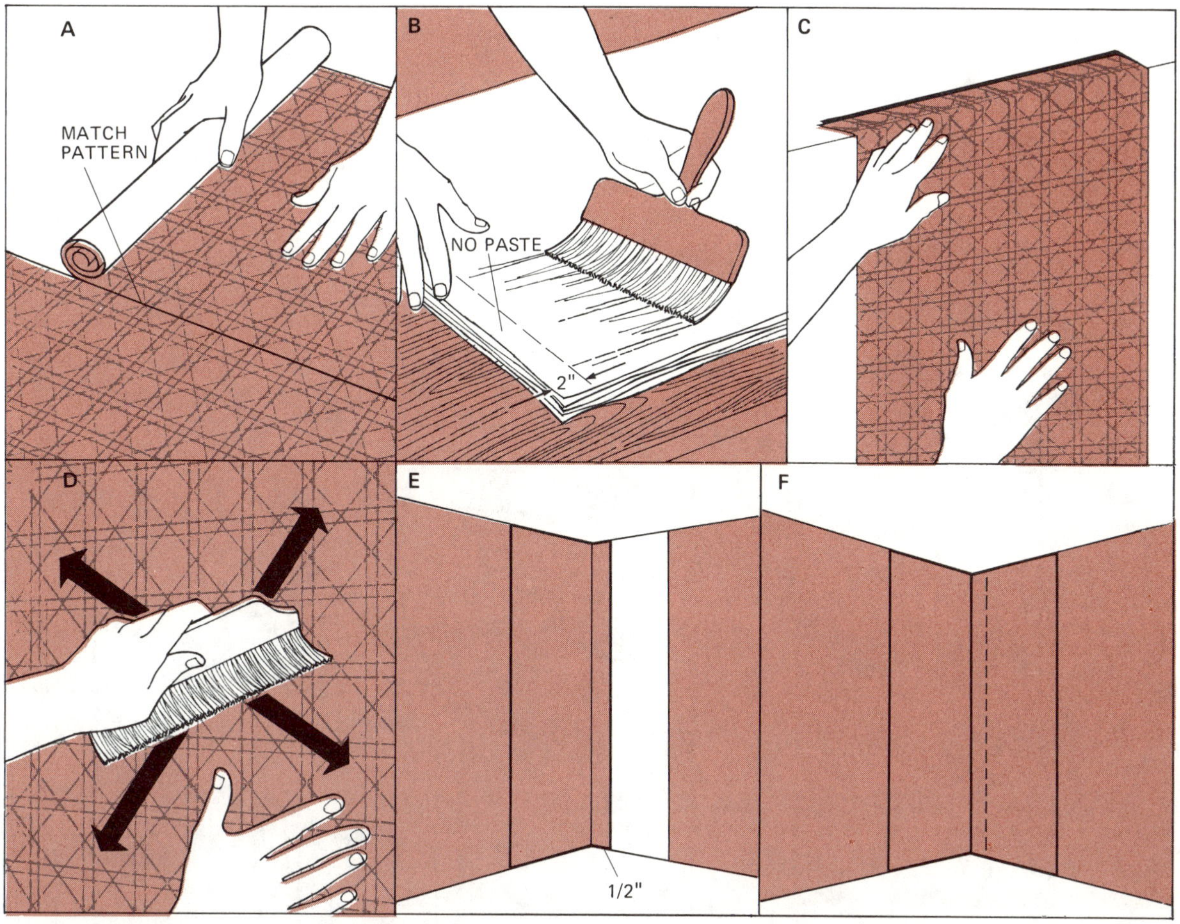

Preparing and hanging the wall covering

Two rules of thumb: If you plan to paper all the way around the room, hang the first strip along the edge of a door or window. If there is a fireplace in the room, center the first strip over it and work in both directions from there.

On an ample-sized table—a 2x6-ft. piece of ¾-in. plywood on sawhorses is fine—unroll the wall covering and lay it face up. Measure out wall height and add 6 in. allowance for trim. Lay the second strip next to the first, match the pattern and cut it to the same length. Lay the second strip on top of the first and continue matching and cutting strips in this manner.

When all strips are cut, turn over the stack of paper. Apply adhesive evenly with a large paste brush. Start at the center and brush toward the bottom. For easier handling, leave a 1-in. strip at the bottom unpasted. Allow about three minutes for the paper to expand before you handle it. Now fold the bottom half of the strip toward the center, paste to paste, without creasing the paper. Stop short of the center so that the fold you later make from the top will be slightly longer than the bottom one. Align the edges carefully. Apply paste to the top half of the strip as to the bottom, wait for paper to expand, and fold the top over to the center. The 1 in. unpasted strip at the top should overlap the bottom edge folded up to the center.

To hang the paper, unfold the top section and place the strip high on the wall, overlapping the ceiling-wall joint by approximately 2 in., and aligning its edge with a vertical snapped with your chalked plumb line. Give the upper section a couple of strokes with your smoothing brush to hold it to the wall. Then open the lower section. When you are satisfied with the paper's alignment, brush the entire strip smooth. Always brush from the center toward edges to get rid of air bubbles. Trim off excess paper at baseboard and ceiling joint and around doors and windows.

To hang the second strip, use the first as a guide, matching the pattern and butting—not overlapping—the seams. Repeat the smoothing procedure, then roll the seam with the seam roller. On flocked or embossed wall covering, seams should not be rolled—instead, tap along the seam with the tips of the smoothing-brush bristles. Clean strips with a damp sponge immediately to remove any paste on the surface, ceiling or baseboard. Hang remaining strips the same way.

To prepare a corner, measure from the last strip to the corner at ceiling level, midpoint and baseboard. Add ½ in. to the widest measurement, cut a strip to this width, and hang it in the usual manner; it will overlap the corner by ½ in. Snap a plumb chalkline over this overlap for use as a guide in hanging the first strip on the other wall of the corner. This technique will give you a true vertical even if the corner is not perfectly straight.

How to fix an automatic washer

■ A MALFUNCTION in your automatic washer usually affects a basic function: fill, wash (agitation), drain or spin.

The troubleshooting charts on these pages will help you pinpoint a problem and correct it. To determine what the common components look like and their location, refer to the large illustration. It's a composite that's typical of most machines.

COMMON WASHER COMPONENTS

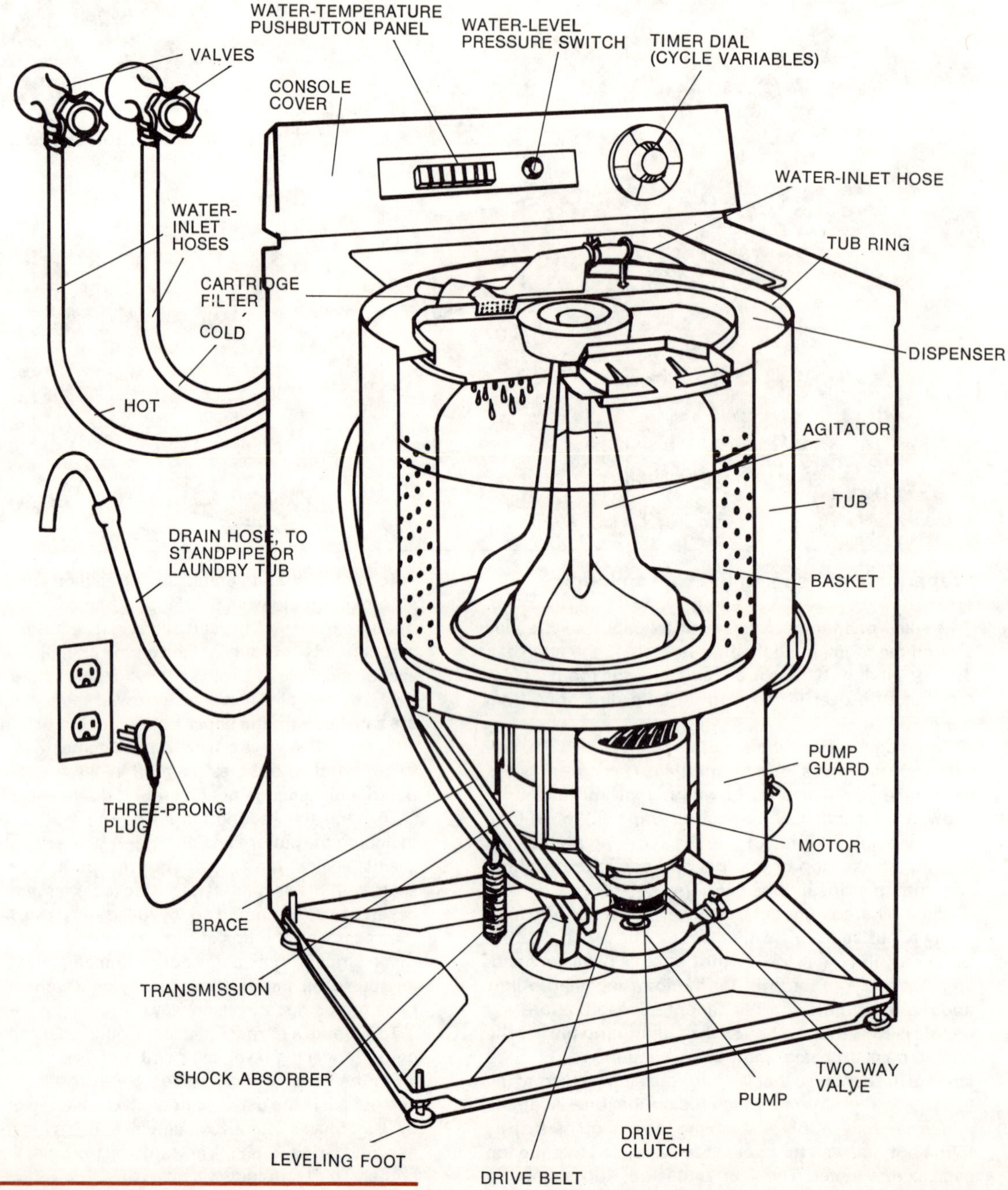

SEE ALSO
Appliance centers . . . Clothes dryers . . . Heaters, water . . . Irons . . . Laundry counters

When testing electrical components, consult your machine's wiring diagram, which is glued on the back of, or inside, the machine. The chart with this article will help you interpret the electrical symbols.

To test the timer, turn the control knob slowly from the "Off" position before the regular cycle to the spot in the cycle where the machine isn't working properly as you count the number of increments (clicks). Count the corresponding increments on the timer cam chart and determine which terminals should be closed. Timer contact terminals are marked on the timer and timer cam chart by a letter or numerical code. Connect a 115-v. test light to the terminals and turn on the machine. If the test light fails to light, the timer is faulty in that model and should be replaced.

Washer doesn't fill

CAUSE	ACTION TO TAKE*
1. Water faucet(s) closed.	Open faucet(s).
2. Water inlet hoses kinked.	Straighten hoses.
3. Clogged water valve screens.	Remove screens and flush out sediment.
4. Damaged water valve solenoid.	Remove leads and connect a 115-v. test light across terminals, turn on electricity and move control knob to "Fill." No light signifies a bad solenoid. Replace.
5. Defective timer.	Test as described in text above.
6. Defective water temperature switch.	Remove leads and connect a 115-v. test light across terminals, turn on electricity and move control knob to "Fill." No light signifies a bad solenoid. Replace.
7. Defective water-level pressure switch.	The switch normally has three terminals. With switch in "Fill" position there is contact between two of the terminals with the third terminal "open." Make sure you connect a 115-v. test light across the terminals affecting "Fill." Consult the wiring diagram. Turn on electricity and move control knob to "Fill." No light signifies a bad solenoid. Replace.
8. Water valve internal malfunction.	Disassemble water valve and check each part for damage, paying particular attention to the guide assembly and diaphragm. Replace the bad part, if possible. If not, replace the whole valve.
9. Open circuit.	Using the wiring diagram as a guide, probe each wire connection with a 115-v. test light to determine if defective wiring or a loose connection is causing the problem. Be sure control knob is at "Fill" position.

*After taking each "action," reconnect power and test operation, but be sure to pull plug from wall receptacle before continuing.

Washer doesn't drain

CAUSE	ACTION TO TAKE
1. Kinked drain hose; clogged drain.	Straighten hose; clear drain.
2. Broken or slipping drive belt.	Replace or tighten.
3. Defective pump.	Usually pump is clogged or impeller goes bad. Pump may be taken apart for cleaning or replacement of defective parts, or it may be replaced as a unit.
4. Defective timer and open circuit.	If the motor doesn't kick into "Drain," test timer as described in text above. Also check for open circuit. Be sure the control knob is set to "Drain" position.

WATER VALVE

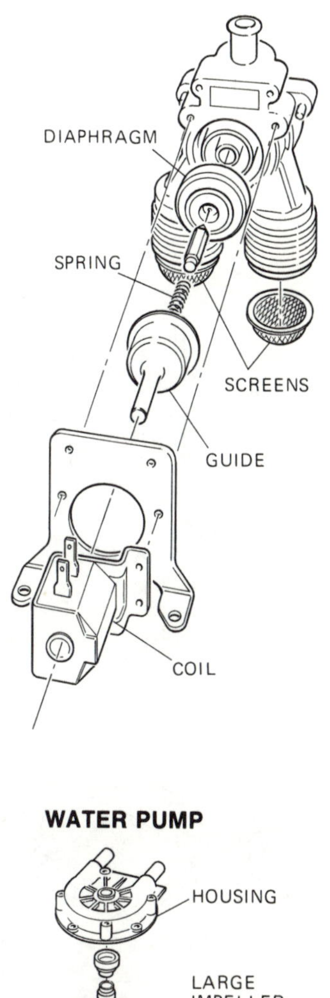

WATER PUMP

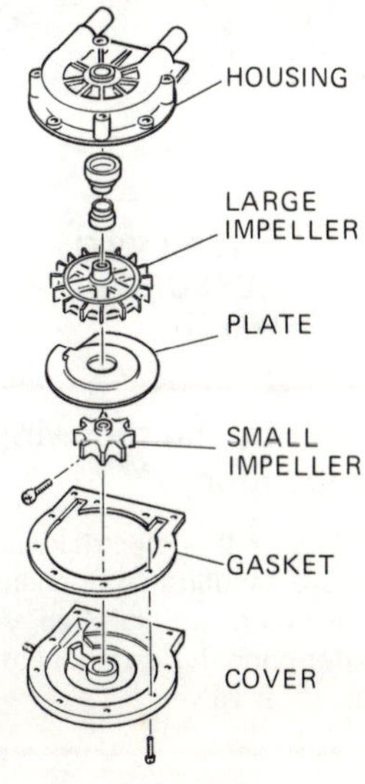

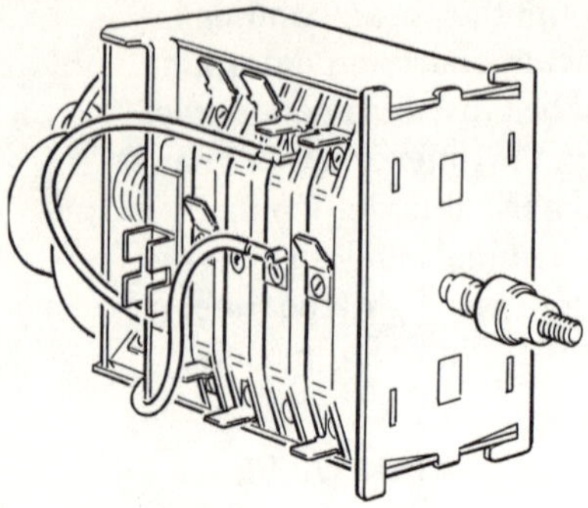

TIMER

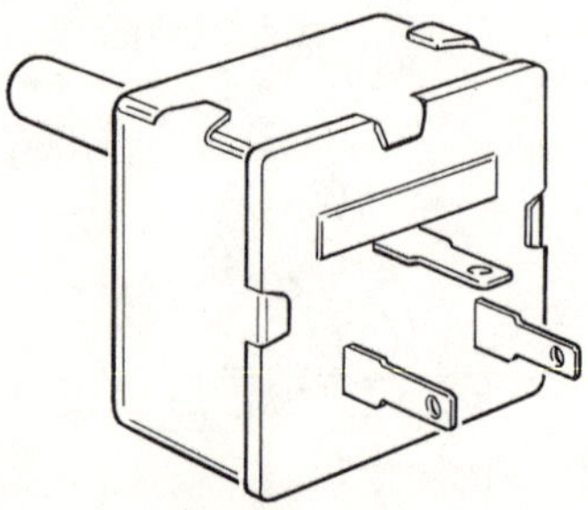

WATER-TEMPERATURE SWITCH

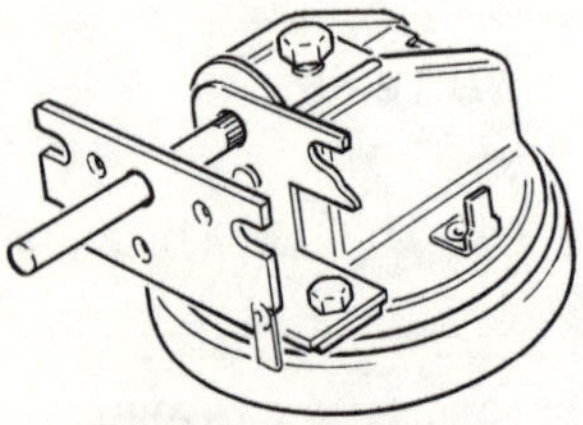

WATER-LEVEL PRESSURE SWITCH

Washer doesn't agitate (wash)

CAUSE	ACTION TO TAKE*
1. Broken or slipping drive belt.	Replace or tighten.
2. Defective drive clutch.	Remove the drive belt and turn the clutch by hand with the control knob in the "Wash" (agitate) position. If there is no "grab," the clutch is defective and should be replaced.
3. Defective transmission.	With the drive belt off, manually rotate the transmission pulley in agitate direction (usually clockwise) with control knob in "Wash" (agitate) position. If this doesn't drive the agitator, the problem is in the transmission.
4. Defective timer.	Test as described in text.
5. Faulty water-level pressure.	When water has filled the tub, contact reverts to the third terminal of this switch and to one of the other two terminals. The remaining terminal reverts to "Open" position. Make sure to connect a 115-v. test light across the terminals affecting "Filled." Consult the wiring diagram. Turn on the electricity and move the control knob to "Wash." No light signifies that you have a bad switch.
6. Open circuit.	Using the wiring diagram as a guide, probe each wire connection with a 115-v. test light to determine if either defective wiring or a loose connection is causing the problem. Make certain that the control knob is set at the "Wash" position.

*After taking each "action," reconnect power and test operation, but be sure to pull plug from wall receptacle before continuing.

Washer doesn't spin or spins slowly

CAUSE	ACTION TO TAKE
1. Broken or slipping drive belt.	Replace or tighten.
2. Loose motor pulley.	Tighten pulley.
3. Defective drive clutch.	Test as described under "Washer doesn't agitate," Cause 2 (above); be sure control knob is in "Spin" position.
4. Spin brake doesn't release or transmission is frozen.	The brake is not part of the transmission, but since they are attached and work together, they are checked as a unit. Set control knob in "Spin" position and remove drive belt. Turn brake stator; it should move freely. If not, the brake assembly or transmission is defective. Both units can be repaired.
5. Defective timer or open circuit.	If motor doesn't kick into "Spin," test timer as in text. Also check for open circuit. Be sure the control knob is set to the "Spin" position.

Abide by the following precautions:

- Be sure that electricity is turned off before handling components.
- Turn off water when working on water-handling components, such as the water valve.
- Before replacing an electrical component you believe is faulty, make certain that a loose connection isn't causing the problem.
- After replacing an electrical component, tighten connections.
- Before reconnecting your electrical service, see to it that ground wires are tightly attached.
- Make sure that water connections are secure.
- Install replacement parts that meet factory specification. You can't go wrong using parts made by the manufacturer of the washer.

Motor doesn't run

CAUSE	ACTION TO TAKE*
1. Electrical service cord isn't plugged in; blown fuse or a tripped circuit breaker; possible malfunction in branch circuit.	Be sure that plug is connected and fuse or circuit breaker is okay. If there is no power at the wall receptacle, check the circuit.
2. Defective timer.	Test as described in text.
3. Defective lid switch.	Many models have a switch in the lid which automatically turns the washer off if door is open during cycling. If the machine refuses to operate with the lid closed, connect a test light across the lid switch. No light indicates a faulty switch. Replace.
4. Defective motor.	Most motors are protected by an internal overload circuit breaker that stops operation if the motor overheats. If this protective device halts motor operation, but the motor can be started again after about 30 minutes, consider the following conditions:
(a) If the motor trips off when the machine goes into the spin cycle, the cause of trouble may be in the clutch, brake or transmission—not the motor. To find out, remove transmission drive belts and let the motor operate. If it doesn't trip off now, there is no motor problem.	(b) If the motor operates in agitate position, but won't operate in spin position or vice versa, check timer and lid switch, and look for broken wire before condemning the motor.
5. Open circuit.	This possibility always exists, so before you rip the motor out of the machine conduct continuity tests with your test light at each wire connection.

*After taking each "action," reconnect power and test operation, but be sure to pull plug from wall receptacle before continuing.

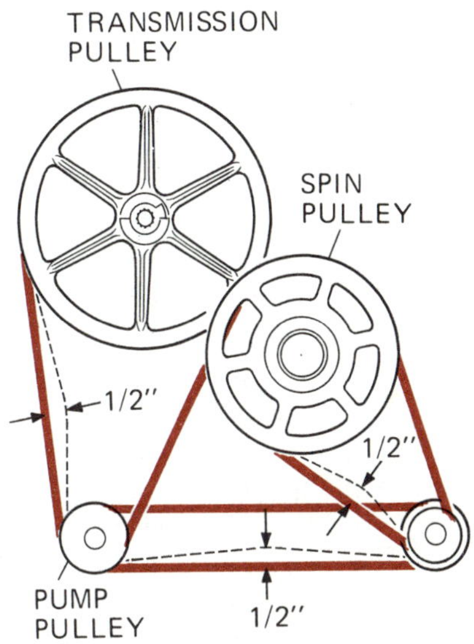

PROPER belt tension is reached when you can deflect it ½ in. Minimum belt tension after extended use should be 15 pounds. To check this, hook spring scale at mid-point and note what force is required to deflect the belt 1 in.

Symbols found in wiring diagrams

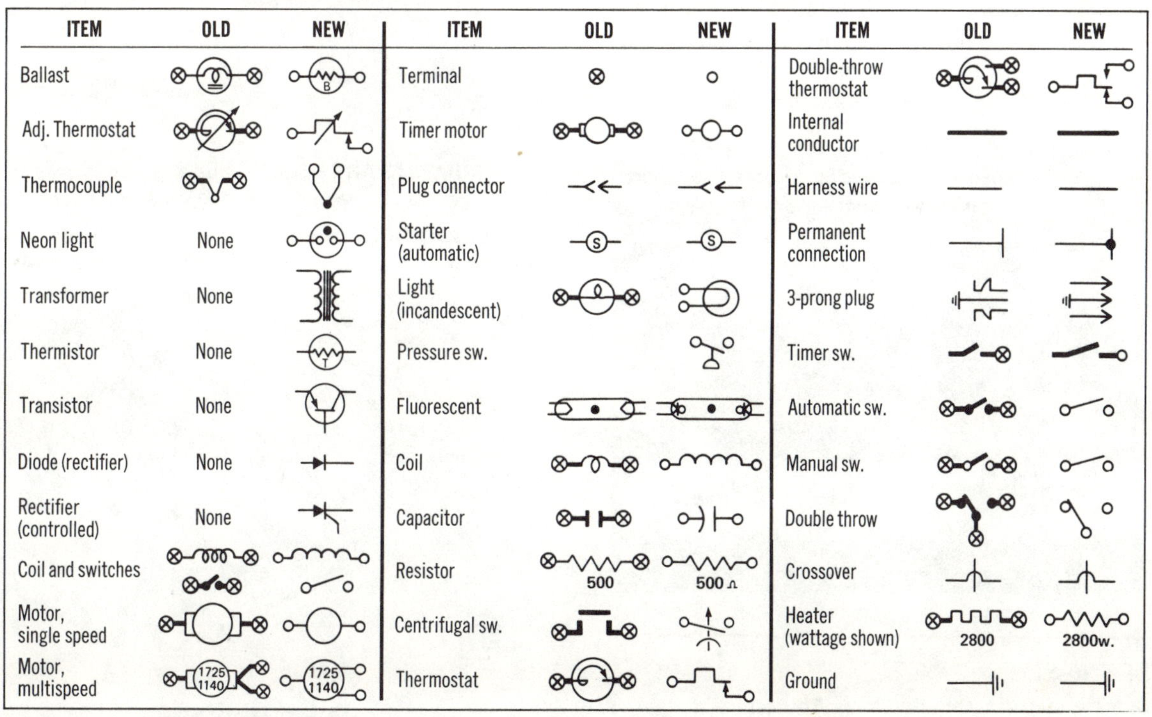

Build a colonial weather station

By JOHN CAPOTOSTO

■ THIS WEATHER STATION not only makes an attractive wall decoration for den or family room; it keeps you posted on relative humidity, temperature and barometric pressure 24 hours a day. The eagle and instrument plaques are cut from knot-free (clear) white pine. To simplify cutting and working the small plaques, gang the three in a row and cut them apart after making the holes and boring the corners.

Holding small pieces for shaping is difficult, especially when the work is smaller than the router base. To do this simply and safely, make a workholder by driving a few brads up through the bottom of a piece of ¼-in. plywood and clamp or nail this to the workbench. The work is simply pressed down on the protruding brads.

Humidity and temperature gauges are merely press-fitted into their holes. A separate flange is provided to hold the barometer bezel. This is pressed over the flange after it is screwed in place.

Since weather instruments must "breathe," wood spacers are glued to the backs. Tiny screweyes and brass chain link the plaques.

You can finish the wood parts as desired; the new antique colors are ideal for pine. The three weather units, plus the eagle are from Armor Co., Box 290, Deer Park NY 11729.

SAWING HOLES for instruments is less of a problem when the three panels are sawed as one, then cut apart.

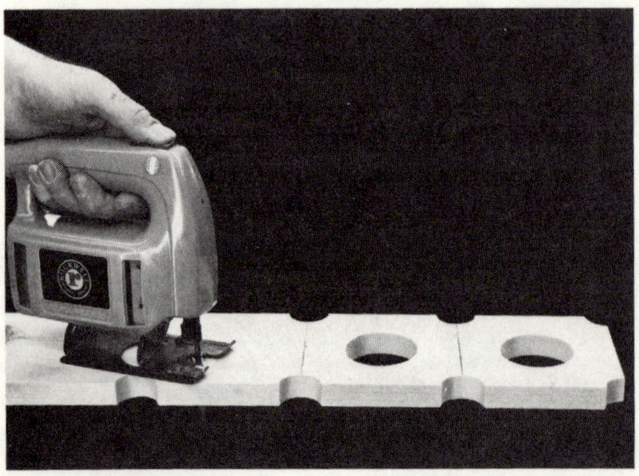

INSTRUMENTS ARE HELD in panels by a snug press-fit. The holes can be sawed, or bored on a drill press.

HOLDING WORK when shaping edge is made easy by resting it on brad points driven up through plywood.

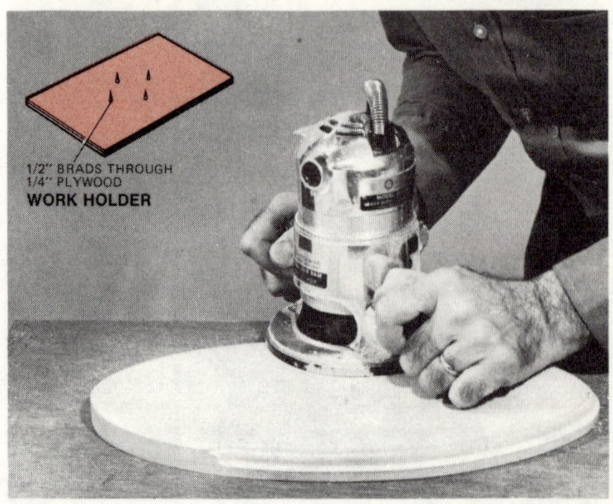

SEE ALSO
Clocks . . . Gifts, Christmas . . . Routers

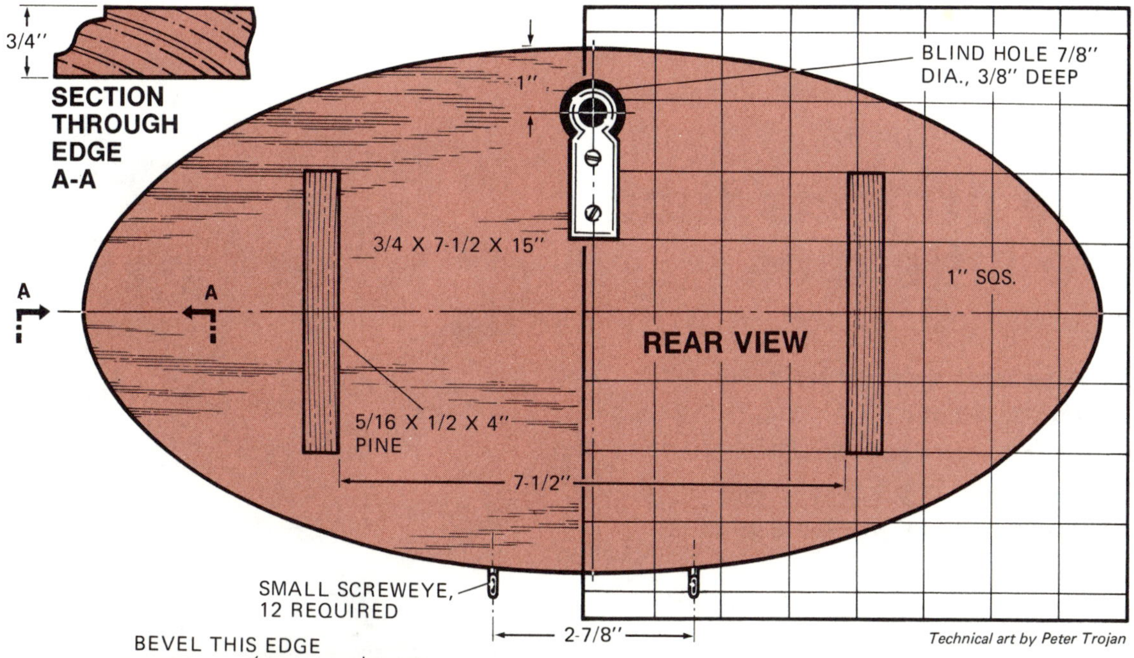

Technical art by Peter Trojan

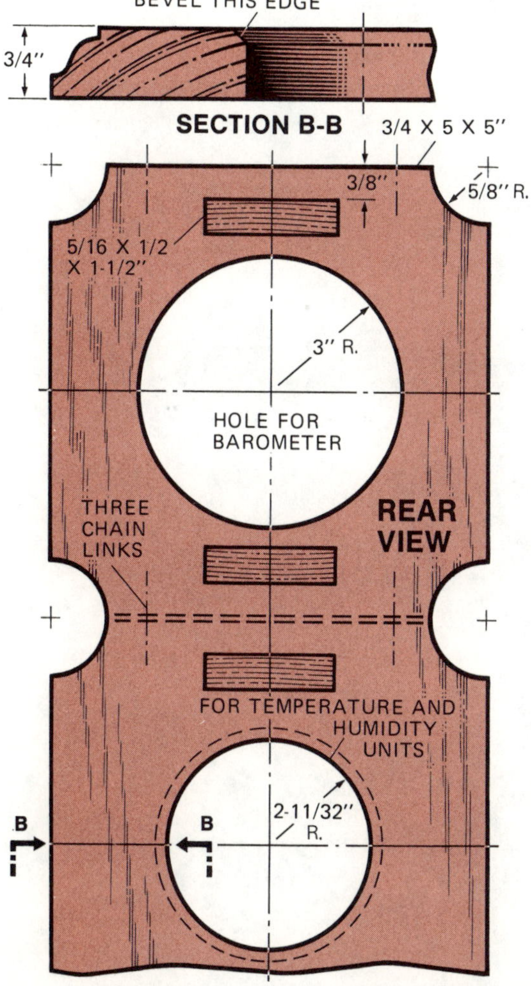

SPACER BLOCKS are glued to the back of the panels to hold instruments out from the wall so they can "breathe."

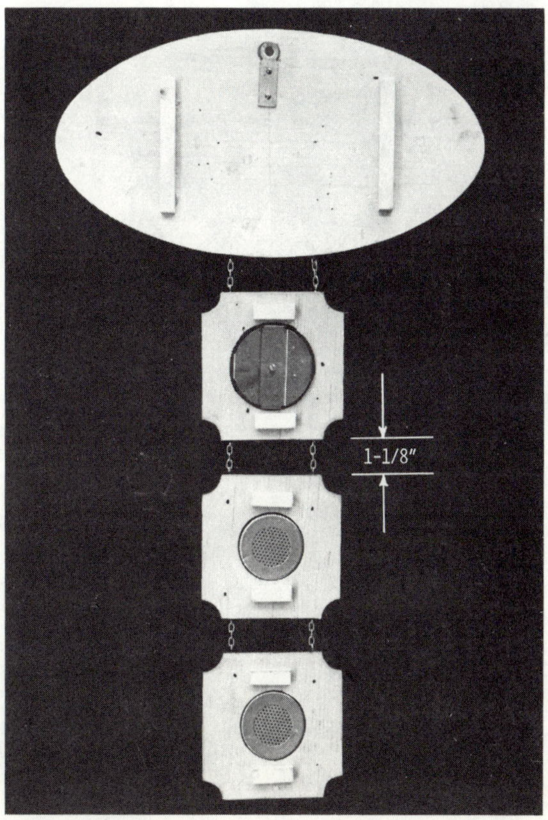

Little projects that take little time

These three projects are designed to give you relatively simple and useful products. You can probably complete any of them in a weekend and use them yourself or give them as gifts

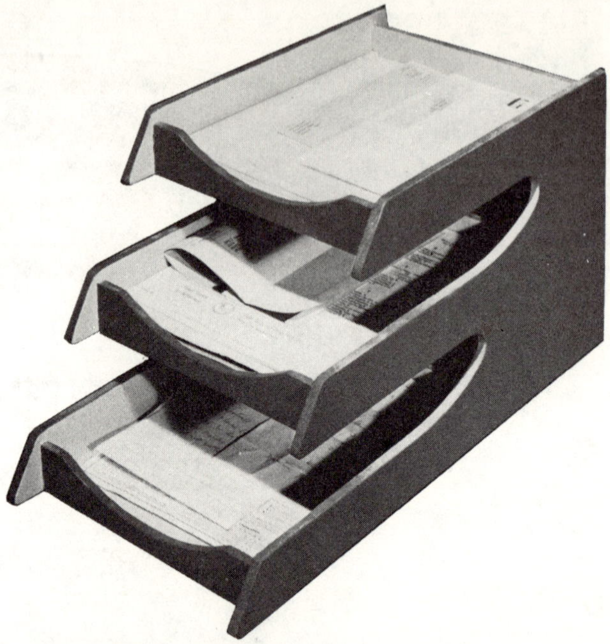

Modern mail organizer

Cue-and-ball rack

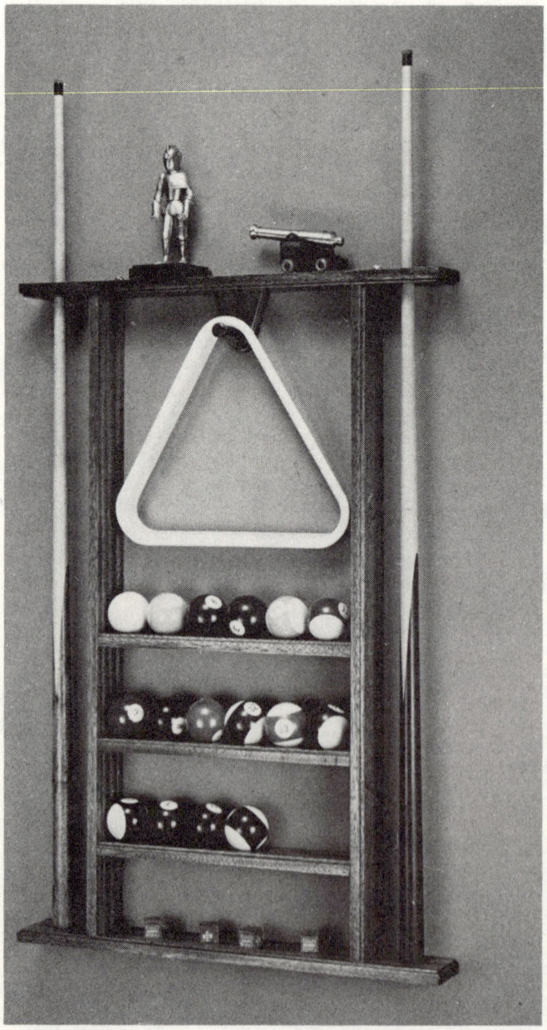

'Swiss-cheese' mountain game

SEE ALSO
Air games . . . Desk accessories . . .
Drill press techniques . . . Gifts, Christmas . . .
Letter racks . . . Pool tables . . . Toys

Cue-and-ball rack

By WAYNE C. LECKEY

■ ROUNDING UP the balls and cues when you're ready to "rack 'em up" is no problem when you store them in a handy wall rack. While this handsome one of walnut holds two cues, it can be built to hold four by making the outboard ends longer and boring extra holes top and bottom. Except for the size of the holes, the top and bottom pieces are alike, as are the sides and the three shelves. Make ball grooves in the shelves by passing the work diagonally across the blade of your table saw. Clamp a wood fence to the table and start with the blade only 1/16 in. high. Raise the blade 1/16 in. with each successive pass until you have a concave groove 1 in. wide. Hand-finish the rough cut by wrapping sandpaper around a large dowel.

If you don't have a lathe, a length of dowel can be substituted for the turned rack peg. All parts are blind-doweled and glued together. Finishing is a lot easier if you do it before the rack is glued together. Apply strips of masking tape to the pieces at the glue joints to keep the wood free of stain. When the finishing is completed, peel off the tape and apply glue to the dowels. Glue and clamp the shelves to the sidepieces first, then add the top and bottom pieces and finally the peg bracket. Add two flat, metal hanging hooks to the rear edge at the top.

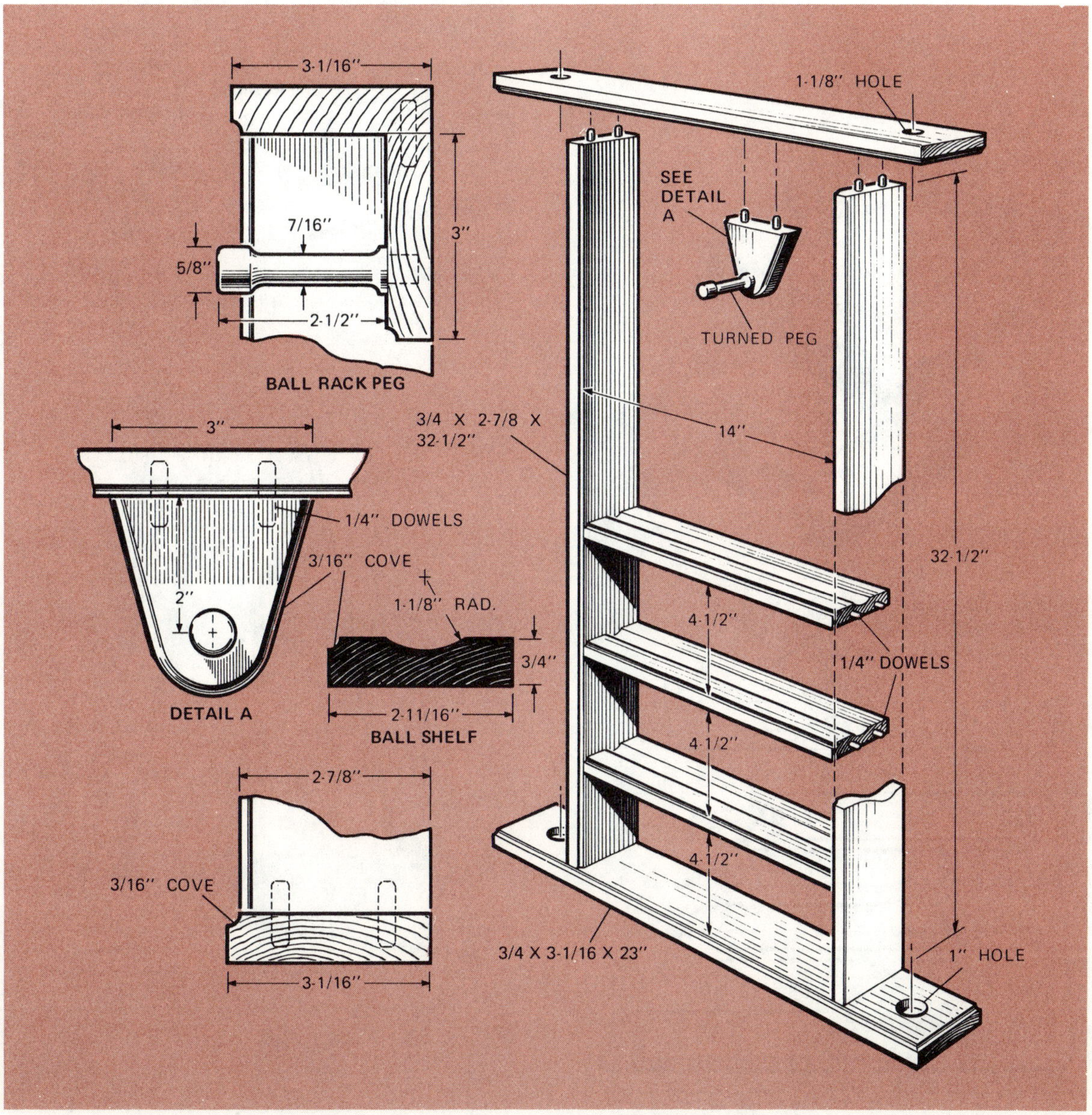

Modern mail organizer

By ROSARIO CAPOTOSTO

■ IN TODAY'S "paper world," almost everyone can use a mail organizer—the chief executive of the house, the housewife, students and, of course, the office worker. For you fellows in the latter category, imagine the impression you'll make with this sleek IN and OUT box on your desk, especially if you paint it fireball fluorescent red.

Use ⅜-in. plywood to make it. Tacknail together the two side pieces and jigsaw or bandsaw both at once. Cut the three shelves, glue and nail the ends to them, then glue on the side panels. Sand a slight soft radius on all edges and corners. Set and putty the nailheads before painting.

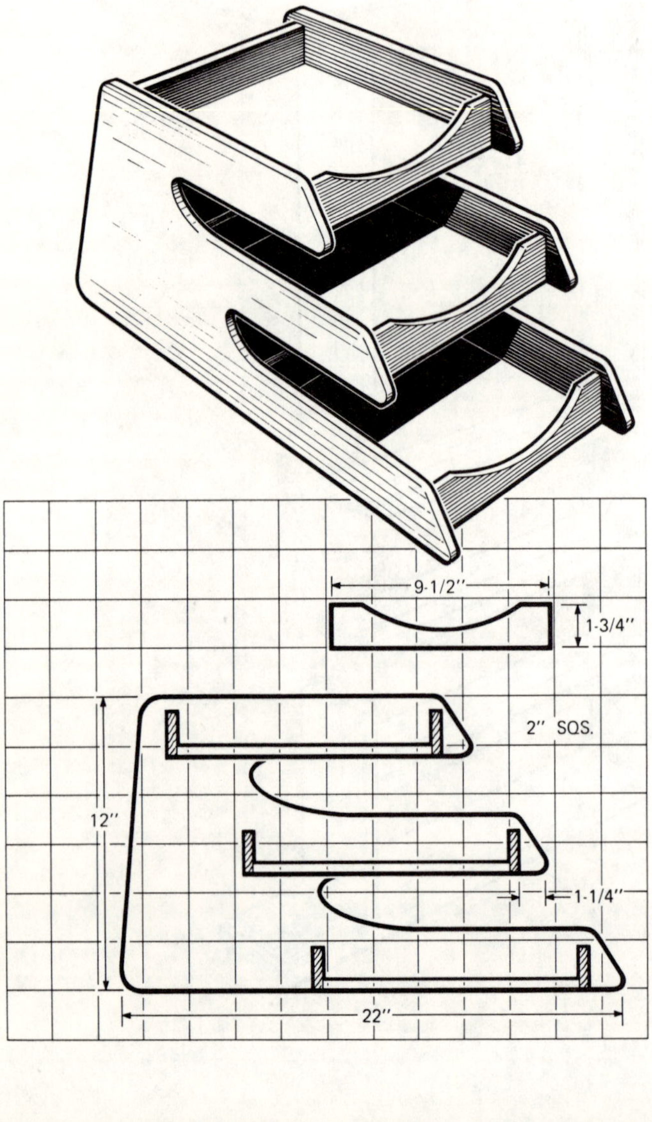

BALL HOLES are bored in hardboard sides with a 1¾-in. hole cutter in a drill press.

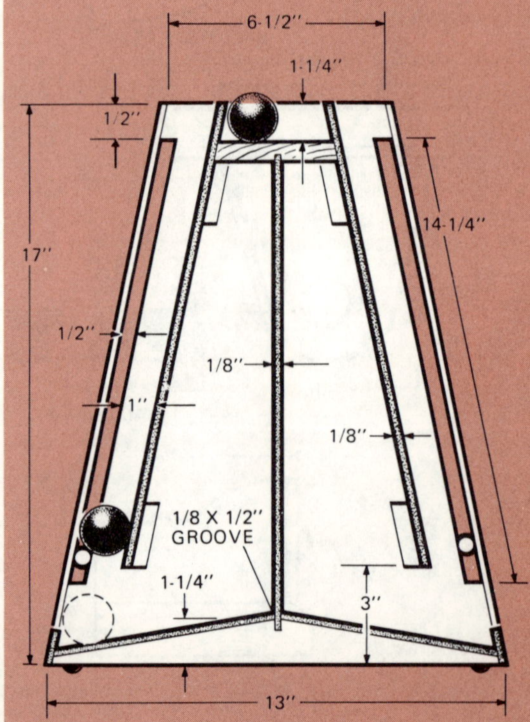

END VIEW SECTION

'Swiss-cheese' mountain game

By MERTON H. SLUTZ

■ IN A RACE to scale this "Swiss-cheese" mountain, climbers on opposite sides must watch their step in maneuvering a table-tennis ball up the treacherous slopes. A slight miscue will send the ball through a hole in the "cheese" and back to the starting point. It's a game for two or four players (two to a team), and the climber (or team) who reaches the summit tray first wins.

Made in the shape of a wedge of cheese, the game consists of two 1/8-in. (or 1/4-in.) hardboard sides that have 19 holes in them. Notice that the side holes are bored 1/4-in. in from the edges and that no hole is more than 1/2 in. from each adjacent one. The section view shows how ramp cleats, glued to the 3/4-in. plywood ends, support a center partition and a sloping floor of 1/8-in. hardboard. A saw groove in the bottom of the summit tray fits over the partition so it is 1 1/4 in. down from the top.

To cut the slots for the dowels in the edges of the slanting plywood ends, set the saw fence a scant more than 1/2 in. from the blade. Then turn on the saw and carefully lower the work over the blade. Run the cut as far as you can, then stop and square it off with a hand or sabre saw. Hardboard strips cover the notches to hold the 1/2-in. dowel handles in place. Short sections of 3/4-in. dowel cap the ends. The dowels should slide freely in the slots.

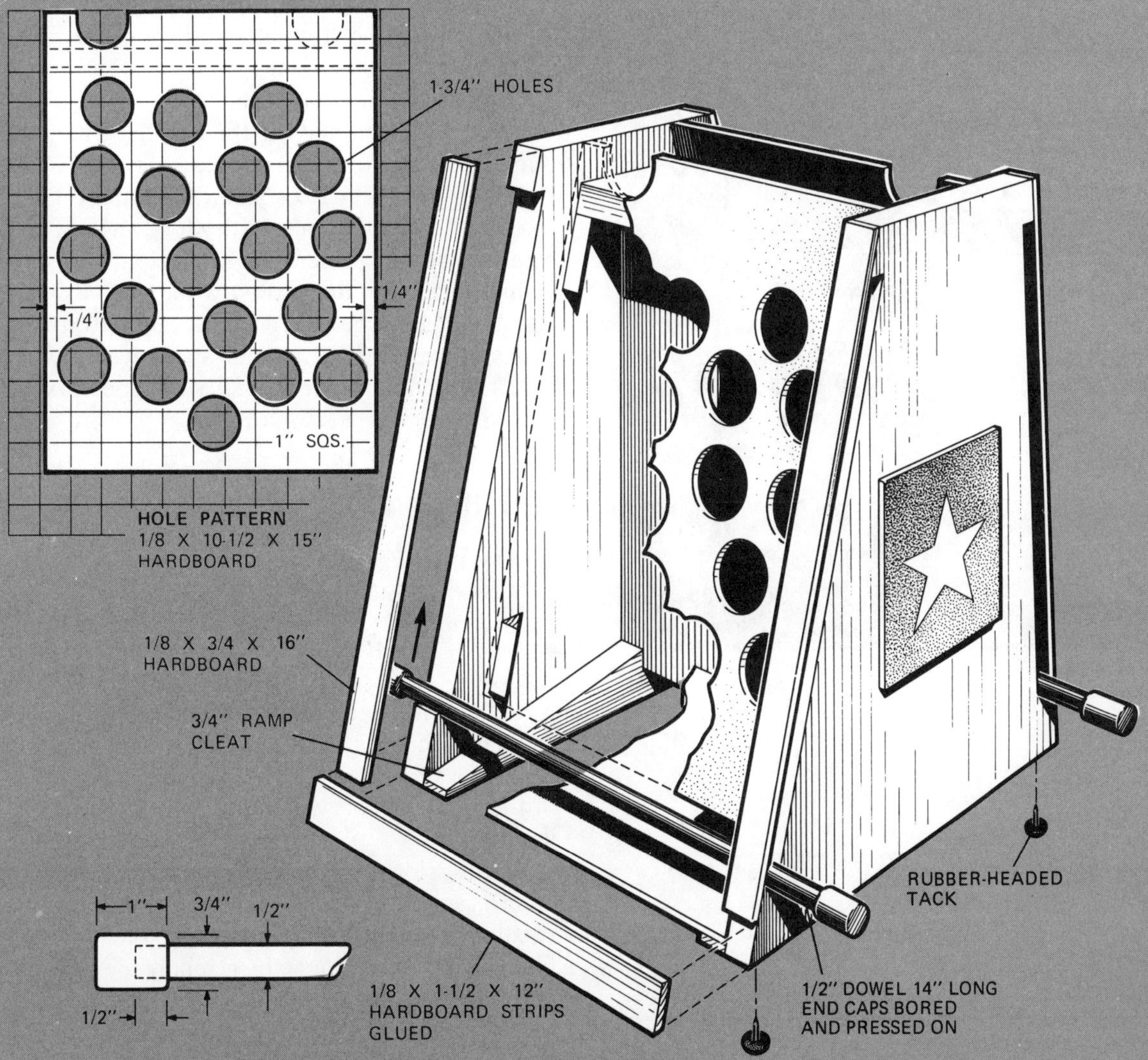

Fun projects

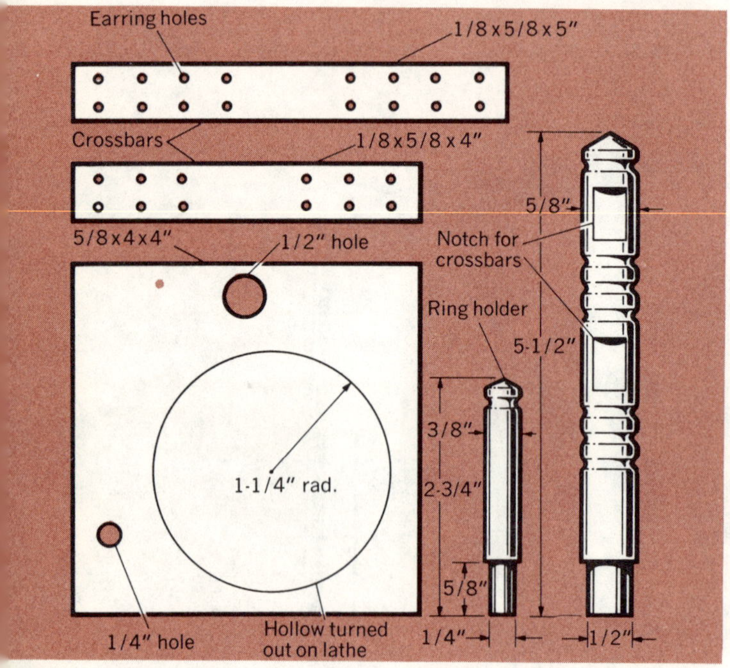

SEE ALSO

Gifts, Christmas . . . House numbers . . . Jewelry . . . Jewelry boxes

Jewelry keeper

By HAROLD JACKSON

■ YOU CAN QUICKLY build a surefire "corral" to keep your wife's small jewelry—earrings, pins, rings and the like—in one handy spot. The keeper shown is a project you can easily turn out in one day.

The "tree" at the back keeps the earrings in pairs; the clamp types on the crossbars, and those for pierced ears in the small drilled holes. Rings are neatly stacked on the short pole at the front, and pendants and pins can be stored in the scooped-out portion of the base.

I recommend using hardwood, such as walnut. The two posts and the dished-out section are turned on a lathe (the latter on the lathe faceplate).

Sand the turnings on the lathe, using a fine-grit sandpaper before making the cutoffs. Then assemble the stand, using glue, and let dry.

Finish with a coat of stain and wipe off the excess. Allow the keeper to dry for 24 hours, and apply wood paste filler. (This is necessary only if you are using an open-grain wood such as walnut, mahogany or oak.) Finally, spray on two coats of clear lacquer. After a two-week "curing," rub with double-0 steel wool and wax.

A baffling puzzle

By KENNETH WELLS

■ HERE'S A PUZZLE that you—and no one but you—will be able to solve unless you reveal its secret. Made as shown in the drawing, the smaller piece (with the dowel glued in) fits into the larger one. The object is to engage the notch in the rubber band which *appears* to be in the large piece.

The illusion that *you* can engage a rubber band is created by the way you withdraw the smaller part. To pull off the gag, you slide the plunger out an inch or so by gripping the tapered end between the thumb and forefinger. Then, when you squeeze, it will snap from your fingers and literally fly back into the block. Then, pass the puzzle to a challenger and sit back and watch as he finds it impossible to hook the band.

Key house number

By C. WAYNE CLOSE

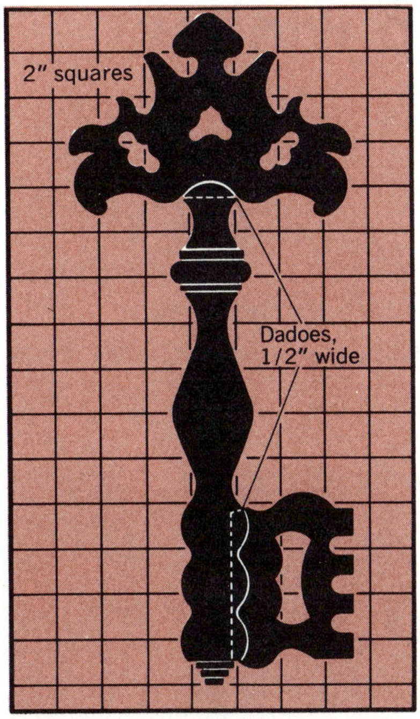

■ LOOKING FOR a novel way to display our house number, my wife and I hit on the idea of making a replica of a keymaker's sign. It's easy to make, and when it's hung from the roof overhang, the early American touch enhances the look of the house.

The turned section is six glued-up 1x5s. While this piece is "square," cut the two ½-in.-wide dadoes for the handle and key sections. Then cut two blocks to fill the dadoes and glue them in place with water-soluble glue and use paper in the joint. Next, the turning is made. After completing the lathe work, the glued-in blocks can be easily pried out with a slight dampening and a chisel. Sand the turned section and set it aside. Now jigsaw the decorative handle and key sections and, after sanding the edges, glue these pieces in place on the turned section with waterproof glue.

The house numbers are jigsawed from ½-in. stock and are glued to a ¾-in. mounting strip fitted with screw eyes to accept the chain as shown. All parts are then assembled with a decorative chain. Though expensive, a solid brass chain is the best choice. But, if you prefer a less expensive chain, you can paint it with flat black enamel.

To finish, stain or paint the key to suit your home's exterior. If you prefer, the key can be antiqued (make distress marks with gouge, chisel or by beating with a chain). Since the key will be exposed to the weather, apply at least two coats of exterior varnish for maximum protection and long life.

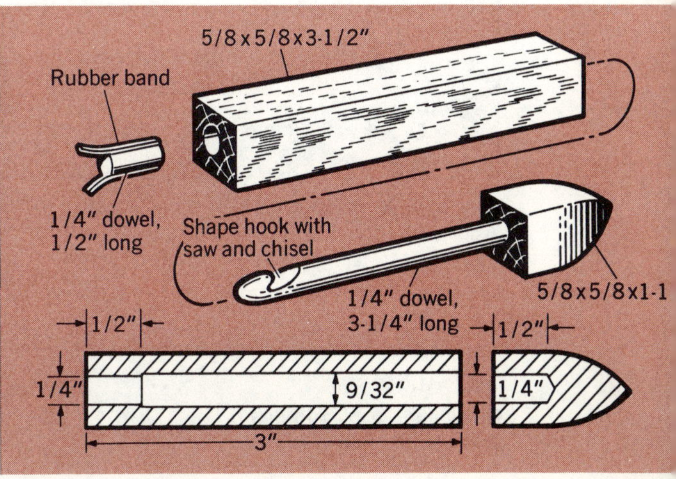

How to replace a broken window pane

Baseballs and other flying objects have a way of finding windows. By learning a few facts about the various weights of glass and how to install them, you can save some money

HEATING OLD PUTTY with the flame of a torch softens it, makes it easier to remove. Avoid scorching the wood by using a shield of scrap tin.

SAFE WAY to remove a cracked pane is to cover it with strips of masking tape and crack further with a hammer. Wear a glove when pulling out broken pieces.

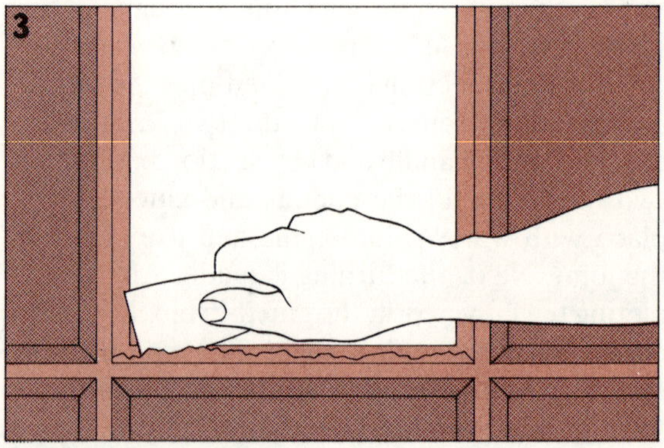

SCRAPE PUTTY CLEAN from rabbet with a knife or chisel, pry out old glazier's points and brush rabbet clean. Seal bare wood with thinned oil-base paint.

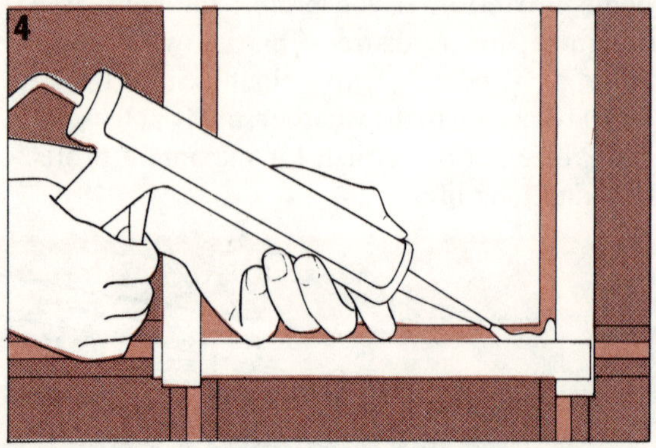

SILICONE RUBBER sealant or regular putty can be used to bed the glass. If silicone is used, outline the opening with tape to keep off adjacent panes.

PRESS NEW PANE (with 1/16 in. allowance on all sides) in place until sealant oozes around edges for tight seal. Remove excess with putty knife.

SEE ALSO
Glass cutting . . . Screens . . . Storm doors and windows

DRIVE GLAZIER'S points, size 1 or 2, using driving tool packaged with points. On small pane use one point along the short sides of glass, two on long sides.

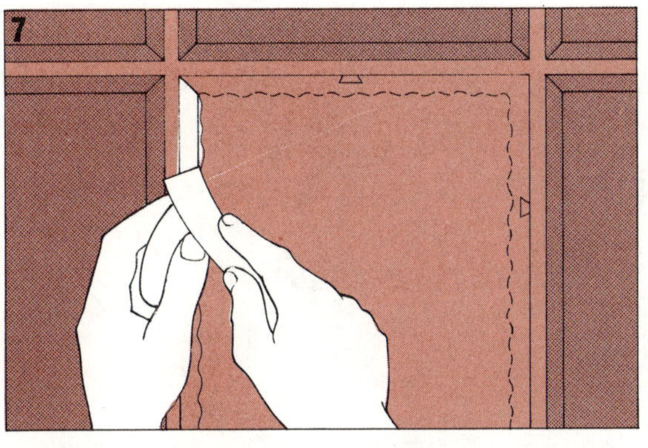

FOR FINAL BEVEL, silicone or putty is smoothed with putty knife dipped in solvent or turpentine to keep material from sticking to the knife blade.

IF PUTTY is used, it should be painted several days later when it's dry. Painting the new putty improves appearance and keeps it from shrinking.

■ SOONER OR LATER most homeowners can count on having to replace a shattered window pane. Knowing how to loosen the old putty, bed the new glass, hold it with glazier's points and strike a neat bevel when applying the putty seal will save you the frustrating job of trying to get someone to come and fix it. A propane torch and caulking gun make the job go faster, but they are not essential. If you work carefully, you can remove the old putty with a sharp chisel, and you can apply the putty by hand without a gun. A hammer and a putty knife are the only other tools you'll need.

The easiest way to get a replacement pane is to take the dimensions to a hardware store or a glass dealer and have the pane cut to fit. Allow 1/16-in. clearance all around so the pane will slip easily into place with no binding.

variety of thicknesses

Glass comes in various thicknesses. *Single-weight* window glass is 3/32-in. thick; it is normally safe to use in sizes up to 2x2 ft. *Double-weight* window glass is 1/8-in. thick; it is normally safe for use in sizes up to 3x5 ft. *Heavyweight* glass is 7/32-in. thick and is recommended where high gusty winds or other hazards may occur. Even heavier glass is available from glass dealers for table and countertops, large sliding doors and other specialized uses.

how to set the window pane

Run a bead of putty or silicone rubber all the way around the rabbet for the pane. Then press the new glass into place, applying equal pressure on all sides. Continue to press until the putty or sealant oozes all the way around the pane.

Next, drive glazier's points into the wood trim to hold the pane in place. You'll find a small driving tool packaged with the points. On a small pane use one point on each of the short sides of glass, two points on the long sides. For larger panes, use your own judgment.

Roll a ribbon of putty between your hands and string it along one side of the pane. Dip your putty knife into turpentine, then form a neat bevel in the putty.

Let the putty dry for several days, then paint it to improve the appearance and keep the putty from shrinking away from the glass and the wood trim.

It is easier to clean the window of putty marks after the putty has hardened for a few days.

Take your choice—three novel wine racks

By ROSARIO CAPOTOSTO

■ HAVING A MODEST selection of wines at hand in one of these handsome racks makes it easy to be a gracious host.

The charming wall rack cradles five bottles. It can hold 10 or more if you lengthen the side members.

You can make it of any hardwood. The best way to cut the cradle side members is to do the holes first. If you have a drill press, use a 1½-in. spade bit and 3⅜-in. adjustable fly cutter; be sure to clamp work securely to the drill-press table. Do not bore the holes with a portable electric drill. Unfortunately circle cutters for portable drills aren't large enough for use here. If you have no drill press, try careful hand-cutting with a jigsaw or sabre saw.

After making the holes, it's easy to cut out the waste by sawing a line tangent to the holes. Sand both surfaces smooth before shaping the edges with a router. Use a *sharp* ⅜-in. corner-rounding pilot cutter; a dull one will tend to chip the wood at the ends of the bottle-holding slots. Finish-sand all parts.

A pair of ⅜-in. dowels are used to join each

Wall-hung rack

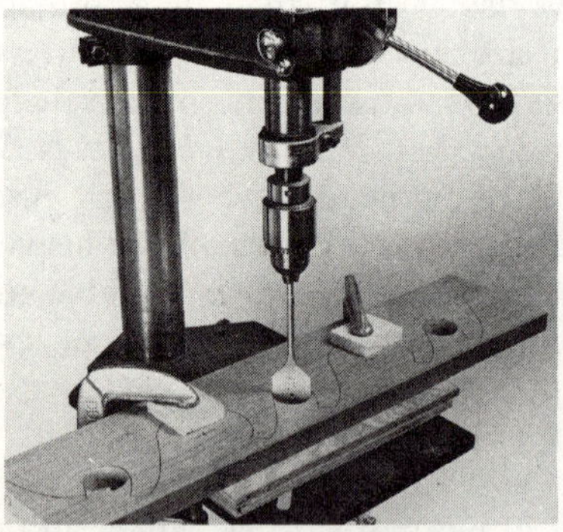

USE A SHARP drill bit and a backup scrap board to obtain a clean-cut hole.

CLAMP WORK securely and keep fingers out of the way when using an adjustable fly cutter.

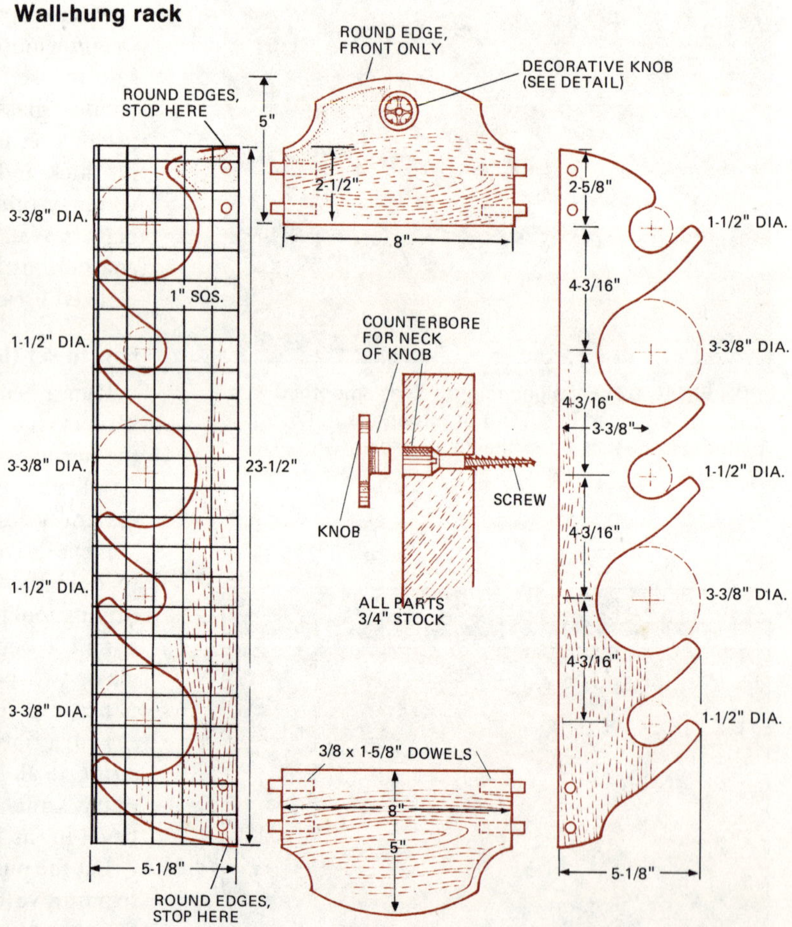

RACK HOLDS five bottles, can be made taller to take more.

SEE ALSO
Bars . . . Plexiglass projects . . . Servers

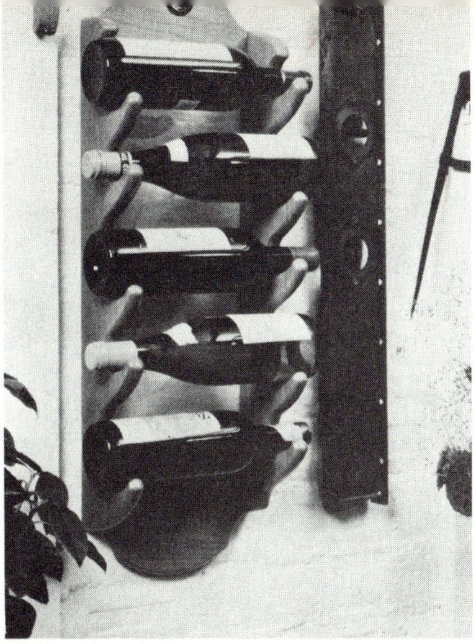

WALL-MOUNTED RACK cradles bottles with their lables in full view. The rack is made of hardwood.

PLEXIGLAS BEAUTY has the look of lustrous glass. At home in the most formal or informal setting, it keeps a sampling of your prize vintages always at hand for any occasion that may arise.

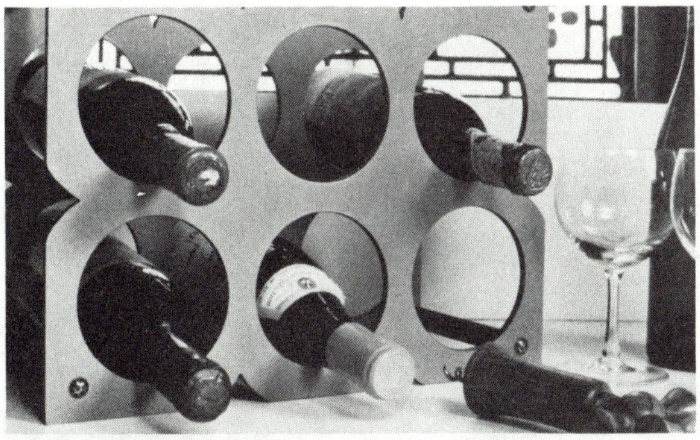

EXTRA SIMPLE TO MAKE, this attractive countertop rack can be very colorful. It is half finished before you begin for it's made from prefinished wall paneling.

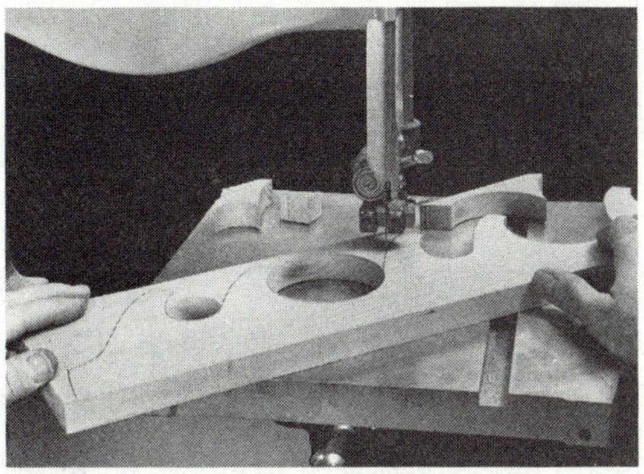

DROP OUT waste by making a pair of cuts tangent to each hole to create a slot.

USE CORNER-ROUNDING bit to shape outer edges. The cutter must be extra sharp.

side to the top and bottom back pieces. Drill holes in the sides first, then insert a pair of dowel centers to transfer and mark the holes accurately in edges of back members. Glue and clamp sides to backs and scrape off any squeezed-out glue before it dries.

The best and safest way to hang the rack is on a screw driven into a wall stud; use an expansion anchor or toggle bolt when you must hang it from a hollow wall. I used a decorative cabinet knob in a counterbored hole to conceal the hanging screw. Apply a coat of sanding sealer to the rack, then two coats of self-rubbing clear finish. Sand with No. 600 paper between coats.

Plexiglas rack. This sparkling see-through wine rack is made by heat-forming a sheet of ¼-in. acrylic plastic into a U shape. Start with a piece 13⅞ x 28-in. Mark centers for the holes, following the drawing, and punch them lightly with an awl. Drill 3⅝-in. holes with an adjustable fly cutter mounted in a drill press. *Never try to use this tool in your portable drill.*

Clamp the workpiece firmly to the press table and run drill about 800 rpm. If your cutter is sharp and clean-cutting, the edges of the holes will come out fairly smooth.

After the holes are bored, clamp the sheet in a bench vise. Scrape all exposed edges with the back of a squarely ground hacksaw blade to remove tool marks. Follow with sanding, starting with No. 400 wet-or-dry abrasive paper, then No. 600, wrapped around a small roll of short-nap carpeting or similar material. Sand until you get a satin edge and then ease all sharp corners.

For a high polish, you'll need polishing compound and a small buffing wheel chucked in a portable drill. Charge the wheel with compound and buff at high speed, but with medium pres-

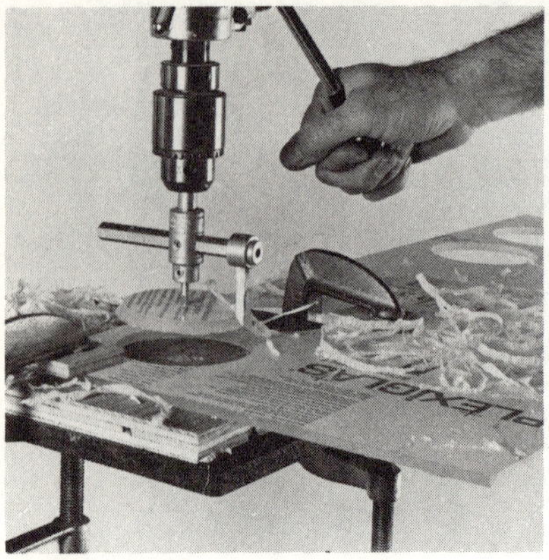

USE FLY CUTTER in drill press to bore holes. Run drill about 7-800 rpm.

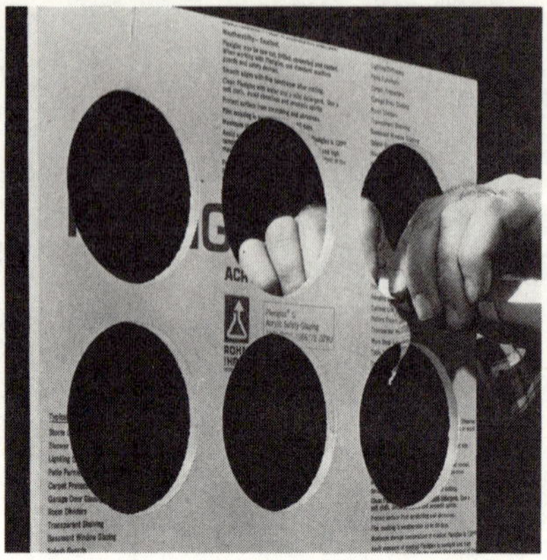

SCRAPE PLASTIC edges with square-ground edge of hacksaw blade.

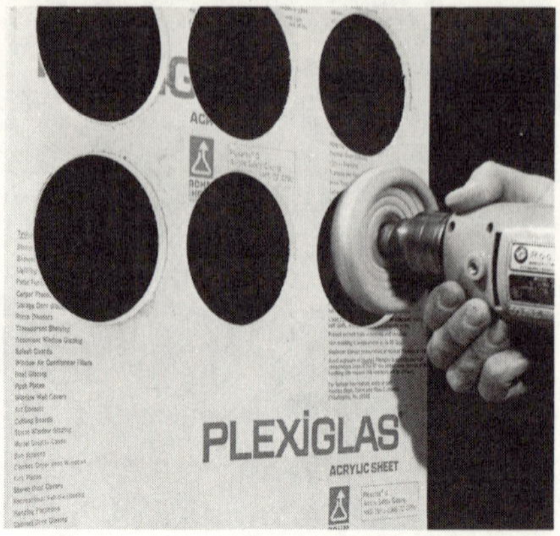

TO POLISH EDGES, buff with polishing compound, cloth buffing wheel.

Plexiglas wine rack

CRYSTAL-CLEAR rack with the look of glass holds six bottles and rests on a wood base.

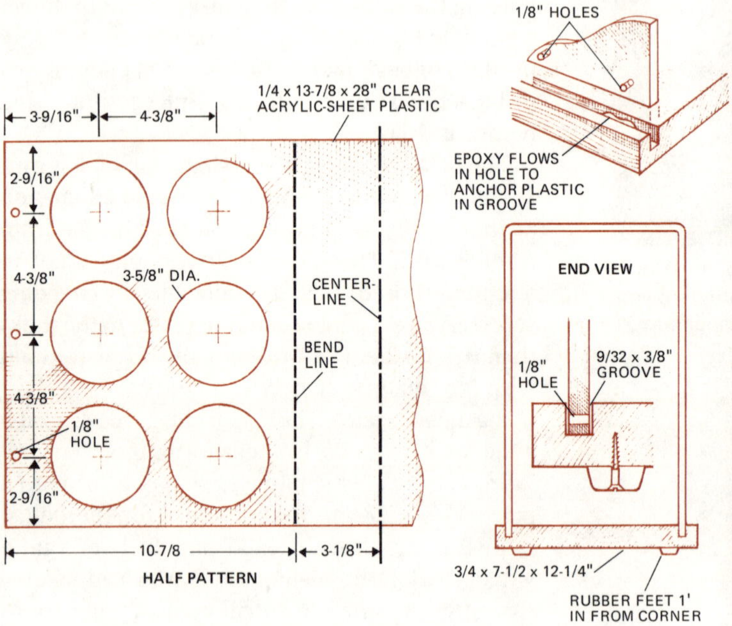

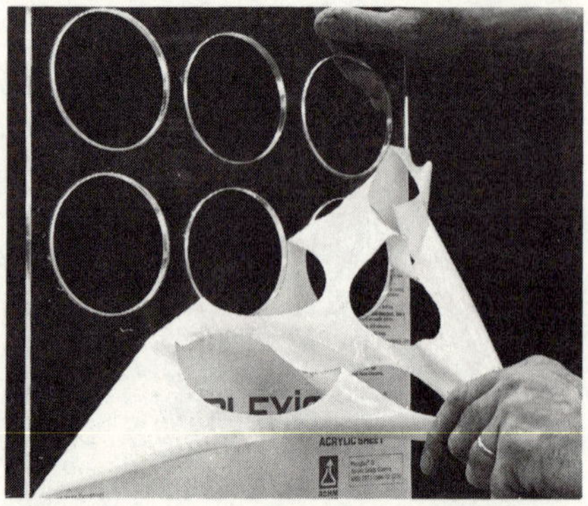

PEEL OFF protective paper, then rinse plastic with soapy water to remove compound.

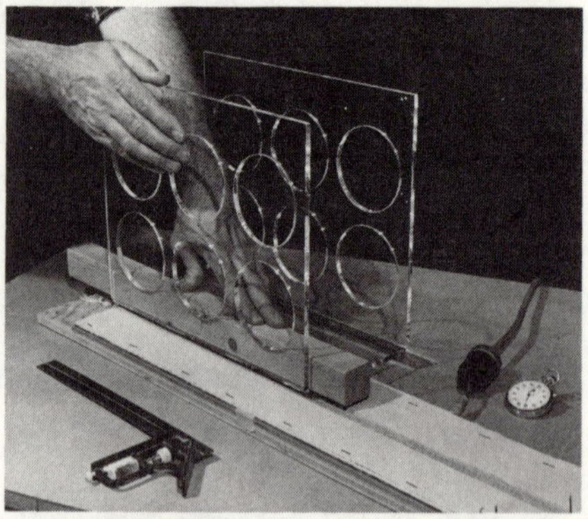

LAY PLASTIC on strip heater; soften 15 minutes. Block insures proper bend.

sure. It won't take much effort to obtain a high gloss. After polishing, peel off the protective masking paper and use a grease pencil to mark the bending lines. Now place the plastic on a strip heater and leave it there for about 15 minutes. When the heat has sufficiently softened the sheet, place a block of wood (with the corner rounded slightly) on the line. Use a square to be sure the block is held at a right angle to the edge of the plastic. Hold the block firmly; then slowly bend the sheet. Once the bend is started properly, you can remove the block and continue the bend a bit beyond the right angle to compensate for spring-back. Remove the work from the heater and hold it (a minute or two) until the plastic cools. Repeat this procedure for the second bend.

If you don't have a strip heater, you can make one with a special heating element (tape) sold at most plastic supply shops.

For the base of the rack, cut two grooves a shade over ¼-in. wide and ⅜-in. deep in a piece of hardwood, sand and apply the finish of your choice.

Finally, drill three ⅛-in. holes along bottom edges of the plastic, wash the piece with soap and lukewarm water, rinse and dry. Mix a bit of quick-drying epoxy and drop three small blobs into each groove so they coincide with the holes in the plastic. The epoxy will flow into the holes and anchor the piece in place.

Marlite rack. A couple scraps of prefinished Marlite wall paneling are used to make this good-looking rack. If you don't happen to have a scrap or two, you can order a single 16x96-in. panel from your lumber dealer; it will give you enough material for four racks. The material is ¼-in. tempered hardboard with a durable baked-on plastic surface.

Mark the centers for the 12 holes and use a fly cutter on the drill press with the work securely clamped. After cutting, sand all edges with No. 220 aluminum-oxide paper, followed with No. 400 and 600-grit, wet-or-dry paper (used dry).

Edges of tempered hardboard can be given an attractive, satin-smooth, dark-brown finish by burnishing. For the outside edges, use a cloth charged with auto-polishing compound. Rub briskly until a good shine is obtained; follow by a hard rub with a dry cloth. To burnish the hole edges, use a buffing wheel in a portable drill.

Four ⅝ x 6-in. dowels are used to assemble the unit. Drill screw pilot holes into the ends of the dowels and clearance holes in the hardboard. Use a very small amount of five-minute epoxy in the dowel ends and drive in screws.

If decorative screws are not available, you might try this: Use a diagonal cutter to snip off the nails from the heads of four ornamental upholstery nails. Then back out the screws after the epoxy has set. Put a drop of epoxy into each of the cupped nailheads and insert screws. After the epoxy has hardened, replace the screws by turning them in by hand.

BORE HOLES with fly cutter, clamp work, use medium speed; don't force feed.

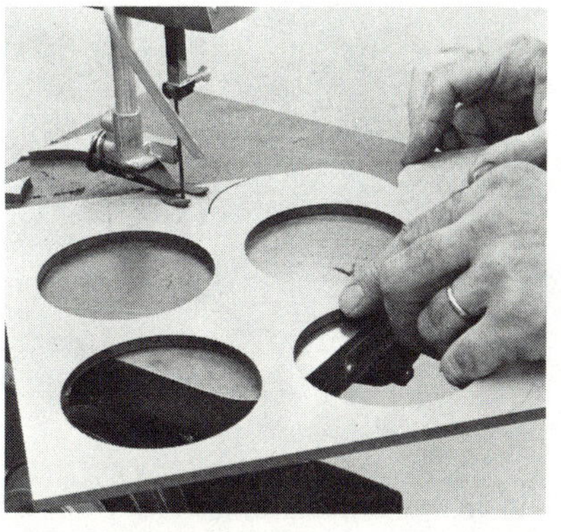

JIGSAW THE OUTER cuts with a fine-tooth blade, saw hardboard with good side up.

BURNISH EDGES shoe-shine fashion with soft cloth and auto-polishing compound.

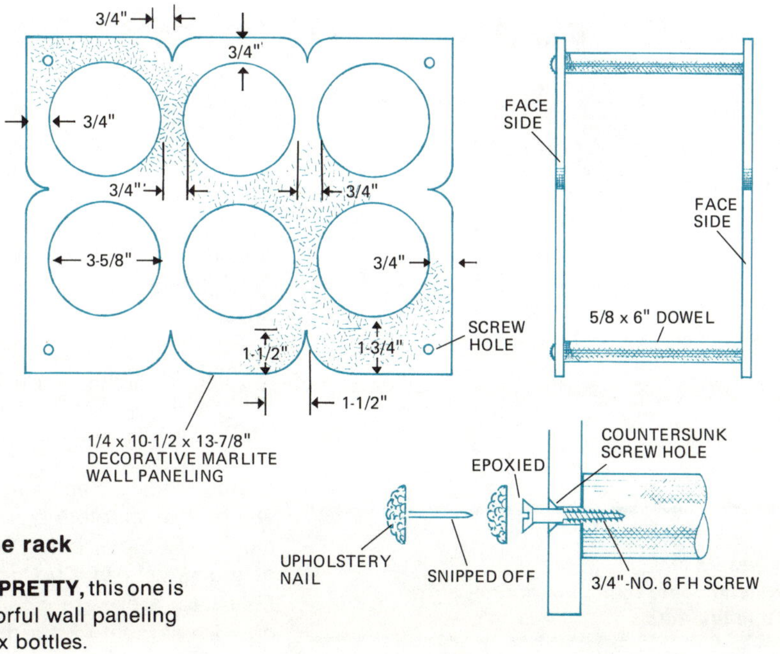

Marlite wine rack

QUICK AND PRETTY, this one is made of colorful wall paneling and holds six bottles.

USE CHARGER, if necessary, to bring your battery up to full charge for winter starting.

How to protect your car against the cold

You'll breeze through the winter if you do the right things to immunize your car against the deep freeze of winter. Here's how to prepare in the fall

By MORT SCHULTZ

SEE ALSO

Auto batteries . . . Battery testers . . . Chains, tire . . . Cooling systems, auto . . . Lubrication, auto . . . Motor oil . . . Tires . . . Tune-up, auto

A STUDY done by the Champion Spark Plug Co. tells us that the number of engine starting failures reaches a peak in winter.

Big deal. Any school kid could have told you that.

But do you know that almost consistently the number of winter starting failures in severely cold Quebec, Canada is less than it is in the warmer southern Atlantic states? Well, it is.

How come? Canadian cars aren't any hardier than ours, so the answer must lie with the fact that 43 percent of the drivers in Quebec are giving their cars a prewinter tune-up, while only 20 percent of the drivers in the southern Atlantic states do the same.

Across the board, the Champion study shows that, where maintenance is practiced, the starting trouble is lowest. In New England, for example, 32 percent of those surveyed winterize their cars and 22 percent have starting failure. Conversely, in seven states taken as a group—Minnesota, North and South Dakota, Missouri, Kansas, Iowa and Nebraska—25 percent of the group surveyed perform prewinter maintenance and 26 percent of them have trouble.

Trying to avert a mechanical problem is just one reason for winterizing a car. Another is to minimize hazards to safety.

To try to touch all the bases in this article—so you don't miss anything when you go to work winterizing your car—we have literally charted a course for you to follow by listing what should be done. Information accompanying each task will allow you to do the work more competently or more easily.

Of course, you may not have to do everything we suggest. It depends on what services you had done in the last couple of months. For instance, if you've just tuned up the engine, you shouldn't have to do it again. However, going into winter with an ignition system which hasn't been serviced since last winter is inviting trouble.

battery checks

■ Replace a battery that is cracked or has eroded terminals.

■ Before testing with a battery hydrometer, add water if the electrolyte level is low and give the battery a high-rate charge for 30 minutes or drive the car for a few hours.

■ A difference of .050 or more specific gravity points between high and low readings signifies a bad battery. Replace it.

■ Remove the battery and scrub it with diluted ammonia or baking soda solution. Flush with water, being sure the vent caps are tight and covered with tape. Clean the battery carrier, too.

■ If the battery shows less than full charge (that is, an overall specific

YOUR BATTERY can't deliver if terminals and posts aren't clean.

gravity of 1.260), charge it on a slow-rate charger.

■ Ideally, a sealed battery should be load-tested to determine its condition. However, in the absence of a 300-amp. load tester and voltmeter, refer to the battery's built-in charge indicator, which provides an indication of battery condition.

service battery cables

■ Replace cables having split or frayed insulation or badly eroded terminals.

■ Disconnect cables using a terminal puller, if necessary. Clean terminals with a wire brush.

■ Reinstall cables, tightening terminals to posts securely. A chief cause of hard starting is improperly secured terminals. If you have a problem getting a terminal to bottom on the battery post, place a wrench socket of suitable size over the terminal and *gently,* very gently, tap the terminal down until it won't go any more.

clean or replace plugs

■ Sparkplugs with worn electrodes, broken insulators or damaged shells should be replaced.

■ Sparkplugs with minimum electrode wear can be cleaned, regapped and returned to service.

replace distributor parts

■ Replace any part—cap, rotor or coil—that shows damage or a sign of damage. "A sign of damage" would be a trail of carbon inside a distributor cap, which signifies a crack.

servicing the distributor

■ If you have to replace breaker points, replace the condenser, too.

■ If new points aren't needed, pass a fine-cut ignition file through the old points one time to clean them before setting gap.

■ An oily smudge on contact points may indicate a clogged PCV system that has caused vapors to be forced into the distributor.

■ Make sure that the condenser and primary wire insulation is in one piece. A bare wire can ground out and bring the engine to a dead stop. See that wires are secured firmly to terminals.

■ If your car has electronic ignition, it has no points and condenser. Setting dwell is not necessary. Setting ignition timing is.

examine secondary cables

■ Replace cables if insulation is cracked, split or brittle.

■ Make sure that cables are firmly seated in the distributor and coil towers and on sparkplugs. "Though lack of contact is involved in most road calls, the problem in most cases is loose wires rather than a defective system," FoMoCo says.

service air and fuel filters

■ Shine a light inside the air filter. If the filter is very dirty, replace it. If it's not too dirty, dislodge particles by slamming the filter on a hard surface.

■ Replace the fuel filter as often as this is stipulated in your owner's manual.

set automatic choke

■ Do this only if the engine becomes hard to start when the weather turns and all other bases have been touched. If the choke is adjustable, turn it one notch at a time to the "rich" side. See if starting gets better.

service cooling system

■ Drain and flush, if necessary.

■ Inspect hoses and test the radiator pressure cap.

■ Add ethylene glycol antifreeze in the proportion necessary to bring protection against freezing in line with the lowest anticipated temperature in your area. *Important:* Use top-quality antifreeze.

■ Inspect drive belts. Replace if cracked or frayed. Adjust if necessary to bring them to adequate tension—¼ to ½-inch play when pressed midway between pulleys.

SPARKPLUGS should be checked for wear, sand-blasted clean and gapped.

lubricate

■ Change oil, if necessary. Drivers in most of the country should select a 10W-30 or 10W-40 motor oil. Where temperatures are consistently between 20° and below 0° F a 5W-30 motor oil may be necessary. If you decide to use a single-viscosity oil and your owner's manual says to use 10W because of the low temperature where you live, avoid sustained high-speed driving.

■ Grease the chassis and body points. Shoot some powdered graphite into door locks to try to avert frozen locks.

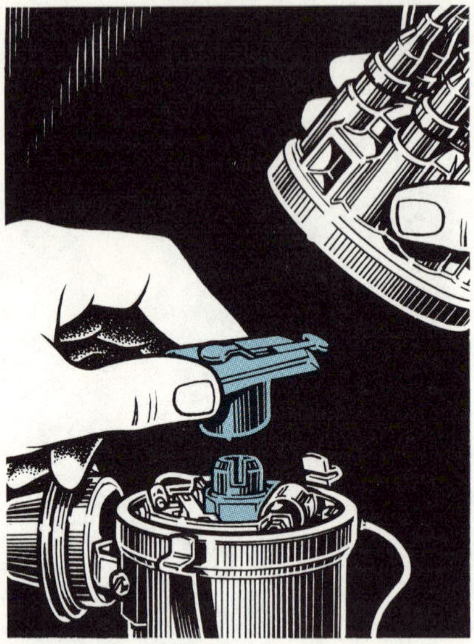

REMOVE distributor cap and rotor and clean and inspect them thoroughly.

get tires in shape

■ Mount snow tires (are they in good shape?), storing the tires you've removed in a clean, dry, cool and closed area away from water, petroleum products, electric motors and heat sources. Place tires on their sidewalls on a flat surface—don't stand them on the tread. Place white sidewall tires whitewall-to-whitewall, one on top of the other to protect the white rubber. If tires remain mounted on wheels, reduce inflation to 12 to 16 p.s.i.

■ If you buy new snow tires and want metal studs, now's the time to get them. The depth of the stud holes molded into winter tire treads and the lengths of studs are carefully matched. In even a few miles of travel, tire treads wear enough, and fill with enough dirt and grit, to disrupt the stud hole-stud relationship. Only new or newly retreaded tires should be studded, if the law in your state permits studded tires.

■ If snow tires were not mounted in storage and are to be put back on wheels, the assemblies should be balanced.

■ Maintain recommended air pressure and check it often. Do not reduce inflation pressure to increase traction. Goodyear says that this is a fallacy "for underinflated tires get less of a grip on slippery surfaces."

CLEAN OR REPLACE the points and replace the condenser if necessary.

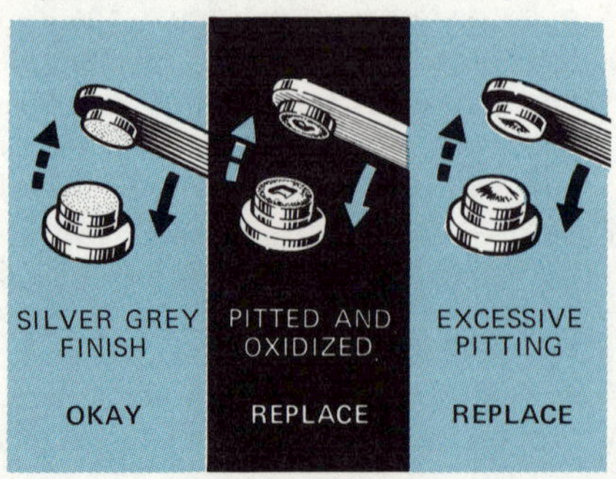

test brakes

■ See that the fluid level in the master cylinder is no less than ¼ inch below the top of the reservoir's lip.

■ Test the hydraulic system for leaks by pressing down on the pedal with the engine running. The pedal should be firm and not fade.

■ If lining (pad) thickness has not been examined in 12,000 miles, remove one front wheel and one rear wheel and do it now. You should have no less than 1/32 inch of lining thickness left. *Important:* If you have to replace the linings (pads) of one wheel, replace the linings of the other wheel on the same axle. Failure to do this will result in unequal braking.

check visual equipment

■ Replace windshield wiper blades if the rubber feels flabby rather than firmly resilient or if blades don't sweep water cleanly away.

■ Make sure the windshield washers work and that nozzles are aimed to squirt water over the area swept by wipers. Nozzles may be bent to aim them properly. If nozzles are clogged, clear the stoppage with a thin piece of wire.

■ Fill the windshield washer reservoir. If your area is subjected to freezing temperatures, the fluid you use should be an antifreeze type. *Caution:* Make certain the label on the container of antifreeze you buy assures you that the product is harmless to paint. If it doesn't, don't use the product.

■ Check to see that all lights and warning signals are working. If one isn't, find out why and fix it.

■ Are defrosters working properly?

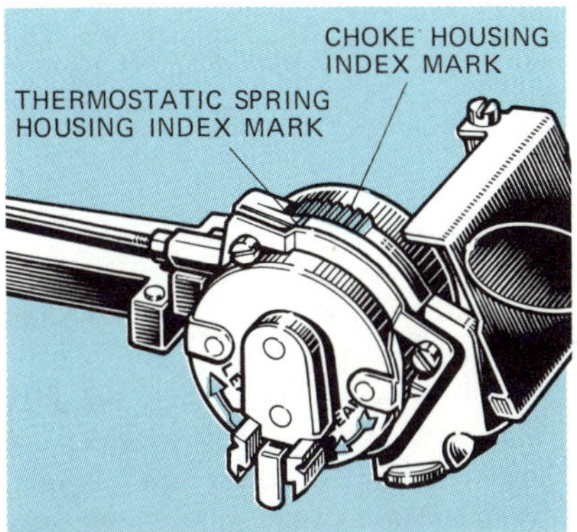

CHOKE ADJUSTMENT is especially important for proper cold starts.

PROPER drive-belt adjustment is necessary for generator and alternator.

■ Test the horn. It may be needed to get you out of a sticky situation one of these winter days.

other checks

■ The exhaust system should be in good shape. There should not be any evidence of holes or rust. Accidental carbon monoxide poisoning cases are more numerous in winter than at any other time.

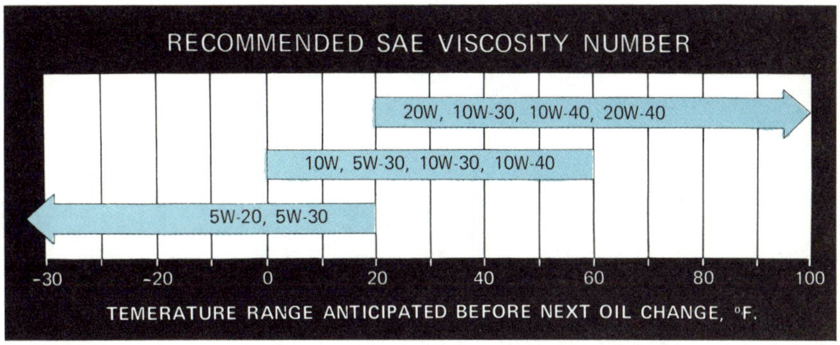

MULTI-VISCOSITY motor oils cover wide ranges of temperature.

■ See that the heater works and throws out enough warm air to make you comfortable.

■ Get winter emergency equipment out of storage and into your car if it isn't already there. This should include a good ice scraper, shovel, extra emergency flares and tire chains (if you use chains). *Important:* If you place extra weight in the rear to attain better traction, make sure it's placed over or ahead of the rear axle. According to Goodyear: "Weight behind the rear axle can reduce vehicle stability and front-wheel traction."

cold-start tips

Once your car is all checked out and ready to go, chances are in your favor that the engine is going to start. But there's always the possibility of a sudden, severe cold snap that could hamper starting. Here are a few extra tips that may help the situation:

■ Don't pump the accelerator pedal. Doing so will send raw gas into the cylinders that will tend to flood the engine on a cold day.

■ If the engine does flood, turn off the ignition key. Hold the accelerator pedal to the floor (do *not* pump it) and turn on the ignition, cranking the engine in five-second bursts. Don't overdo this since you don't want to add a dead battery to your trouble. If the engine won't start after a reasonable number of five-second bursts, allow it to remain idle for 5 to 10 minutes. Then try it again.

■ If the weather is severely cold for a sustained period, a 75 or 100-watt light bulb kept burning under the hood will help keep the temperature of the battery high enough so it will provide a good kick in the morning.

WINDSHIELD-WASHER fluid must be winterized for lowest anticipated temperatures.

■ If you live in really cold country and oil tends to gel overnight so engine cranking is sluggish, you should use a dipstick heater. The heater slides into the dipstick tube and is plugged into house current.

■ Whenever you start a car, keep all lights and accessories turned off. The engine stands a better chance of getting going if it doesn't have to share current with other parts.

The 10 worst heat thieves in your home

Energy experts have pinpointed 10 'fuelish' areas in the average home. We counter with 21 ways to beat heat loss and get the most out of your fuel dollars

By RICHARD F. DEMPEWOLFF

■ THERE MAY BE fluctuations in the rate of rise, but one thing is certain—energy prices keep going up, up, up! Low-cost solar or atomic energy may provide long-range answers, but you can beat the high cost of heat right now by squeezing every last calorie out of your fuel dollar.

For this article, we asked five engineers at the Energy Research and Development Administration (ERDA) to spell out the 10 most common heat-loss areas. You're probably familiar with the big losers like an uninsulated attic and uncaulked openings around windows and doors. But some thieves on ERDA's "10 most-wanted" list may surprise you.

In each category ERDA engineers have estimated a range of dollar savings you can get by following our heat-saving plans. The figures are based on an average, 1750-square-foot house in a northern state and were current at the time this was written.

Savings will vary. You'll get high-range savings in categories where your house is totally deficient and low-range savings where you're improving protection you already have, like adding insulation in your attic. It's not too late to start saving your winter fuel dollars—they'll come in handy for next summer's vacation!

1 DUCT/PIPE INSULATION

Saving per yr., $20–$160

Sheet-metal heat ducts and copper hot-water supply pipes are the two most common types of heat supply. Unfortunately, both act as heat exchangers as well as suppliers. For example, if a duct pipe runs through an unheated area like a crawl space, a substantial amount of heat will be lost through walls of the duct before it reaches the register. ERDA investigators have found extreme cases in contemporary houses with cantilevered upper stories, where hot-air ducts were actually exposed to the weather. One engineer noted: "They lose more heat to the outside air than they convey to the rooms they were installed to serve."

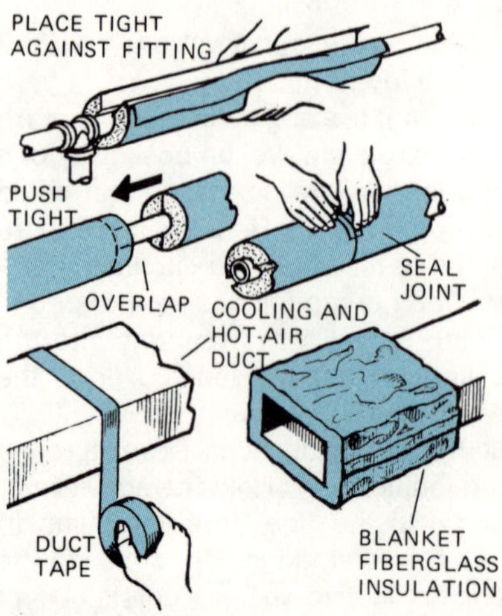

SEE ALSO

Caulking . . . Fireplaces . . . Furnaces . . . Heaters, water . . . Heating systems, home . . . Insulation . . . Storm doors and windows

The solution is duct insulation, available in one and two-inch-thick blankets. For cylindrical ducts, butt collar-like sections of the insulation and secure them with tape. For rectangular ducts, cut sections to fit snugly all the way around, but don't compress the mineral filler. The cut end should be butted flush by the end you bring around to meet it, and then you should seal the entire joint with a sufficiently wide tape. Avoid squeezing the batt. Be sure to check for—and repair with duct tape (see sketch)—all loose joints and split seams in the ducting before insulating.

Note: The ERDA engineers concede that exposed ducting and piping in full basements and crawl spaces help warm the ground floor and, in some cases, serve to heat usable basement areas. If this reasoning is followed, they suggest that the basement itself should be insulated as specified under section 10 of this report.

If you have a full basement with laundry, family room, shop or other facilities that require heat when they're being used in winter, it may pay you to insulate the ducting anyway—but also to run small ducts (insulated) to the areas in question—with terminal registers that can be closed when any of the spaces are not being used.

2 STORM WINDOWS AND DOORS

Saving per yr., $76–$146

Glass acts as a heat exchanger to the outdoors. Single panes in a home with about 18 windows and two glass-lighted doors can lose more than 20 percent of your heat during an average northern winter. This is a "heat leak" any do-it-yourselfer can plug easily. While triple-track combination storm-and-screen sash is convenient and efficient, it costs $30 and up per window, installed. Dead air space is what counts. You can now buy transparent plastic sash in a kit made by Plaskolite, Inc. (see photo). The 1/16-inch polyethylene sheet fits a vinyl mounting frame with pressure-sensitive tape on one side that seals it to the *inside* of the window casing—no ladder acrobatics necessary. The frame, white but paintable to match your color scheme if desired, remains permanently attached to the window. The clear plastic sheet is removable by unsnapping the lip of the vinyl frame—a fingertip operation. The unit comes for basic window sizes, priced accordingly.

Standard single-pane storm sash, which you can make yourself from aluminum framing and regular glass sizes available in hardware stores—or standard wood-framed storm sash available in lumber yards—runs about $10 and up per window. Energy experts point out that all types are about equally effective. The more expensive ones are simply more convenient and generally more attractive in appearance.

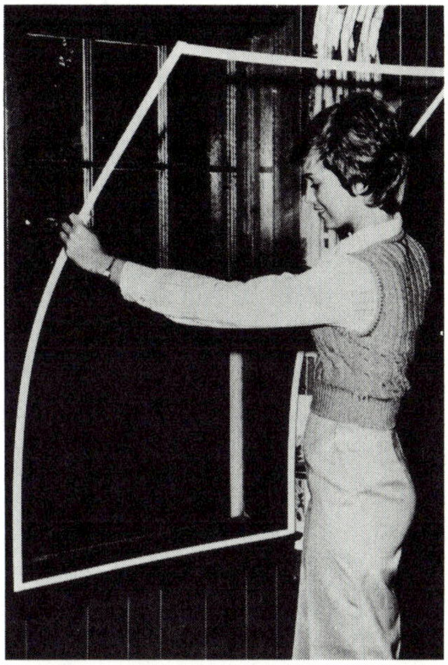

Combination storm and screen doors also are available from building supply yards in metal or wood. It's better to buy them complete since parts are precision cut in order to provide a snug fit for the storm insert, and the better the fit, the less heat will be lost.

3 MAXIMUM ATTIC INSULATION

Saving per yr., $35–$120

One of the most effective ways to cut fuel costs is to insulate your attic. While most homes today have *some* insulation in the overhead, few are equipped with enough, say the experts. ERDA authorities now recommend blanket or batt-type insulation rated R-30 for oil or gas-heated homes in cold winter zones. That's about 10 inches, made up in two layers since batts don't come that thick. Electrically heated homes in cold climes call for R-38 (about 12 inches). Heat engineers point out that if you already have six inches or more, additional thicknesses won't pay off in dollar savings over a reasonable length of time, except in the coldest areas or if you have electric heat. There are three basic systems for insulating attics:

■ **Unfinished, unfloored.** Batts can be layered one atop the other between joists, extending above them as needed.

■ **Unfinished, floored** (with no insulation beneath the boards). Remove the floor, lay batts between and to full depth of joists, and replace floor. If more insulation is needed for maximum protection, staple batts between rafters as well.

■ **Finished attics.** Lay batts between joists above the ceilings of the finished rooms (you may have to cut a ceiling trapdoor to do this). Staple additional batts between the outer roof rafters (see sketch) beyond the knee walls of the rooms. Engineers also recommend that the attic gable-end walls in these triangular spaces also be insulated between studs.

What about sidewall insulation throughout the house? ERDA's experts disagree with some other agencies on retrofitting existing buildings. Their studies have shown that injection of wall insulation must be done commercially; that it is far too expensive for dollar pay-back in a reasonable time and usually proves inadequate.

An energy agency in Minnesota foam-insulated a test wall and later removed interior panels to check the coverage. "There were voids all over the place," reports an ERDA scientist. "Wire cables, electric boxes, fire stops and 'cats' set up barriers that completely blocked the foaming urethane as it tried to spread out."

But attics are another matter. Even if yours *is* insulated, check to see how much you have. If another 4 to 6 inches would bring you up to R-22 or R-30 rating, the investment will pay off if you install it yourself.

4 CAULKING AND WEATHERSTRIPPING

Saving per yr., \$30–\$70

In many homes, ERDA investigators found that up to 70 percent of heat loss was due to infiltration of outside air coming through window and door casings and building sills. herever different materials or parts of a building join, caulking should be applied and regularly renewed. Tube cartridges and a gun are the basic tools, and anyone can do the job. Places to check and caulk if needed:

■ All joints between door and window frames and siding.

■ Along bottom edge of siding where it laps the foundation wall, as well as inside the basement where the sill rests on the foundation.

■ Outside water faucet plates and other penetrations of the outside walls.

■ Joints between wing extensions, porches and main body of the house.

■ Where outside chimney or other masonry joins the house wall.

Large gaps, often found between foundation wall and back of siding, should be packed with oakum, caulking cotton or similar filler before caulking is applied. Most cartridge-type caulks today will do an adequate job. Butyl and silicone types will stay resilient and resist cracking.

Weatherstripping windows and doors —an obvious heat-leak stopper—can be done by amateurs nowadays, using any of the wide variety of materials.

■ **Foam-rubber** stripping backed with adhesive is easiest to install, and least expensive. Applied against door jambs it's good for a year or two but should be replaced when worn. It can't be used on double-hung sash except as a top and bottom stop seal, since it won't stand up under friction of the sliding sections.

■ **Rolled vinyl,** tacked to door jambs and window frames of any type, also is simple to install and provides a long-lasting seal. The only disadvantage is its visibility. On double-hung windows the "roll" should press lightly against the wood frame of the sash at sides, bottom and top. A strip nailed to the underside of the top sash laps and seals the joint between upper and lower window halves. On casement windows the strips are tacked so the window compresses the "roll" when shut.

■ **Thin spring metal** makes a highly durable seal for doors and most types of window, and is invisible when properly installed. It can be handled by do-it-yourselfers, but is difficult and somewhat exacting; doors are much easier than double-hung windows. The strips must be installed by opening the sash and sliding the side strips into the channel behind the sash frame, where it is tacked under the sash cords. Full-width strips are fastened to the underside of the bottom rail on the lower sash, and top of the upper sash top rail, and a full-width strip goes on the inside of the bot-

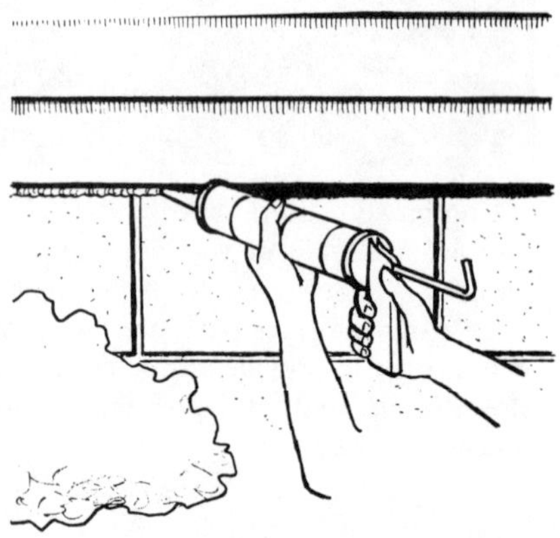

tom rail of the top sash, with nailheads hammered flush so the window will close easily.

■ **Metal J-strips** for doors and casement windows call for critical alignment, but provide durability and an excellent seal.

Door-bottom drafts can be stopped with simple "sweeps" that fasten to the outside of the bottom rail, or "vinyl bulb" thresholds, which require door removal and fitting. Interlocking metal thresholds are even more fussy, and require careful and accurate alignment.

5 INSULATE WATER HEATER

Saving per yr., \$28–\$69

You can save from \$5 to \$45 on this facility just by cutting down the water temperature. Normally, 120° F. is plenty hot. Dishwashers without heating elements, however, demand a 140° supply, but anything above that is wasted and can shorten the life of a glass-lined heater as well. The heat experts have determined that an additional 5 to 8 percent of water-heater energy can be saved by wrapping the unit in an outside

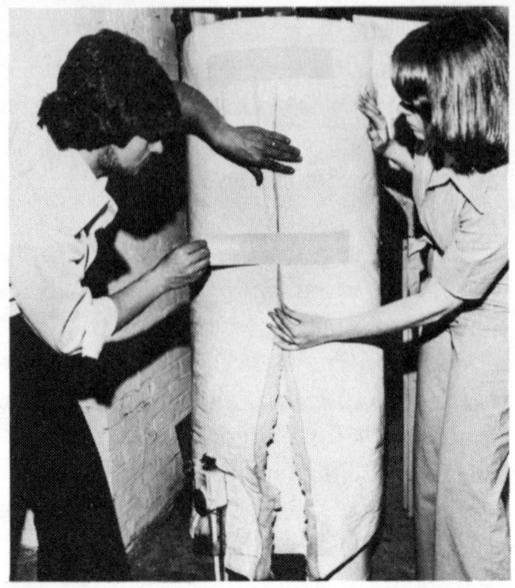

layer of insulation. Johns Manville now has insulation kits that are designed especially for either electric or gas water heaters. ERDA engineers warn that if you wrap your gas heater, take care not to block air vents, and the top of the tank should be left uncovered.

The small cost of doing this job will pay for itself in less than a year. Another saver: drain a gallon of water from the bottom of the tank each year. Sediment that settles in the bottom insulates the water from the heating element.

6 UPGRADE THE FURNACE

Saving per yr., \$25–\$65

According to ERDA, most of what can be done about a furnace should be handled by professionals. To check the efficiency of your setup, the amount of "fuel-in" and "energy-out" must be measured, as must the chemical content of the exhaust. Fuel suppliers may have the instruments to do this. An inefficient furnace will show low carbon dioxide and high temperature in the stack. An efficient oil furnace should run above 14 percent CO_2, and less than 450° F. stack temperature. Gas should run the same for CO_2, but under 330°. Besides the usual filter changes (in forced hot-air systems), air bleeding (in hot-water systems), cleaning and adjustments, several other things can be done to enhance performance of any heating system:

■ **Steam and hot water.** Installation of a "baffle" in the firebox will spread the flame to the sidewalls and heat the medium more quickly. Heat engineers caution that installation should be made by specialists, since exhaust gases are slowed by the device, and it may create a hazard unless properly fitted.

■ **Forced hot air.** Up to 10 percent of a home's total heat loss may result from faulty cyclic operation of the furnace. This can be decreased by setting the fan switch to turn off the fan at five degrees above the thermostat setting, and turn it on as near above that setting as the switch permits.

The old controversy over whether it's better to feed the furnace combustion chamber with preheated inside air, or introduce cold air from outdoors, is settled, according to ERDA. An enclosed duct system bringing cold air directly from outside to the furnace has proven to be the most efficient system. One engineer explained, "A furnace operating on inside air pulls cold air into the house all the time and a significant amount of the warm air it uses is shot up the chimney."

Small-diameter ducts (usually about 4 inches) bringing outside air to the variable draft fan on oil furnaces, for example, will keep the furnace running cleaner and more efficiently.

7 FLUE-PIPE RETROFITS

Saving per yr., $60 plus

A distressing part of any fossil-fueled furnace is that a significant percentage of the heat it produces goes up the flue. Some interesting new devices, however, now recapture some of that lost energy. A typical device is the heat pipe.

■ **Heat pipe.** This compact heat exchanger can be attached to either a vertical or horizontal flue pipe run. What it does is intercept the waste heat on its way to the chimney, extract it from the gases and redirect it to wherever it's wanted—to warm the basement, a particular upstairs room via extra duct, or it can be fed into the house duct system. A danger, scientists point out, is that removing too much heat from exhaust gases can decrease their buoyancy and result in a reverse flow. Hence, heat pipes, too should be installed by specialists, says ERDA.

Lack of proper draft in the chimney, besides producing toxic gas in the house, could also ruin the furnace.

8 FIREPLACE DAMPER

Saving per yr., $60

No builder today would install a fireplace without a damper, but many that are installed fit poorly and don't close snugly. In many old houses, the fireplace chimney is wide open, drawing warm air to the outdoors as effectively as an open window.

While the installation of an effective damper in an existing fireplace is an expensive business, extremely attractive glass fronts for fireplaces are readily available. The glass doors can be opened when a fire is blazing, and closed to seal off the entire opening when the hearth is not in use. Vents across the bottom can be opened to provide a draft if you like your fire behind glass. The units run about $125 up, depending on quality and size of opening. They can save up to 6 percent of the annual heat you put into your house, and will pay for themselves in about two years with the protection that they provide.

9 THERMOSTAT CONTROLS

Saving per yr., $24–$48

Slide-rule wizards have calculated that if everyone in the country set back his thermostat about 10° at bedtime and turned it up at about 5 a.m., the result would be a saving of about 4 percent of the country's total yearly fuel consumption. For each homeowner it would amount to about 10 percent annual saving in the North; 30 percent in the South. Well, now a number of devices on the market will do the work for you.

■ **Clock thermostat.** Several versions are being produced by well-known companies, and most heating supply outlets carry them. They range from about $100 to $150. You set them to drop a given number of degrees at 10:00 or 11:00 p.m., and move up to the desired room temperature again in time for your morning shower.

RESISTOR-TYPE control plugs into a wall outlet to run a clock that triggers a heat unit under the thermostat.

■ **Clock-triggered resistor.** This device does the same job by fooling the thermostat into shutting down the furnace at night and returning it to normal operation before you wake up. Some four manufacturers currently are producing them. They cost from $10 to $30 and are easy to install. The timer unit is simply plugged into a nearby outlet and the unit is mounted directly below your thermostat. Small amounts of electricity cause heat to flow from the resistor at the top of the unit to the temperature sensing controls of the thermostat. The built-in 24-hour timer lets you set the off-on cycle to your convenience.

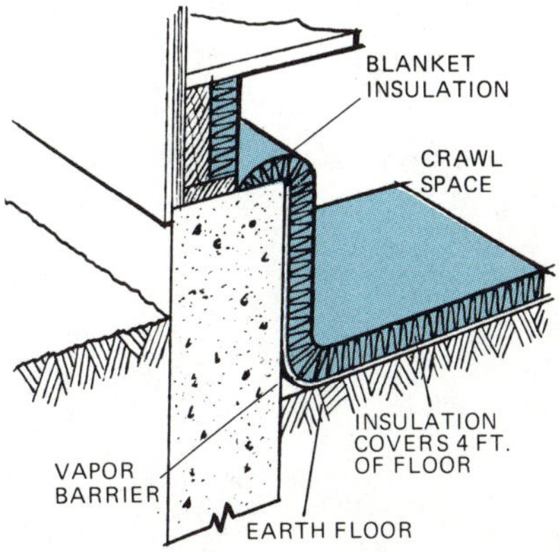

10 BASEMENT INSULATION

Saving per yr., $20–$45

If you've insulated heating ducts or heat-system pipes in your basement or crawl space, it is almost essential to insulate the house foundation walls to protect water pipes and to make the basement livable. In accessible crawl spaces, batts are run between each floor joist, over the sill, down the wall and across three or four feet of the earth floor inside the space. In full basements, 2x3 framing (with sill and plate) is built on two-foot centers, against the foundation with insulation batts run between. The batts need only extend down the wall as far as the frost line for your location. This structure then can be covered with dry-wall panels to accommodate the use to which the space will be put. In both foundation types, a vapor-barrier sheet should be laid against the concrete surface just beneath the insulation.

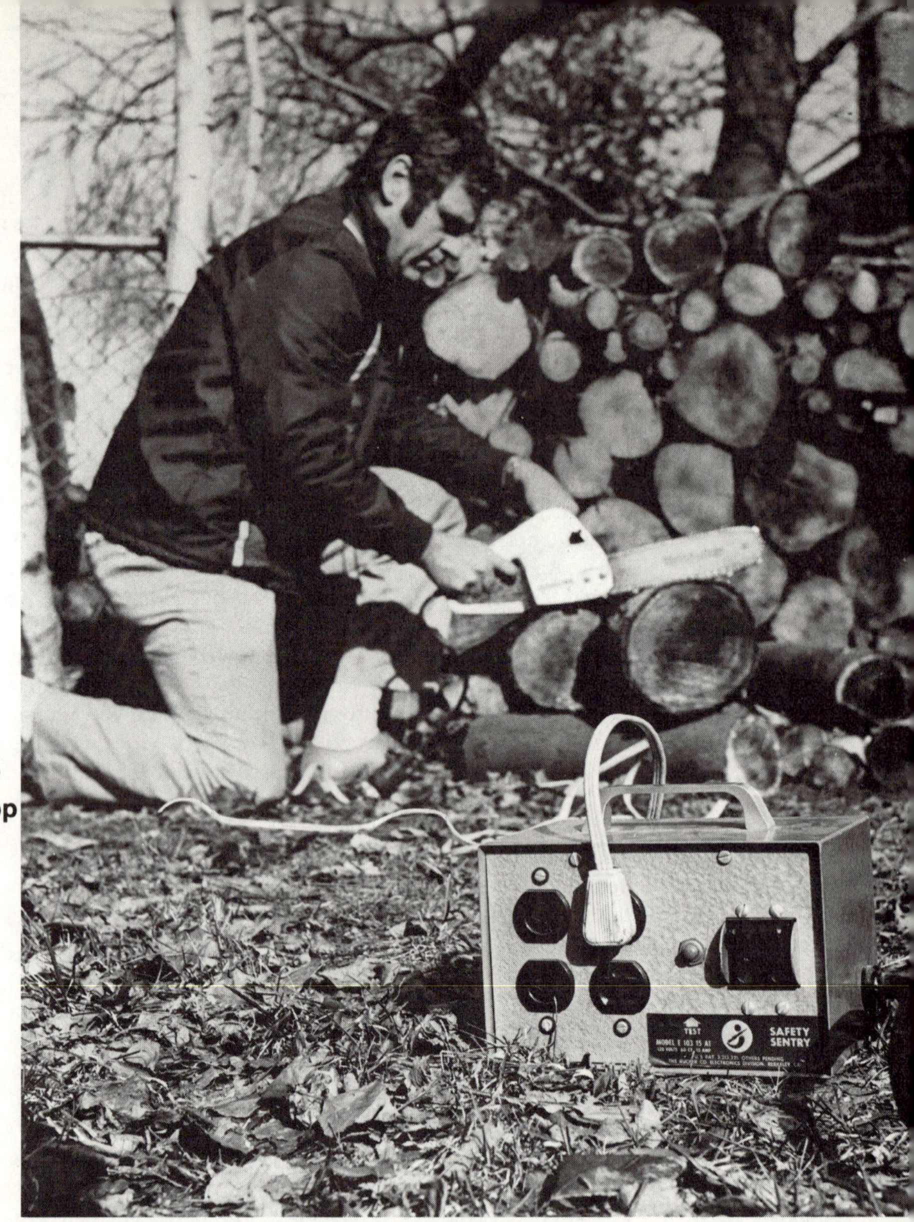

Ground-fault circuit interrupters are required for outdoor and swimming-pool outlets and are worth the investment for workshop or basement. Here's what you need to know about how they work and how to choose one

Protect your family from outdoor electric shock

By D. J. HOLFORD and HARRY WICKS

SEE ALSO

Electrical wiring . . . Extension-cord reels . . . Kitchens . . . Swimming pools . . . Testers, continuity . . . Workshops

■ ON A WARM Saturday morning, your kids head for your back-yard pool. About noon your wife decides to edge-trim the lawn with an electric edger. Later, you're cutting lumber with your portable circular saw (while standing on damp grass).

These are typical family activities on a weekend—yet three times different members of your family were exposed to the risk of serious electrical-shock injury and possible electrocution.

All it would take would be an insulation failure on a pool outlet, the edge trimmer or the electric

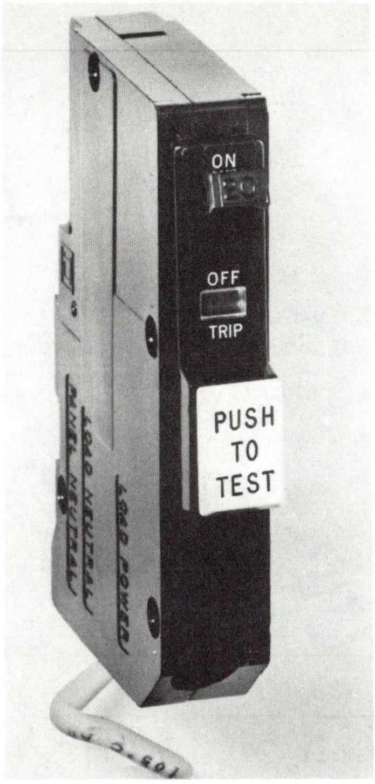

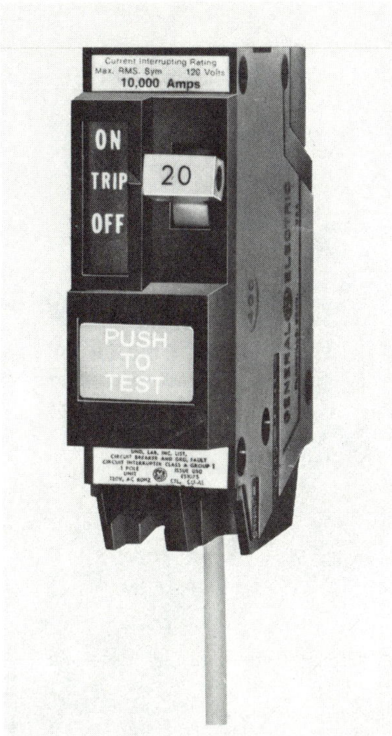

A BRANCH CIRCUIT is completely protected when the breaker in the service panel is a GFCI type. Square D breaker (far left) takes up the same space as the circuit breaker it replaces. This manufacturer has models available for 15, 20, 25 and 30-amp. breakers.

CIRCUIT BREAKER (near left) by General Electric has 5-milliamp. ground-fault protection. It can be used to replace standard plug-on or bolt-on breakers. Available in 15, 20, 25 or 30 amps., 120-v., it has a 10,000-amp. interrupting capacity and a push-to-test feature to provide verification of performance.

Other types of interrupters

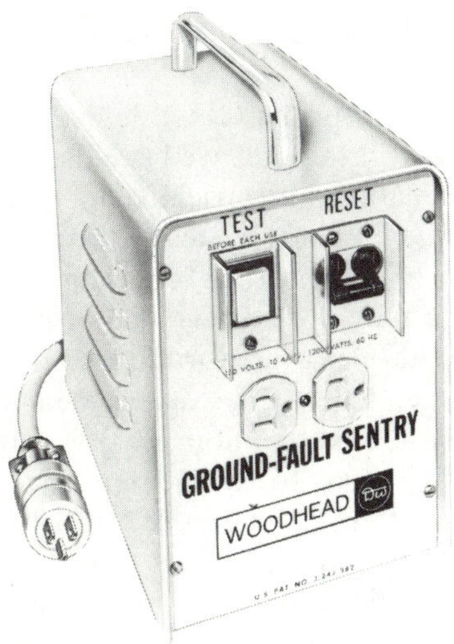

THIS PORTABLE interrupter is designed for on-the-job ground-fault protection. The unit is simply plugged into a power source, and tools plug into it. Model 1670 by Daniel Woodhead is claimed to be the most sensitive GFCI available. It trips on 0.2 ma. of current.

A LOW-PRICED interrupter, the Interrupter/15 by Pass & Seymour, is built into a duplex receptacle and fits a standard outlet box. It's available in two models—dead-end protecting its own outlets, and feed-through for protecting all outlets on the circuit.

THIS PORTABLE GFCI can plug into any 15-amp., 120-v. standard grounded receptacle to provide ground-fault protection; thus it is ideal to keep in your toolbox for use with power tools indoors or out. It's the GFP-115 by Harvey Hubbell.

Other portable interrupters

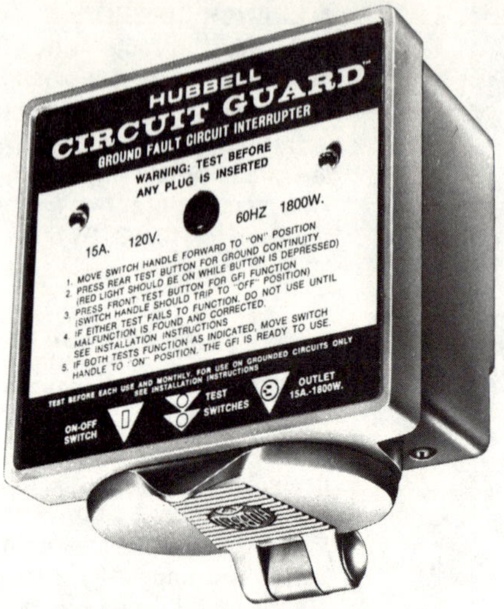

RAINPROOF OUTLET, Hubbell model GFA-315, can be mounted on any existing outdoor receptacle, but you should keep in mind that it has just one ground-fault protected outlet.

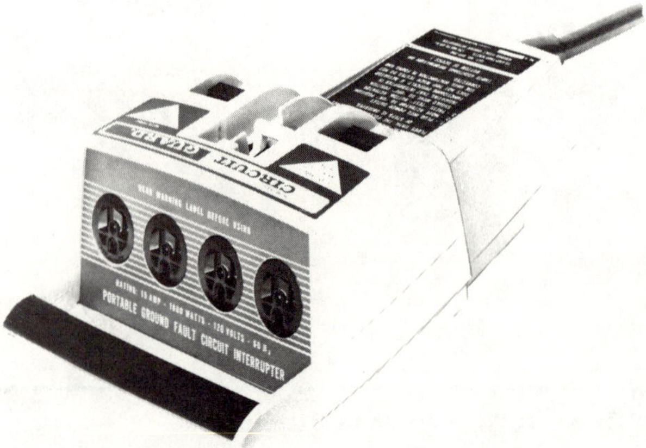

INTENDED FOR CONSTRUCTION SITES, Harvey Hubbell portable GFCI, model GFP-201, is ideal when a number of protected outlets are desirable. Instructions for testing all units before use are clearly spelled out on labels.

saw. Should such a power leakage occur, the user himself becomes the route by which an electrical current will find its way from the tool to ground.

The National Electric Code as of Jan. 1, 1973, changes this picture. All 15 and 20-amp. outdoor receptacles in one and two-family dwellings must be equipped with devices called Ground Fault Circuit Interrupters (they are referred to as GFCI or GFI by the electrical trade).

GFCIs are also required for any receptacle within 10 to 15 ft. of a swimming pool, and all equipment used with storable pools must be on GFI protected circuits. (As of Jan. 1, 1974, GFCI's were required for use on 15 and 20-amp. circuits set up at construction sites.)

Stated simply, a GFI provides protection against serious injury or death caused by contact with damaged or defective electrical equipment such as those tool-insulation failures just mentioned.

And, according to electrical industry sources we have contacted, this is just a beginning. Most experts see a trend toward much greater in-home use of GFIs. It is expected that, eventually, similar devices will be required in kitchens, bathrooms and high-accident areas, such as workshops.

A wide range of the GFCI devices are available, and on these pages we have listed some of those obtainable at electrical suppliers.

What a GFCI does, basically, is compare the currents in milliamps. (ma.) entering and leaving a circuit; if they are not identical it means that some current is leaking to ground. When the tool user is grounded, such leakage means severe shock at best, electrocution at worst. The GFCI upon sensing a leak trips the circuit and turns off the power within 25/1000ths of a second. That's not quite fast enough to avoid your feeling some tingling sensation, but it is fast enough to save your life.

(Once aware of leakage, you must check your electrical equipment to see if the insulation has broken down. If the tool proves to be okay, it means that the problem is in the wiring and you should call in an electrician to trace and correct the problem.)

Where should you install ground-fault protection? Ideally, throughout your house. But that could be expensive. A good rule of thumb is to install a ground-fault circuit interrupter wherever there is moisture present or grounded metal surfaces that the tool user may contact. In short, those high-accident areas mentioned previously.

Total in-home protection is achieved by replacement of all circuit breakers with GFCI breakers. But the installation costs—even on a do-it-yourself basis—will escalate rapidly.

For openers, you should consider replacing your outdoor outlets with one of the weather-proof GFCIs that can be installed in place of an existing duplex.

Or you can choose a portable type, which you can keep in your toolbox so it will be handy anywhere, indoors or out, when you have occasion to use any 110-v. power tool.

How ground-fault interrupter 'guards' circuit

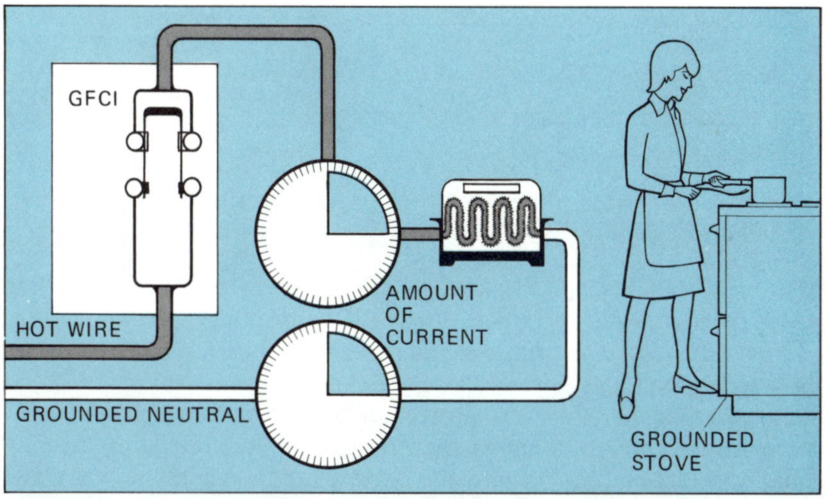

SIMPLIFIED DRAWINGS at left show how a ground-fault circuit interrupter monitors current flow to assure equal current in the wires. Condition shown here is safe.

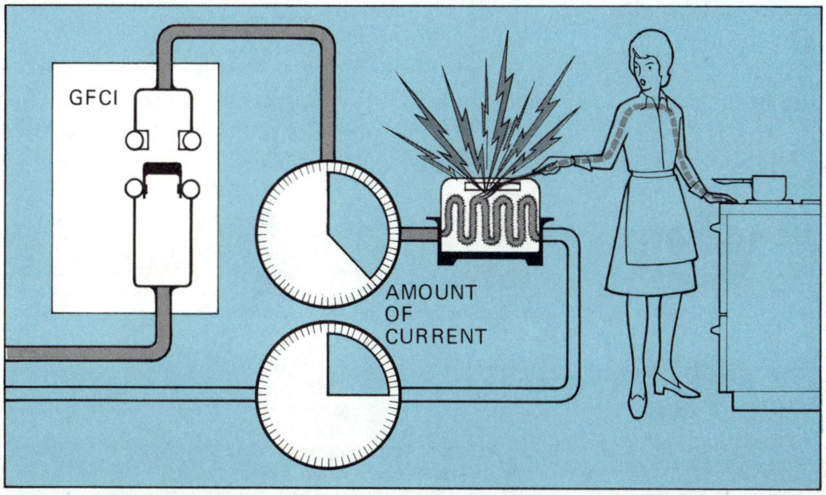

A GROUND FAULT changes current in one wire. Here, housewife wrongly poking a metal object into toaster creates a shock hazard—because she is "grounded" by touching a grounded metal stove. Upon sensing current difference, GFCI acts fast (trips) to shut off current.

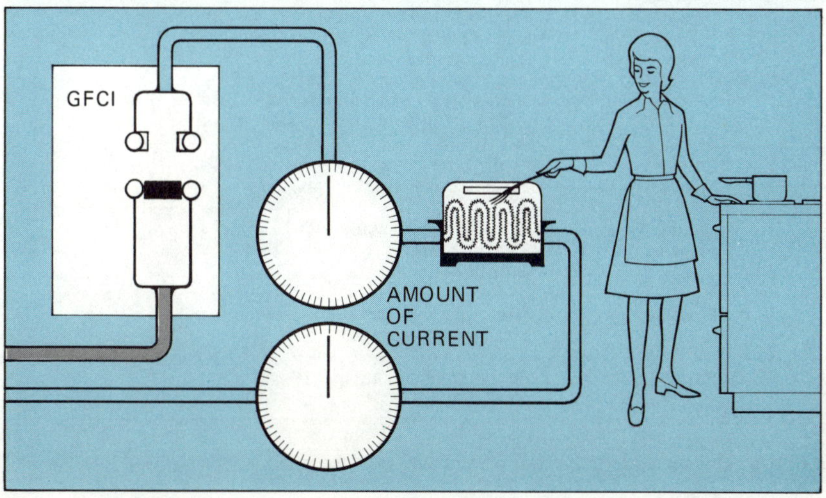

GFCI cuts off the circuit completely to eliminate the shock hazard but 25/1000ths of a second after it senses a ground fault. Thus, the circuit interrupter is, in effect, a circuit "watchdog."

GFCI WIRING DIAGRAM

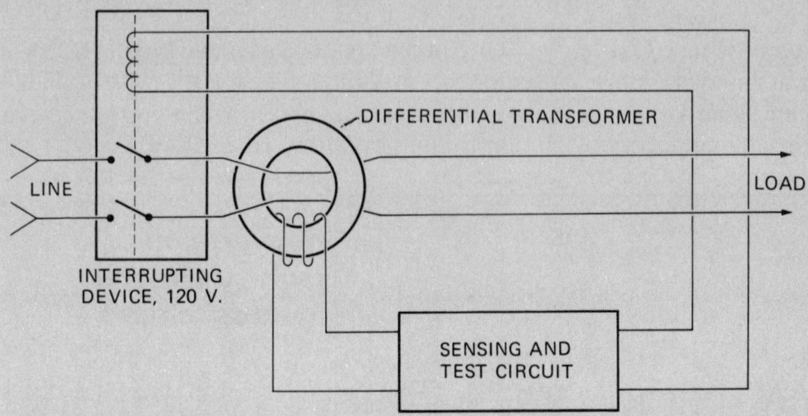

How it works

Current leaking to the ground on the load side of a protected circuit causes an imbalance in the circuit, producing a change of flux in the magnetic care of the interrupter differential current transformer. This induces voltage in the transformer's secondary windings that quickly actuates solid-state circuitry, causing the circuit to open before any bodily harm can occur. The interrupter doesn't depend upon a third ground wire. The diagram is for Pass & Seymour's Interrupter/15.

For indoor high-accident areas, consider replacing receptacles with a GFCI built into a duplex receptacle. One version, the Interrupter/15 from Pass & Seymour, is offered in two models (both intended for 15-amp., 120-v. circuits). One type provides individual outlet protection (dead-end); for a couple of bucks more (see the chart below), you can buy a feed-through version that will protect the entire circuit when it's installed on the first outlet of the branch line.

If, as in most kitchens, the outlet is "split-wired," you cannot simply replace an existing outlet with a GFCI duplex. (A split-wired outlet has a separate wire and fuse for each outlet, but they share the same return wire.)

To protect split-wired outlets, you will need a more expensive dual-voltage GFCI, or you must rewire the outlets for four wires and use two GFCIs for each one. This type of installation is best left in the hands of a licensed electrician.

What it adds up to is that in terms of dollars and cents, GFCI protection is not cheap. But when you consider the safety you have provided your family, the devices are a bargain.

Ground-fault Circuit Interrupters—General Information

Manufacturer	Model No.	Type	Description
Harvey Hubbell, Bridgeport, CT	GFP-115†	Plug-in	Plugs into any outlet, provides one protected outlet.
	GFA-315	Outdoor outlet	Single outlet in rainproof box. Mounts on existing duplex outlet.
	GFP-201	Portable	Four outlets on the end of a 6-ft. extension cord. (Do not confuse with the GFP-221, which looks the same but has special 20-amp. plug.)
Pass & Seymour, Syracuse, NY	Interrupter /15	Dual-outlet dead-end. Feed-through	Replaces standard duplex outlet. Available in black, white, stainless steel. Rainproof cover available for outdoor use. Dead-end model protects its own outlets only. Feed-through model permits protection of all outlets on same circuit.
General Electric, Plainville, CT	CB3	Circuit breaker	Four models available with 15, 20, 25 or 30-amp. breakers.
Square D Co., Park Ridge, IL	QO115	Circuit breaker	Four models available with 15, 20, 25 or 30-amp. breakers. Kits available for outdoor use.
Daniel Woodhead, Northbrook, IL	1670	Portable	Two outlets and circuit breaker. Trips on 0.2-milliamp. leakage.
Rucker Electronics, Concord, CA	E103-15-A1	Portable	Four outlets and circuit breaker in box on end of 6-ft. extension cord.

†Available through Sears, Roebuck; all others at electrical distributors.
Note: Higher-power models are available in ratings up to 100 amps., which could handle a whole house.

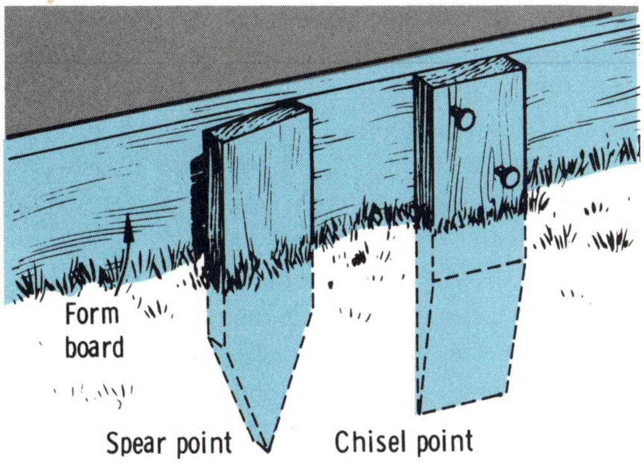

NEXT TIME you're staking form boards for a walk or driveway, remember this stunt. Instead of pointing the stakes in the usual manner, cut them chisel shape. You'll find they won't twist like a pointed stake when driven in place, and will hug the sides of the forms to keep them running straight and parallel.—*G. E. Hendrickson.*

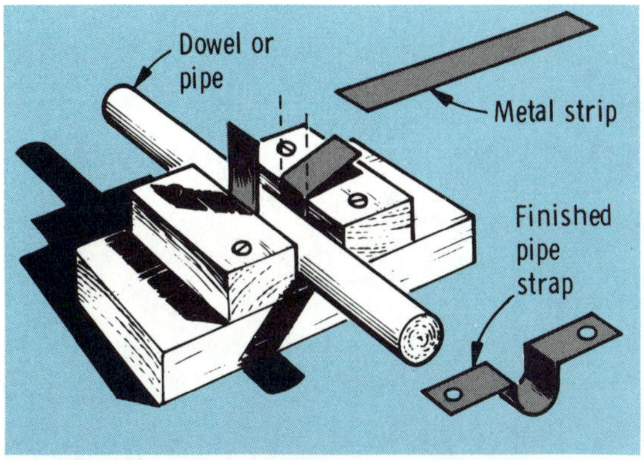

YOU CAN MASS PRODUCE neatly formed pipe straps in jig-time with this block-and-dowel press and they won't cost you a cent if you use metal strapping from cartons. To form a strap, merely center a 4-inch strip over the slot, press down on the dowel and bend the ends down flat. Width of the slot should be twice the thickness of the metal plus the diameter of the dowel for a really neat bend.—*William G. Wrenn.*

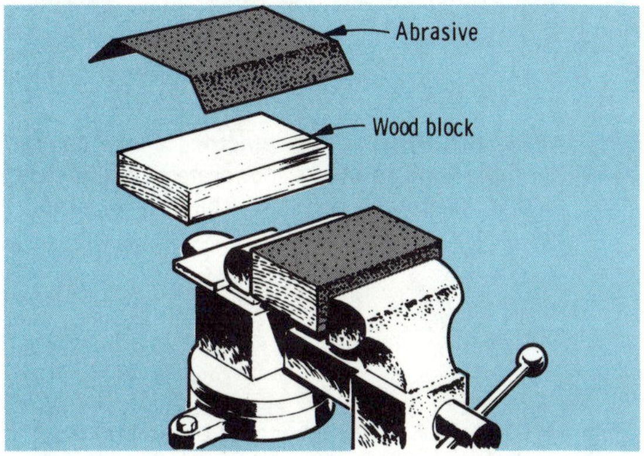

IT'S NOT NECESSARY to tack the abrasive paper to a sanding block when you're going to clamp it in a vise. Simply fold the paper sharply over the edges of the block and let the vise jaws hold it. When the paper has to be renewed, you won't be wasting time removing tacks; the paper will come free as soon as you loosen the vise. This idea is especially handy when switching from one grade of paper to another in order to hand-sand small parts to an extra-fine finish.—*Henry E. Johnson.*

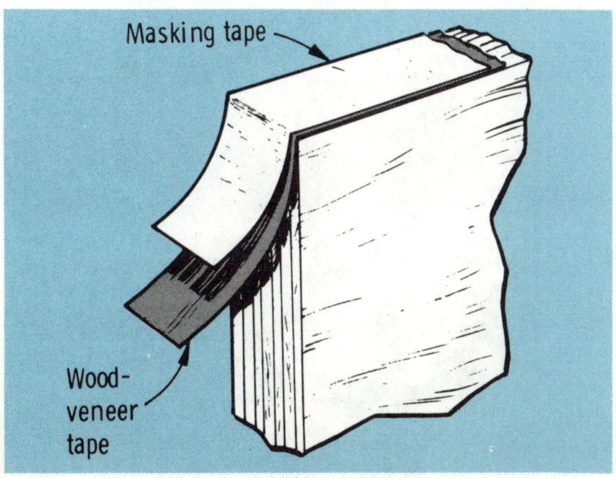

WHEN APPLYING wood tape to the edges of plywood, I found that the material would crack if it was bent around sharp corners. After trying several ways to prevent this, I hit upon the idea of reinforcing the wood tape with masking tape before coating it with quick-setting contact cement. The tape facing did the trick nicely and made it easy to bend the thin veneer perfectly. Once the wood tape was stuck in place, I simply peeled off the masking tape.—*G. E. Hendrickson.*

How to put a bend in wood

By MANLY BANISTER

Simple procedures enable craftsmen to make almost any desired bend in bendable woods

■ OFTEN YOU as a craftsman have admired a fine example of bent woodwork and said to yourself, "if I could only do that . . ." You can. Just look at the two photos below which picture examples of wood bending done with simple, inexpensive equipment that can be assembled by any craftsman. You probably already have some of the necessary equipment such as the household iron, shown in use in bending plywood in Fig. 1, or the radial saw and bandsaw used in kerfing, Figs. 7, 8 and 9. But for kerf bending you don't even need these power tools. Kerfing can be done with a backsaw, using a guide to

1 **APPLYING HEAT** with an electric iron will cause ¼-in. plywood to take a moderate bend. Fasten as you go. Ringed nails work best for this job; they are tough to pull out.

2 **SOLID WOOD** can be bent by kerfing, steaming, boiling or with cauls. Bending by kerfing is well known to old-time carpenters, also cabinetmakers and millwork fabricators.

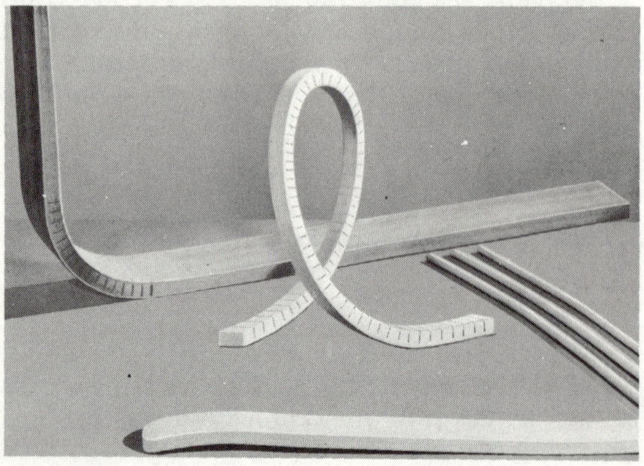

3 **AN EXAMPLE** of wood bending by lamination of layers of thin stock joined layer by layer with glue. Piece will hold bend even though left freestanding, as shown by arms of this chair.

SEE ALSO

Bandsaws . . . Chairs . . . Clamps . . . Finishes, wood . . . Paneling, plywood . . . Plywood . . . Radial-arm saws . . . Sanding . . . Woods

4 **LONG STRIPS** and even wide boards can be bent by soaking or heating part to be bent and staking on any level area in the yard until dry. Degree of bend should be over that required to allow for spring-back. Use wooden stakes.

make sure all the cuts are square across the stock and are made to a uniform depth.

Some kinds of wood bend more readily than others. For example, hickory which has been properly prepared by heating, soaking or steaming, will bend almost back on itself without splintering or breaking. Ash, properly prepared, will bend quite easily. This also is quite generally true of the domestic oaks. On the other hand, the more dense, fine-grained woods such as birch and maple are more difficult to bend in the solid. If you build up to a required thickness by gluing and laminating thin strips of these woods, then bending them is easily done by clamping the strips between shaped cauls, as in the various methods of caul bending, Fig. 18. You can put a sweeping bend in a long strip or board simply by soaking the piece and staking out in the yard as in Fig. 4.

Old-time carpenters and interior trimmers were familiar with the method of kerf bending, Fig. 5. The trick in obtaining the degree of curvature desired is in the spacing, number and depth of the kerfs. As you can see in Fig. 5, detail B, the curvature can be varied by spacing of the kerfs. And the bend can be easily held by applying glue in the kerfs before bending as in detail C, Fig. 5. To determine the space between kerfs you work from the known radius. The bend you plan to make is an arc of a circle. First, determine the circumference of the circle. Then divide 360 by the number of deg. that will be included in the bend (arc). As an example, for a

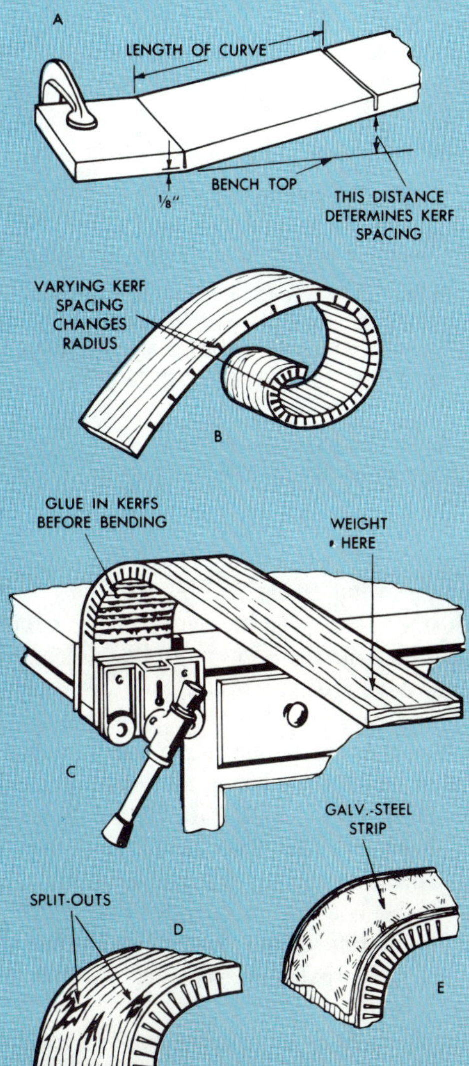

5 **KERF BENDING**

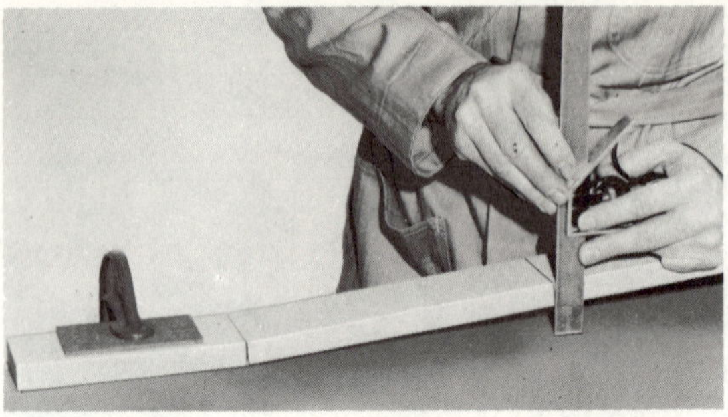

6 **METHOD** of measuring spacing of kerfs. Raise stock until kerf at left closes. Then measure as shown, using a combination square.

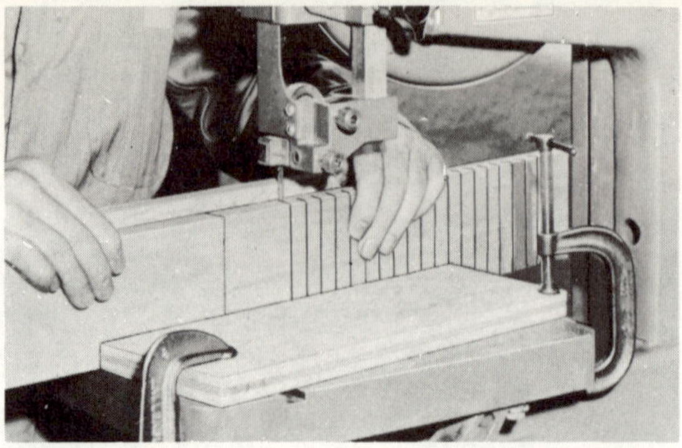

7 **KERFING** is easily done with a bandsaw. Note guide is set at slight angle so stock will clear frame. Push stock into blade.

8 **KERFING** also is easily and quickly done with a radial saw. Here spaced kerfs are cut square across as stock is pushed along fence.

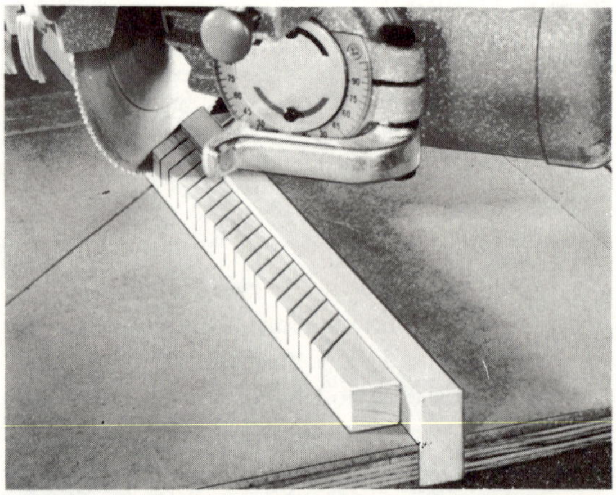

9 **KERFING** stock at an angle results in an advancing spiral bend as in center of photo, Fig. 2. This is done with a radial saw.

right-angle bend divide 360 by 90. The answer, of course, is 4. Divide the length of the circumference by 4 and the answer will be the length of the curve you desire. Mark this distance, or length, on the work where the curve is to be and make the first kerf at one end of the portion that is to be curved. Then clamp the board to a table or bench as in A, Fig. 5, also Fig. 6. Raise the end opposite the kerf until the edges of the kerf meet. Then measure the distance from the lower edge of the board (a second kerf is shown in detail A at this point) to the bench top and you've got the spacing of the kerfs for that particular job.

Kerfing at an angle with the center line of the work, Fig. 9, will give you an advancing spiral form of the type shown at the center of the photo, Fig. 2. In making a right-angle bend, or when making a fairly sharp bend past a right angle, you may have trouble with split-outs on the convex face, Fig. 5, detail D. This usually can be overcome by strapping with a strip of galvanized steel as in Fig. 5 detail E, also detail B, Fig. 18. The metal strap must extend the full length of the work and be clamped at the ends before the bend is made. As the work shortens in bending, the strap will be drawn very tight. This will prevent any split-outs by forcing the surface fibers to take the bend. After the work has thoroughly dried and the fibers have taken a set, split-outs are unlikely. Surface as in Fig. 10.

Plywood, ¼ in. and less in thickness, can be made to take a bend quite easily by alternately sponging and ironing a small area as in Fig. 1. The material is nailed or screwed in place as you go. Apply pressure and keep the iron moving so that its heat is distributed as uniformly as possible over the sponged area.

Short strips of any of the bendable woods, also sections of long strips such as boat chines, can be bent by steaming as in Fig. 11 and in Fig. 12, details A and B. Anything you can devise from

10 **AFTER BENDING,** tension, or face, side of stock is finished by sanding. Be careful not to cut through to the saw kerfs.

materials at hand which will partially confine the steam will serve the purpose. Fig. 11 and detail A, Fig. 12 suggest methods of steaming small pieces. Although necessarily rather crude, both methods are, nevertheless, effective. Note that in both units steam is generated in a separate container, or "boiler," and piped to the steam box. A length of box gutter or a length of square downspout is excellent for steaming long pieces.

Another simpler method of steaming small strips is shown in detail B, Fig. 12. Anything that will hold water, or that can be made to hold water, will do—a length of pipe capped at one end as shown, tubing closed at one end, or even a 3 or 4-in. vent pipe sealed at the joints and capped. Still another method is detailed at C in Fig. 12. Here the stock is subjected to boiling water for 20 min. to a half hour. Use a 55-gal. drum for long pieces, an ordinary wash boiler for short strips.

Caul bending, Figs. 15 through 18, provides a means of bending either thin solid stock, the toboggan slats in Fig. 17 being one example, and the bending of panels or strips laminated from several thicknesses of thin material, Figs. 15, 16 and 18. Detail A, Fig. 18 is a common, workable method of bending a laminate, which consists of several thicknesses of thin stock (veneers in regular thicknesses can be used) glued together and clamped to the form as indicated. Detail B, Fig. 18 shows the method of making toboggan slats and similar bent parts, also pic-

11 **SIMPLE SETUP** for steaming short strips of solid stock. Steam source is 1-gal. can serving as "boiler." Don't let it run dry.

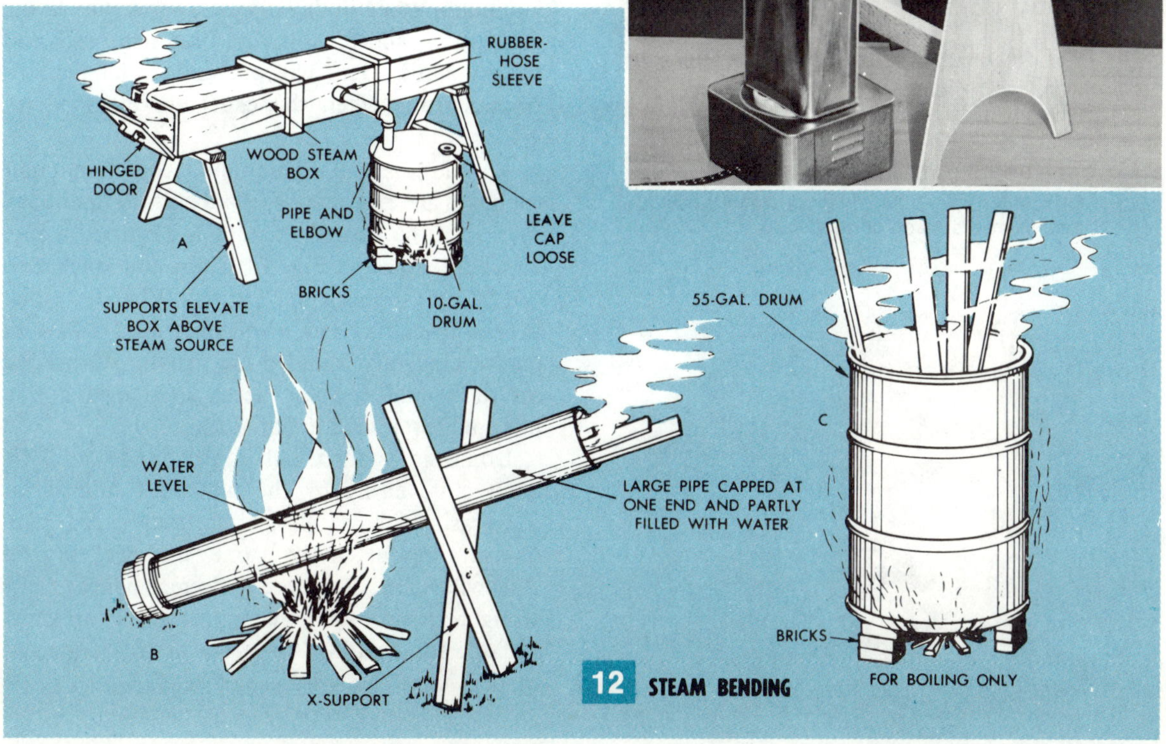

12 **STEAM BENDING**

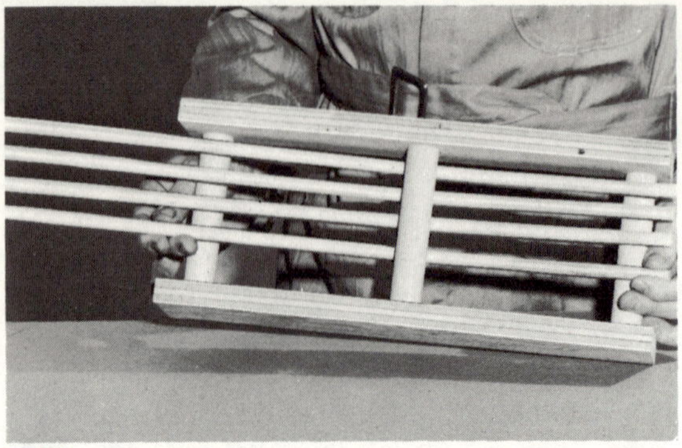

13 **OLD METHOD** of bending chair slats (or splats) and rounds. Stock to be bent is steamed or soaked. See sketch below for bending.

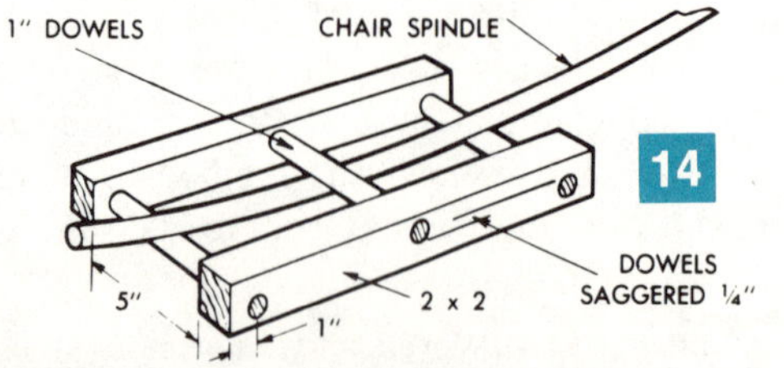

14

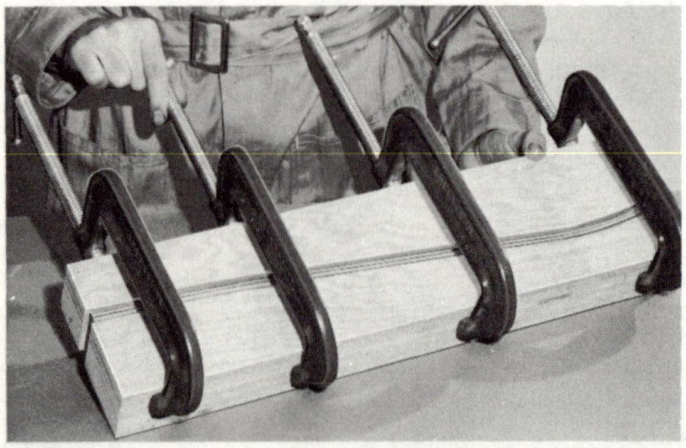

15 **BENDING LAMINATED STOCK** is best done with cauls built up from several thicknesses of plywood. Pressure on C-clamps should be even.

16 **CAUL BENDING** of a panel, the laminations being joined with glue. When dry, panel will hold bend. Frame is made of hardwood.

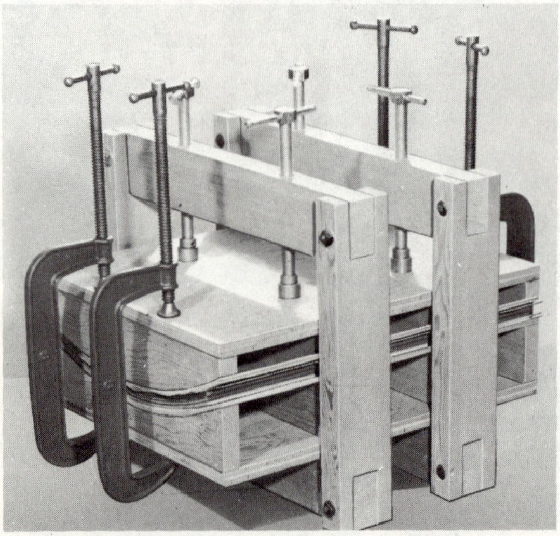

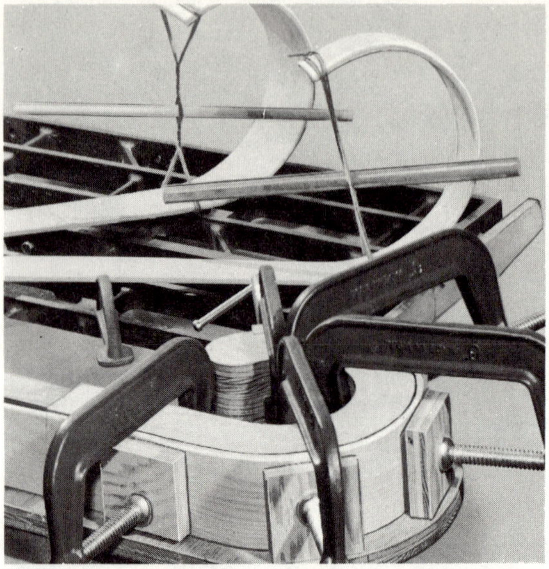

17 **FORM BENDING** is a method commonly used to produce toboggan slats requiring extreme bends. Pad clamps to protect slats.

tured in Fig. 17. A reverse-curve bend can be cauled as in Fig. 18.

Material can be made to take an edgewise bend by first bandsawing a kerf on the center line as in Fig. 18, detail D, and then steaming and bending around a form. After the piece has dried on the form, the kerf can be opened and glue applied and the work clamped until dry. Details E and G show built-up cauls for laminating small panels, both convex and concave forms. When laminating stock in this manner, apply glue to the laminations and then drive a brad near each end as in detail F. This will prevent the laminations from shifting when the cauls are clamped together, Fig. 3 and 16.

An old method of setting a bend in chair rounds (an example is the bend in the back rounds of the Boston rocker) is pictured in Fig. 13 and detailed in Fig. 14. Thin, flat stock also can be bent in this form, Fig. 14. When flat stock is bent in such a form, or bending jig, 1 x 2s with one face slightly rounded are usually substituted for the round dowels. Pieces so shaped give a more uniform bend in flat stock.

Domestic woods which can be made to take a bend quite easily by the methods outlined include ash, hickory, elm, birch, maple, red gum, oak and beech. Of these only ash, hickory and elm will take the more extreme bends. Only straight-grained stock in any of these woods is suitable for bending. Only the fir plywoods can be bent moderately by use of heat.

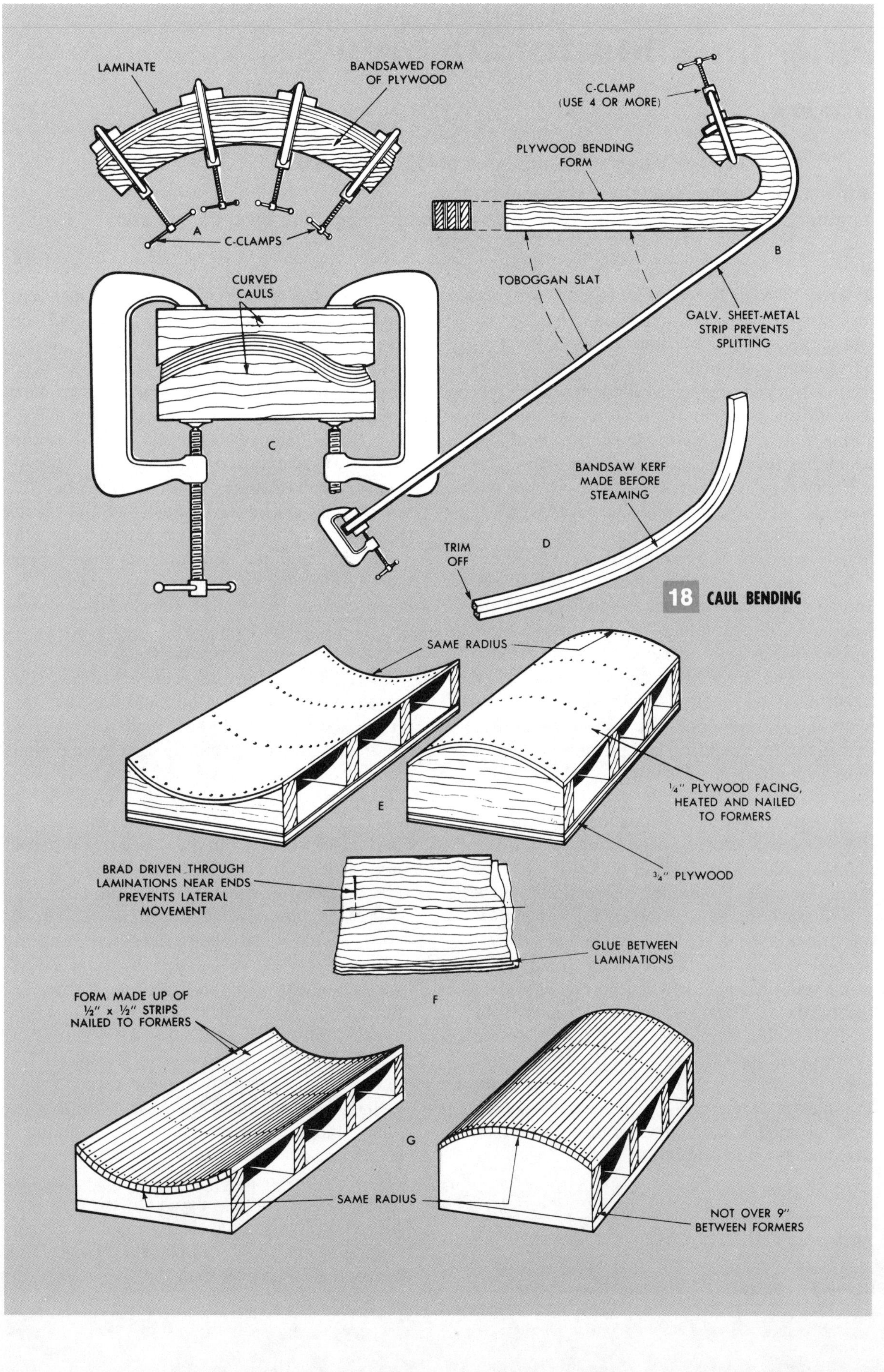

18 CAUL BENDING

Fine finishes for furniture

By LEN HILTS

There are few things more beautiful than furniture with a truly fine finish. With some know-how in selecting the materials and care in applying it, you can produce such fine finishes yourself

THE TRADITIONAL fine finishes for good furniture include hand-rubbed oil finish, shellac and varnish. If you are thinking about finishing or refinishing a good piece of furniture, these are the finishes you consider. Add to them two other good finishes—polyurethane, the modern substitute for varnish, and tung oil, an old finish which has recently become popular again.

Every type of finish, even the best, has bad points as well as good. When deciding which to use, take both sides into account. Here is a quick review of the characteristics of the best finishes.

Hand-rubbed oil. Found today principally on antiques, the hand-rubbed oil finish gives the wood a warm, soft look. The chief drawback of an oil finish is that surfaces collect dust like a magnet. The second drawback is that the oil finish must be renewed about once a year to maintain its appearance. The third consideration is that the true hand-rubbed oil finish takes almost a year to apply. The work isn't difficult, but it takes *time*.

Modern science has rescued the oil finish, and if you shop in stores specializing in finishing materials, you'll find cans of oil finish which go on in one coat. Follow the instructions on the can, since the method of application varies from one brand to the next. These finishes usually are applied to wood which has been stained with a water stain, leaving the wood porous enough to receive the oil. The oil is applied, allowed to soak in, then buffed thoroughly. Although the products can be applied in one coat, you may find several coats, with several days between coats, provides a warmer glow to the wood. A well-kept oil finish looks more beautiful a year later than the day it was applied.

SEE ALSO

Abrasives . . . Finishes, wood . . . Furniture, care of . . . Sanding . . . Scrapers . . . Staining, wood . . . Woods

Shellac. Used for centuries on fine furniture, shellac provides a prized warm depth and very good wearing qualities. Unfortunately, water, alcohol, and many chemicals cause shellac to soften or turn white. Careless guests at a party can ruin a shellac finish by placing drink glasses on it. If you plan to use shellac, do it on furniture not likely to be exposed to this kind of treatment.

Good shellac comes in dated cans, because you should work only with fresh material. Check the top of the can before you buy, and be sure the shellac is "in date." Buy only as much as you will need for any job, because after the can has been opened, the shellac deteriorates. After a few months, it probably won't dry properly.

If you are using shellac for the first time, you need to know about the "cut." Shellac is dissolved in denatured alcohol, and the "cut" refers to the amount of shellac per gallon of alcohol. A 3-lb. cut, for example, is three pounds of shellac in a gallon of alcohol. The average shellac finish is built up layer by layer, and the heavier the cut, the thicker each layer. The 1-lb. cut is easiest to use, but if you use it you should apply at least five coats. With a 3-lb. cut you need only two or three coats (minimum).

When applying shellac, flow it on, don't brush it out as you would paint. Excessive brushing creates tiny bubbles which mar the surface. Shellac dries quickly, so you can apply a new coat after an hour or so. Sand between coats with a very fine finishing paper (5/0 or 400 are designations to look for). As you sand, the paper will clog quickly, so have plenty on hand. In most sanding, you can clean the paper with a brush when it clogs, but not when you are sanding a shellac finish.

Buff the finish as a final step, using a good paste wax and a buffer in your electric drill—but buff lightly. If you hold the pad against the surface too hard or hold it in place too long, you'll develop heat that may melt the shellac right off the surface.

EASY WAY to cut sandpaper when sanding between finish coats is to draw an awl, guided by a ruler, across the back of the paper, then tear.

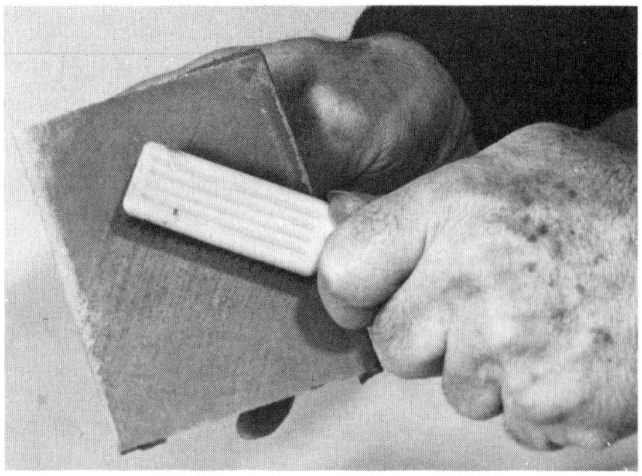

KEEP SANDPAPER efficient when sanding wood or finishes by cleaning it occasionally. A stiff brush will remove accumulated clots of dust.

SANDING LEGS and other curved surfaces, finished or unfinished, is easily done using strips of emery cloth cut to fit the situation.

INSTEAD OF SANDING between coats of varnish, you can rub the finish down with a mixture of light oil and pumice. Wipe very clean.

Varnish. Good varnish has long been rated as the best clear finish which can be applied to furniture. A couple of coats of good varnish, hand-rubbed to develop a warm glow, will enhance any piece of furniture. Varnish flows easily, doesn't leave brush marks when applied correctly, and is waterproof, heatproof and alcohol resistant.

A good varnish finish, however, isn't easy to apply. Standard varnish is slow drying and collects dust as it dries. It takes a certain amount of experience to flow varnish on a surface to get a perfect finish.

These remarks apply to the old standard natural-resin varnishes. Today, these have been replaced by varnishes based on manmade resins—the alkyds, phenolics and urethanes. The urethanes have received the widest acceptance for use by the home finisher.

These new varnishes dry in four to six hours and so collect less dust. They still must be applied with care to get a good final result. They come in glossy, satin, and flat finishes, and produce a very tough and durable final coat. Most important, the finish is slightly flexible, so it doesn't scratch nearly as easily as old-time varnishes. Whichever type you decide to use, *be sure to follow the instructions on the can.* The manufacturer wants you to get the best possible results, and his instructions are aimed at helping you.

Urethane varnishes can be applied to bare wood, to wood which has been filled and stained, and over an old finish which needs rejuvenation. Remember that varnish is transparent, and should not be applied over blemishes or dirt marks, since these will show through. If you are applying varnish over an old finish, make sure you have cleaned off all the accumulated wax and dirt. Otherwise, the varnish may not adhere, may not dry properly, and may show evidence of the underlying materials. If the old surface is glossy, prepare it for the new finish by sanding to remove the gloss, or wipe down all surfaces with

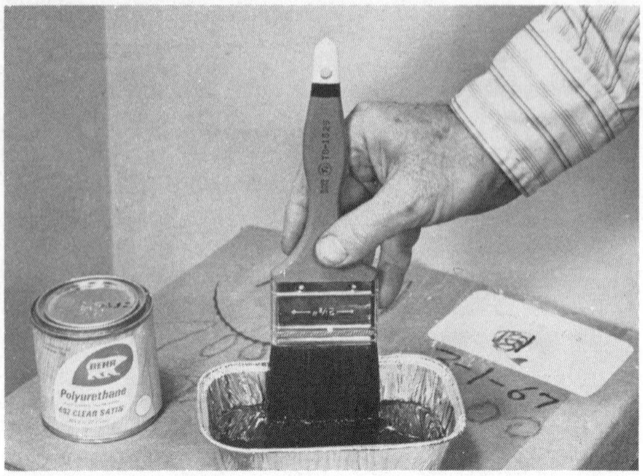

BEGIN VARNISHING by dipping brush about a third of the bristle length into varnish. Brush should be a soft, natural-bristle type.

LIFT THE BRUSH straight up from the pan of varnish and carry it to the surface. Don't wipe the bristles on the pan lip to remove varnish.

APPLY THE VARNISH across the grain of the surface, flowing it on in an easy motion. Do not brush out the varnish as you would paint.

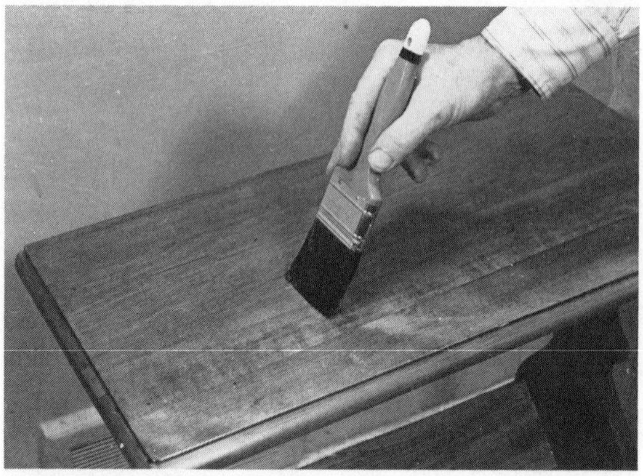

AFTER COATING the entire surface across the grain, go back over, using only the tip of the brush bristles, working with the grain.

a gloss-removing product such as Liquid Sandpaper. This provides a "tooth" for the new finish.

Do your varnishing indoors, in a room 70 deg. F. or warmer. By all means clean the room thoroughly a day or two before you begin. Get rid of all the dust. Use a tack rag to wipe window sills and other surfaces. Vacuum dust from the corners. Make the room as dust free as possible. And while the coats of varnish are drying, keep the room closed to prevent the entry of more dust.

Don't apply a urethane varnish over a heavy coat of shellac or lacquer. Check the label of the product you buy for instructions. Some varnishes must be used with certain types of stains. Also read the label for drying times. Most specify that the second coat must be applied within four to six hours of the first; if you miss that deadline, you have to wait 24 to 48 hours before applying the second coat, and you have to scruff-sand between coats. Again, *read the instructions*, because formulations vary widely.

Most varnishers recommend that the first coat be thinned using one part thinner to four parts varnish. But once again, read the instructions. Use only the thinner recommended by the manufacturer, and if the label tells you to use the material unthinned, then do just that.

Apply urethane with a soft, natural-bristle brush which has never been used with paint. Apply the varnish to horizontal surfaces, and allow each surface to dry before turning the piece to get at the next surface. Give all surfaces one coat, then proceed to the second coat. Plan a minimum of two coats, and use three for the best results. Because you varnish only the horizontal surfaces, and must wait for each to dry before turning the piece, you can see that it might take a week to do a good varnish job on a chest. But be patient and do the job right. Keep in mind that you are trying for a *fine* finish, not a quick one.

When applying urethane varnish, pour the material into an open container—a small baking dish is fine. Dip the brush straight in about one-third the depth of the bristles, then lift it straight

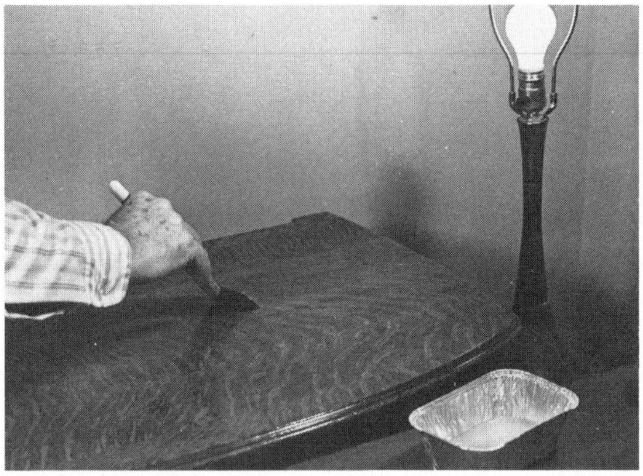

WHEN VARNISHING or shellacking, place a light at the opposite end of the work. You can then see any spots you have missed.

BETWEEN COATS, use a fine 5/0 or 400 sandpaper to dress surface, or use a mixture of pumice and light oil, applied as shown here.

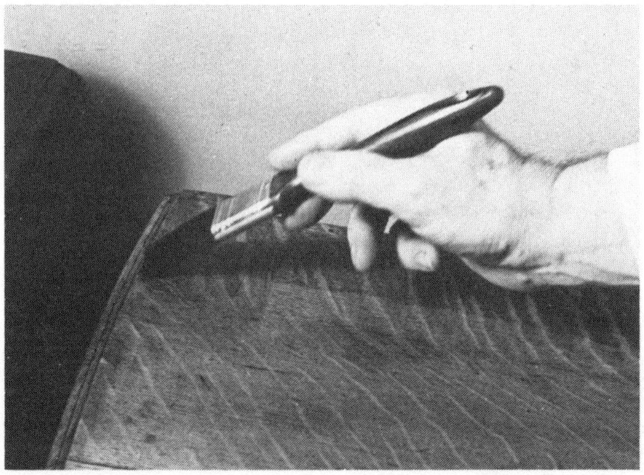

BE CAREFUL when starting a brush run near an edge. Touch the tip of the brush to the edge. Don't allow varnish to run down.

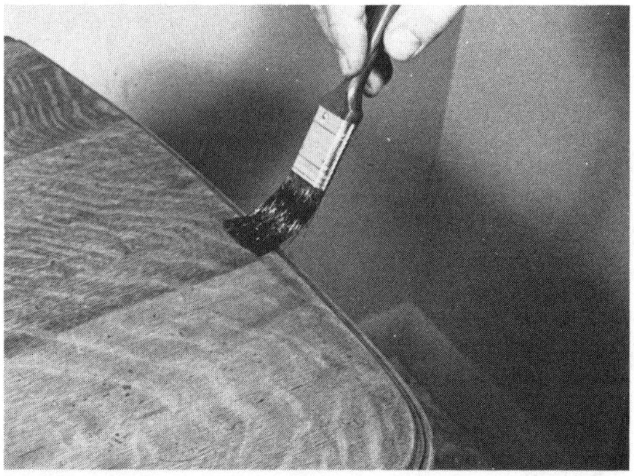

WHEN COMPLETING a brush stroke during shellacking or varnishing, don't press brush too hard. You'll leave a puddle behind.

up and take it to the surface. Apply the coat *across the grain* in a flowing motion. When the whole surface has been covered, go back over it *with the grain* touching the brush lightly to the surface, using only the tips of the bristles.

You'll find it best to place a light across the work, so you can see the light reflected in the varnish. This will show you any surface area that you might have missed. Keep going over the surface with the tip of the brush until the coverage is even and no dull spots show.

Allow the surface to dry the required time. If it dries too long, wet-sand the coat before applying the second one. Use wet-or-dry sandpaper or a mixture of fine pumice and mineral oil, and sand just enough to give the surface a dull look. Don't work so hard at it that you take the varnish off. Wipe the surface clean after sanding, using a tack cloth following sandpaper, or a damp cloth after pumice and mineral oil.

When brushing, be specially careful near the edges. You don't want varnish running down the edges. Put your brush close to the edge and draw it away from the edge, being careful not to allow the varnish to run down the side. Never attempt to rebrush varnish after it has begun to set.

To get that final soft glow, rub the finish down with rottenstone and mineral oil after the last coat has dried thoroughly. Apply the mixture with a soft, unused rubbing pad, rubbing generally with the grain of the wood. Allow the finish to dry for a week or so, then complete the job by applying a good paste wax.

Tung oil. Tung oil comes from the nut of the tung tree, is transparent, penetrates deeply into the wood, and builds up a tough, glossy finish similar to varnish. It resists alcohol, grease and water, and is extremely durable. It can be applied over most stains, old finishes which have been thoroughly cleaned, and over bare wood.

Tung oil is expensive and takes a long time to dry—up to 36 hours per coat. But the final result is long-lasting and worth the effort. It tends to deepen the color of the wood to which it is applied, so be careful. You could get a darker result that you want.

THE LAST STEP in a good finishing job is a coat of paste wax, applied to the surface, allowed to dry, and then buffed.

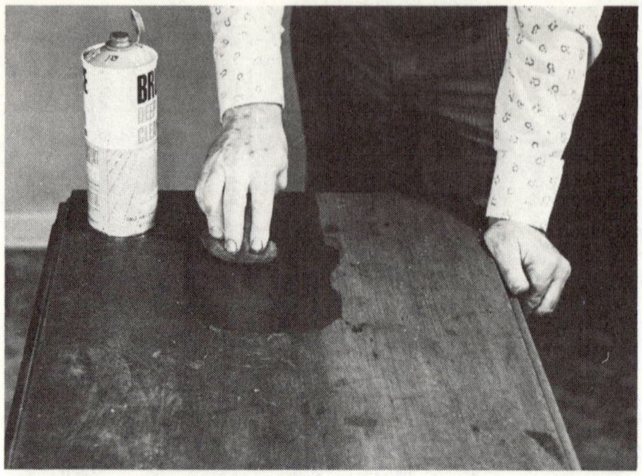

BEFORE ANYTHING ELSE, clean the furniture. A lot of dirt and wax will come off and you may find the finish better than you thought.

IF DENTS are a problem during refinishing, you sometimes can raise them by applying a wet washcloth and heating it with an electric iron.

VAT STRIPPING takes off everything, but finishers report it may take the life from the wood, making a fine finish difficult to apply.

fine finishes continued

When purchasing tung oil finishes, read the labels. The oil may have driers and other additives which call for completely different methods of handling. As before, follow the instructions to the letter.

You apply tung oil with your bare hands, a cloth pad, or a brush. Bare wood will soak up the stuff like a sponge. Stained wood will drink it in, but not as fast. If you are applying the oil to an oil finish, it won't soak in at all. Very dry wood may take five coats, with each coat providing a little more gloss than the last. You may be able to get a good gloss on new wood in three coats.

Other finishes. Most furniture you buy at the store, and most furniture made since 1920, is finished with spray lacquer. Lacquer, like shellac, turns white when water penetrates it. Other than that, a lacquer finish is good and durable. However, the best lacquer finishes are sprayed on and oven-dried. There are lacquers available for brushing, but you won't get the same kind of finish that was achieved at the factory.

Penetrating resin finishes soak into the wood and harden between the fibers, providing a plastic-hard finish but at the same time, leaving a natural wood look. They are among the most durable of all finishes. You flow them on the surface and leave them as long as the directions specify, then wipe the excess liquid from the surface. These resins are not a traditional finish. They are practical on furniture which willl get tough treatment, but if used on antiques, will reduce the value.

Finishing considerations. Don't be in a hurry to strip the finish from a good piece of furniture, especially old furniture. Old furniture has a rich patina, the result of the aging of the wood and the finish. By all means, try to save the old finish, and only strip down and completely refinish a piece when the old finish is a total disaster.

Begin by cleaning the piece thoroughly, using mineral spirits or a wax stripping wood cleaner

WHILE WAITING for a coat of varnish to dry, keep your brush soft and pliable by suspending it in a container of mineral spirits.

TO ADD CHARACTER to a finish, you can add fly specks by splattering stain on the surface with a tooth brush. Practice first on an old board.

TO DECIDE what final color you want, apply several different stains to a board, then coat them with shellac.

A NEAT TRICK for touching up a finish is to rub artists' colors over a blemish. Mix the colors to match the finish. Allow several days for drying.

formulated for the job. Allow the cleaner to soak on the surface for a few minutes, then use a lot of elbow grease. Remove all the old wax and dirt. If there are blemishes which can be removed by scraping lightly with a knife blade (paint droplets, for example), work at them carefully.

When you have finished with the cleaning, the old finish will look dull, but don't be fooled. The luster can be restored by waxing. The thing you are looking for is the soundness of the finish. Expect a moderate number of dents and scratches; these lend character to the finish, and are not a reason for stripping off the old finish. After all, you pay a good price for "distressing" when you buy new furniture.

Ask yourself these questions: If I just wax and buff, will I be happy with the look? Many times the answer will be yes. Or should I simply apply a new varnish coat over the existing finish—without stripping? This is a better solution than stripping and works in the majority of cases. The old scars will show through, but once again, that's a part of the character of the piece. Should I remove the old finish only, leaving the stain and filler in place? This requires semi-stripping, and you lose much of the patina—but you won't goof up the basic color of the piece. If the previous solutions don't work, consider it. As an absolute last resort, strip the piece down to bare wood.

When you do, carefully build the new finish. If needed, use a wood filler to level the surface and fill the wood pores. Apply a stain of the desired color. Then apply your final finish as described earlier. When finished, you'll have a piece of furniture that looks good—but new. You'll have to wait years for a patina to develop.

Amateur furniture finishers often make the mistake of thinking that a fine finish is the same as a new finish. It is not. A fine finish is sound, but can show its age through dents and marks. In the eyes of an old pro, a new finish is too new.

However, *you* are the one who must be pleased with the result. Finish a piece so *you'll* be satisfied—and proud.

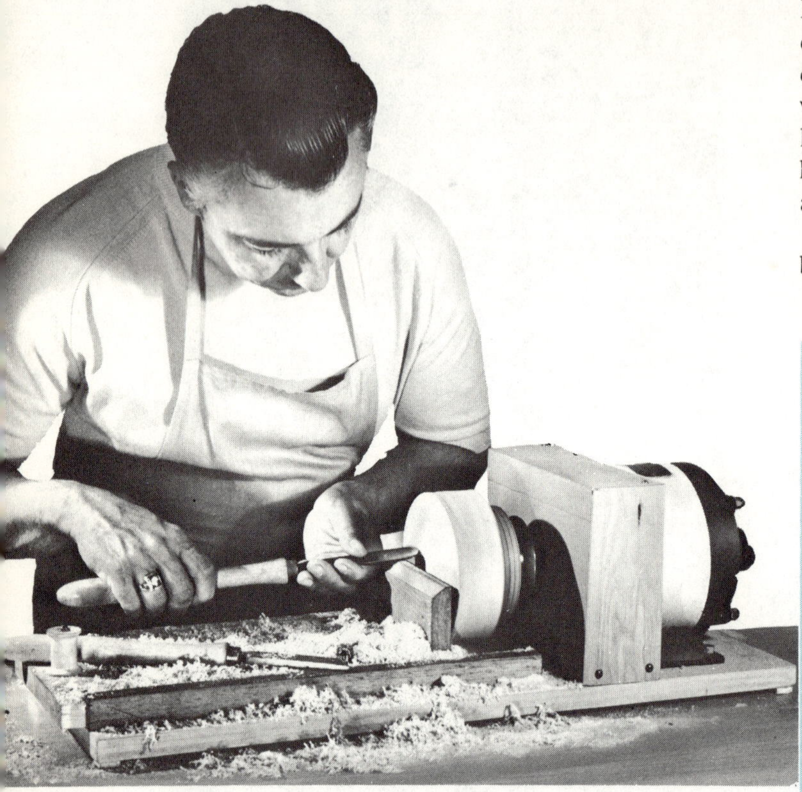

Make a faceplate lathe from odds and ends

■ A FACEPLATE LATHE for wood turning is a rather simple machine intended for making things that can only be faceplate-mounted. But that doesn't limit its capabilities. For example, possible projects include wooden bowls, plates, wheels, trivets, candlesticks, knobs, door stops, decorative plaques, round boxes and lids and other items loosely classified as discs or short knobs. Since this little lathe has no tailstock, it will not handle work between centers.

The lathe shown was built around a design suggested by John A. Roznick of Milwaukee. The headstock is an electric motor with a sheave (V-belt pulley) securely mounted on its shaft. Fastened to this sheave is a wooden disc that becomes the faceplate. If thick enough, it can be converted into a chuck for holding partly turned workpieces for final turning. Through a center hole in the disc, a wood screw can be inserted for holding small-workpiece blanks. Large pieces are fastened with several screws.

The motor is bolted near one end of the baseboard. Most of the remainder of this board is

SEE ALSO
Motors, shop . . . Wood-lathe techniques . . . Workbenches . . . Workshops

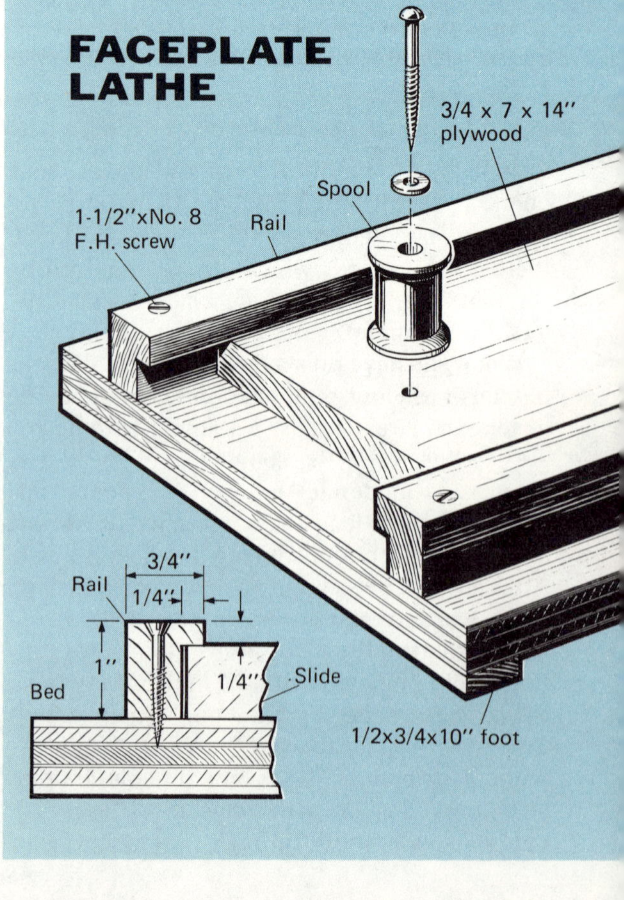

occupied by a sliding panel on which is mounted a toolrest—a piece of ¾-in. wood extending crosswise, parallel to the faceplate with its top edge about ⅛ in. below its center. Because it is sometimes desirable to turn the side or edge of a mounted workpiece, small auxiliary toolrests can be clamped to the main rest.

Though dimensions of the various lathe elements are shown in the drawing, modifications may be necessary to suit a particular motor. In the model shown, the motor has a base-to-shaft height sufficient to permit the turning of bowls and the like a little over 6 in. in diameter. One possible drawback is that a motor usually provides only one turning speed. But no trouble was experienced in producing smooth work at 1425 rpm. Conventional single-phase motors often operate at 1725 rpm. Speed higher than

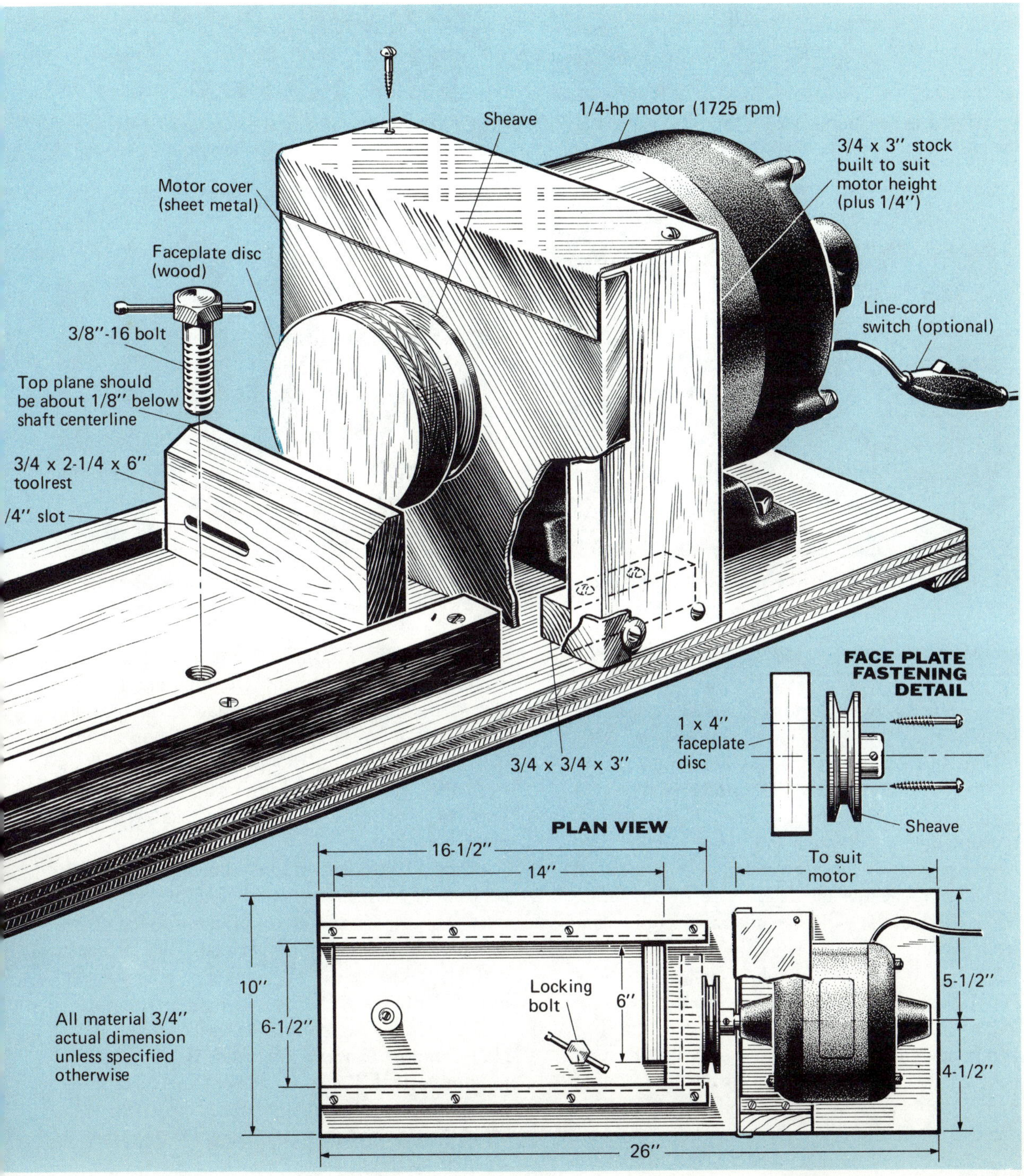

TO TURN A BOWL, the auxiliary rest is bolt-fastened to the main rest. The blank is held on with screws.

THE FACEPLATE consists of glued-together plywood discs. Here, an auxiliary rest is used to true its edge.

A CENTER SCREW through the faceplate held this knob. The auxiliary rest in the foreground was used.

FOR FINISHING, bottom is anchored with a center screw in a shallow cavity turned in the faceplate disc.

faceplate lathe, continued

that, particularly for a novice, would be less desirable.

The baseboard can be any unwarped plank ¾ in. thick or thicker. The motor is mounted so its outer end is about even with one end of the baseboard. Although the motor can be centered front-to-back, our version was positioned about 1 in. nearer the back edge of the base, while the toolrest slide was mounted equidistant from front and back. Thus the toolrest, somewhat forward of the faceplate center, provides better support for the turning chisels.

The main toolrest can be fastened to the sliding panel with nails or screws across the end next to the faceplate. Channels for the sliding panel are formed by two L-section strips as indicated in the drawing.

A large spool or other knob is mounted with a wood screw near the outer end of the sliding panel to aid in adjustment. Optional is a locking screw to clamp the panel in place. This can be a bolt operating through a threaded hole at any convenient point on the panel. That shown is near the rear edge and toolrest; its end bears (not too forcibly) against the base when the panel is locked.

A shield installed around the motor helps to prevent it from being smothered by chips and dust. This consists of two upright wooden strips to which is fastened an L-shaped piece of sheet metal (tin-can material) having a hole for the motor shaft.

A sturdy sheave should be used for the faceplate support. Sheave diameter is not particularly important, if it has sufficient space for drilling three or more equally spaced holes through which husky wood screws can pass to secure a wooden faceplate disc or chuck to the sheave.

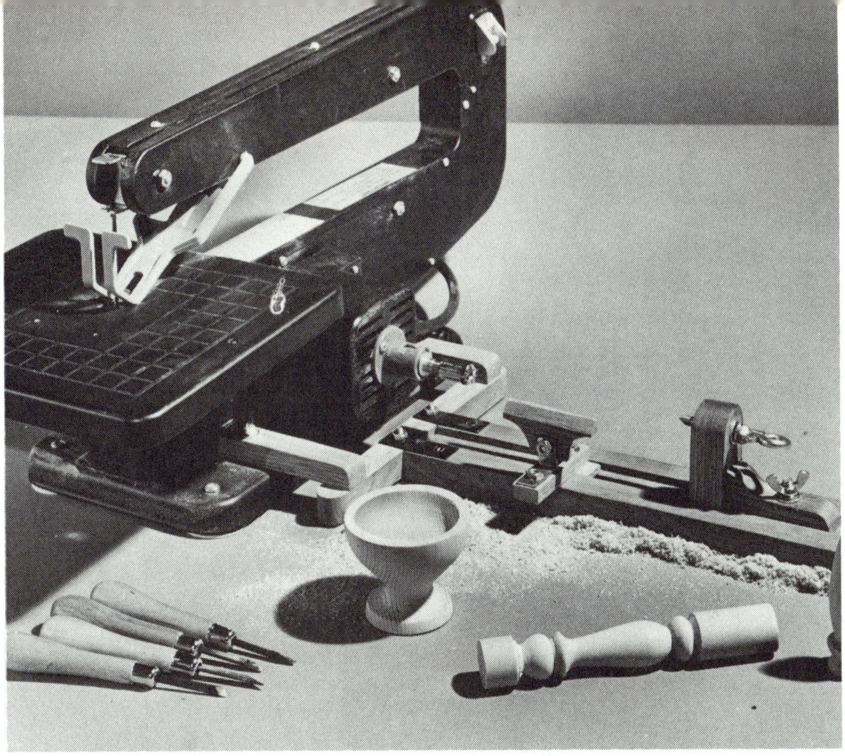

OUR LATHE PROJECT is designed around Dremel's Moto-Shop; you will have as much fun building the lathe as you will creating turnings on it.

Build a miniature tabletop lathe

By JOHN GAYNOR

■ THE CHIPS REALLY FLY when you go to work on this little, homemade hobby lathe. The tool turns small wood parts for toys, models and other miniatures with precision.

Although the lathe is designed to be powered

SEE ALSO
Finishes, wood . . . Power-tool maintenance . . . Sanding . . . Sharpening, tool . . . Shop tools . . . Wood finishes . . . Wood lathes

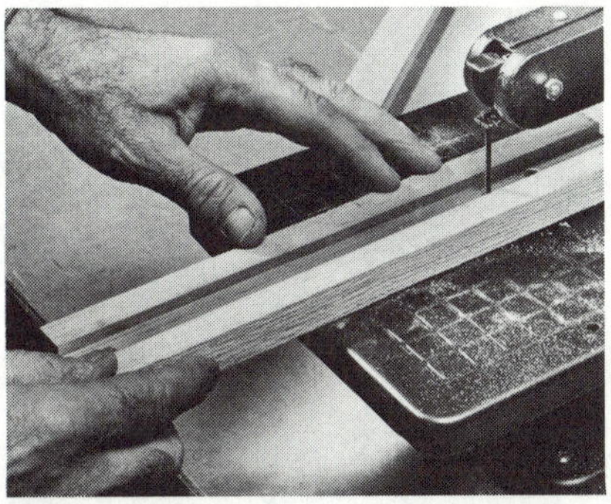

1 GROOVE the lathe bed and cut a slot with the Moto-Shop. Bore holes at the slot for blade entry.

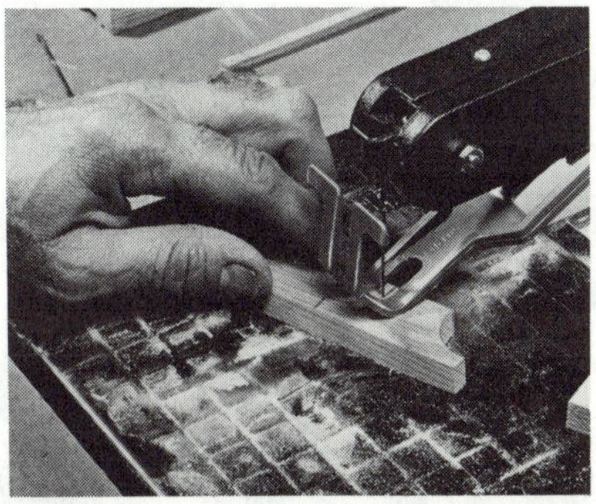

2 NEXT, cut out the toolrest with a jigsaw; bevel face after sanding.

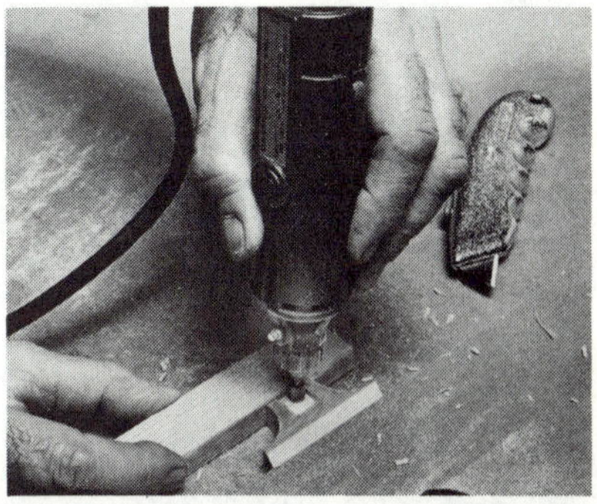

3 USE A hand grinder and end-milling bit to shape the small recess on the toolrest. First mark borders with knife.

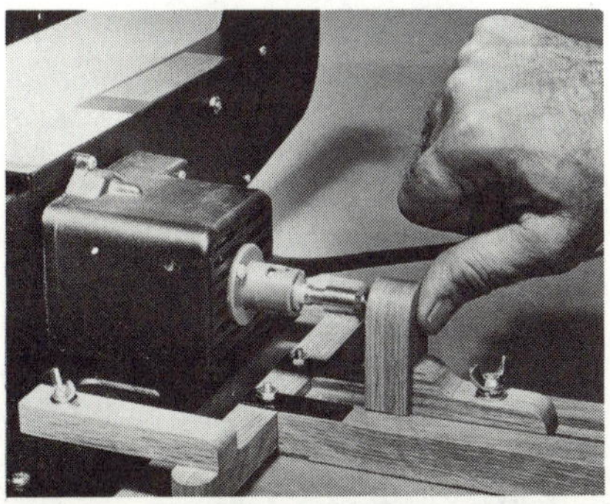

4 TO GUARANTEE alignment, locate hole for dead center by pushing tailstock into live-center spur point.

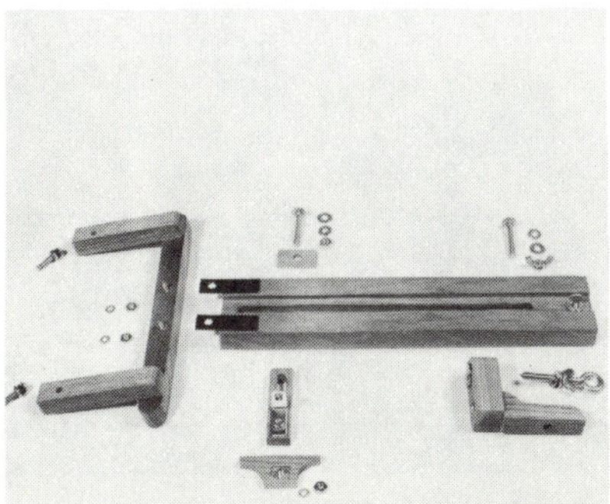

5 PARTS are ready to assemble. Stock is oak, but you can use any hardwood.

6 BORE mounting holes in saw base after centering attaching bracket.

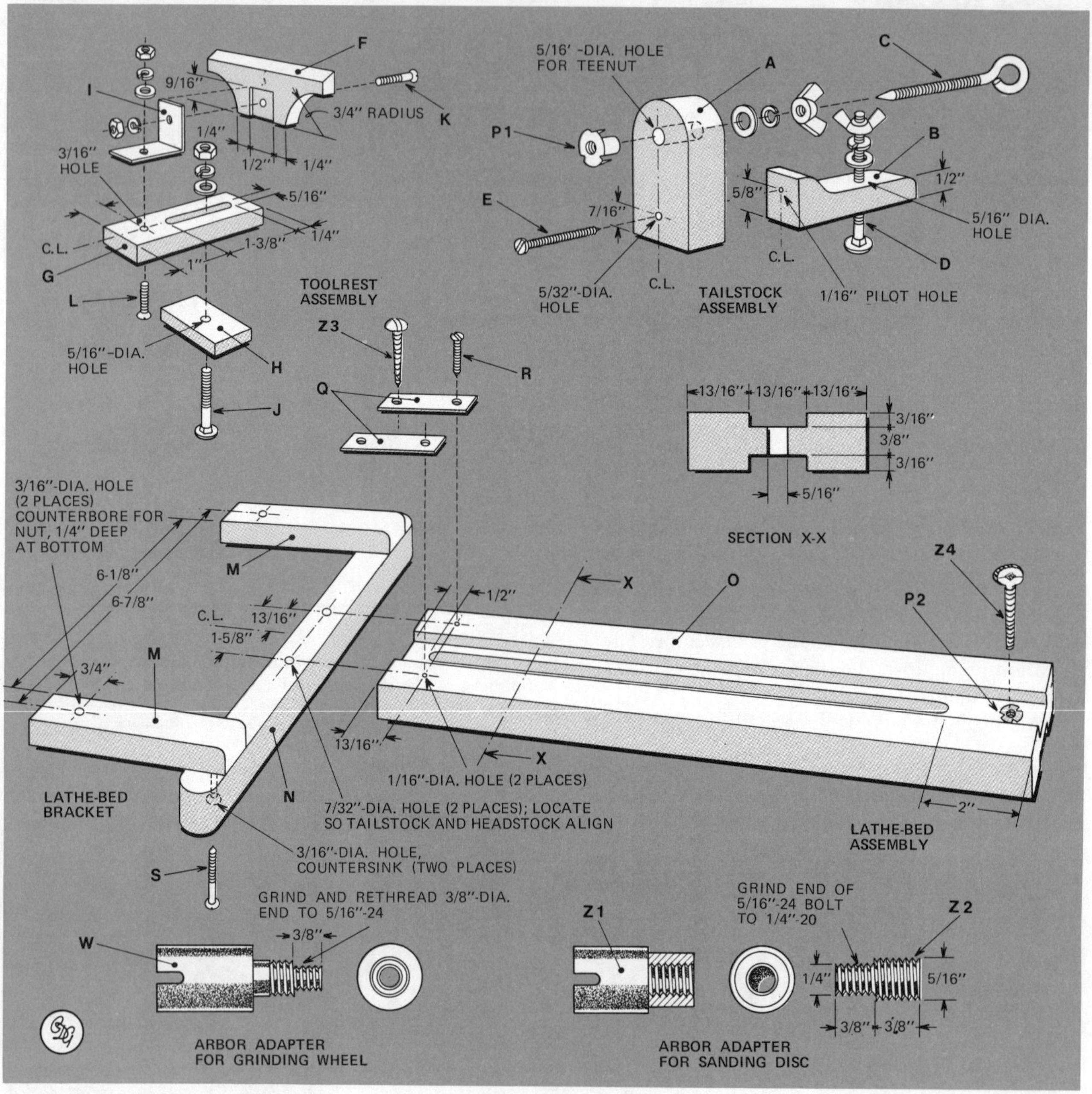

7 FINISHED lathe is ready for use. You can purchase live-center spur and chisels at any Dremel supplier.

8 YOU CAN TURN quite intricate spindles using your small chisels.

9 WITH PRACTICE, you can do excellent faceplate turning.

by a Dremel Moto-Shop, it works with any motor of about 3400 rpm. If the motor has a higher speed, a variable-speed control allows you to dial the rpm setting to suit. Cost of materials, including the spur center and faceplate (both from Dremel), is about $6.

For a smooth finish, sand all parts with 120-grit sandpaper and dust with a tack cloth. Spray with two coats of Krylon No. 1301 clear lacquer, rubbing with 4/0 steel wool and dusting with a tack cloth between coats.

Cut the motor bracket parts (M and N) and assemble with glue and screws. To assure alignment of live point (C) with spur point, bore holes for the lathe-bed fasteners only after the bed and tailstock are assembled.

Cut the groove in the lathe bed (O). This groove receives the tailstock carriage bolt (D) and the toolrest carriage bolt (J). Bore a hole near the end of the lathe bed for the leveling Teenut (P2).

Cut tailstock parts (A and B). You can determine the height of the live (bolt) center (C) after fastening together the bed, bracket and motor. To avoid splitting, round off the top of the tailstock only after tapping in the Teenut (P1).

Cut toolrest parts (F, G, H). Floating spacer (H) is primarily used to retain the toolrest height when using a faceplate. Bevel the top edge of the toolrest at a 45° angle.

Dremel's spur center and faceplate receive a 5/16-in.-dia. x 24-thread shaft (W). If you use power other than the Moto-Shop, you must adapt it to these accessories.

With a 5/16-in.-dia. x 24-thread die (about $1.50), you can grind most shafts or arbors by holding a flat file against the turning shaft until a 5/16-in. dia. is reached. By chucking a ¼-in. eyebolt in your drill, you can grind a live point (C).

For information on Dremel products or parts, write: Dremel Manufacturing Div., Emerson Electric Co., 4915 21st. St., Racine, WI 53406.

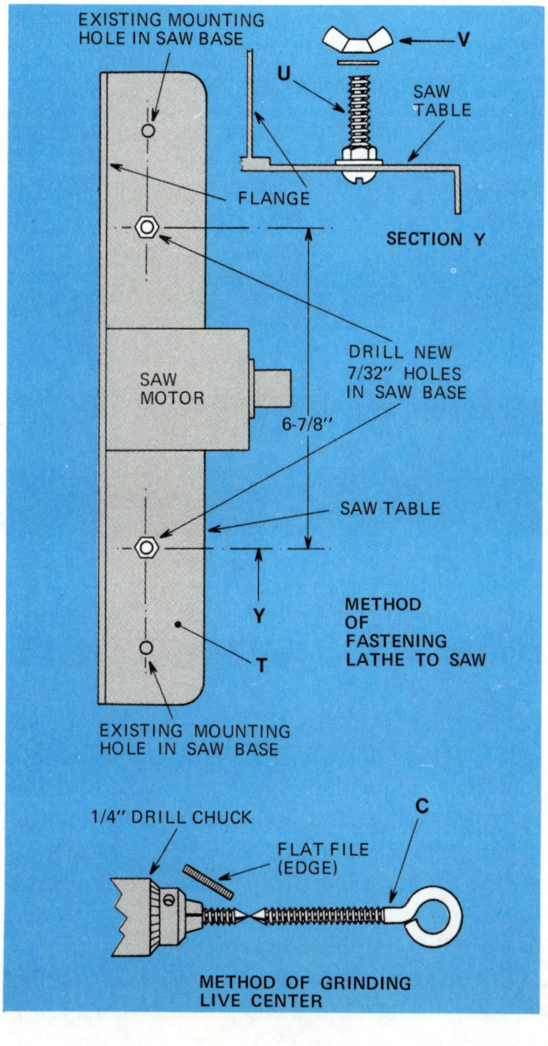

MATERIALS LIST—TABLETOP LATHE

Key	Amt.	Size and description (use)
A	1 pc.	¾ × 1⅛ × 2¼" hardwood (tailstock)
B	1 pc.	¾ × 1 × 2½" hardwood (tailstock guide)
C	1	¼-20 × 2½" eyebolt and corresponding washer, lock washer and wingnut; grind end to point (live center)
D	1	¼ × 1½" carriage bolt and corresponding washer, lock washer and wingnut
E	1	1¼" × No. 6 panhead screw
F	1 pc.	¼ × 1⅛ × 2½" hardwood (toolrest)
G	1 pc.	⅜ × ¾ x 2⅝" hardwood (toolrest base)
H	1 pc.	3/16 × ¾ × 1⅜" hardwood (floating spacer)
I	1	1 × 1" steel corner brace; grind leg attached to F to 9/16" length
J	1	¼ × 1½" carriage bolt and corresponding washer, lock washer and hex nut
K	1	No. 8-32 × ½" fh machine screw and corresponding lock washer and hex nut
L	1	No. 8-32 × ½" fh machine screw and corresponding washer, lock washer and hex nut
M	2 pcs.	⅝ × ¾ × 4" hardwood (bracket)
N	1 pc.	¾ × ¾ × 8¾" hardwood (bracket crosspiece)
O	1 pc.	¾ × 2 7/16 × 12⅜" hardwood (lathe bed)
P1	1	¼-20 Teenut
P2	1	No. 8-32 Teenut
Q	2	½ × 2" mending plates
R	2	⅝" × No. 6 fh wood screws
S	2	1" × No. 8 fh wood screws
T	1	Dremel Moto-Shop
U	2	No. 10-24 × 1" rh machine screws and corresponding lock washers and hex nuts
V	2	No. 10-24 wingnuts and washers
W	1	Dremel Moto-Shop modified arbor adapter
Z1	1	Dremel Moto-Shop arbor adapter
Z2	1	Sanding-disc fastening stud
Z3	2	1" × No. 6 panhead sheet-metal screws
Z4	1	No. 8-32 × 1" thumbscrew

Misc.: Franklin Titebond glue; Krylon No. 1301 clear lacquer; 4/0 steel wool; 120-grit sandpaper.

How to use your wood lathe like an expert

By HARRY WICKS

SEE ALSO

Finishes, wood . . . Power-tool maintenance . . . Sanding . . . Sharpening, tool . . . Shop tools . . . Wood finishes . . . Wood lathes

■ THOUGH A WOOD LATHE is the one shop tool that almost guarantees shop satisfaction, many workshoppers shy away from the tool because they believe it takes some kind of "special" skill to master a lathe. If you have such reservations, you are depriving yourself of a great deal of shop fun and creative satisfaction.

For openers, the lathe is the *only* shop tool that will let you turn out a completed product all by

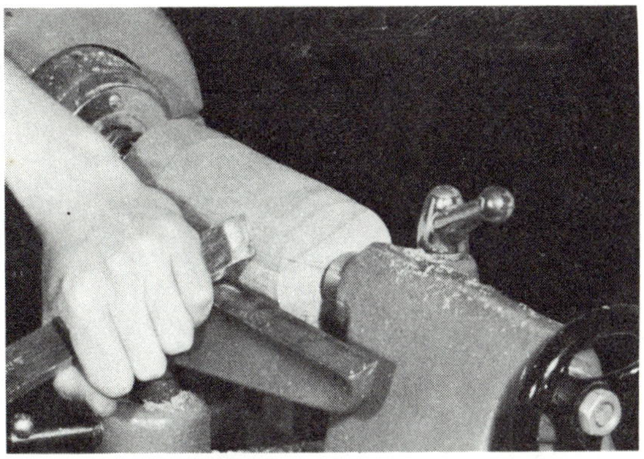

1 SHAPING TO ROUGH round is done with a gouge; deep gouge used here works great and is fast.

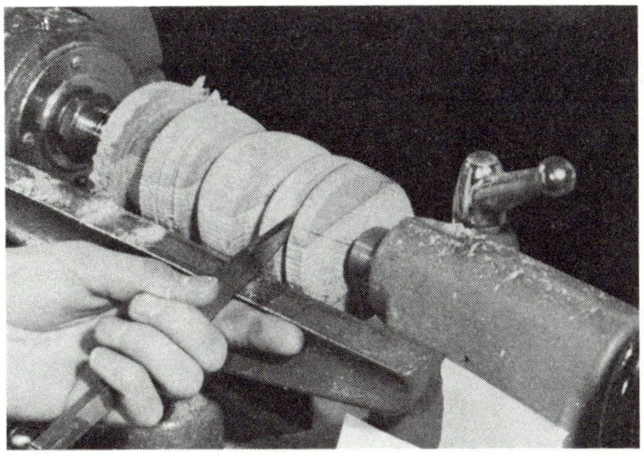

2 NEXT, USE the parting tool to cut to desired depths. Stop lathe and check cut often with a caliper.

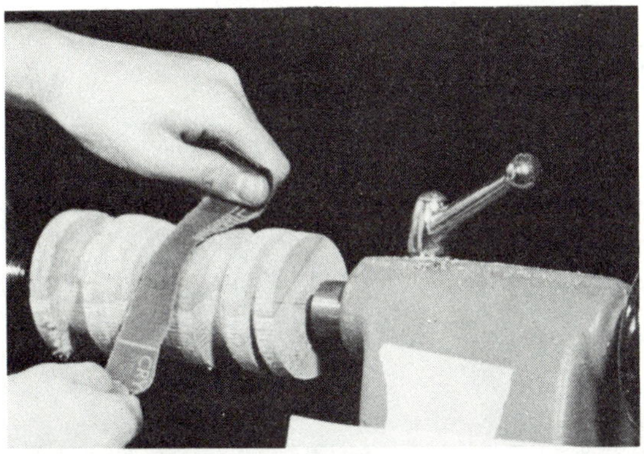

3 USE FINE, then very-fine sandpaper shoeshine fashion to smooth the turning spindle.

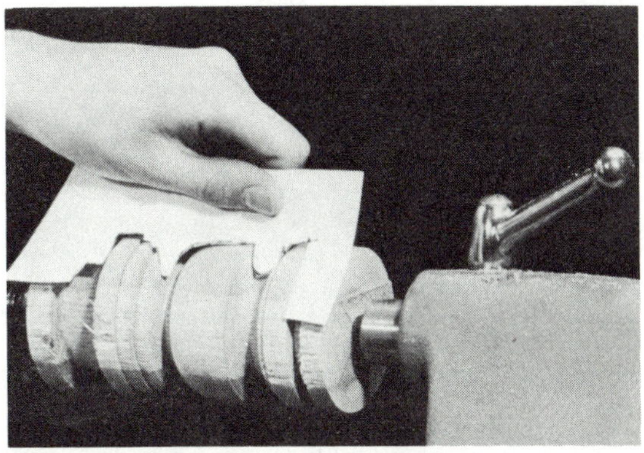

4 BEFORE REMOVING piece from the lathe, check its shape against a pattern for the turning.

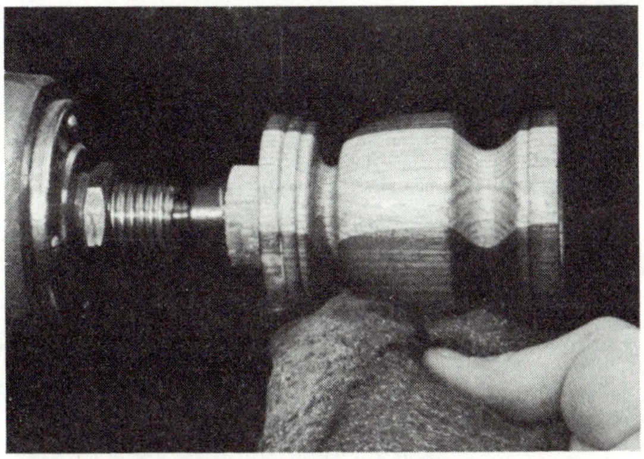

5 FINAL SMOOTHING is done with 000 steel wool; note that the turning is now faceplate mounted.

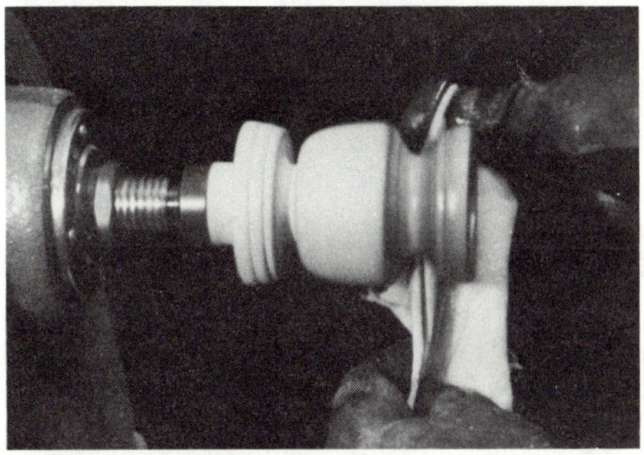

6 FINISH IS APPLIED before stand is removed from lathe; next, it is glued into turned base.

OBJECTS FOR daily use are easy to turn.

HOLDING GOUGE in a shearing position gives clean, smooth cut, but scraping is better for beginners.

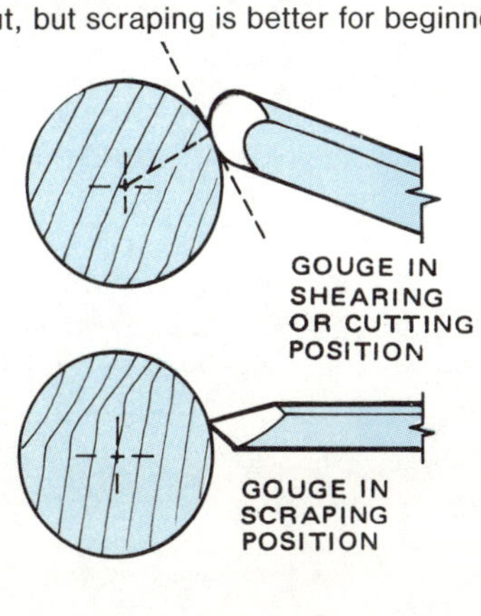

TOOLS OF THE WOODTURNER'S TRADE

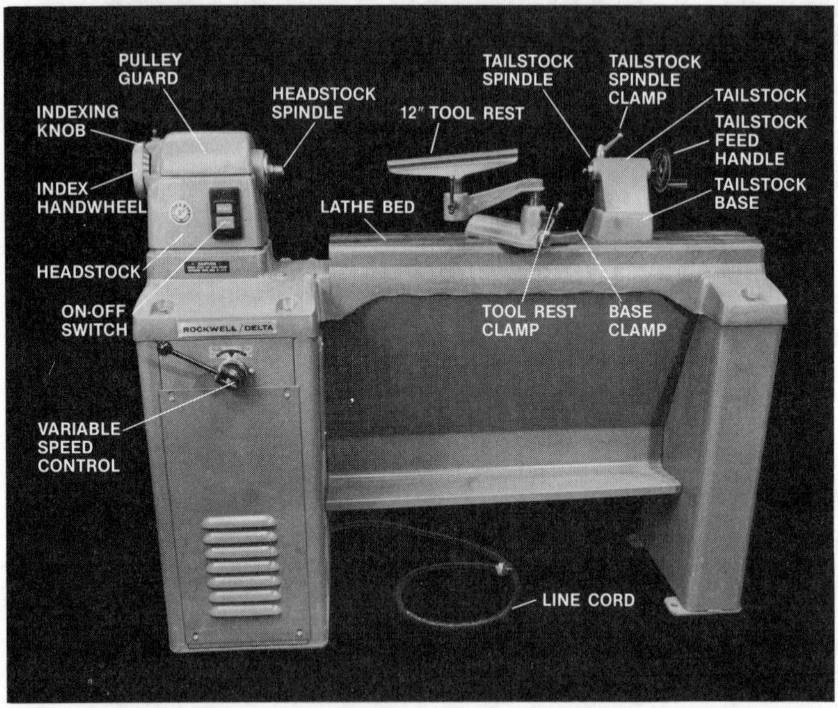

FAMILIARIZE YOURSELF with names and purposes of lathe components identified.

DRIVE CENTER fits into headstock spindle, turns the work between centers.

CUP, OR DEAD, center is used at tailstock to support outboard end of spindle.

TOOLRESTS come in various sizes, shapes. Shown are 6- and 12-in., and right angle.

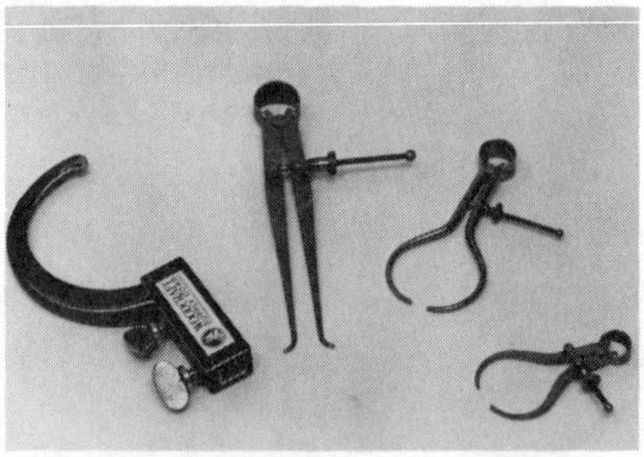

ASSORTMENT of inside and outside calipers is needed to check diameter of work.

FACEPLATE is used for turning bowls; it is threaded onto the headstock spindle.

SCREW (LEFT), drive and spur centers; first is for small faceplate work.

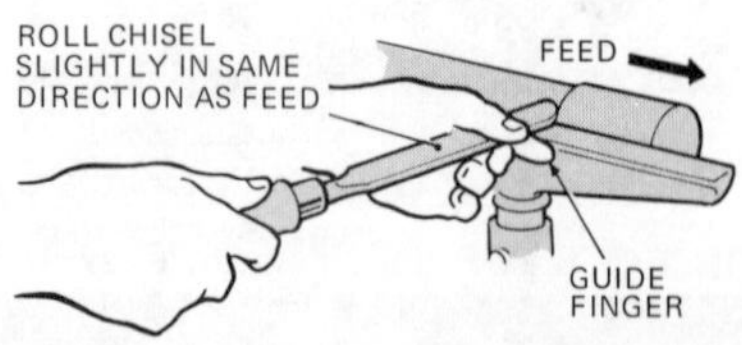

RIGHT WAY to rough a blank round; gouge is rolled slightly.

itself. You can shape, glue, assemble and finish without ever leaving this remarkable tool. The items in the photo at the bottom of page 3107 were all turned out using only the Delta/Rockwell lathe shown.

It is not an exaggeration to say that you can, in fact, turn out a handsome project on your very first try by using scraping methods. I have students in my woodworking class who have proven that fact semester after semester. But you do owe it to yourself to learn the basics before switching on the lathe.

The quickest and easiest way to get yourself into safe and satisfying woodturning is with the help of a good book of instructions. One of the best that I have come across is *Creative Woodturning* by Dale Nish, Brigham Young University Press. I like Nish's technique of showing attractive and sensible projects, and then giving instructions for duplicating them. The book is available from Woodcraft Supply Corp., Dept. PM 778, 313 Montvale Ave., Woburn, MA 01801.

about wood lathes

The label *wood lathe* is generally used when referring to a woodturning lathe to avoid any mixup or confusion with its cousin, the screw-cutting metalturning lathe.

A wood lathe is designated according to the maximum diameter of work which can be swung over its bed. Thus, a lathe that can handle a 12-in. diameter piece of wood is called a 12-in. lathe.

The important parts of a lathe can be seen in the photos on page 3108. Basically, a lathe consists of a headstock, a tailstock and a toolrest. The latter is comprised of the rest itself mounted in a base that slides along the bed. There is a variety of rests available and these can be interchanged to suit the task at hand. At the least you should have both 6- and 12-in. rests, as well as the right-angle rest for faceplate turning.

Though there are two types of headstock spindles, solid and hollow, most—like the lathe shown at top of this page—are hollow. The hollow spindle is internally tapered at both ends for a No. 2 Morse shank (see drive center photo, page 3108). Small lathes usually have a No. 1 Morse taper. Most manufacturers make the tailstock spindle to match the headstock so that the various attachments can be used at either end of the lathe if desired.

adjustable tailstock

The tailstock is adjustable, of course, to suit the length of the work to be turned between centers; the headstock is fixed. The former can be moved along the bed and across the bed (slightly), and its spindle can be projected or retracted by turning the feed handle. Any and all tailstock spindle positions can be fixed by clamping.

GUIDE TO THE LATHE CHISELS YOU'LL NEED

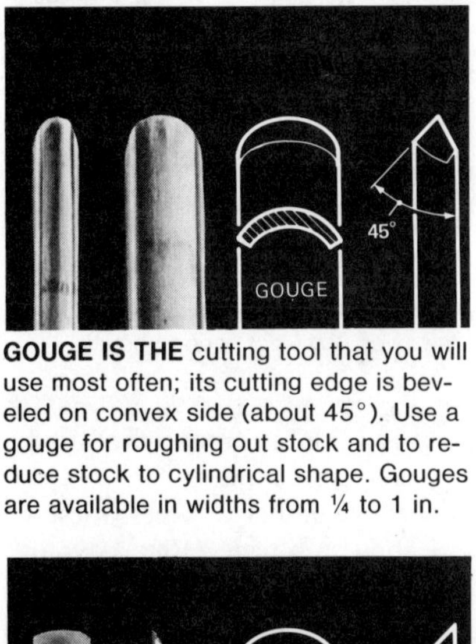

GOUGE IS THE cutting tool that you will use most often; its cutting edge is beveled on convex side (about 45°). Use a gouge for roughing out stock and to reduce stock to cylindrical shape. Gouges are available in widths from ¼ to 1 in.

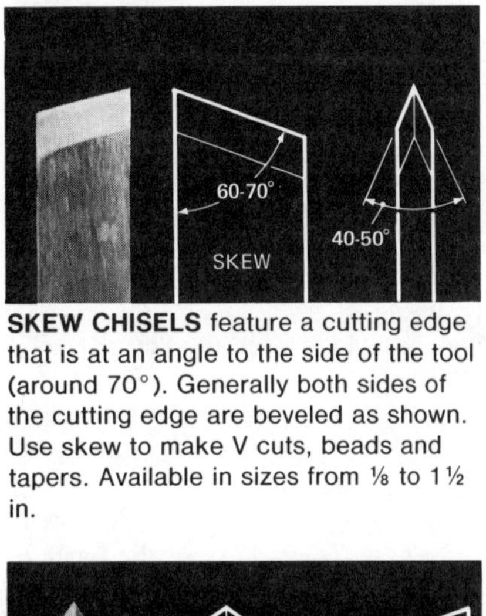

SKEW CHISELS feature a cutting edge that is at an angle to the side of the tool (around 70°). Generally both sides of the cutting edge are beveled as shown. Use skew to make V cuts, beads and tapers. Available in sizes from ⅛ to 1½ in.

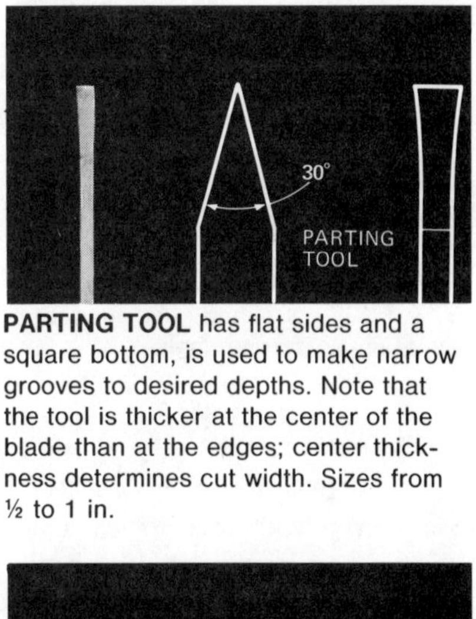

PARTING TOOL has flat sides and a square bottom, is used to make narrow grooves to desired depths. Note that the tool is thicker at the center of the blade than at the edges; center thickness determines cut width. Sizes from ½ to 1 in.

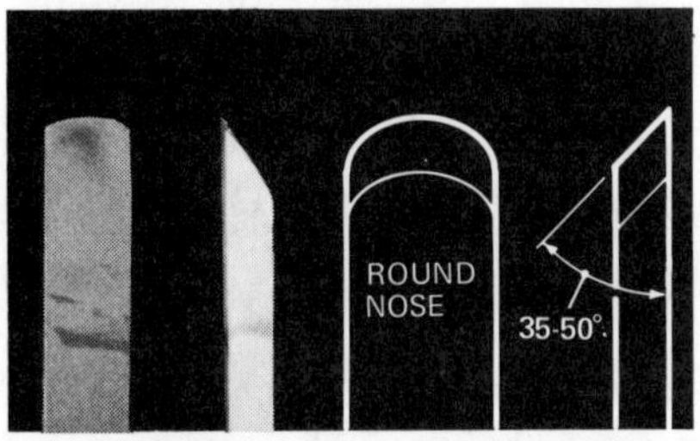

ROUND-NOSE chisel can be used for coves and the like in spindle turning, for concave cutting in faceplate turning (bowl interiors). The tool is used with a scraping action; a sharp one produces a very smooth cut. Sizes from ⅛ to 1 in.

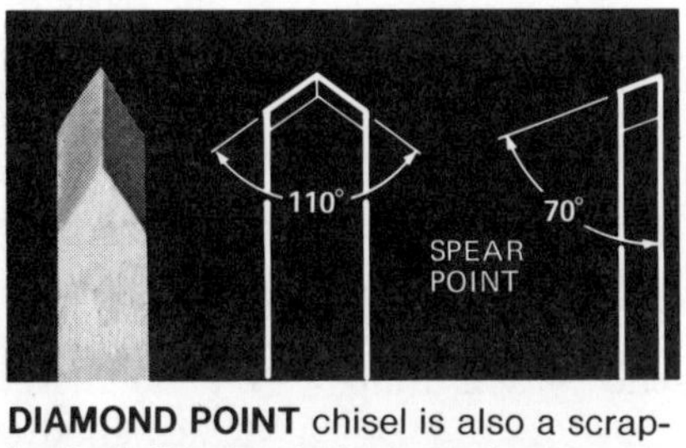

DIAMOND POINT chisel is also a scraping tool. It is used whenever its shape is needed to fit the turning being worked. The most common size used is ½ in. but you can grind other chisels to a diamond point to custom-suit the job at hand.

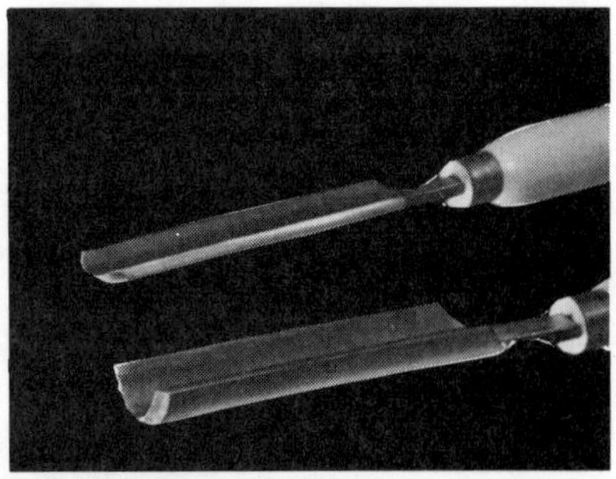

STANDARD GOUGE (top) and extra-deep gouge from Woodcraft Supply. The latter lets you rough-round stock incredibly fast.

HOW TO SHARPEN YOUR TURNING TOOLS

TO RESTORE cutting edge to correct angle, grind tool on wheel with true face.

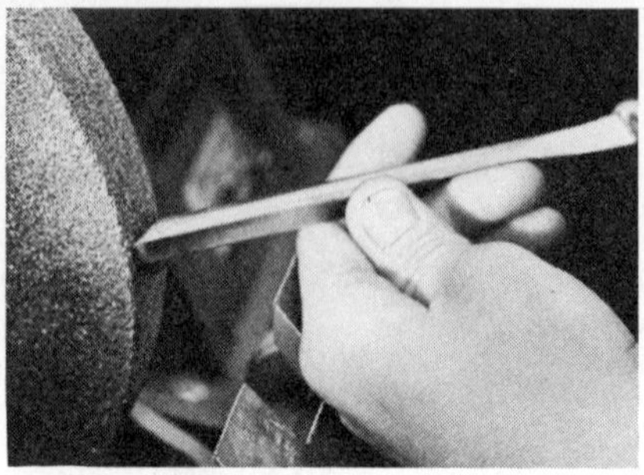

GOUGE BEVEL can be ground as above or as in photo at left. Watch bevel carefully.

TO WHET gouge, pour oil on stone, stroke gouge using a circular motion.

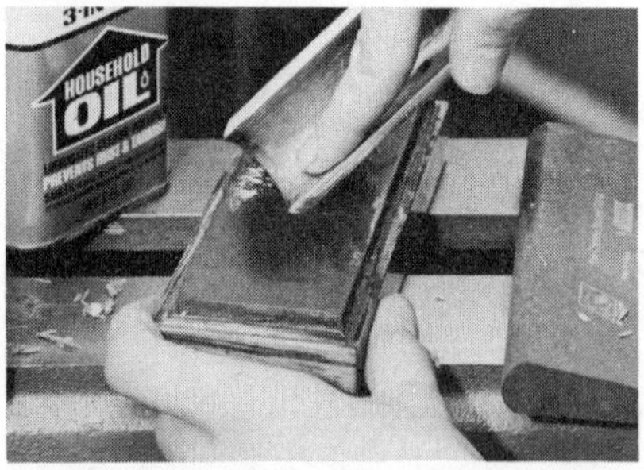

AS GOUGE is moved in circular motion, rotate the edge from left to right.

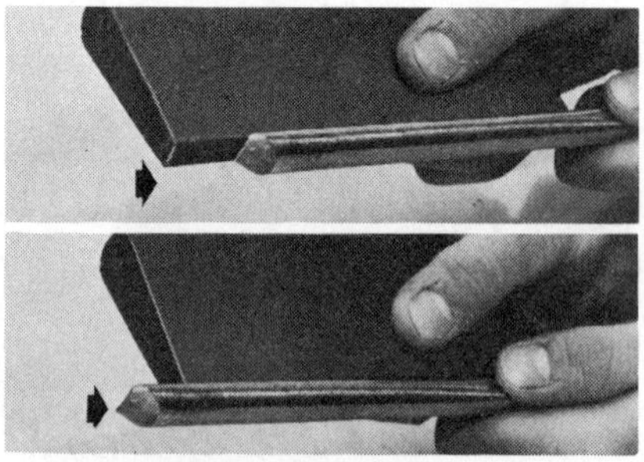

NEXT, SLIPSTONE is placed on concave side as at top, then pulled downward (bottom).

TO GRIND a skew, let bevel contact wheel face then move it back and forth.

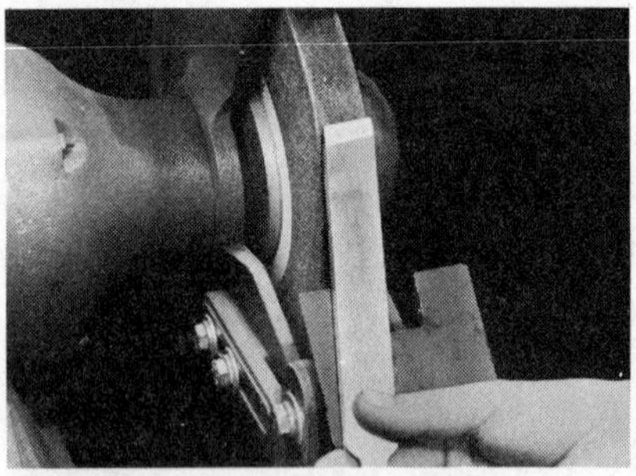

NEXT, FLOP chisel and grind second side. Maintain correct angle.

TO WHET SKEW, pour oil on stone, keep bevel in contact, use figure-8 motion.

WHEN "WIRE" forms on edge, turn skew over and whet second bevel.

cutting tools

Basically, there are five shapes of chisels that you will have to learn about *and master.* The most important—and probably the first one that you will use—is the gouge. This is used for roughing cuts, making coves and other operations. The skew chisel is also important because it does the best job of smoothing cylinders and cutting beads, shoulders, V grooves and the like. It is also the most difficult chisel to master, which means that you should first practice with it using inexpensive scrap wood.

The spear (or diamond point) is used when its conformation matches the shape of the work. The round-nose chisel is also used to suit work configuration. Both chisels are used with a scraping action.

The parting tool is a double-ground tool used for making sizing cuts and cutoffs.

You will also need a number of accessories—the basic ones are shown on page 3108. As your skills and knowledge develop, you will want to add other important accessories to your lathe setup.

wood lathe safety

The lathe is a safe tool to use when you practice good shop safety habits. The usual power-tool rules apply—make certain tool is solidly affixed to a rigid base or cabinet, assure its being properly grounded to avoid chance of shock, and do wear clothes that are suitable for workshop activities: no dangling neckties, loose sleeves or

CONTRARY TO POPULAR misconception, it doesn't take a small fortune to get started in woodturning. A four-speed lathe (left) from Sears sells for about $200; a decent set of chisels costs about $75. Items in photos above were turned on lathe at left. On page 3116 you'll find plans for candleholder with chimney.

long hairdos that could be caught in the spinning workpiece.

Several safety rules that apply especially to the lathe:

■ Develop the technique of always spinning the work by hand before turning on power, to check clearance.

■ Keep chisels sharp for easy cutting operations.

■ Run all work at a safe, high (top) speed. More often than not, this means at speeds below 1000 rpm.

■ Using a dust or respiratory mask is a personal choice; I generally don't when cutting but *always wear one* when filing, sanding, dusting or finishing. I opt for the low-cost mask with throwaway filter liner (such as that made by 3M). Those with allergy problems should probably keep the mask on during all lathe operations.

■ Lathe purists also argue that safety glasses are unnecessary because a tool torn from the operator's grip or a workpiece flung from the lathe tends to follow a downward path. Though the trajectory argument is valid, I prefer wearing safety goggles—and insist that students in my woodworking class do, too. I urge readers to adopt the same attitude.

HOW TO GET A PROFESSIONAL FINISH

POUR A SMALL amount of shellac from a paper cup into a clean, lint-free cloth as a first step.

IMMEDIATELY ADD a couple of drops of boiled linseed oil to the shellac-dampened rag.

APPLY BY MOVING the rag across work with lathe at slow speed. Replenish the rag as needed.

APPLY RAG to all wide, easy-to-get-at surfaces on the cylinder's top and base.

TO WORK the finish into any crevices, wrap piece of rag around small-diameter stick.

REPEAT THE SAME procedure on the base; keep rag moving or you may create burn marks.

turning on the faceplate

When the work cannot be turned between centers, it must be mounted on a faceplate or other workholding device. All cutting in faceplate work is done with chisels in the scraping manner.

If you should try to apply a shearing cut on the edge of a piece of faceplate-mounted work, you will probably produce a hogging cut. That is, the chisel will tear a chunk from the wood and, in turn, be torn from your hands because the end grain is presented twice to the operator on every revolution.

Once you have selected the stock for a faceplate turning, cut it square. Then cut the rough-round shape on a bandsaw, keeping the blade on the waste side of the line. Select the largest-diameter faceplate you can use on the workpiece. Mount the block as shown in the photos. Always use the heaviest possible screws to mount wood on a faceplate.

Make certain that screws are of the right length for the project; they mustn't come in contact with the chisels. (For some designs, conventional faceplate mounting cannot be used. Glue mounting, glue-chuck or ring-clamp methods are then required.) To turn the hurricane lamp base shown on page 3111 (drawing, page 3116) you *can* use conventional faceplate mounting.

With the block securely fastened, turn the faceplate all the way onto the lathe spindle. If your lathe has a system for locking the spindle while you tighten the faceplate, use it. Adjust the toolrest so it is about ⅛ in. away from the work and the chisel's cutting edge will be at the center line. Rotate the work by hand to make certain it clears the toolrest. Run the machine at slow speed. Check the lathe manufacturer's speed chart because the roughing speed varies with the type and diameter of the wood.

Generally, a woodturner shapes the outside diameter first with a square-nose chisel. Since there are no square-nose chisels available commercially (that I know of), you'll have to grind your own. The best tool for final smoothing of an outside edge is the spear-point chisel. Use it to pick

FACEPLATE TURNING BASICS

SQUARE UP STOCK, find center by marking diagonals using a straightedge.

MAKE A permanent mark at the center by tapping a punch lightly.

WITH COMPASS, lay out and mark circle $\frac{1}{8}$ in. larger than finished size.

USE BANDSAW to cut stock to rough dimension; cut on the waste side.

SELECT faceplate, set compass $\frac{1}{16}$ in. more than its radius and draw a circle.

CENTER faceplate on stock, line up two screws with grain, mark for screwholes.

BORE PILOT holes for faceplate screws; use tape stop on bit at desired depth.

USE HEFTIEST possible screws to secure to faceplate; choose length carefully.

HOLDING LATHE spindle rigid, mount workpiece on lathe, tighten with wrench.

SET MACHINE at low speed, and scrape across edge of stock.

TO SHAPE the outside corner, a skew can be used in a scraping fashion.

AFTER SMOOTHING face with square-nose chisel, use pencil to mark cuts.

SMALL ROUND-NOSE chisel is used to turn decorative half-round groove.

BORE MORTISE for spindle stub with work still on lathe.

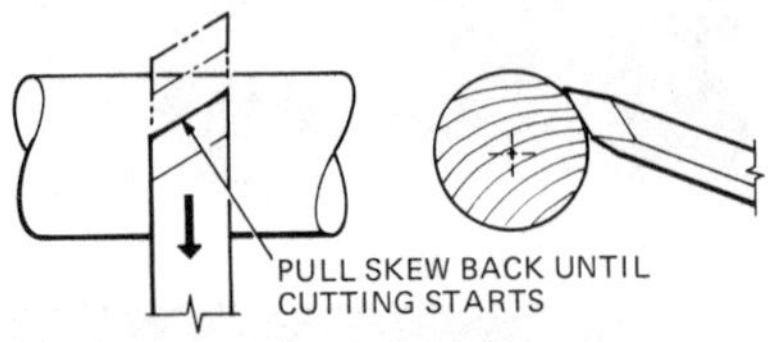

FOR SMOOTHEST finish, you must master the skew.

up a scant bite at one corner and carry the bite right across the edge.

Truing the work's face can be done with either a skew, square-nose or diamond-point chisel held in the scraping attitude. Move the tool from the center of the workpiece to its outside edge. You can shape the face with whatever chisel best fits the shape you want. Work from the center toward the edge. Remember, the outer edge is spinning much faster than the center. Thus, it is good practice to take light cuts only when working on the face.

turning a spindle

Work turned between centers is called spindle turning. Make it your practice to square the wood you will use for a spindle turning; this makes it easier to rough-round a cylinder with a deep gouge. Steps for spindle turning are illustrated on these pages. It is important to determine the centers of both ends in order to mount the workpiece in the lathe properly. Other key points include:

■ Always cut saw kerfs for the drive center, as shown on page 3115. Use a wooden mallet to seat the drive center well into the wood. (A metal hammer will damage the center.)

■ Apply a lubricant to the cup center to reduce friction. You can use light machine oil. I prefer a candle stub—which won't stain wood.

When mounting a piece to be spindle-turned, insert the spur center into the spindle and support the outboard end of the workpiece with your left hand. Move the tailstock within an inch of the work and clamp it. Advance the cup center by turning the handwheel; make certain its point enters the prepunched center. Continue to advance the center while slowly rotating the work with your left hand until the work is difficult to turn. Then back off the wheel ⅛ to ¼ turn and lock the tailstock spindle. Set the toolrest, rotate the work by hand to clear the rest and turn lathe on.

Turn the work to a rough cylinder using the gouge and a slow speed. To smooth the cylinder, use the skew, a tool that requires effort and practice to master. Here's the easiest way for learning how: With the work spinning in the lathe, rest the skew on the toolrest so its point is well *over* the cylinder. Grip its handle with your right hand and the blade—close to toolrest—with your left hand. Curl your fingers over the blade so your thumb is toward you. (See photo, page 3116.) Slowly lower the skew until its bevel rides on work and shearing cut is made at blade's center. Maintain blade position as you move skew across the cylinder.

getting a professional finish

First, the wood should be thoroughly sanded, dusted and wiped with a tack rag. Next, prepare a clean, lint-free cloth with a small amount of shellac and boiled linseed oil. Then, upon application, set the lathe at slow to medium speed (about 600 rpm) and keep the rag moving to avoid burn marks in the shellac (see photos, p. 3112).

TURNING A SPINDLE

TO GLUE UP stock for spindle turning, apply liberal amount to surfaces.

USE A NUMBER of clamps to hold the work tight until glue dries.

IMMEDIATELY wipe off squeezed-out excess glue and set aside for 24 hours.

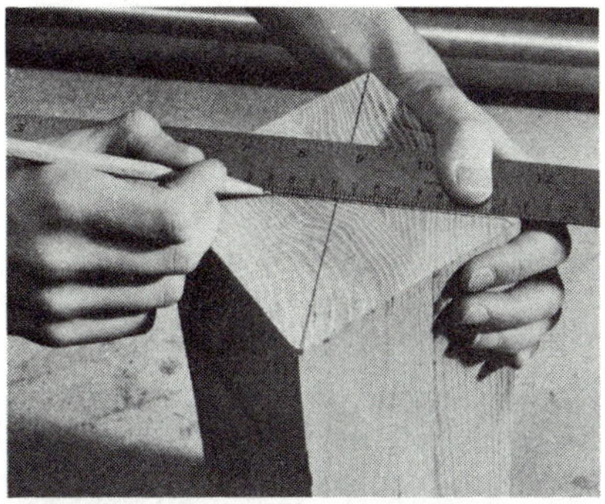

FIND CENTERS on both ends using diagonal lines method as shown here.

ON SPUR CENTER end of work, saw ⅛-in.-deep kerfs along diagonal lines.

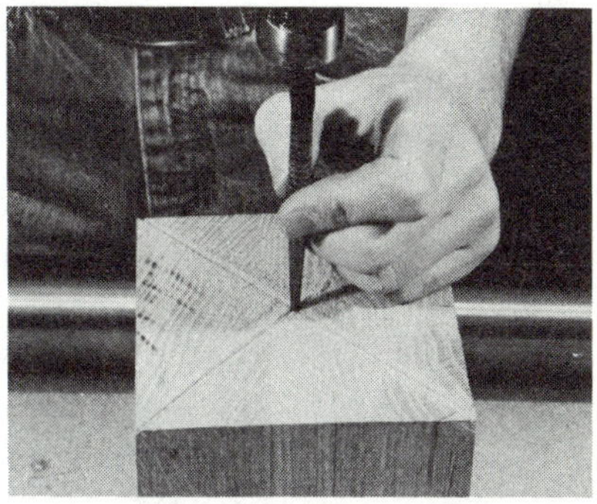

ON BOTH ENDS, center-punch holes at exact center (about 1/16 in. dia.)

USE A WOOD mallet, which won't damage center, to drive center into stock.

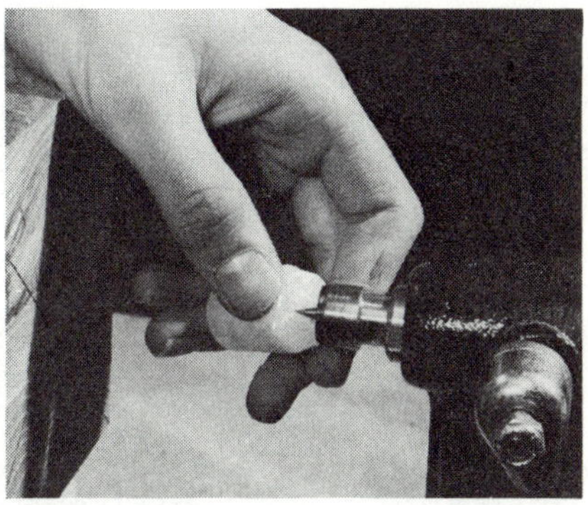

MOUNT WORK in lathe; before advancing cup center, apply lubricant.

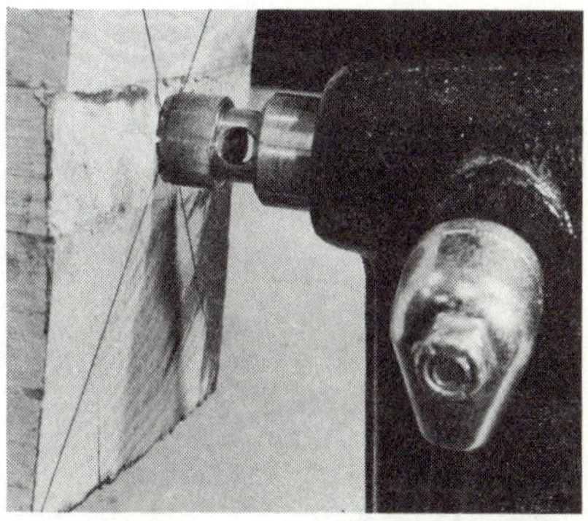

ADVANCE cup center into stock until secure, back off ⅛th turn, lock.

IF WORK MUST be removed, mark at headstock using reference on spur.

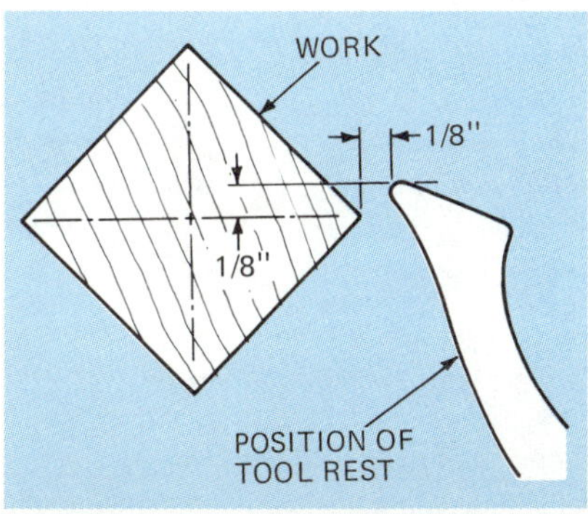

ADJUST toolrest as shown, clamp. Turn work by hand to make sure it clears.

USING GOUGE, rough-round right end, mark to determine cylinder size.

using the wood lathe, continued

START LATHE and use gouge to make a series of 1½ to 2-in.-long cuts.

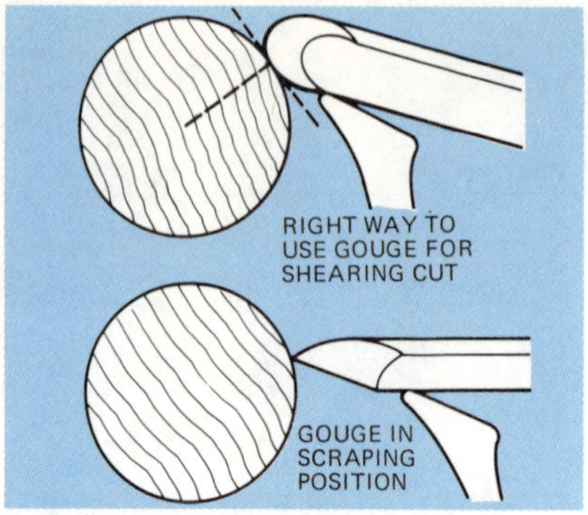

GOUGE can be used to make a shearing or scraping cut; make light cuts.

WHEN YOU'RE about 2 in. from left end, roll gouge and work toward left.

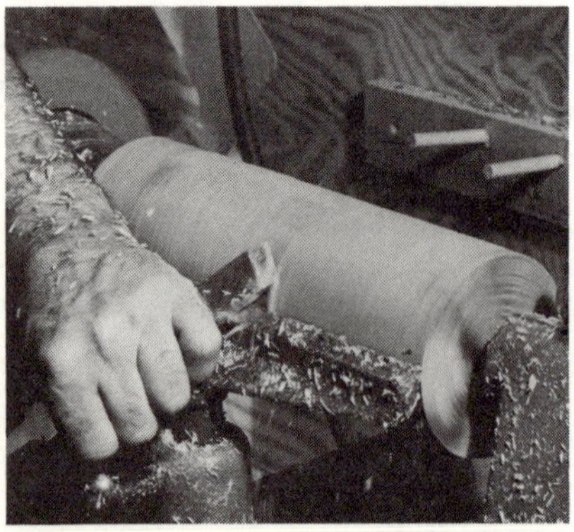

USE SKEW with light shearing cut to turn cylinder smooth.

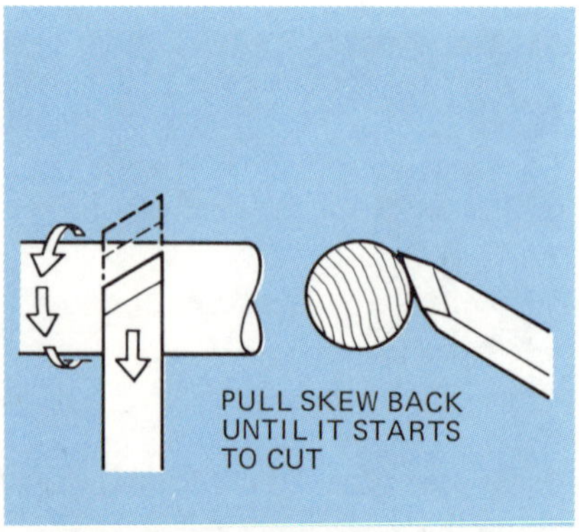

TO USE SKEW, place it over work, draw it back until bevel rides work.

OR, MAKE smoothing cut using skew in scraping position.

USE A SQUARE to check cylinder flatness; remove stock as required.

CUT TEMPLATE and use it to lay out basic shape on cylinder.

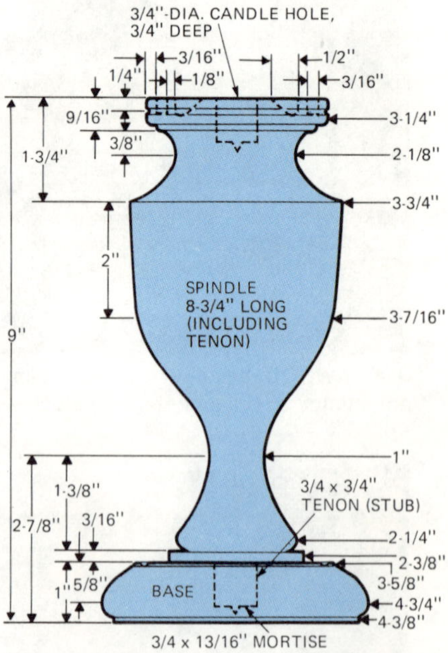

USE THIS PATTERN to make candleholder shown in photos on page 3111.

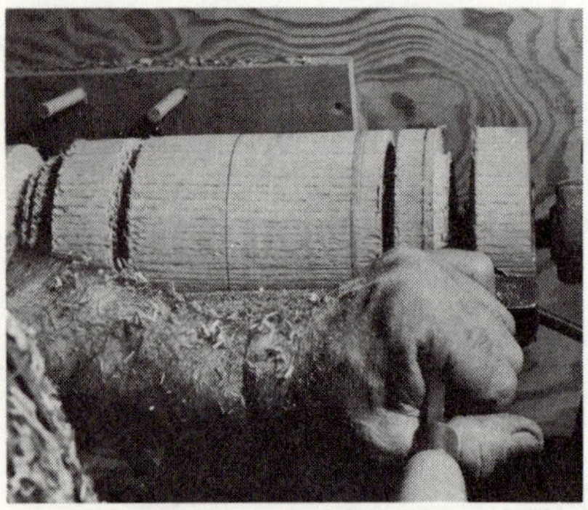

CUT VARIOUS segments to correct diameter using the parting tool.

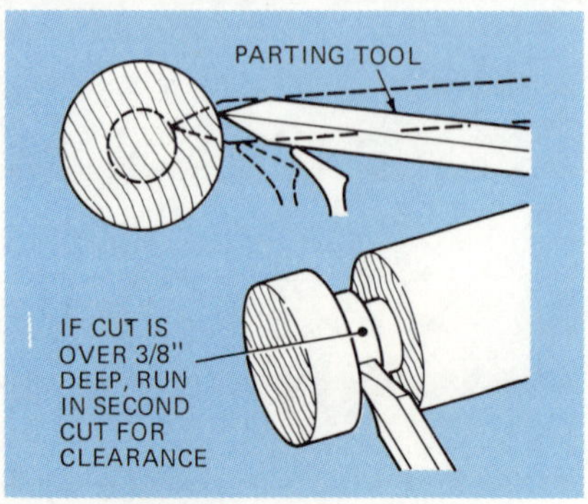

HOLD PARTING tool 90° to work. Raise handle slightly as you push tool.

LAY OUT and cut groove for chimney using a small round-nose chisel.

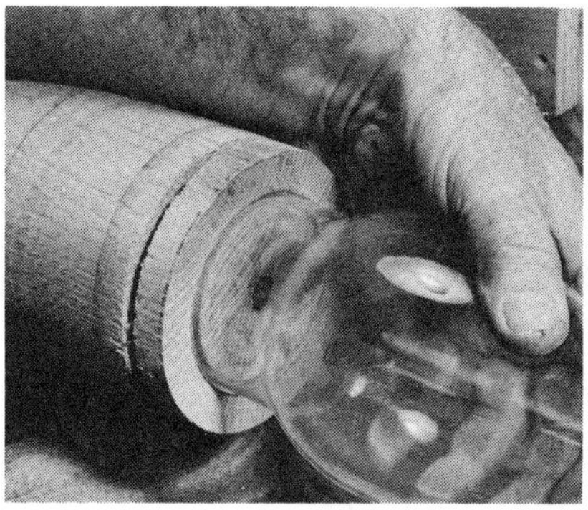

PERIODICALLY check globe in the groove. Back off tailstock to do it.

NEXT, SHAPE the surface between the groove and the candle hole.

SHAPE COVE portion by working from both shoulders down to the center.

SKEW IN scraping attitude is an effective way to control shape.

SHARP GOUGE with shearing cut produced desirable results.

USING THE PARTING tool, make a cut to the desired tenon depth.

CHECK STUB diameter with caliper. When satisfied, turn to initial cut.

FILE, SUPPORTED by toolrest, is an excellent way to start smoothing.

FOR FINAL smoothing, use 220-grit paper (or emery cloth).

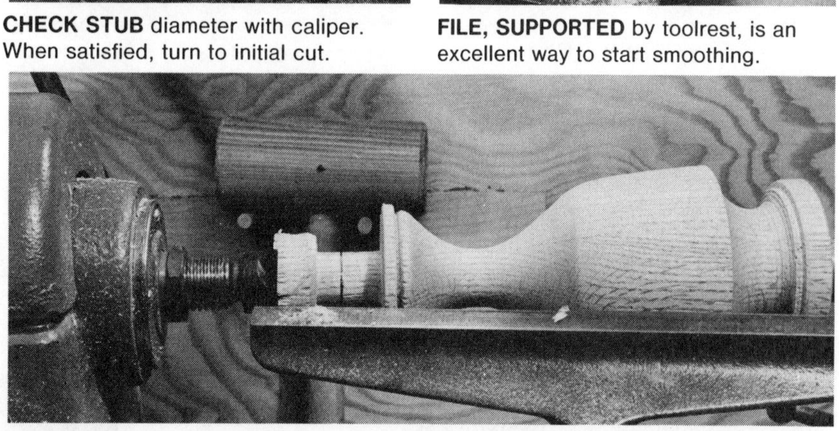

TO FINISH, remove the work from the lathe and bore the candle hole (or bore on the lathe with a chuck mounted in lathe) and cut off tenon on the bandsaw.

Interlocking wood sculpture—an ancient art

By KENNETH WELLS

■ YOUR FRIENDS are certain to marvel at this fascinating carved-wood sculpture. And they'll be curious to know just how you created it. Actually, the concept is based on the hand carvings made in the bazaars of India and elsewhere in the East by native craftsmen using primitive tools. Unlike them, you can use power tools to remove the waste wood quickly and almost effortlessly.

SEE ALSO

Candle stands . . . Centerpieces . . . Gifts, Christmas . . . Sanding . . . Tools, hand . . . Wood finishes . . . Wood-lathe techniques

1. AFTER SELECTING stock, clamp wood in the vise and rough-shape it round using a chisel and plane.

BASE FOR CANDY OR HORS D'OEUVRE DISH

DECORATIVE CANDLE BASE

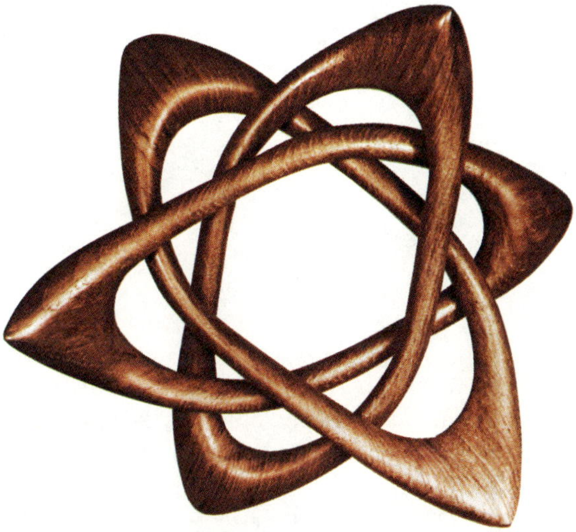

WALL DISPLAY

INTRIGUING SCULPTURE is a grand exercise in woodworking, and produces a finished product that can be used functionally (above) or simply as a conversation piece. Work with a piece of well-seasoned hardwood such as walnut or maple.

2. ROUGH-HEWN BLOCK is then mounted in a lathe and turned to true size—4 in. dia. by 7 in. long.

3. FOR ACCURACY, a large centerhole is bored on the lathe. If drill press is used, clamp the workpiece.

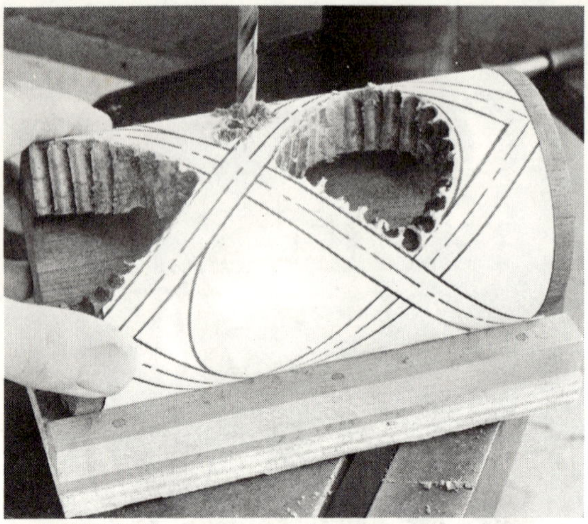

4. MOST OF the waste wood is removed by chain-drilling. Notice the support stand beneath the wood.

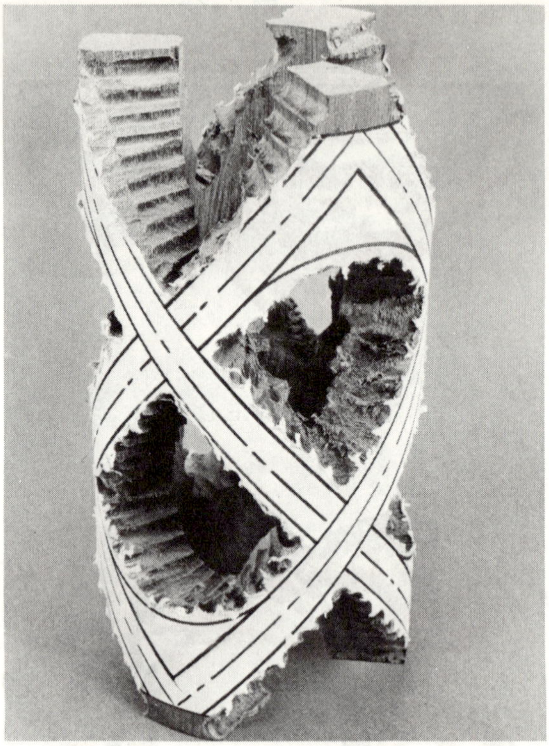

5. CYLINDER looks like this when waste has been drilled away. Drilling must be vertically accurate.

Making the link is a welcome change from the disciplines of precise measurement and accurate working so necessary for most sophisticated workshop projects. The finished sculpture is attractive as an art piece or it can be put to work as a dish or candy base.

It will pay you to select well-seasoned hardwood for this project. Walnut or maple are good choices because both are strong, yet not too tough to carve. After selecting stock to use, rough-round it by sawing, chiseling and planing. Next, shape the block to a cylinder by turning on the lathe.

The large hole through the center can be bored (in from both ends) in the lathe, by bench drill, or, most laboriously, by hand with an expansive or center bit in a brace.

Next, wrap a piece of paper around the wood

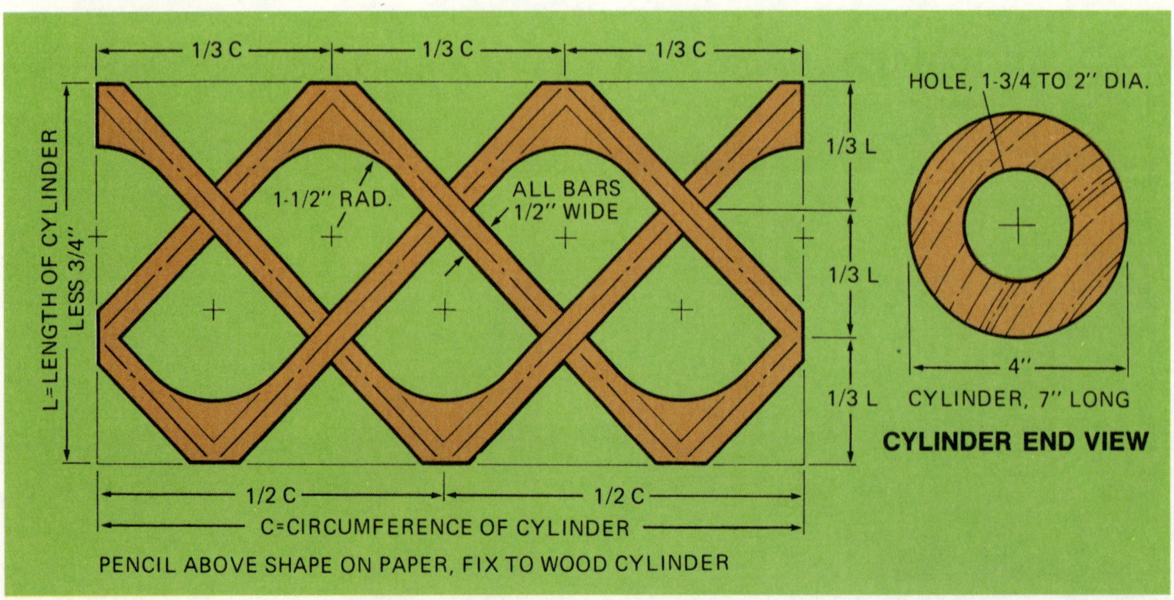

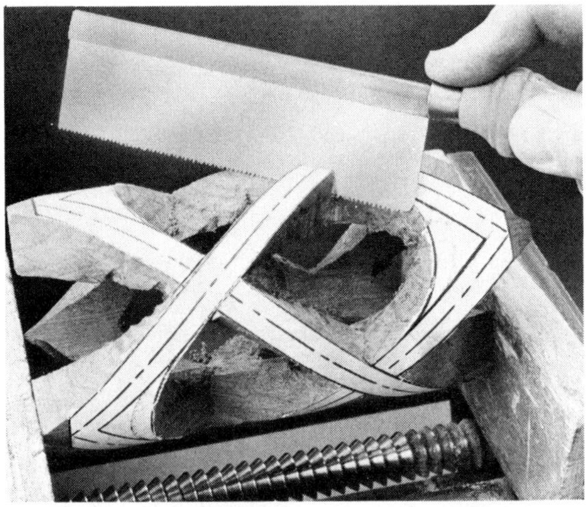

6. WOOD IS GRIPPED on end in vise, and backsaw is used to saw halfway through the underpass bars.

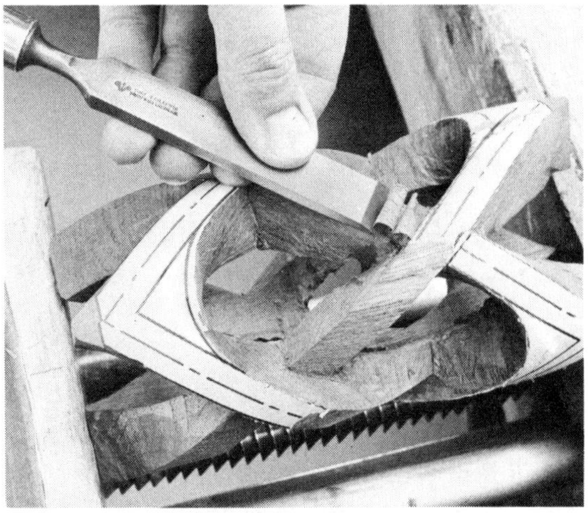

7. WITH WORK still in the vise, upper surfaces of the underpass bars are then chiseled away.

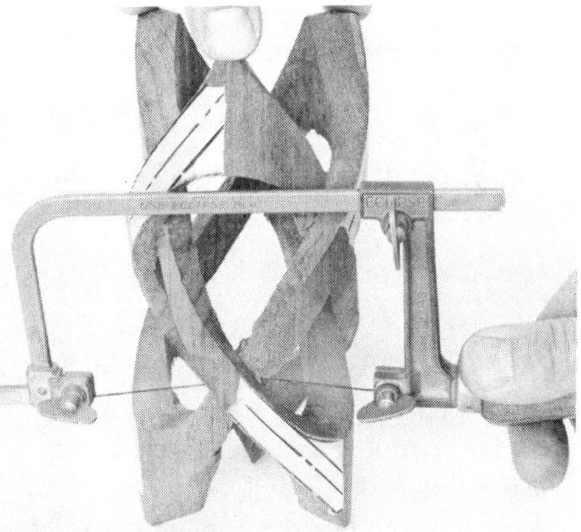

8. UNDERPASS AND OVERPASS bars are separated with a fine-bladed saw. Bars are now easier to work.

and carefully mark and cut away any overlap to leave edges that just meet. Mark out the lattice-work shape shown in the diagram using light pencil lines initially; then, after checking, boldly line in the bars with a felt-tip pen. Secure the paper to the wood with white glue or library paste. When it's dry, most of the waste wood can be removed by chain-drilling a series of holes with the cylinder resting on a channel-section stand. When you're drilling, *it is important* to judge that the center line of the bar adjacent to each hole being drilled is precisely in the "top dead center" position. This assures that the holes in each side of the bars will be parallel down through the thickness of the cylinder walls. The uneven edges left by the drilling can be smoothed with a sharp chisel and penknife.

Grip the wood on end in the vise and saw halfway through the thickness of the cylinder wall (underpass bars) each side of the *overpass* bars (see photo No. 6.) Pare away the waste wood in such a way that each *underpass* bar descends to the halfway position against each *overpass* bar.

It will now be obvious that similar—though more difficult—paring is required inside the cylinder to shape the inner surfaces of the overpass bars to clear the underpass ones.

A fret or piercing saw is used to saw through between the underpass and overpass bars where they cross as shown in step No. 8. The three separated, but interlocked, pieces are now easier to deal with as the bars are made roughly round or elliptical in section by careful whittling with a chisel or penknife. The points at one end can be shaped inward to give a horn-shaped single point support most suitable if the sculpture is used as a base for a dish. With the sculpture arranged in its natural resting position, the base ends can be carved or sanded to give an area of contact with the surface under them.

Final smoothing is made by diligent use of medium-grade, then fine-grade glass or garnet paper. The carving can be finished with two or three coats of shellac or varnish applied with a soft brush. Each coat, including the last, should be lightly rubbed with steel wool. After the last coat apply a little wax polish to bring out the full beauty of the grain and your carving.

Working properties of common woods

Do you need a wood that bends easily, or one that works easily with hand tools? The first step in any do-it-yourself project is to select the right wood

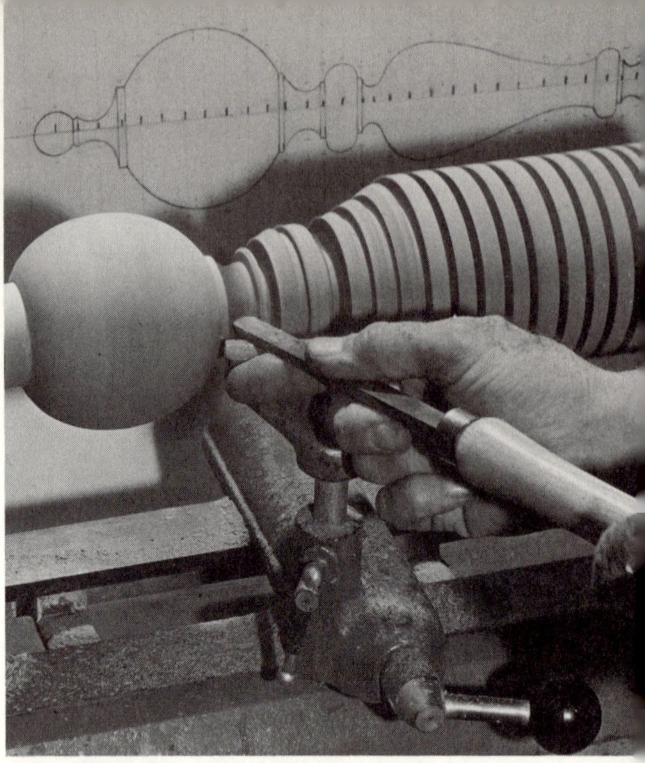

WILL THE WOOD you choose for your project work easily? Check the chart to find out.

WHEN SELECTING A WOOD to use in a project, your choice is likely to be governed by two major considerations: the final appearance of the wood after you finish it, and the strength and workability of the wood.

To make a durable piece of furniture, for example, you want wood which is hard and will stand up to everyday usage. It should take turning on a lathe, and take a fine finish sanding. Then, when you apply the final finish, it should offer an attractive grain, take staining evenly, and then take the final finish attractively.

The chart on the opposite page was developed as a result of experimental work at Forest Products Laboratory, and was designed to provide a guide to lead you to the right wood for each project. You should note that even cuts of wood from the same log vary considerably, so that the values given here are averages.

Under the heading "Planing and Jointing" you will see figures. These tell you the cutting angles which have been found best when using edge tools (chisels, for example, or a jointer or molding head) to shape each type of wood.

The grade of sandpaper shown for each species is the paper which has been found best for the final smooth sanding. Paper of the grade shown will not leave scratches on the surface. On some samples of any of these woods, you may have to go one step finer in sandpaper grade to produce the best final finish.

SEE ALSO

Abrasives . . . Finishes, wood . . . Lumber . . . Plywood . . . Sanding . . . Staining, wood . . . Veneering . . . Wood bending . . . Wood finishes

You can use any color of stain on any wood, of course. The colors recommended here are those which produce a traditional color in the wood. In many cases, the traditional look is actually an imitation of another wood. Birch, for example, is most often stained to look like walnut, maple or mahogany. Walnut, on the other hand, is always finished to look like walnut.

Before making your selection, read the notes in the "Remarks" column, which give you an additional insight into the appearance and working qualities of each wood. You'll find references to such things as uniformity of color, principal uses, and how well the wood can be worked by hand or power tools.

The chart does not indicate the availability of the listed woods. Some, such as pine and fir, can be purchased locally in a variety of sizes. Most, however, must be ordered from woodworking supply houses such as Albert Constantine and Sons, 2050 E. Chester Road, Bronx, NY 10461; and Craftsman Wood Service, 2124 S. Mary St., Chicago, IL 60608. Send for the latest catalog published by each and order from it.

Fine woods are short in supply and can be hard to find, especially in large pieces. You would have difficulty, for example, in finding top quality walnut in 2 x 8-in. planks. Smaller pieces of the fine woods are available and considerably less expensive. Keep this in mind when planning a purchase. Some of the rare woods can be had only in veneers, and then perhaps only in sheets of 4 x 36 in.

CHARACTERISTICS OF WORKABLE WOODS

General Characteristics — Note: NGR = Non-Grain Raising (Applies to stain)

Name of Wood	Weight Per Cubic Foot	Hardness	Planing and Jointing	Turning	Sanding	Natural Color	Usual Grain Figure	Stain: Type	Stain: Color	Bleach	Remarks
Ash (U.S.A.)	35	Med.	Good 10-25	Fair	Best 2/0	White to Brown	Plain or Fiddleback	Any	Any	Yes	A tough, grainy wood quite uniform in color. Bends quite easily when steamed. Will take stain, but finishes best in natural color
Basswood	24	Soft	Good 20-30	Poor	Poor 4/0	Cream	Very Mild	NGR	Red or Brown	Not Nec.	Light, softwood usually uniform in color. Fine texture, fairly strong, takes paint well. Used for drawing boards and as veneered core stock
Birch	39	Hard	Good 15-20	Good	Fair 4/0	Cream	Mild	Any	Walnut or Mahogany	Yes	Similar in texture to hard maple. Takes the maple finish very well. Widely used in furniture construction. Fairly Uniform color
Butternut	25	Soft	Good 10-25	Good	Fair 4/0	Heart: Amber Sap: Cream	Like Walnut	Water	Walnut or Oak	Yes	Similar in grain and texture to black walnut. Relatively easy to work with hand and power tools, except as noted
Cherry	36	Med.	Best 10-30	Best	Best 4/0	Red to Brown	Good	Water	Red or Brown	No	One of the finest domestic cabinet woods. Fine texture, dense grain, often wavy or curly. Takes natural, stain, fine enamel finishes
Cedar (Aromatic Red)	23	Soft	Poor 5-15	Fair	Good 3/0	Heart: Red Sap: Cream	Knotty	None		No	Universally used for cedar chests and clothes-closet linings, also novelties. Finishes best in its natural color
Chestnut	27	Soft	Good 15-20	Best	Best 3/0	Gray-Brown	Heavy Grain	Oil or Wiping	Red or Brown	No	Rather coarse grained, often worm-holed. Used as picture frames and sometimes as random paneling. Machines well, takes novelty finishes
Cypress	29	Soft	Good 15-25	Poor	Fair 2/0	Heart: Brown Sap: Cream	Plain or Figured	Water, Oil or Wiping	Red or Brown	No	Tends to splinter when worked by hand or machine. Most durable in outdoor exposures. Will take natural or novelty finishes quite well
Elm (Southern)	34	Med.	Poor 15-20	Poor	Good 2/0	Brown to Cream	Heavy Grain	Water	Red or Brown	No	A good furniture wood but difficult to work either by hand or machine. Takes stain fairly well. Some pieces attractively grained
Fir (Douglas)	26	Soft	Fair 10-25	Poor	Fair 3/0	Cream to Red	Plain or Wild	Wiping or Oil	Brown	No	Widely used in home construction, especially framing. Universally available as plywood in varying thicknesses. Best sealed and painted
Gum (Red)	33	Med.	Fair 10-20	Best	Fair 4/0	Heart: Br. Red Sap: Cream	Plain or Figured	Any	Red or Brown	Yes	Dense-grained wood, smooth texture. Occasional attractive figure in heartwood, easily worked. Widely used in furniture construction
Hickory	42	Hard	Good 10-25	Good	Best 2/0	White to Cream	Usually Straight	Water	Red or Brown	Yes	Among best domestic woods for steam bending, tool handles. Usually straight grained and of a fairly uniform color and texture
Holly	33	Hard	Good 10-25	Good	Best 3/0	Silver White	Mild	Water	Amber	Not Nec.	Similar to basswood in color and texture. Works easily. Can be stained. Once widely used in inlay and marquetry in early construction
Mahogany	35	Med.	Good 5-25	Best	Good 4/0	Brown to Red-Brown	Stripe	Water	Red or Brown	Yes	One of the choicest cabinet woods. Select pieces beautifully grained. Works easily. Takes both red and brown stains. An imported wood
Mahogany (Philippine)	33	Med.	Good 5-25	Good	Poor 3/0	Brown to Red-Brown	Stripe	Water or Wiping	Red or Brown	Yes	Similar to true mahoganies but coarser in grain and softer. Serves well as boat planking, also used as trim and in core-door construction
Maple	41	Hard	Fair 15-20	Good	Good 4/0	Cream	Varied	Water and Wiping	Maple	Yes	One of the best domestic hardwoods. Widely used in fine furniture construction, also as flooring, turnings, bowling pins
Oak (English Brown)	40	Hard	Best 10-20	Good	Good 2/0	Deep Brown	Plain, Flake or Swirl	NGR	Brown	Yes	One of the finest of the oaks. An imported wood, most commonly available as veneer. Very attractively grained. Takes stains well
Oak (Red)	39	Hard	Best 10-25	Good	Best 2/0	Red-Brown	Plain or Flake	NGR	Green Toner	Yes	Perhaps the most common of the domestic oaks. Heavy, strong and tough. Open-grained, used in furniture where durability comes first.
Oak (White)	40	Hard	Best 10-20	Good	Best 2/0	White to Light Brown	Plain or Flake	NGR	Brown	Yes	Perhaps the finest domestic oak of exceptional strength and durability. Beautiful graining when quarter-sawed. Takes fine finishes
Pine (White)	25	Soft	Good 10-25	Good	Fair 2/0	White to Cream	Mild	Water or Oil	Brown Only	No	One of the most popular woods almost universally used for trim, paneling and furniture. Perhaps the best all around domestic softwood
Poplar	29	Soft	Good 5-20	Good	Poor 4/0	White to Cream	Occ. Dark Stripe	NGR	Brown	No	Another of the most useful domestic softwoods. Widely used as a secondary wood in both early and late furniture construction
Redwood	29	Soft	Good 10-25	Fair	Poor 2/0	Red	Mild St. Grain	Red only for toning		No	An exceptionally durable softwood when used in outdoor applications as house siding, outdoor furniture, fencing, industrial applications
Sycamore	35	Med.	Poor 5-15	Good	Poor 3/0	White to Pink	Flake	Water	Amber or Brown	Seldom	Difficult to work with either hand or power tools. Beautiful, flaky grain when quarter-sawed. Most attractive in natural finish
Walnut	36	Med.	Good 15-20	Best	Best 4/0	Heart: Brown Sap: Cream	Varied	Water	Walnut	Yes	Rated by most as the finest domestic cabinet wood. Used by best cabinetmakers from earliest times. Has every desirable feature

The basic workbench

In any shop planning, the workbench must come first. If it's to be any better than a discarded kitchen chair, then it must be solid, sound and stable. Here's a bench that fills the requirements

By W. CLYDE LAMMEY

■ BUY A STATION-WAGON LOAD of sound 2 x 4s, a short 2 x 8, a few pieces of hardwood, a vise screw and a few bolts—and you're in business. If you don't already have a radial or bench saw, then it will pay you to buy a miterbox to cut ends square. You'll have plenty of use for this tool later.

It's best to be a little picky when selecting the 2 x 4s and the one short 2 x 8, especially the 2 x 4s for the top. You'll need stock that's well-seasoned, straight, and with a minimum of knots. A few sound knots are no problem, but loose knots that may fall out should be avoided.

The details in the drawing show the construction and give a size for the top which is about the minimum. You can make it longer or wider, or both, if you wish.

The first step is cutting the parts for the top to precise lengths so that, when the bench is assembled, there will be a minimum planing of end grain. Notice that the top is cross-bolted, using threaded rod you can buy in your hardware store. This can be eliminated if you take care to do a good job of gluing up the parts.

Glue the long section of the top first, spreading the glue uniformly and as quickly as possible. Or, glue only four pieces at a time and then finish with a single glue joint at the center. In either case you'll need at least four bar clamps, placed two on top and two underneath, the clamps evenly spaced and drawn uniformly tight. Wipe off all excess glue and allow ample drying time.

Next, glue up the extension sections separately and then glue these to the top, front and back.

Notice that the front extension has a hardwood facing which forms the inner, or stationary jaw, of the front vise. The latter is duplicated if an end vise is desired. Otherwise the end piece, or cleat, at the rear end of the top can be made from pine.

The backboard, which forms a side of the tool well is made of softwood. These parts are both glued and screwed in place. Drill spaced ¾-in. holes in the top and one in the vise jaw for planing stops. Make two of the latter for clamping stock across the width of the bench.

Construction of the vise and the leg units is shown in the details. Notice especially the manner of joining the parts with bolts. Plane the top smooth to eliminate the slightly rounded edges of the 2 x 4s. Finish with a high-gloss varnish or an oil finish.

SEE ALSO
Hobby centers . . . Sawhorses . . . Shop tools . . . Shops, modelmaking . . . Varnish . . . Workshops

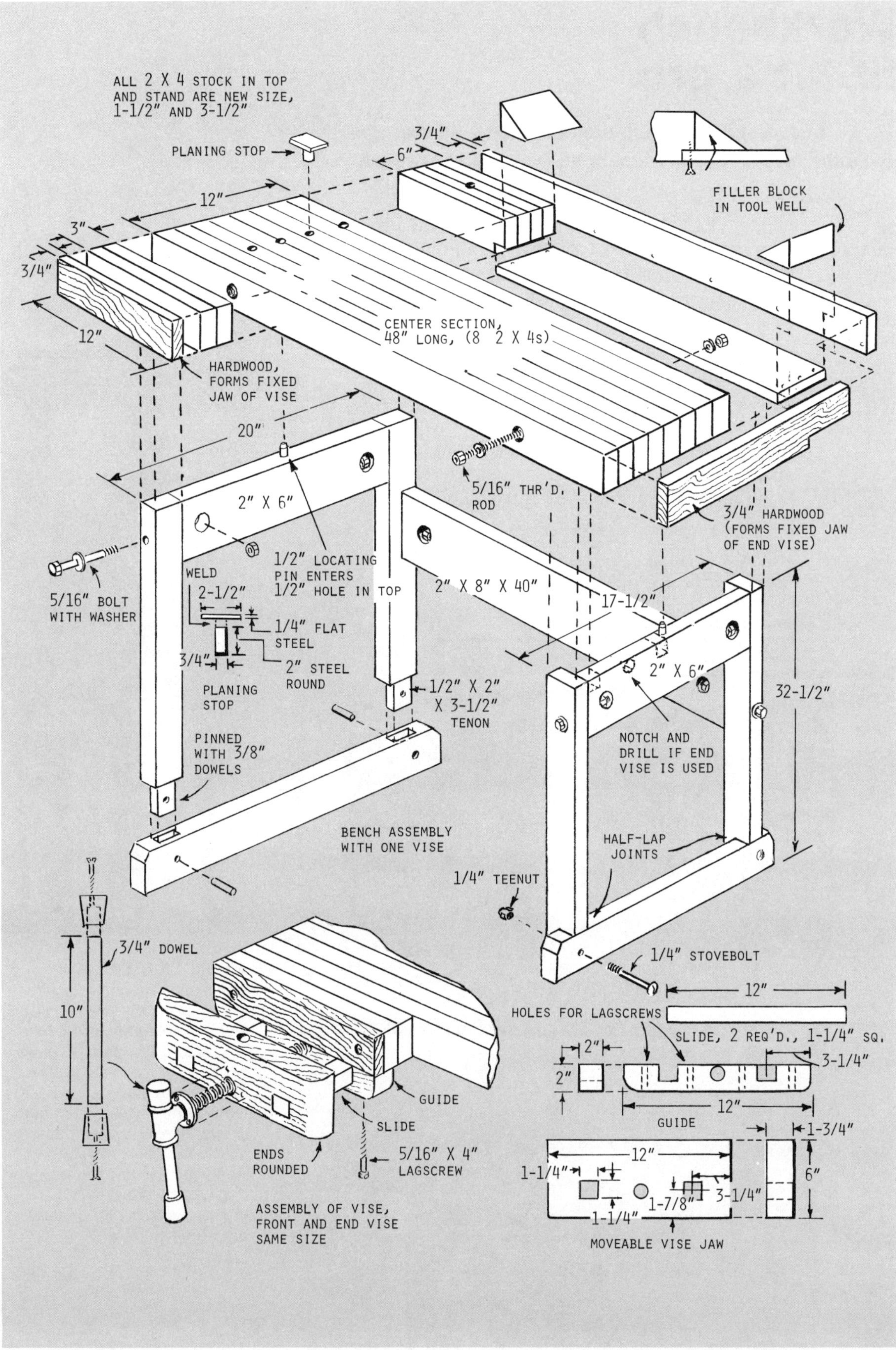

ALL 2 X 4 STOCK IN TOP AND STAND ARE NEW SIZE, 1-1/2" AND 3-1/2"
PLANING STOP
3/4"
6"
12"
3"
3/4"
12"
FILLER BLOCK IN TOOL WELL
CENTER SECTION, 48" LONG, (8 2 X 4s)
HARDWOOD, FORMS FIXED JAW OF VISE
20"
2" X 6"
5/16" THR'D. ROD
3/4" HARDWOOD (FORMS FIXED JAW OF END VISE)
5/16" BOLT WITH WASHER
WELD
2-1/2"
1/2" LOCATING PIN ENTERS 1/2" HOLE IN TOP
2" X 8" X 40"
17-1/2"
1/4" FLAT STEEL
3/4"
2" STEEL ROUND
PLANING STOP
2" X 6"
32-1/2"
1/2" X 2" X 3-1/2" TENON
NOTCH AND DRILL IF END VISE IS USED
PINNED WITH 3/8" DOWELS
BENCH ASSEMBLY WITH ONE VISE
HALF-LAP JOINTS
1/4" TEENUT
3/4" DOWEL
10"
1/4" STOVEBOLT
12"
HOLES FOR LAGSCREWS
SLIDE, 2 REQ'D., 1-1/4" SQ.
2"
2"
3-1/4"
GUIDE
12"
GUIDE
SLIDE
ENDS ROUNDED
5/16" X 4" LAGSCREW
1-3/4"
12"
1-1/4"
6"
1-7/8"
3-1/4"
1-1/4"
MOVEABLE VISE JAW
ASSEMBLY OF VISE, FRONT AND END VISE SAME SIZE

Workbench fit for a pro

Successful workshop projects start with the right tools. Here's the most important tool of all—a good workbench

A WELL-PLANNED WORKBENCH is what a good shop is all about, regardless of whether you are fortunate enough to have more than enough space or are shoehorned into a small work area. The bench is where your projects—big and little—will start, be labored over and, in all probability, be finished. Because a poor bench can easily diminish your interest as well as craftsmanship, use foresight when you build. Know what comprises a good shop setup and, if necessary, vary details and dimensions so they suit your own needs and preferences. Con-

SEE ALSO

Fluorescent lamps . . . Power-tool stands . . . Sawhorses . . . Shop tools . . . Small-parts storage . . . Workshops

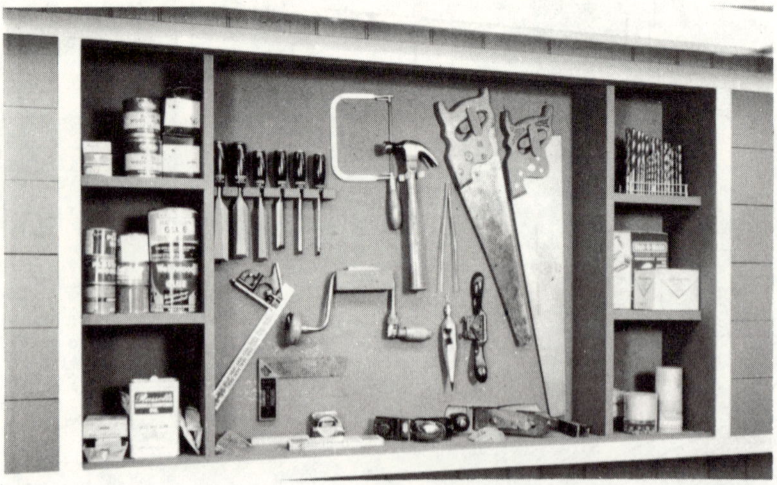

A WELL-LIGHTED SETUP in pleasant surroundings makes work a pleasure. The end vise and bench board-stops let the user keep both hands on power tools where they belong. The roomy wall cabinet (above left) features rails, stiles, doors and drawer fronts covered with plastic laminate. The sturdy workbench boasts two vises, three roomy drawers and goodsize shelves for portable powertool storage.

By HARRY WICKS

sidered by most experts to be the heart of the shop, a good workbench will include:

- A spacious, smooth work surface atop a sturdy and rigid base.
- At least one woodworking vise.
- Maximum small-parts and tool storage.

Because the approach here to building a workbench has been total—a setup rather than a workbench alone—you'll see more features than the three points just mentioned, including:

- A smooth top of more than 1100 sq. in., with an 8-in.-wide shaving trough.
- Two vises, provisions for bench dogs in the top and dowel supports in the apron to support long, vise-held workpieces.
- Storage galore. The base has three roomy, compartmentalized drawers and three shelves for portable-tool storage. Each end is finished with perforated board for extra tool hanging. The wall cabinet has 12 drawers, 6 shelves and a tool panel for fingertip convenience. There's also an overhead shop-built light fixture, a kickplate between bench feet to prevent dropped tools from rolling under the bench and plastic laminate on all exposed surfaces to minimize maintenance.

With minimum upkeep in mind, cabinet, bench and drawer interiors were left natural, merely varnished to make less obvious those inevitable smudge marks from tools and hands. Johns-Manville Melamite plastic laminate was used on exposed surfaces; marks and dirt will sponge off.

The bench, cabinet and light fixture were built

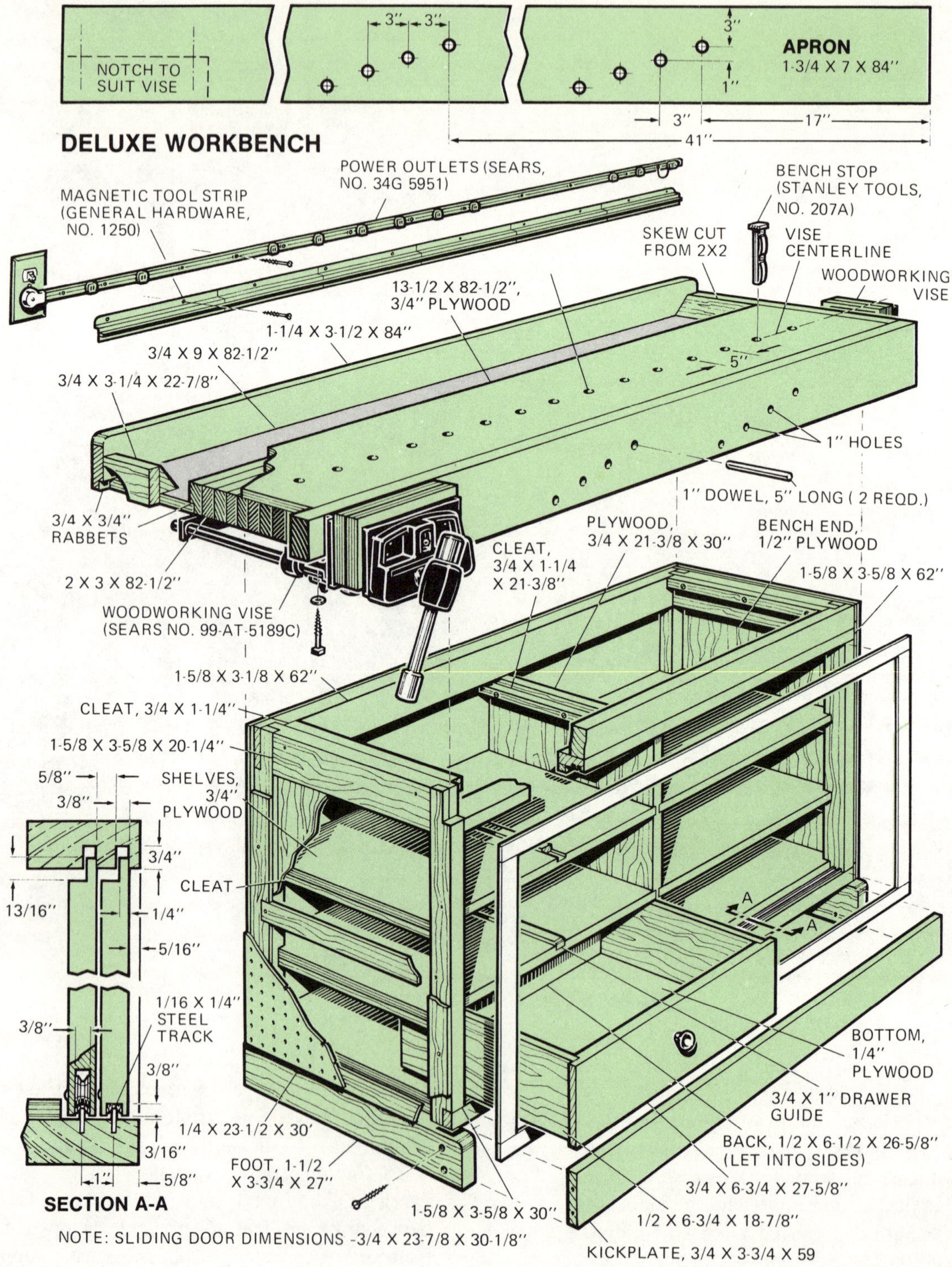

from stock lumberyard items. For parts you may have to order, such as plexiglass and board stops, check the source list on page 3130.

Sliding doors of the bench ride sheaves that roll on steel tracks that parallel the full length of the bottom front rail. Each door is fitted with two sheaves set in 2 in. from the ends. Its top edge is rabbeted to engage grooves along the underside of the top rail. The ¾-in.-deep grooves allow ample clearance to place sheaves on the tracks when you install the doors. If you wish, you could alter dimensions and install com-

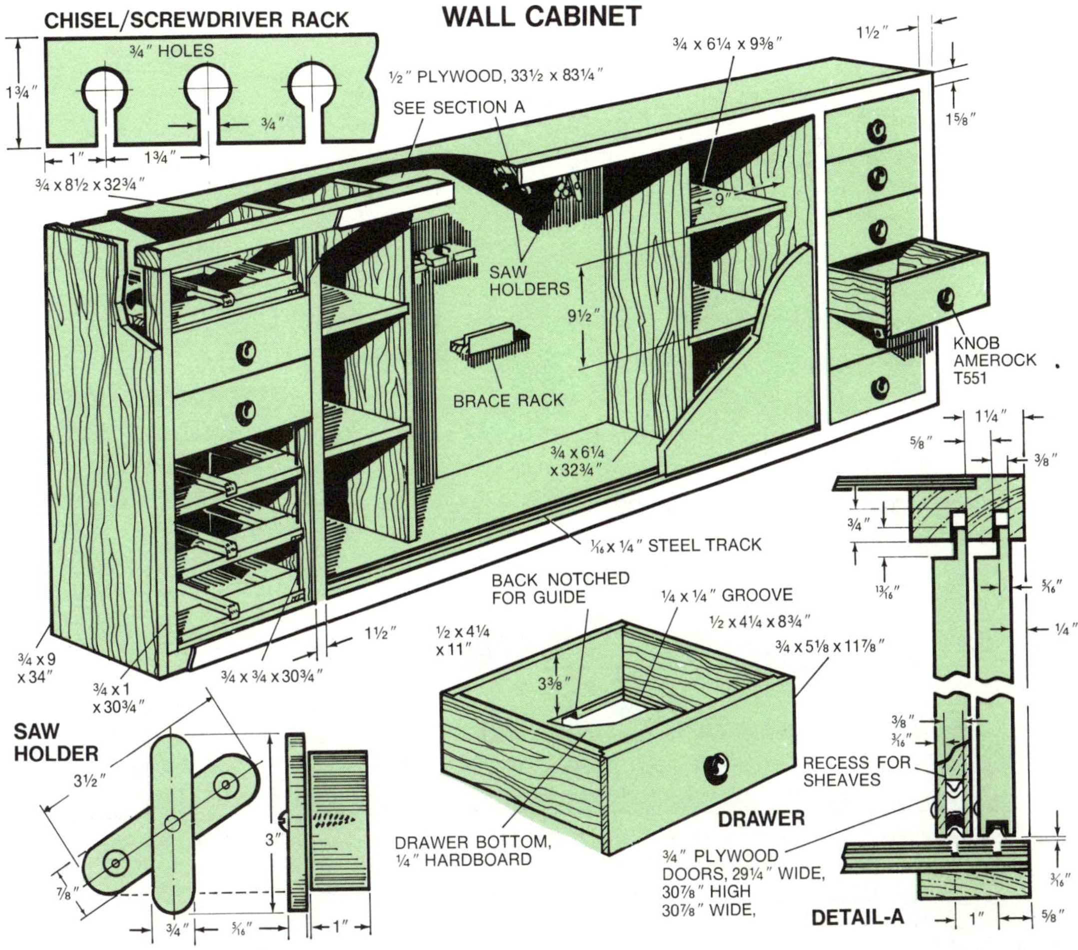

mercially available sliding-door hardware packaged in kits. But don't skimp on quality; these doors will get considerable hard use.

The original design of the workbench and wall cabinet had square holes in the benchtop. We've replaced these with ⅝-in.-dia. holes for use with bench board stops. You may not find these stops readily at hardware stores but they can be ordered through your local hardware dealer. Essentially, they are industrial-school-shop items.

Unused space at the ends of the bench made little sense so we furred both ends and covered

BOTH WORKBENCH ENDS are furred and covered with perforated board for extra tool storage. Two rows of diagonal holes drilled in the bench apron receive 1-in. dowels for supporting long boards.

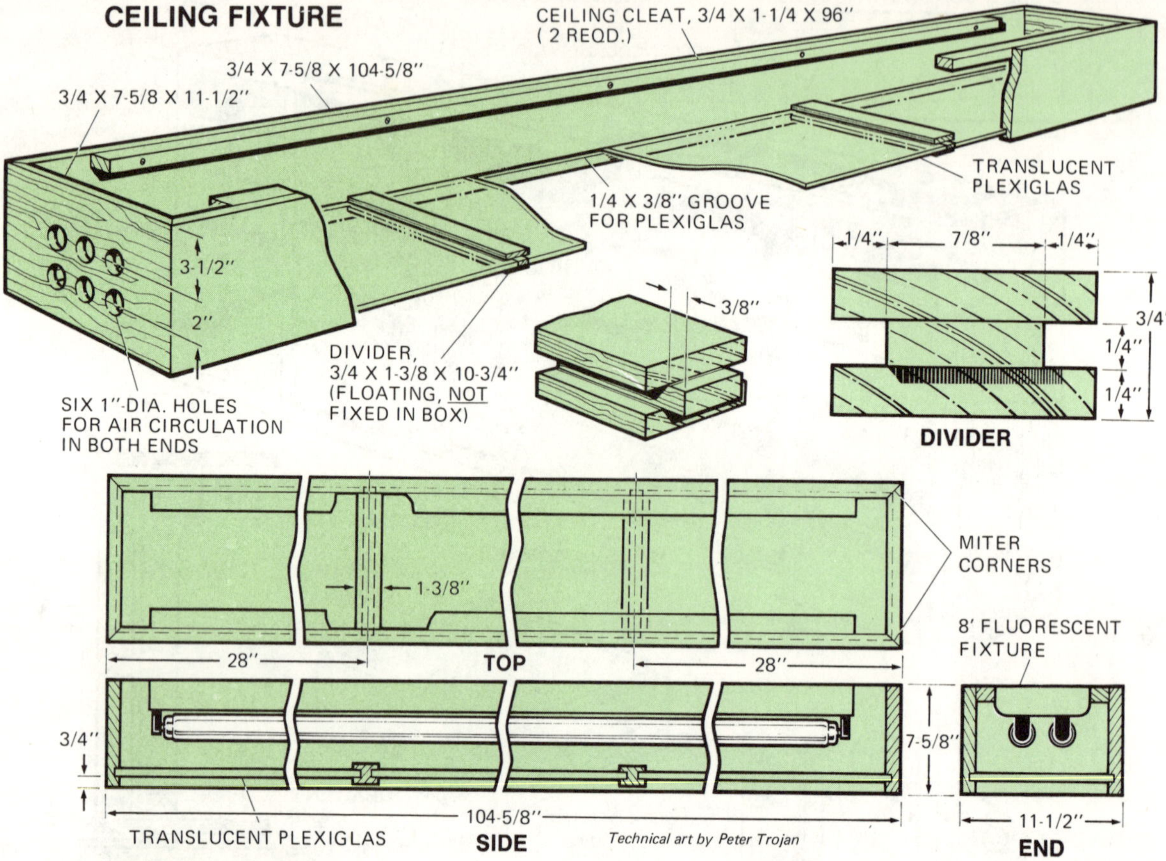

Technical art by Peter Trojan

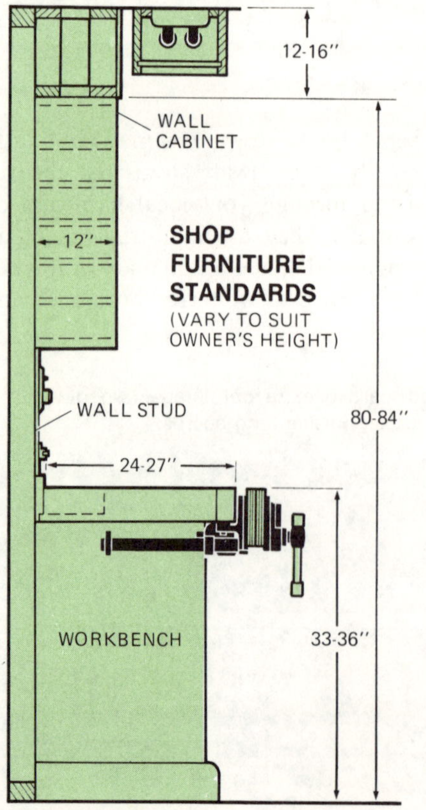

them with perforated board. After applying two coats of semigloss varnish, we used the boards to hold tools and supplies that are needed infrequently. The fixture shown on page 3127 was purchased without a hood and fastened directly to the ceiling. The surrounding box of 1x8 pine was grooved to receive removable plexiglass panels. The wood was simply stained and given two coats of semigloss varnish.

Consider adding a power outlet strip and magnetic toolholders to the wall between bench and cabinet. You can plug in several tools while you work on a project without having to switch power back and forth, and the holders keep your frequently used tools at hand in full view.

SPECIALTY ITEMS USED IN CONSTRUCTION

Drawer knobs, Amerock Corp., Rockford Ill. *No. T551*
Board stops, Stanley Tools, New Britain, Conn. *No. 207A*
Power outlets, Sears, Roebuck and Co. *Cat. No. 34G 5951*
Magnetic tool strip, General Hardware, 80 White St., New York, N.Y. 10013. *No. 1250*
Plastic laminate, Johns-Manville, 300 Canal St., Lawrence, Mass. 01840. *Melamite*
Woodworking vise, Sears. *Cat. No. 99-AT-5189C*
Sheet acrylics (light fixture), Rohm & Haas, Box 9730, Philadelphia, Pa. 19140. *Translucent Plexiglas*
Walls, Masonite Corp., 29 North Wacker Dr., Chicago, Ill. 60606. *Georgetown White 1900*

Tailgate workbench

By H. M. THOMAS

VISE ON THE WORKBENCH is an on-the-job bonus. Benchtop here is 36 in. from the ground, but can be built to suit the user. Left, space under the top stores large tools not in use. When the tailgate is closed, shear panel holds large tools in bench for transport.

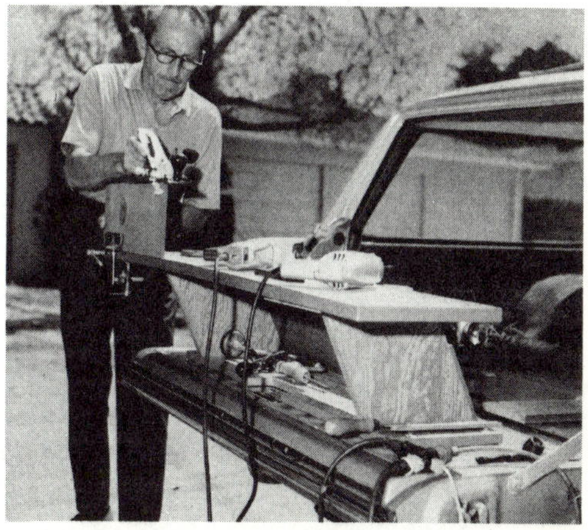

TRAVELING CARPENTERS will immediately spot the useful advantages of this portable —yet sturdy—workbench: 1.) Bench work can be handled at a comfortable-to-work-at height. and 2.) Portable electric tools can be neatly tucked between the top and tailgate for over-the-road storage. If you have a weekend retreat or are frequently called upon to bail out a neighbor with a do-it-yourself problem, the bench could become a valuable addition to your home workshop.

Dimensioned lumber may be used instead of plywood for base and top, if desired. To give the bench a convenient overhang when in use, mount it as close as possible to the edge of the tailgate. Start by removing the gate's inner panel, then clamp the base to it and drill through both for four capscrews. Finally, rivet the nut plates to the underside of the panel.

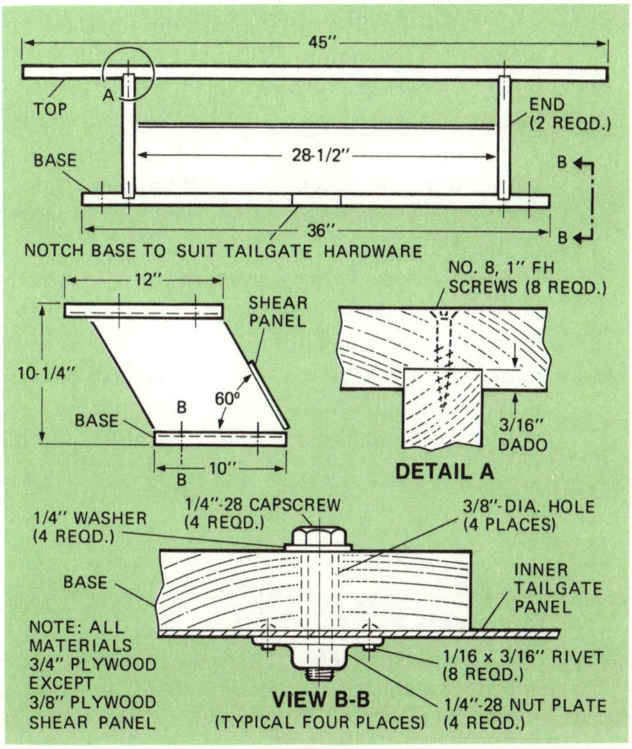

SEE ALSO

Cabinets, tailgate . . . Sawhorses . . . Vacation homes . . . Workshops

Build a shop inside a bench

By WAYNE C. LECKEY

Serving as a combination tool stand and workbench, this space-saving work center becomes a workshop in itself

IF YOU HAVE a hankering to get started in the rewarding and relaxing hobby of making and fixing things but are stymied for a place to work, here's the perfect answer to the question of space.

We call it a shop-in-a-bench and that's just what it is—a self-contained island work center which can be equipped with both hand and power tools to let you have the time of your life in just 3 x 4 ft. of space.

Not only do you have a king-size workbench with a top that's accessible from all four sides, but a bench which serves as a power-tool stand at the drop of a hat.

A drill press, a 4-in. jointer and an 8-in. circular saw are conveniently parked in stalls in the base of the bench. Thus when you want to saw, plane or drill a board with the accuracy of a power tool, you simply reach down, grab the tool you want, plunk it in predrilled holes in the bench top, plug it in, and away you go. It's not necessary to bolt the power tool in place.

When you want to clear the deck and use the big 3 x 4-ft. top for layout and assembly work, you can do it in a jiffy by returning the tools to their respective stalls.

In addition to all this, the bench has five roomy drawers, plus four shelves, where you can store all the hand and portable electric tools you'll ever need, all within easy reach.

While these stalls are dimensioned to accommodate Rockwell's three Compactools, they can be made to suit other small-size, self-contained machines.

The quick-change, no-fastening feature of the machines is accomplished by fitting their bases with 3/8 x 2-in. bolts which are left projecting. Registering holes drilled in the benchtop for the projecting bolts on each machine are all that's needed to anchor the machines. When through using them, you simply lift the machines out of the holes and park them in their stalls.

Two sets of holes are provided for the circular saw which let you position it to suit the shape of the room and the size of the work. This way you can make the most of cramped quarters and be less restricted in the size of the work you can handle.

In the case of the drill press and jointer you merely have to drill out the original holes in the machine bases to accept the 3/8-in. bolts. How-

BY CAREFULLY positioning the saw on the bench with relation to the room's size you can rip and crosscut long boards easily and without hindrance.

SEE ALSO

**Circular saws, portable . . . Drawers . . .
Drill press techniques . . . Motors, shop . . .
Power-tool stands . . . Tools, hand . . . Workshops**

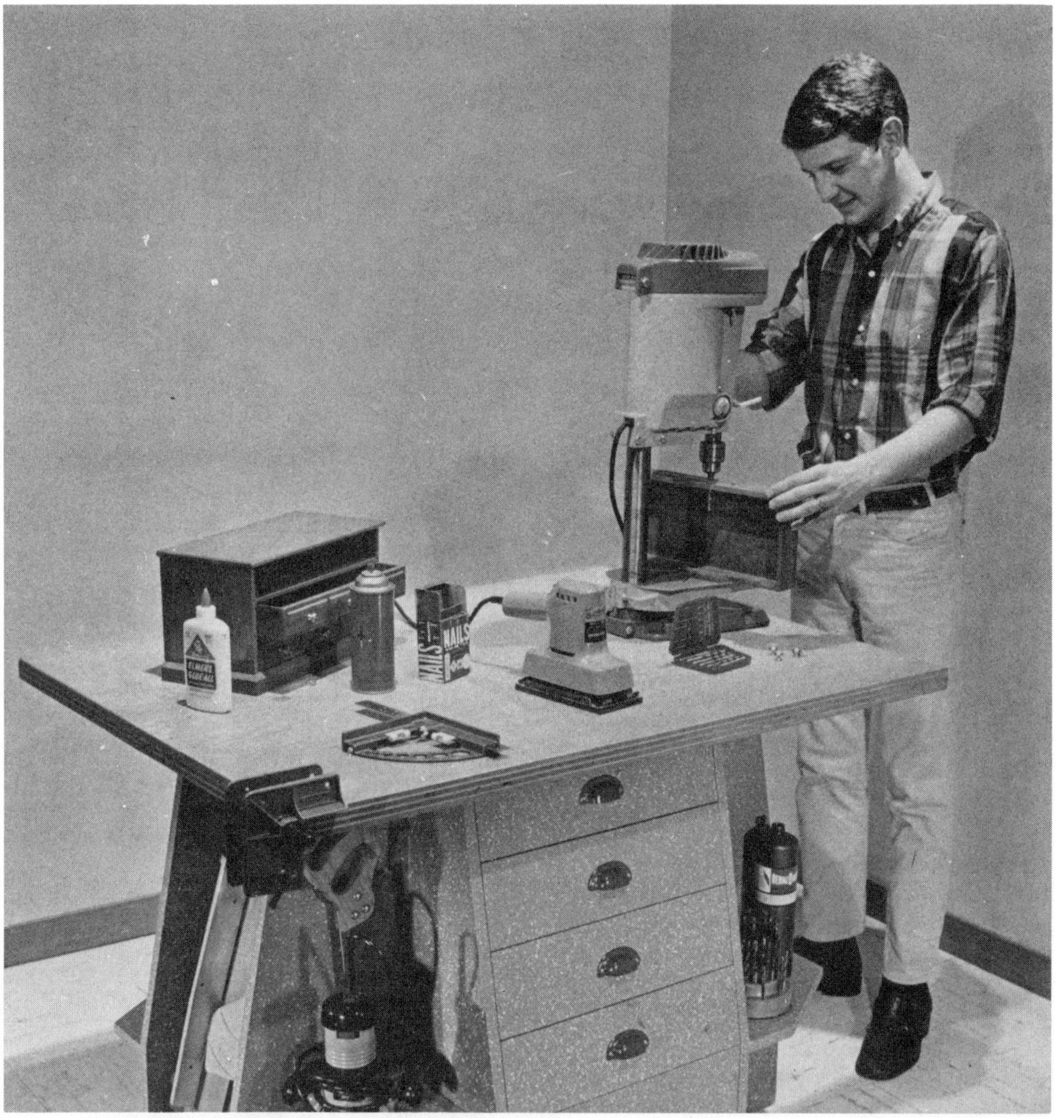

THE BENCH becomes a tool stand when you want to drill a hole. The lightweight drill press is lifted from its stall in the base and set in anchor holes drilled to receive it in the benchtop.

WITH POWER TOOLS parked in the base, the workbench top offers a big uncluttered work area which lets you spread out layout and assembly jobs. Note the stall in the front of the bench for the saw.

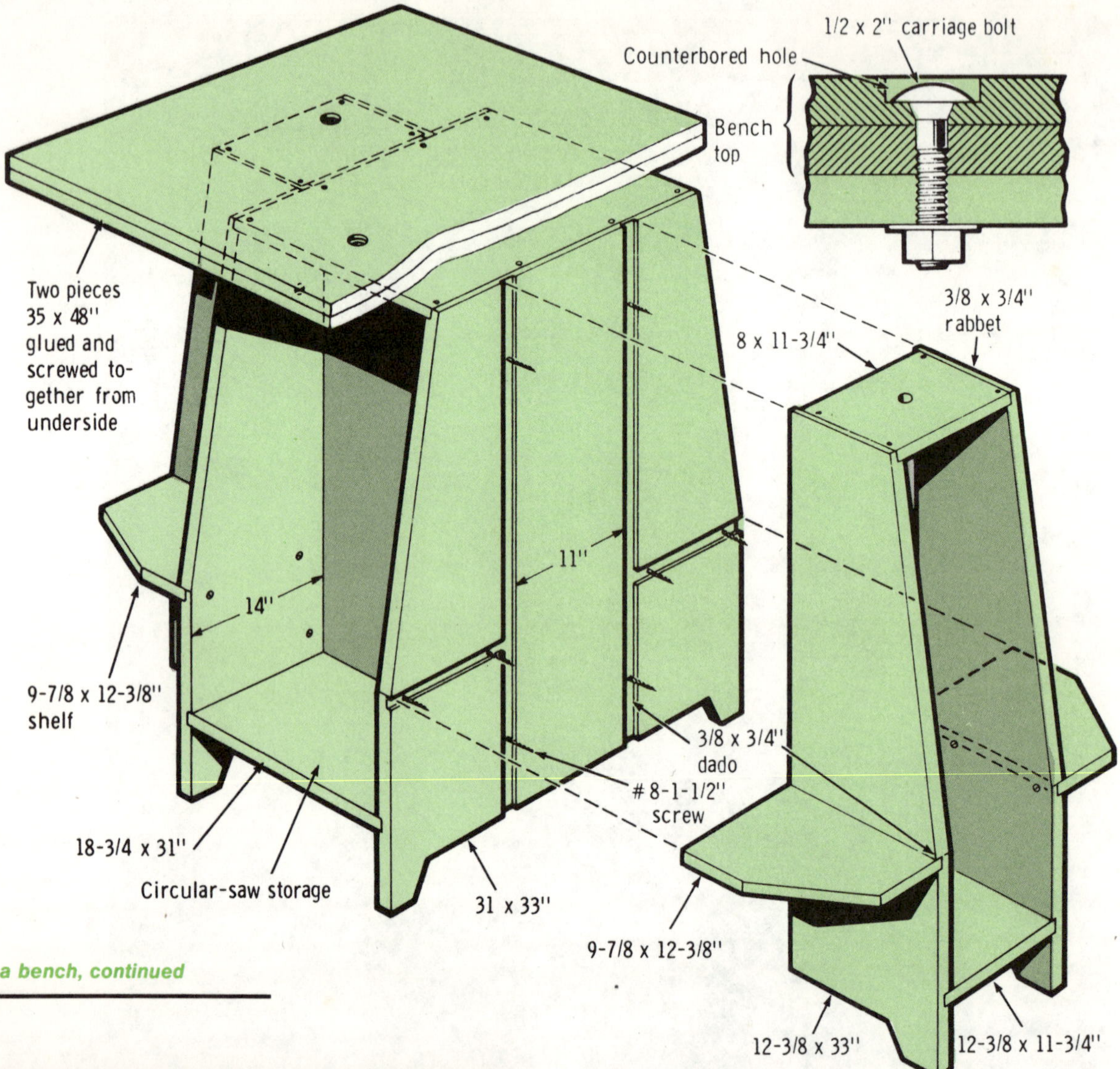

shop in a bench, continued

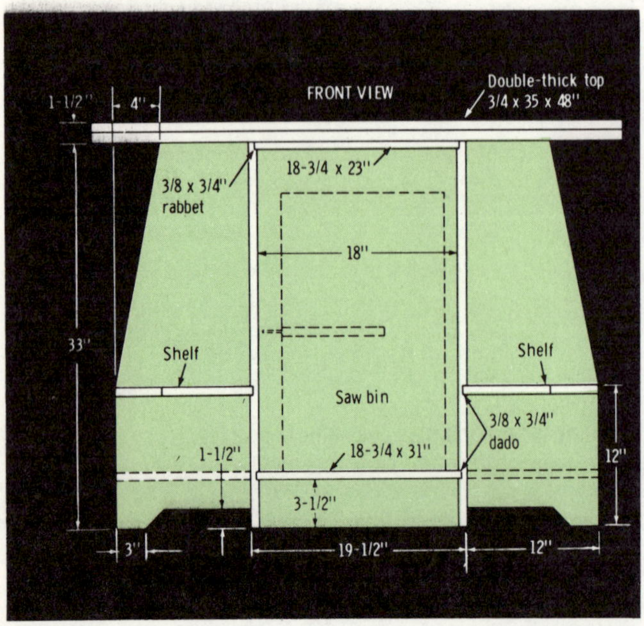

ever, the circular saw requires bolting a ¾ x 9½ x 12-in. plywood base to the saw's sheetmetal base. Four holes for the ⅜-in. bolts are first bored through the plywood and counterbored ¼-in. deep on the underside for the nuts. Next, the holes in the saw's base are marked on the plywood, then drilled for 3/16 x ¾-in. stovebolts and also counterbored for their nuts. The stovebolts are used to attach the plywood base to the saw.

The bench, entirely of ¾-in. fir plywood, is made in four sections; a main drawer section, a jointer stall, a drill-press stall and a double-thick top. The four sections are designed to bolt and screw together so the bench can be dismantled for easy transporting and for negotiating turns, doorways and stairs.

Start making the main drawer section first by laying out the two dadoed ends. These are made in pairs and the dadoes cut before the members

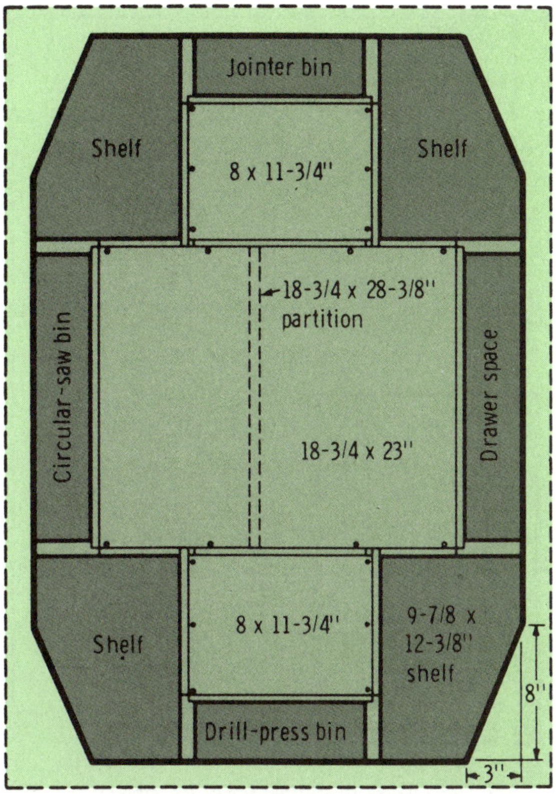

TOP VIEW

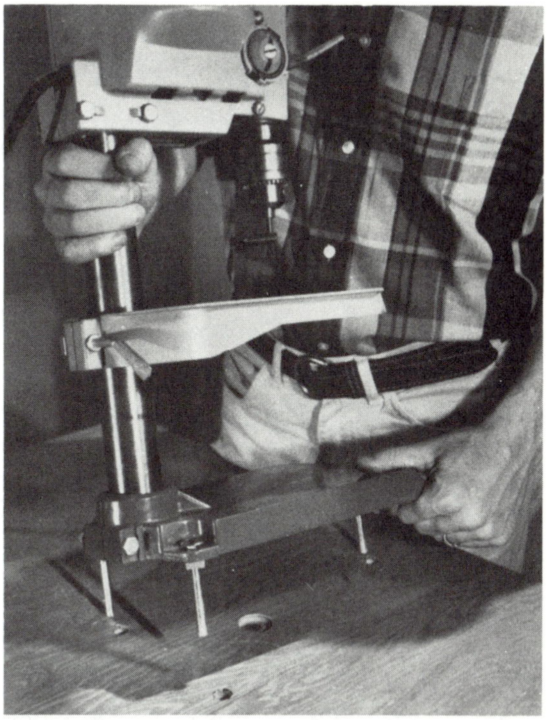

REGISTERING HOLES in the benchtop receive projecting studs on each machine to anchor it for use.

are tapered. Dadoed joints make the sturdiest bench, but you can skip them and use plain butt joints. Likewise, the rabbeted joints across the top of the ends can be butt joints. The partition, in turn, fits a dado in the bottom member and dadoes in the side members, although these, too, can be mere butt joints. Nail and glue the five

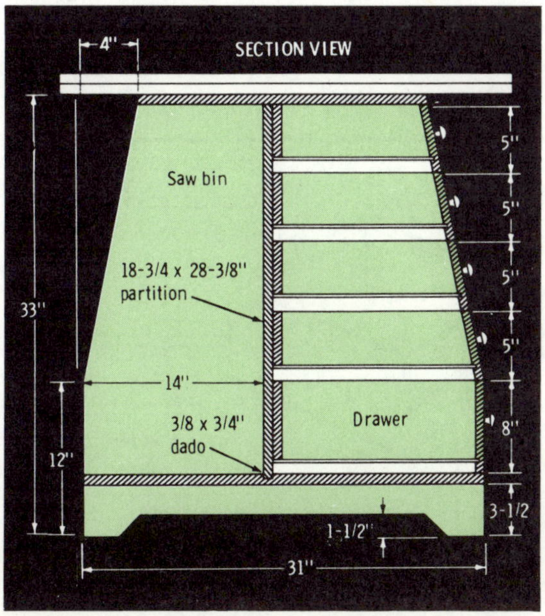

parts together, leaving the drawer runners until later.

The drill-press and jointer stalls are twins and identical in size. Should you not join them to the main section in dadoes, you don't have to deduct the ¼-in. depth of the grooves from the dimensions given, everything will still fit. In either case, 1½-in. flathead wood screws are used to attach the stalls to the main section. Note that the stalls slant inward at the top to match the main section.

Short lengths of dowel glued in blind holes in the side of the stalls, as well as in the sides of the main section, provide pegs for hanging saw blades, the saw's rip fence and miter gauge, and countless hand tools, which will save drawer space.

The benchtop is made extra solid by gluing and screwing together two thicknesses of plywood. The screws are driven from the underside. The top is attached to the base with three husky ½ x 2-in. carriage bolts set flush in counterbored holes. A bolt is located over each of the three stalls. Either a clamp-on or edge-mounted vise can be added to the top.

Except for the bottom drawer, the drawer fronts are slanted to match the slant of the main section. Fronts, sides and backs are cut from

A PLYWOOD BASE is added to the saw's base to accommodate the four studs which fit holes in the benchtop.

¾-in. plywood, while the bottoms are ¼-in. hardboard. The sides are dadoed for the backs and join the fronts in rabbets. Top and bottom edges of the slanting fronts are beveled so they are level, and the drawer-bottom grooves which are cut in the backs of the drawer fronts, are cut at the same angle. Similar grooves are cut in the drawer sides but these are made at right angles. Finally, ⅜ x ¾-in. grooves are run down the center of all drawer sides for the runners on which they slide.

Now assemble the drawers with glue and nails

FIVE ROOMY DRAWERS provide lots of storage for hand and portable tools, sandpaper, nails and screws.

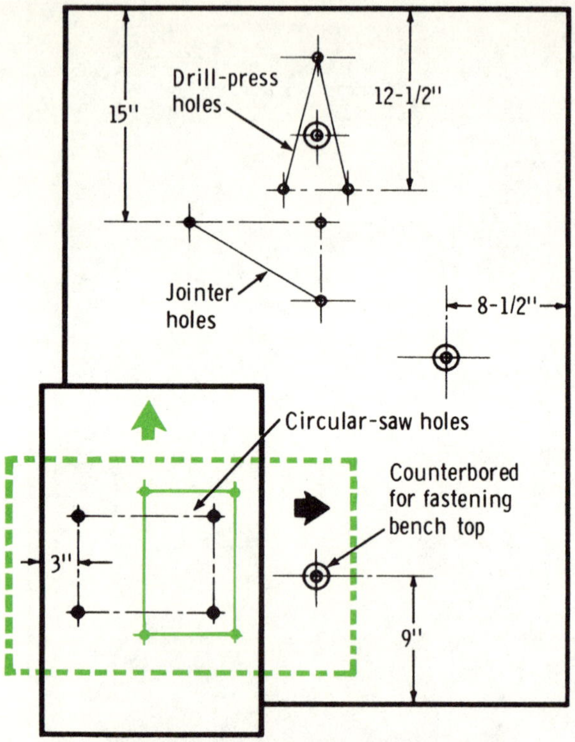

● Saw placed in black holes for crosscutting
● Saw placed in orange holes for ripping

and add knobs or pulls. Cardboard shims between the drawers will help position the runner's so the drawers will have proper clearance. If they should rub or bind, a skimming cut through the saw will do the trick. Wax applied to the runners and grooves will make the drawers slide freely when loaded.

A 4-in. junction box screwed to the side of the bench and fitted with four cover-mounted outlets, plus a 10-ft. cord, will make it handy to plug-in your power tools right at the bench.

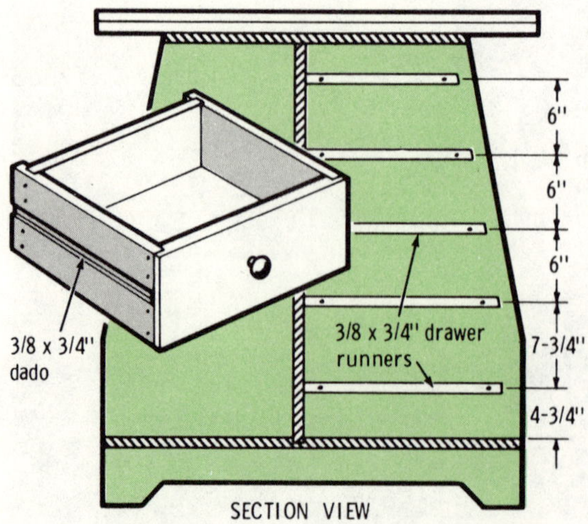

Sharpening lawn mower

Can you tell me how to sharpen a reel-type lawn mower?—Vernon Sheff, Racine, Wis.

Place the mower on a table or bench. Clamp or tie the handle securely. Remove the wheel, pinion and other parts, making sure that you keep them in order. Hold the reel shaft with lever-jaw pliers. Mix valve-grinding compound (obtainable from an auto-parts supplier) with oil to make a paste; brush this on the blades and bed knife. Adjust these parts for light contact and turn the reel backward with the pliers. Keep the bed knife and reel blades in contact by repeated adjustment. When properly sharpened, they should contact smoothly along their whole length. Then readjust so that blades just clear the knife. Reassemble the parts in reverse order to that of their removal and lubricate.

Making varnish vanish

I spilled nearly a pint of dark varnish stain on my basement floor. I mopped it up with paper towels and then scrubbed with a detergent, but much of the stain remains. Can this be removed?—L.N., Ill.

You may be able to get off most, if not all, of the remaining residue with a paint and varnish remover of the nonflammable, wash-off type. Be sure the remover is of the type specified. Brush it on in the normal fashion—a fairly heavy, uniform coating over the whole affected area. Allow it to "work" for 10 minutes or more, then wash it off with a wet cloth. Go over the area several times with the wet cloth to make sure you get up all the remover residue. Then wipe the surface and let it dry. A second application might be necessary.

"Waterproofing" a furnace

I get a little seepage into my basement when there are heavy rains, and this heads directly for my furnace, seeps inside and causes rust. Is there any way to seal the water out?—D.T., Ind.

If you can be sure the water seepage is never more than a half inch or so in depth, you might paint, or enamel, a strip around the bottom of the furnace jacket. Or, if there's a metal trim strip at the bottom, coat this. Use masking tape to get a neat job.

While you're painting the jacket, allow the edge of the brush to apply a narrow strip of paint to the floor as well. Then form a fillet of glazier's putty all the way around to close openings between the metal and the floor. If you're careful to seal all openings, this might do it.

Those sweating windows

Windows in my home sweat and the water runs down over the sills to give the wood a dark, moldy color and streak the plaster below. The house is quite new and has wood casement sash. I'm told wood windows don't sweat, but mine do. And my bathroom is literally swampy wet. What causes this and is there a simple, inexpensive cure?—S.T., Ga.

The cause is the relatively high moisture level in the air. Everyone in your home contributes to this by bathing, showering, food preparation and simply by breathing. For example, if yours is a family of four and you are all at home for a weekend, the four of you will add about three gallons of moisture during that time just by breathing. All other normal activities—meal preparation, tub bathing or showering, laundering and washing dishes by hand—can add 4 to 10 gallons more.

In present-day homes with insulation and tight construction throughout, this moisture cannot escape at the same rate as it does in older structures. Window sash, particularly the glass panes, are at a lower temperature than room air, so the moisture condenses on these surfaces.

Some homeowners with this problem operate an automatic (humidistat-controlled) dehumidifier to keep moisture at lower levels. In some cases tight-fitting storm sash will prevent, or at least minimize, condensation on casements. On warmer days open windows and doors and allow air to circulate for short periods. If your heating equipment is gas-fired (a gas kitchen range will contribute to the moisture level) make sure it is properly vented to the outside.

Toilet tank leaks

Recently my plumber installed a new ball cock and float in my toilet tank. This worked for a time but now water in the tank rises above the overflow, resulting in a constant leak into the bowl. The float is nearly submerged before the thing shuts off. Can I correct this trouble myself?—Manly Benson, Des Moines, Iowa.

Hold the float arm in closed position and unscrew the float. There may be water in it. If not, turn it back on the rod tightly. Then bend the rod down slightly and flush to check. If water still rises above the water-level mark, bend the rod a little more. This usually solves the problem, but not always.

At the end of the pivoted arm that actuates the ball valve you'll see an adjusting screw. Turn this down a turn or two and flush to check. If not sufficient, turn the screw down until the valve shuts off completely at, or slightly below, the water-level mark.

Cabinet bench for a small shop

By WAYNE C. LECKEY

Ideal for anyone with limited shop space this handsome little bench has lots of storage built into its 30-in. length

SEE ALSO

Drawers . . . Motors, shop . . . Power-tool stands . . . Radial-arm saws . . . Shop tools . . . Small-parts storage . . . Tools, hand . . . Workshops

IF YOU HAVE BEEN LOOKING for a workbench that's suitable for a small shop—one that will serve as a tinkerer's bench and let you store your tools in it—this little one should fill the bill perfectly. It features a sturdy top which will withstand a lot of hammering, a sunken tool trough across the back, a roomy drawer with a lift-out nail and screw tray and a storage compartment that will hold a raft of workshop gear.

While its cabinet base is about 30 in. long, its basic design lets you make it longer if you wish merely by increasing its length and fitting it with two drawers instead of one. There's no reason why you couldn't make it 48 in. long if your shop can stand a larger bench.

If you don't need a workbench, but are in the market for a stand for a radial saw, particularly such as the bench-type shown at the right, the cabinet, with its roomy drawer and storage compartment, makes a dandy place to keep saw accessories within easy reach. Here you forget the benchtop and close in the top with plywood.

To build the bench from scratch will cost you about $50—for the tempered hardboard that's used for the doors, end panels and back, plywood for the double-thick top, pine for the drawer, 2 x 4s for the framing members, lagscrews and paint. You may already have scrap wood you can use.

Aside from being made right and left-hand, the two ends are identical. In studying the drawings you'll see that the 2 x 4 members are grooved to receive ¼-in. tempered-hardboard panels (actually a strong 3/16 in. in thickness) which are installed as the ends are assembled.

The connecting front and back rails are also alike, with the exception of front rails (B) and (D). These are grooved to receive the two tempered-hardboard doors which bypass in

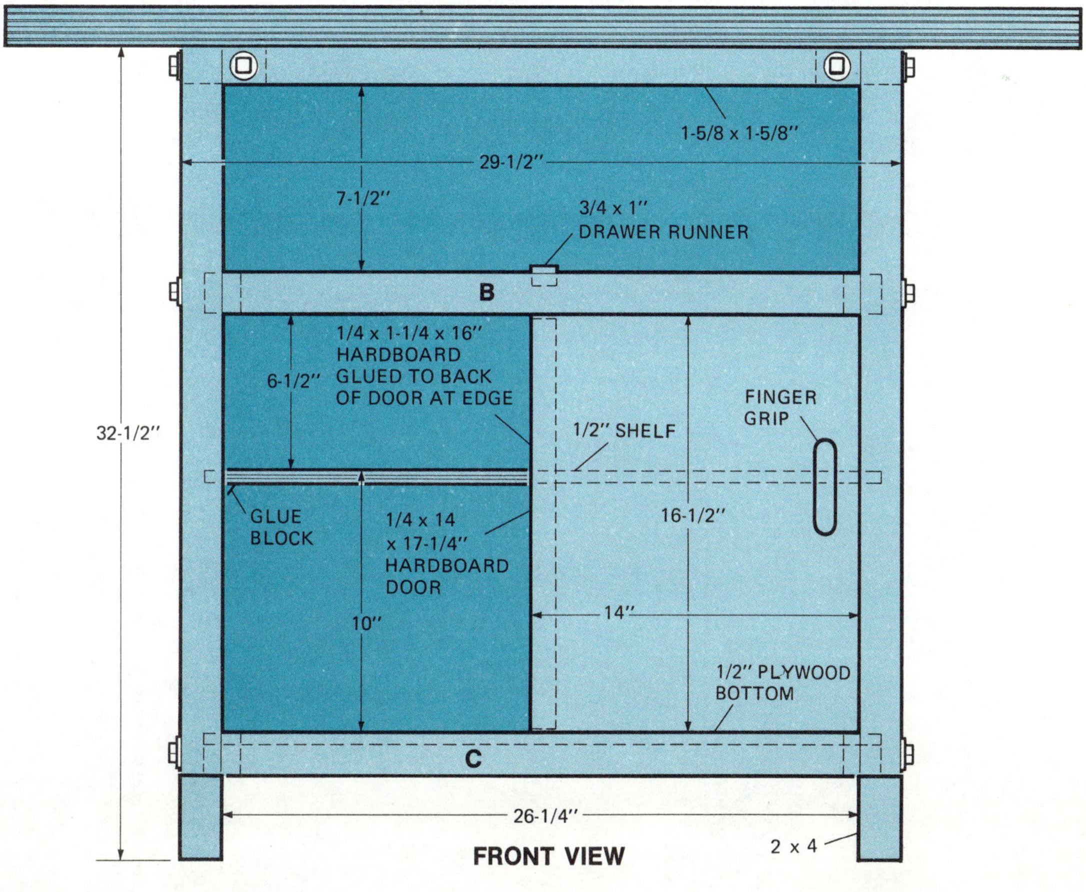

FRONT VIEW

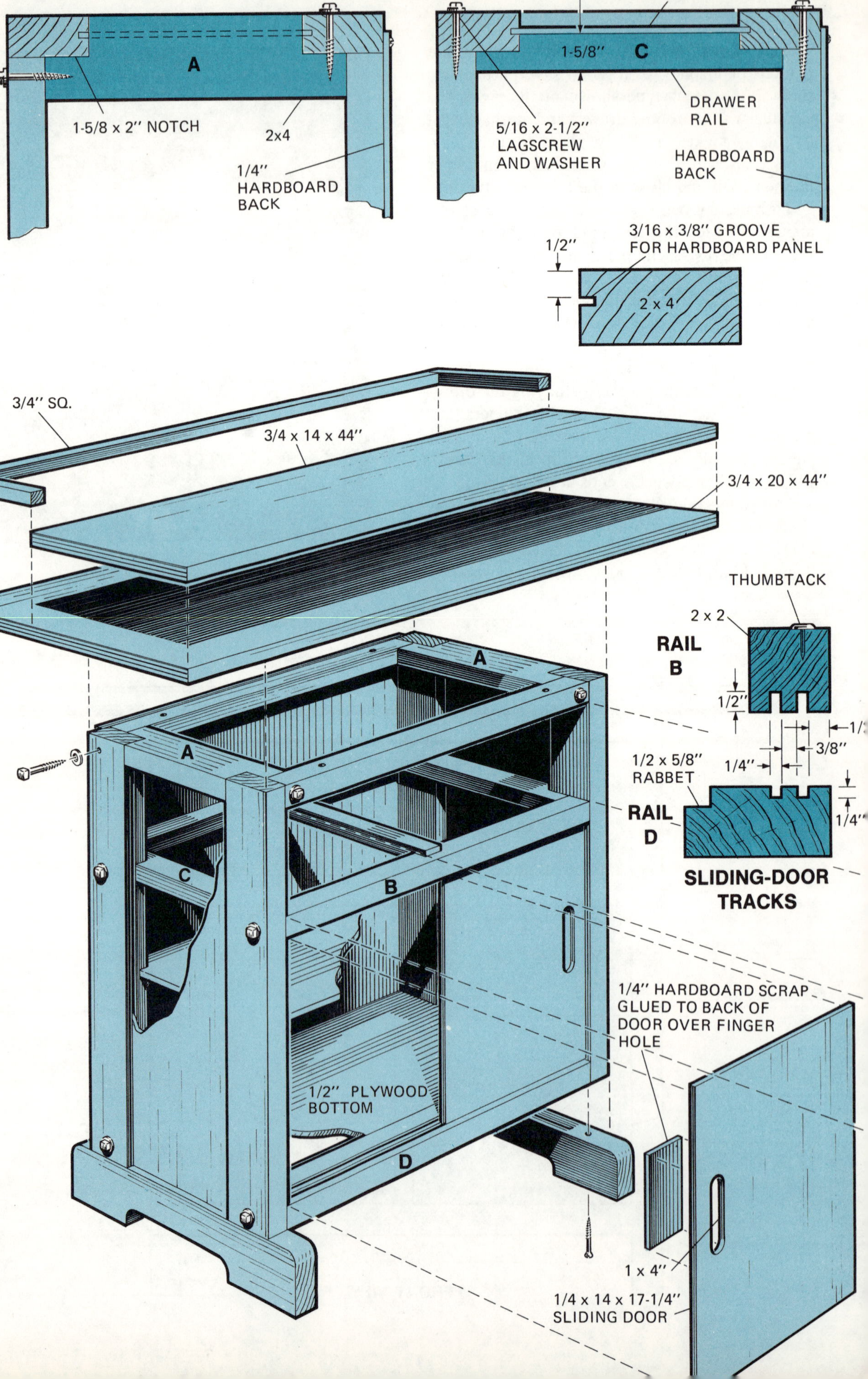
A
1-5/8 x 2'' NOTCH
2x4
1/4''
HARDBOARD
BACK
END PANEL
1-5/8''
C
DRAWER
RAIL
5/16 x 2-1/2''
LAGSCREW
AND WASHER
HARDBOARD
BACK
1/2''
3/16 x 3/8'' GROOVE
FOR HARDBOARD PANEL
2 x 4
3/4'' SQ.
3/4 x 14 x 44''
3/4 x 20 x 44''
THUMBTACK
2 x 2
RAIL
B
1/2''
3/8''
1/4''
1/2 x 5/8''
RABBET
RAIL
D
SLIDING-DOOR
TRACKS
A
A
C
B
1/4'' HARDBOARD SCRAP
GLUED TO BACK OF
DOOR OVER FINGER
HOLE
1/2'' PLYWOOD
BOTTOM
D
1 x 4''
1/4 x 14 x 17-1/4''
SLIDING DOOR

grooves. For the most part, the rails are made in pairs, all of the same length. They are joined to the end assemblies with glue and lagscrews. Notice that rails (D), front and back, are rabbeted along the inner edges to receive flush a ½-in. plywood bottom. The hardboard back is simply applied and screwed to the surface.

The drawer follows typical drawer construction. It's made of ¾-in. pine and has cleats nailed to the inside 3 in. down from the top to support a lift-out sliding tray. Hardboard is used for the bottom, and the drawer is guided by a grooved member that's glued to the underside.

The benchtop consists of two thicknesses of ¾-in. plywood, glued and clamped, then screwed together from the underside. The sunken tool and shavings trough is formed by gluing and nailing ¾-in.-sq. strips to three sides. The top is attached to the cabinet with screws driven up through the front and back crossrails.

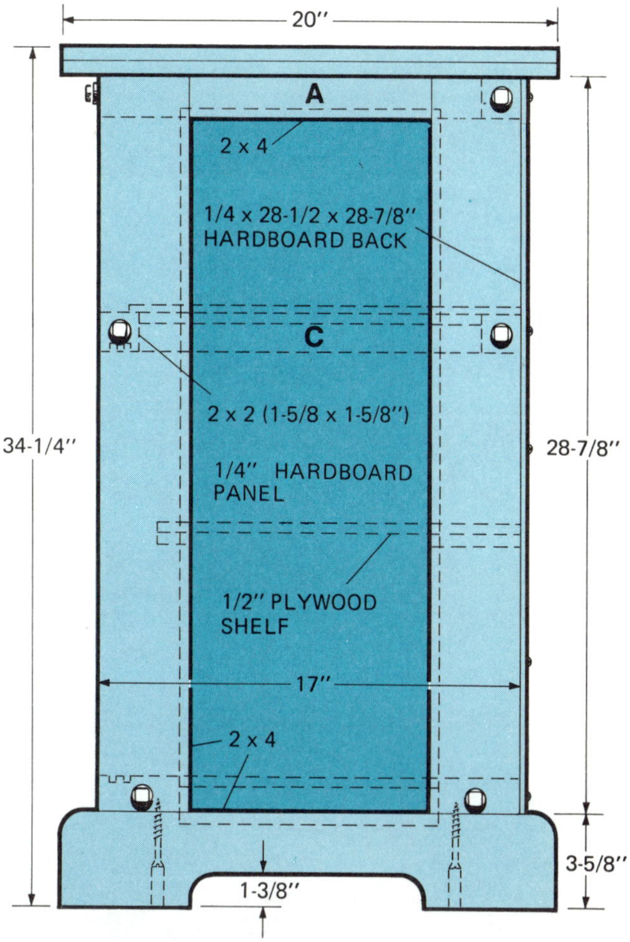

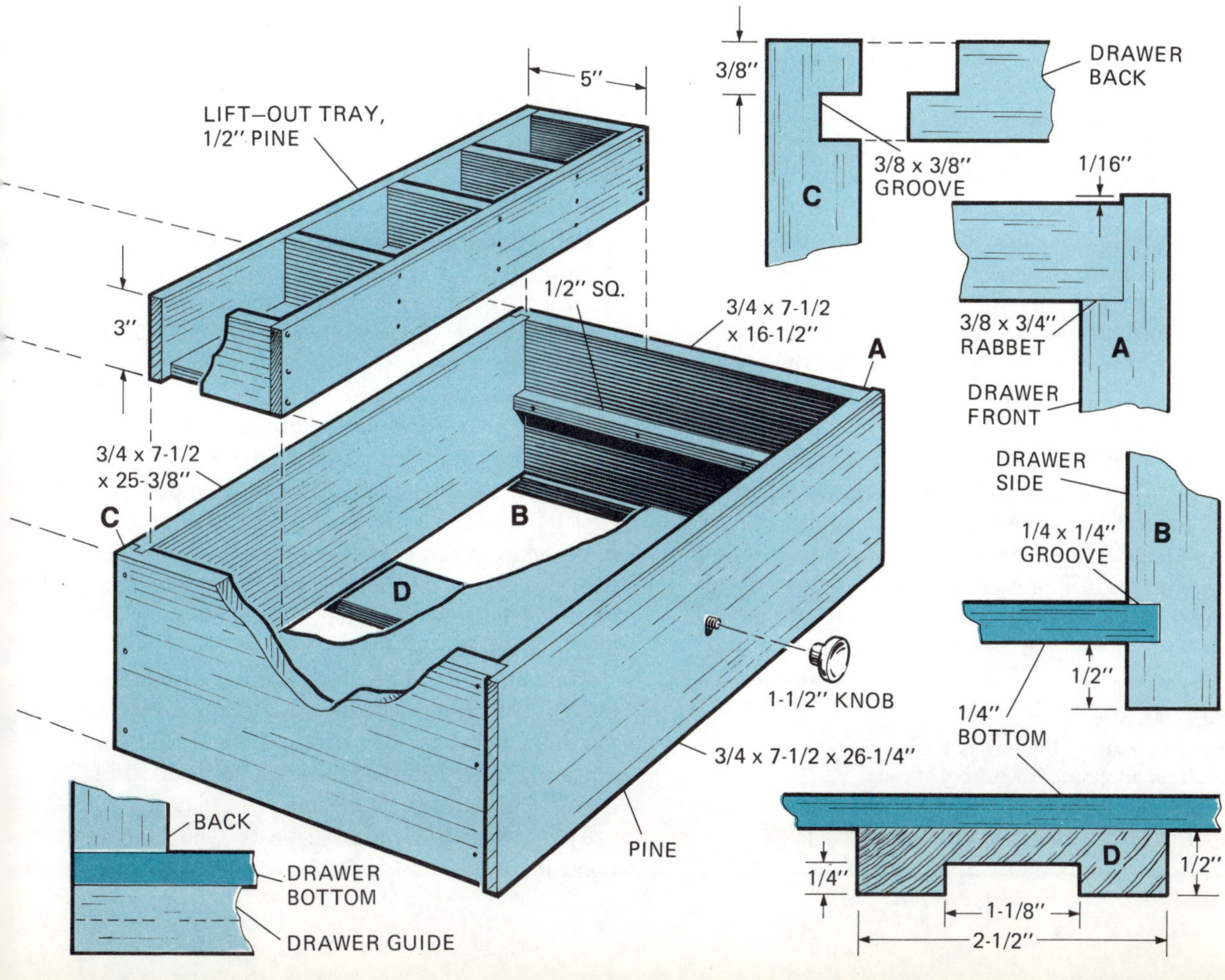

How to lay out your workshop

By W. CLYDE LAMMEY

IN ANY WORKSHOP layout, you need not only handy placement of your power tools but planned space in which to use them efficiently.

The upper floor plan on the opposite page offers suggestions for use of relatively unrestricted space such as may be available by partitioning a part of the basement. The lower plan indicates what can be done where available space must be restricted to a corner of the basement or perhaps one wall in a 1½-car garage.

In the first plan all the power tools are the large, stationary workshop size, and are on floor stands, legs or pedestals. The bandsaw, grinder, jigsaw and drill press are shown in places calculated to give the maximum working space; but should it be necessary to work longer material, these units are relatively easy to move.

In the average workshop most of the work will be done with the circular saw and jointer, and as these are usually first operations on any woodworking project, these two units should be placed side by side with the maximum working space all around.

Where possible a lathe should be placed so that the unit and the work are back lighted. A window is the cheapest and in some respects the best lighting for lathe work, either on the faceplate or between centers. Otherwise overhead lighting, preferably fluorescent, must be substituted over the workbench and those units that are located in the center of the shop.

The shop should be wired with electrical outlets at convenient locations. Outlet strips are handy at benches. Be sure that the wiring is of ample size to handle any load imposed. If in doubt consult your electrician.

The lower floor plan suggests what can be done in restricted space. Here a radial saw is

SEE ALSO
Bench saws . . . Drill press techniques . . . Motors, shop . . . Power-tool stands . . . Radial-arm saws . . . Sawhorses . . . Storage ideas . . . Table saws . . . Tools, hand . . . Workbenches

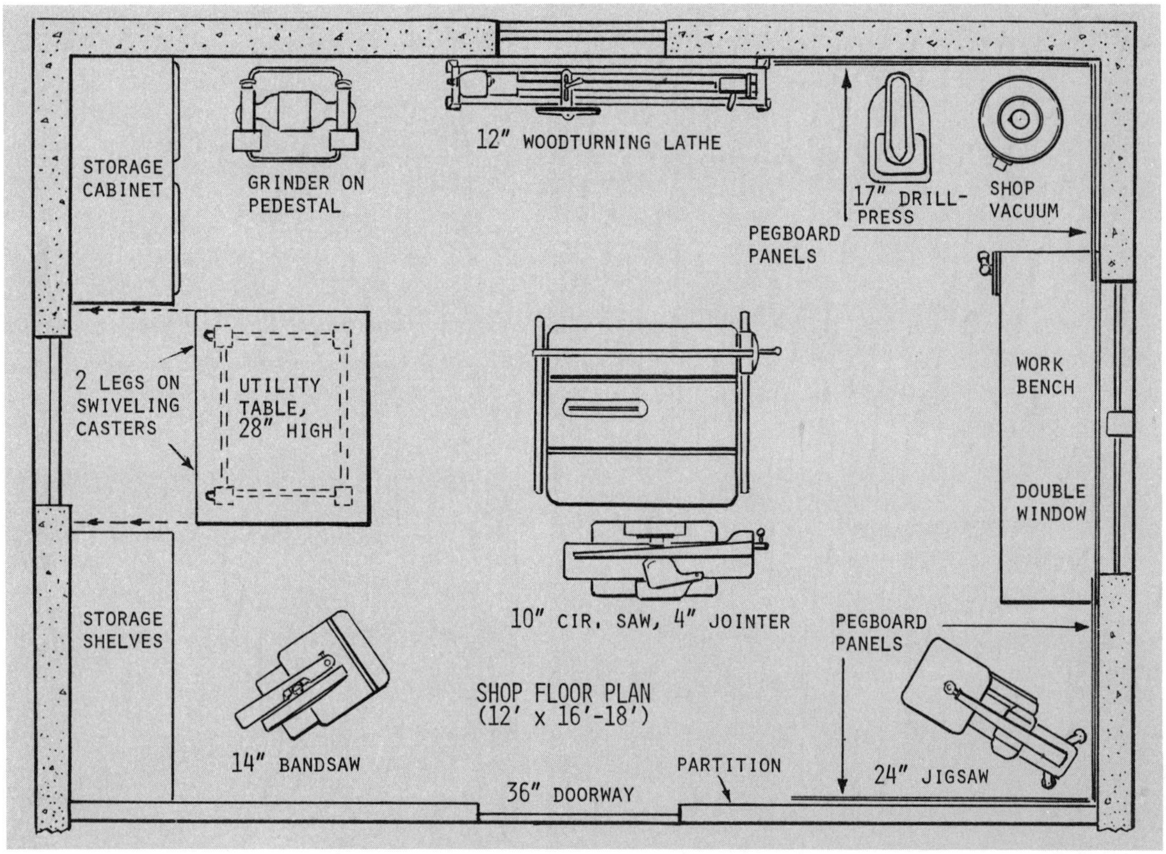

centered along one wall under a window with a cabinet bench on one side of the saw table and an open bench on the other. Both bench tops are at precisely the same height as the saw table, which permits the handling of long stock with ample support. One bench has the back legs on swiveling casters so it can be pulled out and placed in a more convenient position for using the vise, or for project assembly. A similar lower bench, or work table, is also provided in the upper, larger plan. Benches and worktables provided with casters on two legs are useful in any shop, as they are readily portable. This smaller plan features an overhead lumber rack. Where there is ample head room this is a handy addition to shop equipment as it can provide visible storage for both long and short pieces of stock.

Rather than storing hand tools in drawers, utilize the wall space by installing pegboard panels large enough to keep all the hand tools on hangers where they are readily seen and always available for use. Hanging or standing storage cabinets and shelves can be made after the shop is equipped with power tools. Provide a wide door for easy access to the shop and a shop vacuum for quick cleanup of chips and shavings.

IN THE FLOOR PLAN above there's space for larger, floor type power units, but in the restricted space below the radial saw is your best bet.

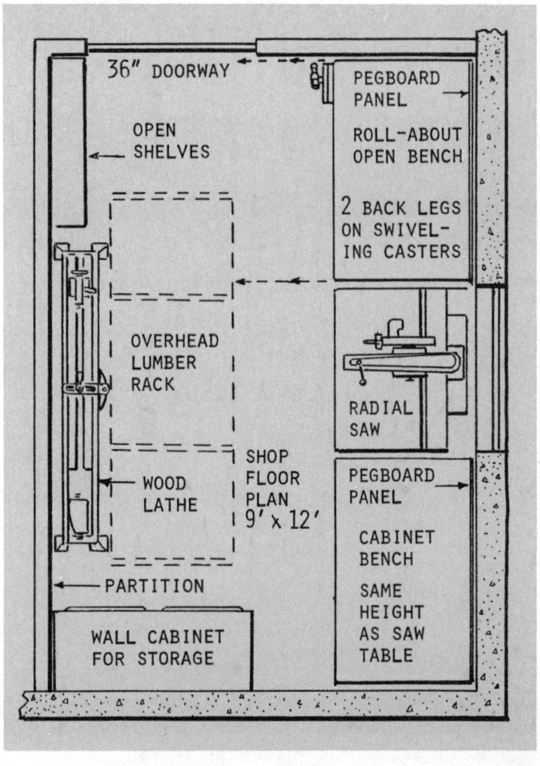

1

2

3

Transform your yard with night lighting

By HARRY WICKS

Creative use of yard lighting can turn your yard into a nighttime wonderland. The secret is to place the lights properly. Here's how to design a plan for your yard

SEE ALSO

Electrical wiring . . . Gardening . . . Gazebos . . . Insect traps . . . Lawns . . . Patios . . . Planters . . . Post lamps . . . Screened summer rooms

NOT TOO LONG AGO, outdoor residential lighting consisted of little more than placing a few floodlights around the grounds in rather bare-looking fixtures. Usually, these functional lights were affixed to buildings or parked on poles to provide broad, general illumination for safety and security for family and visitors.

Though safety and security are both still good and valid reasons for lighting your property at night, a third consideration—beautification—now plays an equally important role in outdoor lighting. Actually, "lightscaping" is simply an outside extension of indoor lighting. But if it's carefully done, you can add new dimensions to your home environment to create, in effect, a totally new living area.

Don't think that lighting your property automatically means that you will be using energy capriciously. For one thing, when exterior lights are turned on for outdoor family use, it means that indoor lights can be turned off or used minimally.

Additionally, you can save even more by installing a low-voltage outdoor system. How such systems work is explained on the next page.

This article shows you how to create attractive outdoor lighting effects—for greater safety and enjoyment—through the variety of fixtures and lamps now available. With these, plus a generous helping of your own imagination, you will be able to turn your backyard into a nighttime wonderland.

basics of outdoor lighting

There is no great mystery to successful outdoor lighting, but there are basic principles you should know about. For example, be aware that it is important to avoid flat lighting—a look that is inevitable if you try to duplicate daylight. Instead, plan light placement so you create a scene with highlights and shadows that has a painting or sketchlike quality.

Generally, a touch of light here and there, cast by the appropriate fixture, is the kind of lighting that will give your nighttime setting a charm of its own. And that's what you should aim for—a look that is distinctly different from your yard's daytime appearance.

Shielding fixtures are frequently used today

4

5

USED CREATIVELY, night lighting will beautify your yard as well as make it safer. The lighting shown includes: 1. Illuminated steps with a light distribution pattern that permits a clear view along the entranceway; 2. Underwater lighting with lily-pad fixtures; 3. Area lighting which emphasizes shadows; 4. A spotlight on a focal point; 5. Silhouetting dark objects against light, achieved by beaming light through translucent materials; 6. A pond illuminated by low-voltage incandescent at the pond bottom; 7 and 8. Wall and ground mounted fixtures for small-area lighting. Photos 1 through 6 are from General Electric Co., Nela Park, Cleveland, OH; Photos 7 and 8 were furnished by Intermatic, Inc. of Spring Grove, IL.

7

8

6

THIS ROOFTOP view shows the position of three 300-watt PAR units aimed at the lawn and trees for dramatic effect.

A BAMBOO trellis is cross-lighted by two floodlamps. A 75-watt lamp adds interesting shadow shapes.

ABOUT LOW-VOLTAGE LIGHTING SYSTEMS

A low-voltage lighting system has two advantages—economy and safety. Such systems generally use low-wattage bulbs that are intended for accent lighting; these, of course, will use less electricity. The equipment is also lower in cost than comparable high-voltage counterparts. And you also save because ease of installation makes this a do-it-yourself task all the way. Safety is good because the transformer reduces voltage from the standard 117 volts to 6 or 12 volts. Dangerous shocks are less likely.

The transformer is the heart of the low-voltage system. A simple device, it comes with a timer that automatically turns lights on and off. The components shown are part of a system called Malibu. The cable can be attached to the floodlight with the floodlight turned on, as shown at left. Or you can attach the power cable to the short fixture cable using Malibu cable connector (right). To determine the proper-size transformer, add up the wattage of all fixtures and select one that closely matches the total load. The load wattage should not be less than half the transformer capacity. For the best lighting results, combine regular voltage equipment with low-voltage equipment. Low voltage is best used for lighting small areas and for accent. For more information on the Malibu system, write Intermatic, Inc., Dept. PM, Spring Grove, Ill. 60081

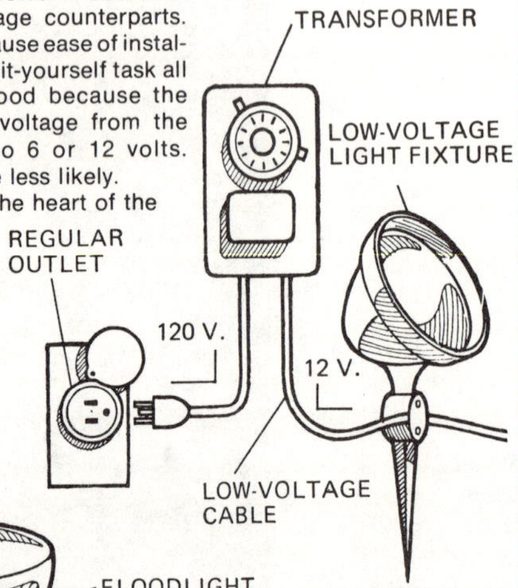

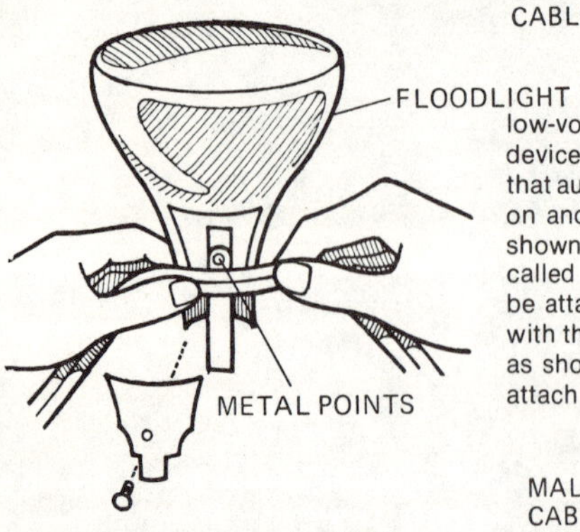

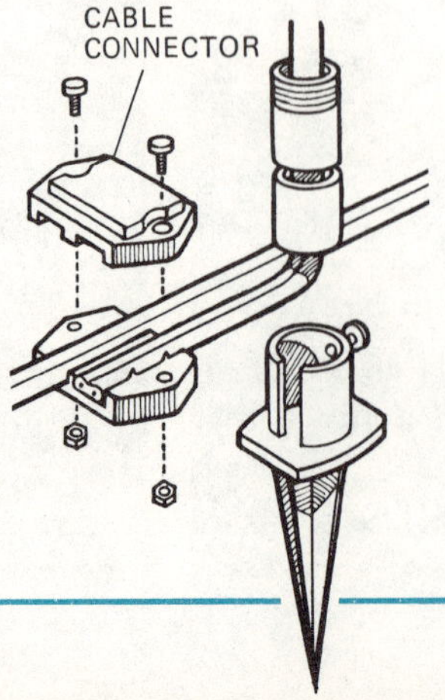

even though they're slightly less efficient and, thus, more expensive to operate. On the plus side, however, these do eliminate irritating glare yet provide illumination where it is wanted. Local or border lighting and spotlighting are usually based more upon esthetics than the ability to see.

One way to determine how and where to place various light fixtures is by working with long extension cords and incandescent lamps. By using this trick you can fiddle with a number of lighting arrangements until you find a setup you'd like to make permanent.

Play it safe. All electric fixtures and wiring used for outside lighting must be weatherproof and installed in accordance with the National Electric Code (as well as your local building department).

about outdoor lamps

Currently, many installations use a floodlight holder for incandescent lamps with built-in reflectors (PAR). Some holders shield the entire lamp so that indoor lamps can be used. Others shield only the lamp base; with these you must use outdoor (weatherproof) lamps.

Outdoor incandescents are available in colors if you want to emphasize color, control insect attraction or create special-effect foliage lighting.

Tungsten halogen lamps are generally tubular in shape. These longer-life incandescents are generally used in higher-wattage floodlights.

You can use fluorescents outdoors provided you meet three criteria:

- Use only weatherproof fixtures.
- Make certain ballasts and fixtures are designed for use at below-freezing temperatures.
- Lamps exposed to temperatures ranging from 32° to 50° F. must be enclosed.

High-intensity discharge lamps (HID) are

LOW-VOLTAGE UNITS under an overhang light planters and a rock garden. The transformer is in the soffit.

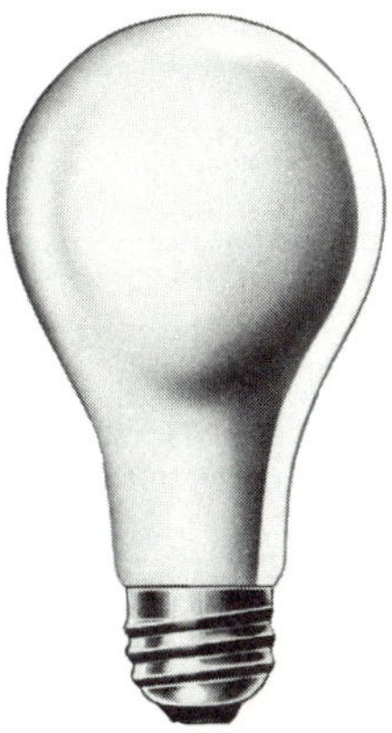

The Bug Chaser bulb above by Duro-Lite has a special yellow coating. GE border lights (left) seem to sparkle because of perforated housings. These come in varied heights

used for floodlighting larger areas and are not commonly used in residential outdoor lighting.

There is a wide variety of lamps and fixtures available to suit all outdoor lighting needs; typical shapes are shown on these pages.

ideas for lightscaping

• *Automation.* Consider installing equipment which will turn lights on and off automatically. It is relatively inexpensive and can save many dollars over the course of a season by completely eliminating wasted electricity.

• *Accent lighting.* Trees, shrubbery and the like can be mood-lighted by directing accent lights from above or below. Use such lights in addition to soft tinted, directed or reflected lighting. Keep in mind that overall floodlighting tends to "whitewash" a garden; accent lights are your

OUTDOOR LIGHTING FIXTURES AND KNOW-HOW

Many lamps and fixtures are available. The typical units shown here are usually made of brass, steel, copper or aluminum. The bulbs shown at right are the most commonly used 115-120-volt types. The reflector bulbs must be used in fixtures, while the PAR type (not shown) need no shielding because they are made of hard glass that will not crack due to weather

LIGHT BULBS

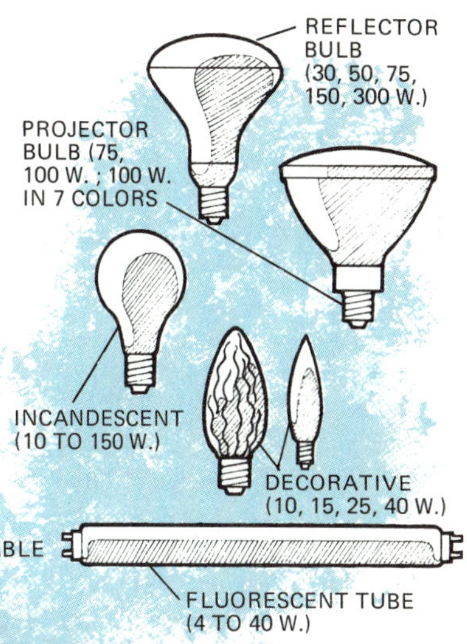

FLOODLIGHT HOLDERS

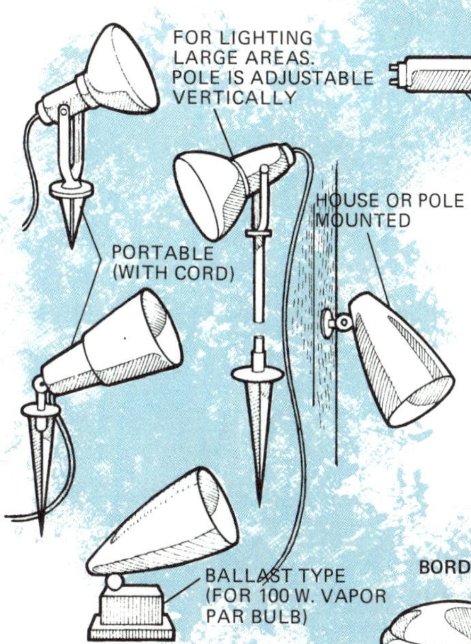

Floodlighting and spotlighting, either up or down, usually is accomplished with projector (PAR) bulbs in adjustable holders. The fixtures shown are widely used today. Two portables come with a cord and ground spike; others can be mounted on a house or pole. A light with an adjustable-height pole is ideal for large-area illumination

BORDER AND STEP FIXTURES

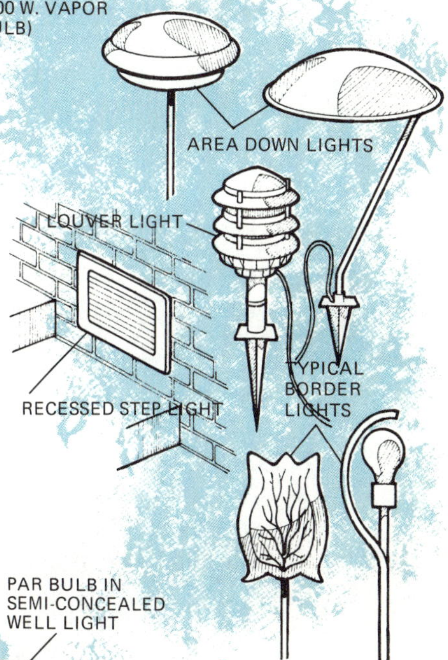

To light steps, paths and borders, select fixtures having neither glass nor plastic parts because the resulting glare will be annoying. Fixtures for this use range from 6 to 18 in. in diameter and 8 to 30 in. tall. From a wide selection you can pick fixtures that give downlighting for steps, borders or low plantings. Designs vary considerably; simply choose fixtures compatible with your garden and lighting needs

UP-LIGHT FIXTURES

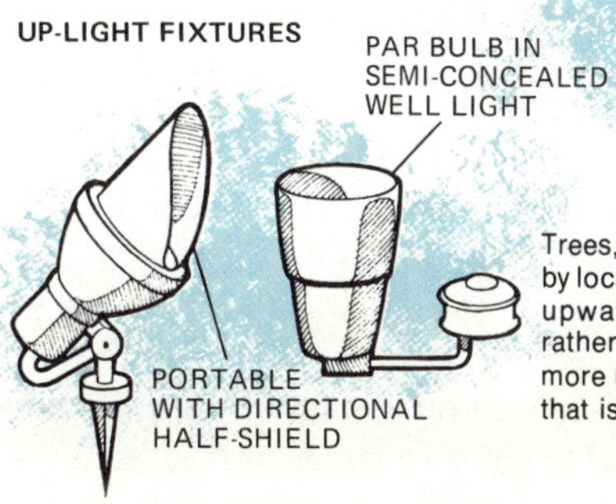

Trees, shrubbery and fences are lighted by locating fixtures on the ground, aimed upward. To produce a dimensional rather than flat appearance, direct two or more up-lights at an angle to the feature that is being specially lighted

FIXTURES AND KNOW-HOW continued

To illuminate large areas such as patio, terrace, driveway, lawn or garden, consider using fixtures suspended from tree branches. Those designed for hanging are available in many shapes and sizes. They add sparkle, color and charm

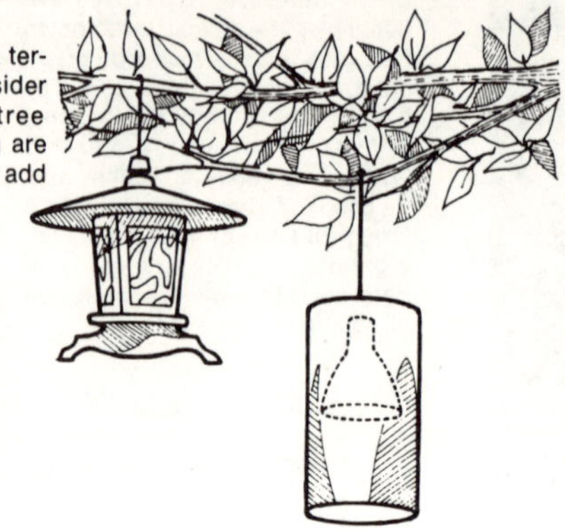

A tree light can be angled with wire fastened to a limb on one end and the bottom of the light on the other

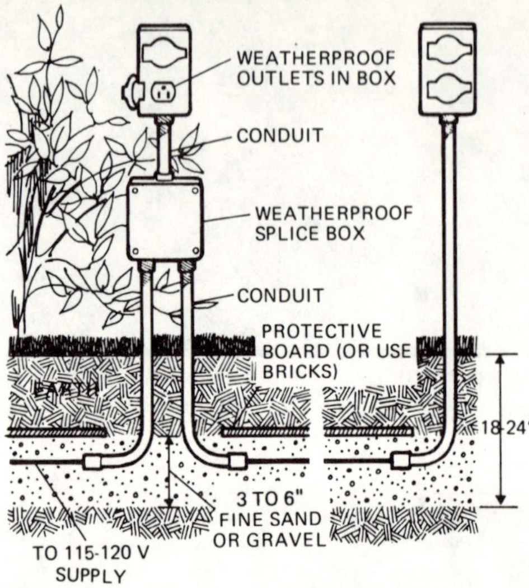

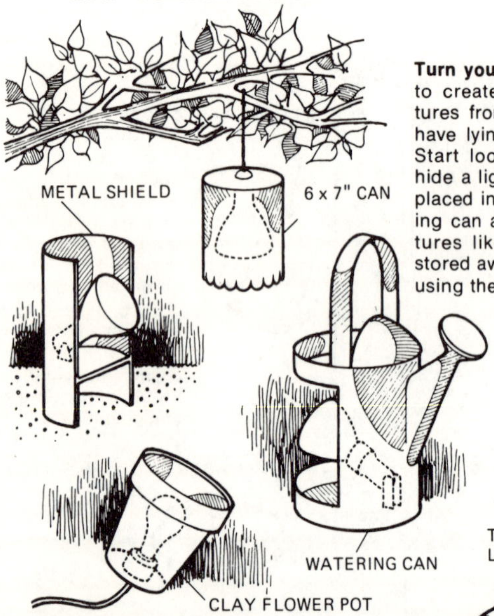

Turn your imagination loose to create do-it-yourself fixtures from objects you may have lying about your yard. Start looking for places to hide a light; here, lamps are placed in a flowerpot, watering can and coffee can. Fixtures like these should be stored away when you're not using them for a while

Unless you're experienced at electrical work and familiar with the codes, leave permanent outdoor wiring chores to the professionals. Use ground burial cable (type UF) in trenches to areas to be lighted. The cable is then connected to weatherproof outlet boxes or to underground junction boxes for fixtures

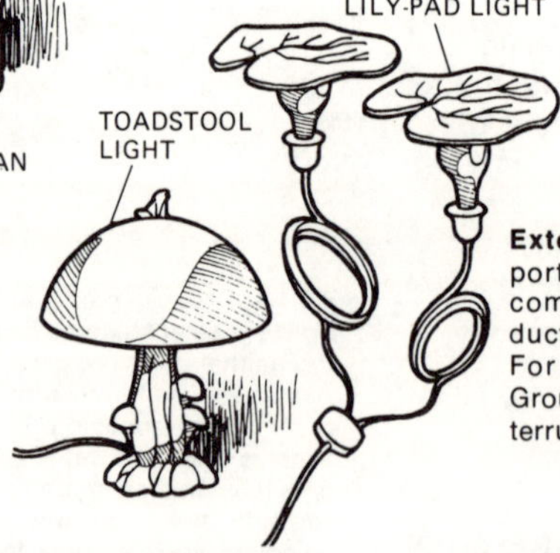

Accent lighting is fun and usually provides the final touch. Fixtures are often shaped to resemble common garden elements such as lily pads and toadstools. Lily-pad fixtures are designed for use in the water; follow the maker's instructions

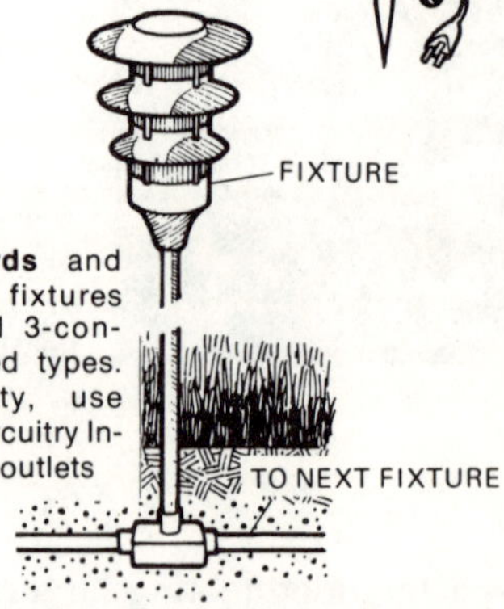

Extension cords and portable outlet fixtures come in 2 and 3-conductor grounded types. For top safety, use Ground Fault Circuitry Interrupter (GFCI) outlets

best tools for avoiding that much-dreaded look.

• *Eliminate hazards.* Walks, steps and paths should be lighted to avoid any chance of missteps, falls and injuries. Do not use any bright or glaring fixtures on steps because they are too likely to blind step users. Ideally, fixtures for step lighting conceal all bulbs yet provide desired safety lighting. Often the locating of fixtures behind foliage will hide lamps, too.

• *Dining out.* For patios and the like, you want lighting that will draw everyone together into a group. Try for good visibility without harsh, irritating light.

Keep in mind that you should also have some transitional lighting on the fringe area so that the change from lighted to dark areas will not be too sudden.

• *Lawn games.* Most games can be adequately illuminated using two poles 18 to 20 ft. high with two or more 150-watt flood bulbs per pole. For net games, light poles should be about 3 ft. from each end of the net. Regardless of the game, place fixtures so light will not shine in players' eyes.

A final word. When you plan your outdoor lighting arrangement, don't overlook your neighbors' right to privacy. Aim all of the lights toward your own property—not theirs—or you will almost certainly trigger squabbles every time you turn on your lights.

How to light a game area

By HARRY WICKS

Adequate lighting properly installed around those yard games will add hours of fun to your vacation at home

continued

LAWN GAMES are often more fun when played in the evening. But avoid glare on neighbor's yard.

ONCE YOU DECIDE to set aside a portion of your property for lawn games, it makes good sense to extend their use into the evening by providing adequate illumination. In fact, during the blistering hot months, you'll probably find the youngsters using the games more during the cool after-dinner hours.

There are other factors to bear in mind when laying out your lighting. There may be times when you do not wish to light a game but want to

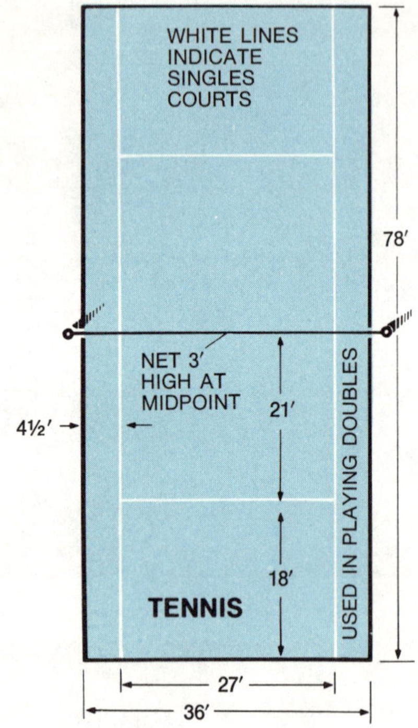

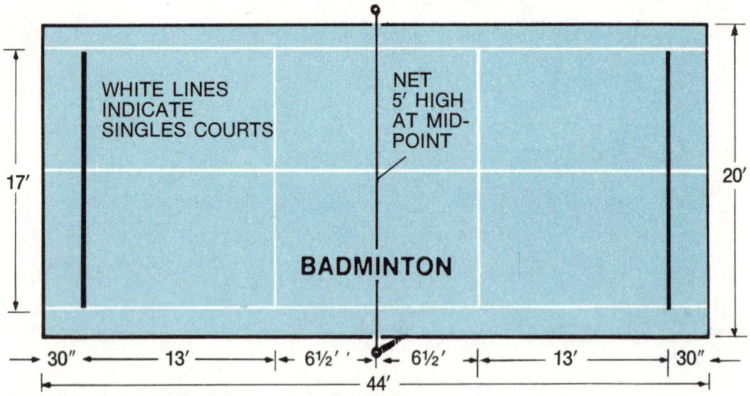

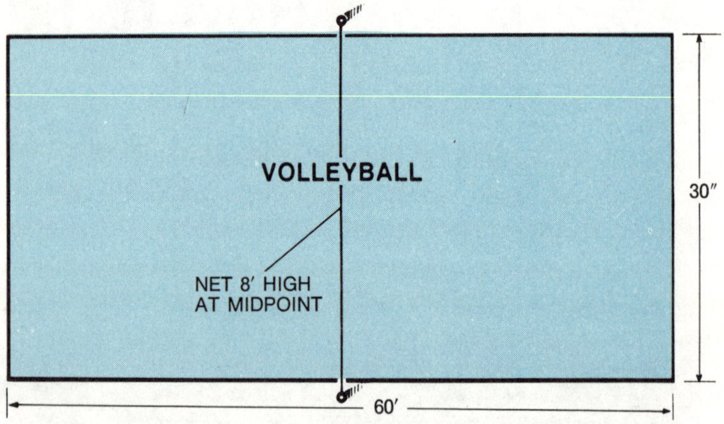

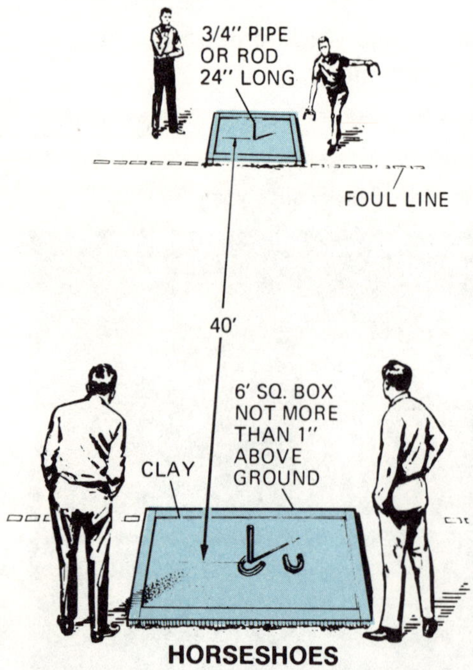

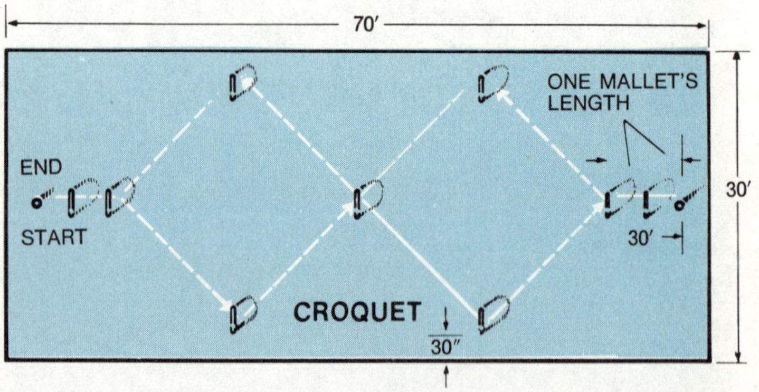

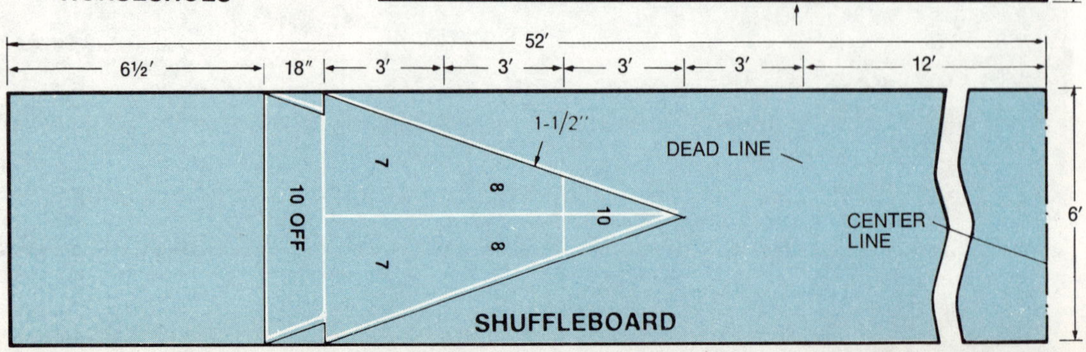

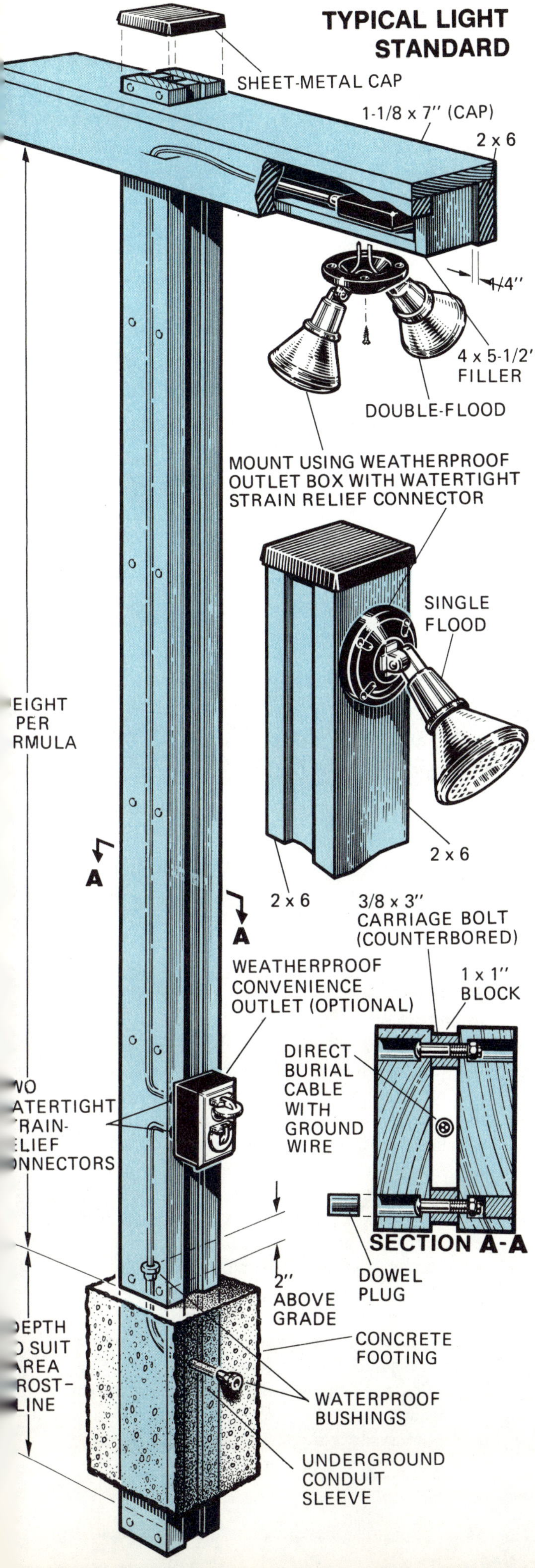

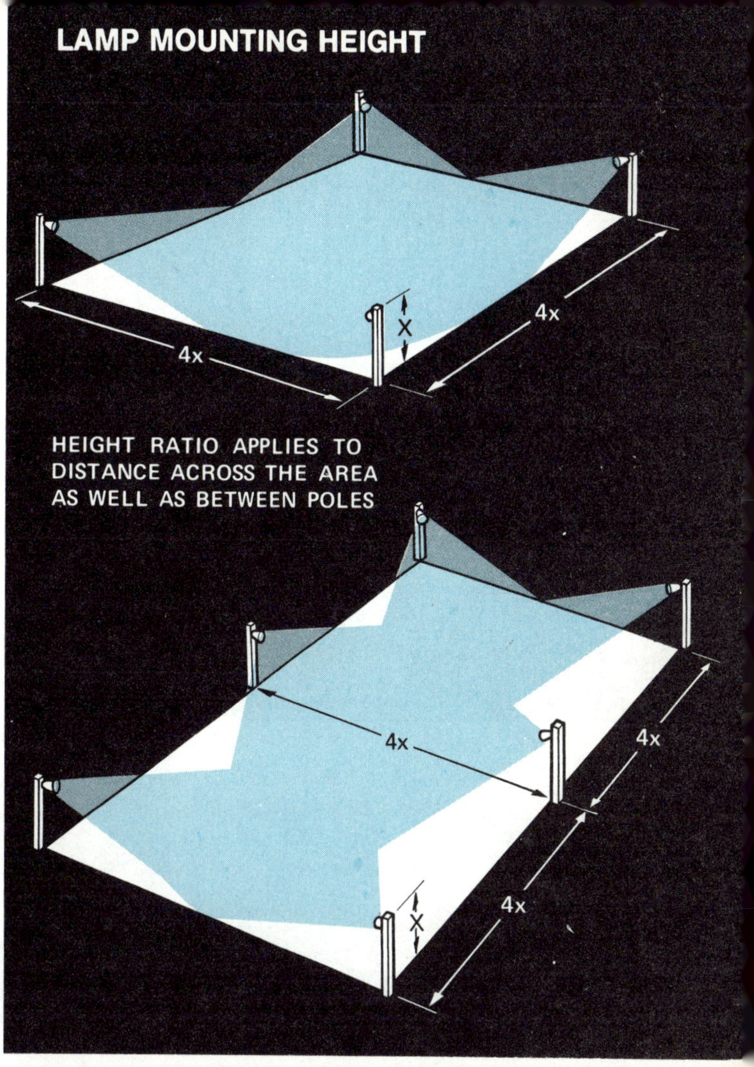

TYPICAL YARD-LIGHT STANCHION shown at left, as conceived by the author, can be varied to suit house architecture. The four-times mounting ratio shown above applies to the width of area as well as the distance between the poles. For example, if the court width is 40 ft., the pole height should be 10 ft. and the poles should be spaced no more than 40 ft. apart whether mercury or filament bulbs are used for light. Any activity area should be bathed with illumination, and standards should be attractive during daylight.

make aesthetic use of the light for highlighting rock gardens, fish pools and the like. For barbecues, picnics and social gatherings you will want a lower level of illumination. Thus, when possible, utilize dimmer switches in your controls. And, as shown on the previous page in the typical light standard if at all possible, provide watertight convenience outlets. At some later date, you might decide to relocate a patio or purchase an electric mower.

• First, the game's location—which of course will determine the placement of lighting standards—should be considered carefully to avoid annoying neighbors.

• A major consideration in the design of any direct-lighting system is the uniformity of illumination over the entire playing surface. A "hot

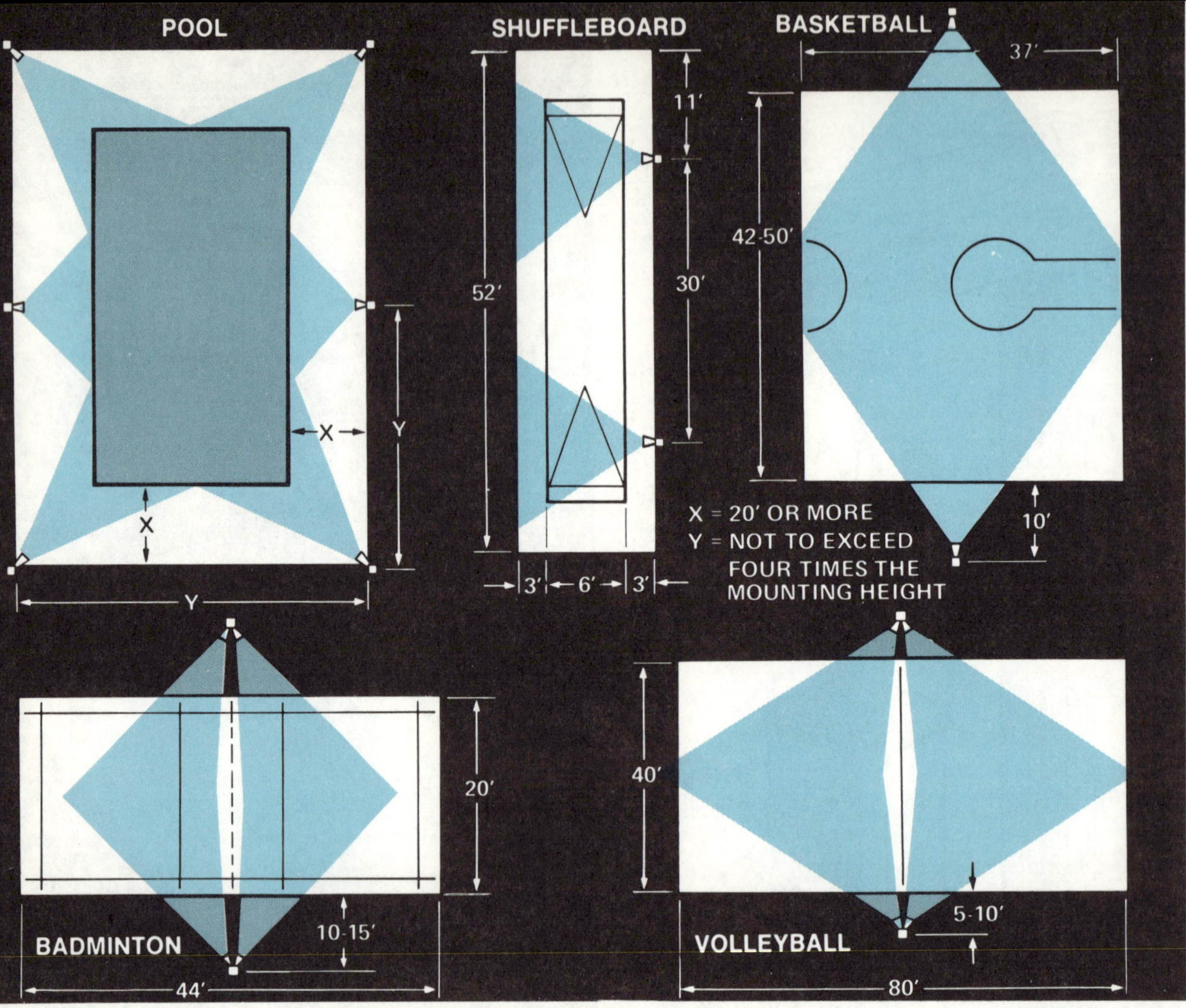

spot" can be as distracting to a player as staring into the sun.

- Since filament lamps tend to have a short lamp life, mercury luminaires, designed for 24,000 burning hours per year, are recommended by most experts.

There are other factors to bear in mind when laying out your lighting. There may be times when you do not wish to light a game but want to make aesthetic use of the light for highlighting rock gardens, fish pools and the like. For barbecues, picnics and social gatherings you will want a lower level of illumination. Thus, when possible, utilize dimmer switches in your controls. And, as shown illustrated at left in the typical light standard if at all possible, provide watertight convenience outlets. At some later date, you might decide to relocate a patio or purchase an electric mower.

Though good illumination for a particular game is of primary concern, do give some thought to how the lights (and their poles) will look during the day.

Above are shown the most common back-yard games and the lighting setup best suited for each. Normally, 10 foot-candles of illumination are recommended for all activities shown except shuffleboard. For this game, five footcandles are sufficient. Tennis courts (not illustrated above) require 10 footcandles of illumination. Swimming-pool lighting refers to pole lights placed around the pool.

Another advantage of well-planned activity and general outdoor lighting, is that such illumination can be utilized for security. So, you might also consider installing timers or light-sensitive switches that will turn lights on and off at predetermined times.

Outdoor floodlighting can be installed with either overhead or underground wiring, but from the standpoint of appearance, and for minimal interference, the latter is more desirable. An underground system can use either direct-burial cable conductors or wire in conduit. While overhead lines can be less costly, they may require additional items. For example, extra poles may be needed to keep wires from dangling into a playing area, or guys may be required on poles where there is a change in direction of feeders or where the feeders dead-end.

INDEX

Entries in regular type refer to feature articles of one page or more. *Entries in italics refer to short items—hints, tips, kinks and time-saving ideas—that are printed on "Easy Does It!" and "Here's the Answer" pages.* The first number refers to the volume, the second number to the page: 9/1312, for example, refers to the article in volume 9 on page 1312.

A

A-frames
garden shelters, 9/1330
spartan vacation home, 19/3016
split-level vacation home, 19/3016
weekend vacation home, 19/3010
Abrasive cutoff machines
how to make, 6/892
made from portable circular saw, 6/894
Abrasives
metal finishes for lathe projects, 12/1808
sanding block clamped in vise, 20/3087
sanding techniques, 16/2503
selecting and using, 1/20
Access panels: basement walls, 2/202
Accidents: drowning, hypothermia prevention, 1/24
Acoustical tile
how to clean, 15/2381
painting, 4/573
Acrobatic water skiing: guide to, 18/2756
Acrylic plastic: see Plexiglass
Additions, house
adding new story, 10/1474
adding new story over attached garage, 10/1484
adding wing to house, 10/1476
garage remodeled into family room, 9/1312
greenhouse addition, 1/30
measurements guide, 12/1784
planning your addition, 1/28
remodeling and adding to old house, 16/2421
Address numbers
displayed on keymaker's sign, 20/3066
how to illuminate, 10/1487
Addresses, mailing: *writing on rolled magazine, 2/291*
Adhesives
gluing plywood panels, 4/553
selecting and using, 1/35
spread with plastic forks, 2/232
waterproof adhesive for basement floor tile, 15/2341
Adult games
backgammon and chess table, 1/146
backgammon board, veneer-covered, 20/3044
bridge table, 3/453
checkerboard cube-stools, 8/1186
chess set and cabinet, 5/658
cribbage board, pocket, 6/877
game table, circular, 9/1304
playing-card holder, 3/452
pool, cue-and-ball wall rack, 20/3062
pool table, bumper-pool, 15/2264
pool table, full-size, 15/2256
shuffleboard table, 17/2678
'Swiss-cheese' mountain game, 20/3062
table tennis, playback for solo practice, 8/1157
table tennis ball and paddle caddy, 4/509
tabletop hockey, 1/58
yard lighting for game areas, 20/3149
Adzes: making and using, 4/624
Aerosol valves: *cleaning, 1/34*
Air compressors: how to build, 6/826
Air games: tabletop hockey, 1/58
Air leaks, auto: stopping, 11/1706
Airconditioners
attic insulation needed for central airconditioning, 16/2523
autos, troubleshooting, 1/56
burglar proofing, 3/460
compressor, covering in winter, 3/338
energy costs, cutting, 7/1093
exterior unit, covering, 1/125
heat pumps, how they work, 9/1404
repair, servicing, 1/50
repairing with tape, 18/2842
room, building in, 1/43
room, choosing, using, 1/46
solar energy guide, 18/2730
Airplane: block toy, 19/2921
Airplane models
control-line models, 12/1886
radio-controlled, 1/62
Alarm clocks: *using alarm on old shelf clock, 19/2979*
Alarms, burglar
buzzer alarm, 3/460
home protection guide, 16/2547
Alarms, fire
home protection guide, 16/2547
smoke detectors, choosing, 1/66
Alarms, smoke: choosing, 1/66
Allen screws: *permanent handles for setscrews, 14/2240*
Allen wrenches
T-handle for wrench, 16/2502
used as door bolt-latch, 10/1555
used on nuts in tight quarters, 11/1644
Alligator clips: *soldered to screwdriver, 10/1555*
Alphabet toybox: 3/430
Alternators, auto
how they work, 10/1524
repairing, 1/70
Aluminum
aluminum gutters, soldering, 1/125
corrugated aluminum roofing, cutting, 13/2069
punching with paper punch, 12/1853
stopping oxide coating, 15/2381
Aluminum siding
aluminum or vinyl, choosing, 4/544
painting, 19/2889
re-siding over asbestos shingles, 16/2557
repainting, 5/800
selecting, 17/2680
won't make house cold, 18/2809
Aluminum-faced tape: home repairs, 18/2842
Amplifiers: for transistor radio, 1/74
Anchors, wall
fasteners, types and sizes, 8/1193
screw anchors, removing from wall, 17/2600
Angle blocksfor table-saw miter cuts, 12/1854
Angle iron: *cutting with hacksaw, 17/2639*
Angled holes
drilling, 1/78
drilling on drill press, 7/1040
drilling with doweling jig, 10/1515
Angles: combination square, using, 6/825
Angles, compound: wood, cutting, 1/76
Animal photography: outdoor photo tips, 13/2006
Animals, wild: calling wild game, 10/1512
Antennas
light, for CB radio, 5/737
masts, from thinwall conduit, 12/1782
putting up, 1/86
repair and maintenance, 18/2848
TV, choosing the right one, 1/82
Antique ceiling beams: making and installing, 4/624
Antique reproductions
bench, pine and maple, 1/90
bootjack, 5/650
chair, splint-seat, 5/650
nesting tables, four Sheraton replicas, 13/1958
shaving mirror, Lincoln's, 12/1840
vanity mirror, Lincoln's, 12/1840
Antiquing: furniture refinishing, 8/1208
Ants, carpenter: *found in firewood, 14/2186*
Anvils: *mini-anvil, from pipe fitting, 5/689*
Apartment darkrooms: portable, 6/904
Apple-cider presses: how to make, 5/710
Appliance centers: patio cookout cart, 11/1622
Appliances
appliance center and snack bar, 18/2794
average wattage used, 7/1085
cart, built-in, 3/454
clothes dryers, electric, repairing, 5/788
clothes dryers, gas, repairing, 5/794
coffee percolators, repairing, 5/782
cords, cleats for storing, 1/119
cords, stored in tube, 2/251
dishwashers, at counter level, 3/454
dishwashers, built-in, 11/1608
dishwashers, cabinet, 13/1948
dishwashers, repairing, 7/1002
energy costs, cutting, 7/1093
food mixers, how to repair, 12/1858
food mixers, portable, how to repair, 8/1260
food processors, how to repair, 8/1262
food-processor-parts rack, 1/99
freezers, repairing, 9/1286
garbage disposers, installing, 11/1608
garbage disposers, installing, 9/1323
garbage disposers, repairing, 9/1326
hose clamps, reinstalling, 11/1644
humidifiers, need attic vapor barrier, 16/2557
humidifiers, selecting and installing, 10/1508
irons, how to repair, 10/1548
laundry center, 18/2794
laundry center for kitchen, 10/1464
ovens, hood for wall oven over range, 13/2018
patio cookout center, 11/1622
ranges, electric, repairing, 15/2391
refrigerator tune-up, 1/100
small-appliance repair, 1/96
toasters, how to repair, 19/2890
toasters, magnet holds plug, 2/291
vacuum cleaners, how to repair, 19/3028
vacuum cleaners, shop, dollies, 19/3032
vacuum cleaners, tube for hard-to-reach places, 10/1499
washing machines, how to repair, 20/3056
water heaters, insulating, 20/3078
water heaters, maintenance and repair, 9/1410
water heaters, must be vented, 11/1760

water heaters, noises, cause and cure, 1/95
water heaters, plastic pipe connections, 14/2182
water heaters, solar system, 9/1416
water heaters, solar, installing, 18/2739
wattage ratings, 12/1784
Appliances, toy: refrigerator, sink, stove, 19/2908
Aquariums
coffee-table aquarium, 6/810
plexiglass wall fish tank, 14/2205
wall-mounted, 6/810
Archways: entryway, restyling, 8/1148
Armchairs: colonial, cherry wood, 1/102
Art frames
barn-siding frames, 9/1284
fancy overlays, repairing, 8/1278
floater frames, making, 8/1277
prints, mounting and framing, 8/1264
Artificial turf: used for putting greens, 15/2356
Asbestos shingles: *re-siding over, 16/2557*
Ashtrays: cut from bottles, 3/418
Asphalt driveways
patching, resurfacing, 1/112
when to seal, 19/2889
Asphalt paths: for garden and yard, 14/2084
Asphalt shingles
installing on roof, 16/2450
wood vs. asphalt shingles, 1/45
Asphalt tile: *varnish spill, not removable, 14/2105*
Astronomy: telescope, made from camera lens, 18/2846
Attache cases: made into camera bag, 4/514
Attics
condensation, cause and cure, 19/2937
condensation inside roof, stopping, 3/338
cooling with fans and ventilators, 1/120
dormers, how to frame, 1/116
fans, using, 1/46
insulation, adding batts to blown-in, 8/1280
insulation needed for central airconditioning, 16/2523
insulation stops heat loss, 20/3078
insulation vapor barrier, needed for house humidifier, 16/2557
shelves, installing, 17/2630
shutters hide under-eaves storage, 18/2794
skylights, condensation from, 11/1621
storage space under eaves, 18/2794
vents, open in winter, 17/2720
Audio mixers: choosing and using, 12/1856
Augers: *screw-point protector, 3/389*
Auto racetrack, toy: for plastic cars, 19/2922
Automatic chokes, auto: maintenance, 5/680
Automatic transmissions, auto: fluid, changing, 19/2938
Autos, airconditioners: troubleshooting, 1/56
Autos, alternators
how they work, 10/1524
repairing, 1/70
Autos, ball joints: lubricating, 11/1740
Autos, batteries
basic auto tune-up, 19/2960
cables maintenance, 4/506
how they work, 10/1524
'maintenance-free' battery care, 1/126
prewinter maintenance, 20/3074
tester, 2/240
Autos, belts: drive-belt maintenance, 2/262
Autos, bodies
lubricating, 11/1740
rust, repairing, 16/2480
Autos, body care
dents, repairing, 1/130
maintenance, 3/384
waxing, 3/388
Autos, brakes
checking lubricant, 11/1740
checkout inspection and road test, 3/434
disc brakes, replacing pads, 3/446
drum brakes, overhauling, 3/440
four-wheel drive tune-up, 19/2970
noises, stopping, 13/1967
prewinter maintenance, 20/3074
troubleshooting, 3/438
Autos, bumpers: snowplow, how to make, 18/2724
Autos, buying: used-car buying tips, 19/3006
Autos, cables: cables and wiring maintenance, 4/506
Autos, carburetors
chokes, automatic, maintenance, 5/680
troubleshooting, 4/585
tune-up zip kit, 4/590
Autos, catalytic converters: servicing, 4/610
Autos, CB radio
antenna light, 5/737
mounting in car, 5/730
using on vacation trips, 5/734
Autos, chokes
automatic, maintenance, 5/680
troubleshooting, 4/585
Autos, clutches: noise, diagnosing, 15/2324
Autos, coolant: recovery system, 6/872
Autos, cooling systems
airconditioners, troubleshooting, 1/56
basic auto tune-up, 19/2960
coolant recovery system, 6/872
engine-overheating causes, 6/867
maintenance, 6/868
prewinter maintenance, 20/3074
Autos, dieseling
causes, 13/1971
how to stop, 7/974
Autos, differentials
noise, diagnosing, 15/2324
troubleshooting, 7/978
Autos, distributors
basic auto tune-up, 19/2960
how they work, 10/1524
ignition cables, testing and replacing, 10/1528
maintenance, 7/1010
prewinter maintenance, 20/3074
servicing, 10/1525
Autos, doors: wind noise and water leaks, stopping, 11/1706
Autos, drive belts: maintenance, 2/262
Autos, drive trains: differentials, troubleshooting, 7/978
Autos, driving
blizzards, surviving in car, 3/351
CB radio, on vacation trips, 5/734
gas mileage, improving, 1/134
tire chains, selecting and using, 4/638
Autos, EGR systems
servicing, 4/610
valve servicing, 7/1088
Autos, electrical systems
alternators, repair, 1/70
batteries, tester, 2/240
how they work, 10/1524
ignition cables, testing and replacing, 10/1528
Autos, electronic ignition systems
servicing, 10/1532
troubleshooting, 7/1075
Autos, emissions controls
basic auto tune-up, 19/2960
servicing, 4/610
servicing, 7/1088
Autos, engines
basic tune-up procedure, 19/2960
dieseling, causes, 13/1971
dieseling, how to stop, 7/974
hesitation problems, solving, 7/1100
lubricating, 11/1740
misfiring, troubleshooting, 12/1846
missing engine, curing, 7/1112
noise, diagnosing, 15/2324
noises, diagnosing, 13/1971
noises, stopping, 13/1967
oil consumption, diagnosing, 12/1912
overhauling engine, 8/1124
stalling problems, solving, 7/1100
stalls, stopping, 18/2780
starting problems, solving, 7/1100
surging, curing, 7/1112
Autos, exhaust systems
catalytic converters, servicing, 4/610
replacing, 8/1166
Autos, filters: oil filters, changing, 11/1740
Autos, four-wheel drive: tune-up, 19/2970
Autos, front-end alignment: servicing, 18/2786
Autos, fuel pumps: gaskets, replacing, 9/1342
Autos, fuel systems
basic auto tune-up, 19/2960
care and repair, 9/1292
gas mileage, improving, 1/134
Autos, gas mileage: improving, 1/134
Autos, gaskets: replacing, 9/1342
Autos, hesitation: troubleshooting, 7/1100
Autos, ignition systems
basic auto tune-up, 19/2960
battery care, 'maintenance-free', 1/126
cables and wiring maintenance, 4/506
dieseling, how to stop, 7/974
distributors, maintenance, 7/1010
electronic, troubleshooting, 7/1075
electronic ignition, servicing, 10/1532
how they work, 10/1524
ignition cables, testing and replacing, 10/1528
servicing, 10/1525
sparkplugs, guide to, 18/2746
Autos, leaks
body leaks, 3/384
wind noise and water leaks, stopping, 11/1706
Autos, lubrication
four-wheel drive tune-up, 19/2970
how to lubricate, 11/1740
oil consumption, diagnosing, 12/1912
prewinter maintenance, 20/3074
Autos, misfiring: troubleshooting, 12/1846
Autos, model: Stutz Bearcat made from tin cans, 18/2875
Autos, motorcycle carrier: 12/1915
Autos, mufflers: replacing, 8/1166
Autos, noises: rattles, stopping, 3/384
Autos, oil filters
changing, 11/1740
gaskets, replacing, 9/1342
Autos, oil pans: gaskets, replacing, 9/1342
Autos, PCV systems: servicing, 7/1088
Autos, power trains: noise, diagnosing, 15/2324
Autos, radiators
coolant recovery system, 6/872

maintenance, 6/868
Autos, radios: interference, 3/384
Autos, ramps: folding, how to build, 1/142
Autos, repair
airconditioners, 1/56
alternators, 1/70
basic auto tune-up, 19/2960
body care, 3/384
body rust, repairing, 16/2480
brakes, disc, replacing pads, 3/446
brakes, drum, overhauling, 3/440
brakes, inspection and road test, 3/434
brakes, troubleshooting, 3/438
cables and wiring maintenance, 4/506
carburetor tune-up zip kit, 4/590
carburetors, troubleshooting, 4/585
catalytic converters, servicing, 4/610
chokes, maintenance, 5/680
cooling systems, maintenance, 6/868
dents, repairing, 1/130
dieseling, how to stop, 7/974
differentials, troubleshooting, 7/978
distributors, maintenance, 7/1010
drive-belt maintenance, 2/262
EGR systems, servicing, 4/610
electronic ignition systems, troubleshooting, 7/1075
emissions controls, servicing, 7/1088
engine misfiring, troubleshooting, 12/1846
engine overhaul, 8/1124
engine-overheating causes, 6/867
exhaust system, replacing, 8/1166
fuel-system care and repair, 9/1292
gaskets and seals, replacing, 9/1342
hesitation problems, solving, 7/1100
ignition systems, servicing, 10/1525
maintenance, routine, 1/138
missing engine, curing, 7/1112
ramps, folding, 1/142
rocker 'car pit' ramp, 15/2390
shock absorbers, checking, selecting, and replacing, 17/2647
stalling, how to stop, 18/2780
stalling problems, solving, 7/1100
starting problems, solving, 7/1100
steering and suspension systems, 18/2786
surging, curing, 7/1112
windshield-wiper maintenance, 1/143
Autos, rocker arm covers: gaskets, replacing, 9/1342
Autos, roofs: bicycle carrier, 2/300
Autos, rust
removing, 3/384
repairing, 16/2480
Autos, safety
blizzards, surviving in car, 3/351
tire chains, selecting and using, 4/638
Autos, seals: replacing, 9/1342
Autos, seats: *foil keeps seats cool, 4/584*
Autos, shock absorbers
checking, selecting, and replacing, 17/2647
servicing, 18/2786
Autos, sparkplugs
basic auto tune-up, 19/2960
cables maintenance, 4/506
complete guide to plugs, 18/2746
replacing, 7/1112
Autos, stalling
stopping stalls, 18/2780
troubleshooting, 7/1100
Autos, starters: how they work, 10/1524
Autos, starting, hard: troubleshooting, 7/1100
Autos, steering: servicing steering system, 18/2786
Autos, stereo speakers: installing, 18/2753
Autos, surging: curing, 7/1112
Autos, suspension
servicing suspension system, 18/2786
shock absorbers, checking, selecting, and replacing, 17/2647
Autos, tailgates: picnic chest, 4/494
Autos, tailpipes: replacing, 8/1166
Autos, thermostats: gaskets, replacing, 9/1342
Autos, tires
care and maintenance, 19/2886
chains, selecting and using, 4/638
'fork' aids in removal, 1/150
labels, how to read, 19/2884
noises, stopping, 13/1967
pressure gauge, stored in glovebox, 6/887
pressure-gauge rack, 7/1009
prewinter maintenance, 20/3074
rotation patterns, 19/2886
spreader made from open-end wrench, 8/1192
steering and suspension, servicing, 18/2786
Autos, trail-bike carrier: 12/1915
Autos, transmissions
automatic-transmission fluid, changing, 19/2938
checking lubricant, 11/1740
differentials, troubleshooting, 7/978
four-wheel drive tune-up, 19/2970
noise, diagnosing, 15/2324
noises, stopping, 13/1967
Autos, trunks: water leaks, stopping, 11/1706
Autos, tune-up
basic tune-up procedure, 19/2960
carburetor zip kit, 4/590
electronic ignition systems, servicing, 10/1532
four-wheel drive tune-up, 19/2970
ignition systems, servicing, 10/1525
Autos, universal joints
noise, diagnosing, 15/2324
noises, stopping, 13/1967
Autos, used: buying tips, 19/3006
Autos, vacuum gauges: gas mileage, improving, 1/134
Autos, waxing: when and how, 3/388
Autos, wheels
four-wheel drive tune-up, 19/2970
noises, stopping, 13/1967
seals, replacing, 9/1342
steering and suspension, servicing, 18/2786
wheel covers, stopping rattle, 1/34
Autos, windows: wind noise and water leaks, stopping, 11/1706
Autos, windshield wipers: maintenance, 1/143
Autos, windshields
wind noise and water leaks, stopping, 11/1706
wiper maintenance, 1/143
Autos, winterizing: prewinter maintenance, 20/3074
Autos, workbenches: mounted on station-wagon tailgate, 20/3131
Awls: *pilot holes for screws, 13/1936*
Awnings: *for mail slot in door, 17/2697*
Axes: *logs held upright inside tires, 19/2989*

B

Baby bottles: *make glue or paint-applicator bottles, 9/1297*
Backgammon
backgammon and chess table, 1/146
board, veneer-covered, 20/3044
Backpacking
backpacks, selecting, 4/540
camera, hung from backpack frame, 4/513
clothing, sew-your-own kits, 4/538
exercises to get in shape, 8/1158
map reading, 12/1764
new gear, 1/151
wilderness-area camping, 4/545
Backup boards: for installing ceramic wall tile, 20/3049
Badminton
restringing rackets, 18/2851
yard lighting for game areas, 20/3149
Bait, fishing: *bait can, double-ended, 6/819*
Baitfish lures: how to make, 11/1755
Ball joints, auto: lubricating, 11/1740
Ball-and-chain gates: *self-closing, 3/416*
Ball-and-cue wall rack: 20/3062
Ball-and-cup ornaments: for Christmas tree, 5/702
Balloon ornaments: for Christmas, 5/702
Ballpoint pens
cut into washers and spacers, 16/2543
needles stored in cap, 13/2012
refills used to draw parallel lines, 9/1322
Bandsaws
basics of using, 2/164
blades, sharpening jig, 2/168
cabinet-stand, 15/2316
cutoff jig, 17/2660
glue dowels, cutting spiral kerfs, 17/2660
maintenance, 15/2310
rip fence, 2/167
table, king-size, 2/170
used to make wood discs, 7/1001
using, 8 tricks, 1/154
Banjo barometers: 2/182
Bar clamps
how to lengthen, 16/2523
making, 5/744
Bar stock: drilling on drill press, 7/1040
Barbecues
barbecue bar for family room, 2/171
cookout bar, 6/862
firepit, brick, 8/1222
gas-fired, 2/176
gazebo cookout center, 9/1346
indoor portable electric grill, 9/1370
mobile cooking center, 12/1865
shelter-house for grill, 9/1375
wraparound table, 2/174
Barn-siding picture frames: 9/1284
Barometers
banjo type, 2/182
colonial weather station, 20/3060
mercury tube, replacing, 7/1023
water type, 2/180
Barrels
whiskey-barrel bar, 2/190
whiskey-barrel planter tubs, 14/2168
Barrels, strawberry: how to make, 18/2816
Bars
'antiqued' family room, 2/188
barbecue bar for family room, 2/171
basement, under heat pipes, 2/185
built from module, 12/1890
cabinet bar, 2/194
mobile bar with running water, 12/1865
modules from kitchen cabinets, 4/484
split-level, for family room, 8/1182
whiskey-barrel bar, 2/190
Baseboards
guide to molding shapes, 12/1901
valuables hidden behind, 16/2558
Basements
bar, under heat pipes, 2/185
ceiling beams, paneling, 2/202

concrete floor, paint instead of cleaning, 11/1685
concrete wall, boring holes, 3/338
concrete wall, patching air-bubble holes, 11/1685
concrete-block walls, waterproofing, 3/369
condensation on floor, 11/1621
doors, eliminating water marks from flood, 6/847
dry rot, preventing, 11/1735
family room ideas, 8/1182
floor, concrete, how to paint, 18/2809
floor, installing sheet flooring over tile, 4/544
floor, removing fuel-oil stain, 1/65
floor-joist bracing, replacing, 5/800
floor tile, needs waterproof adhesive, 15/2341
furnace, keeping flood water out, 20/3137
garden-hose storage, 8/1192
insulation stops heat loss, 20/3078
mini projection booth, 18/2794
moisture caused by outside landfill, 11/1760
moisture on wall, 12/1821
musty odors, removing, 12/1920
partition walls, framing, 2/200
remodeling, family rooms, 8/1186
remodeling, finish details, 2/202
remodeling ideas, 2/198
screens hide furnace, laundry, fuel-tank, 8/1186
shelves, installing, 17/2630
shelves, sliding doors for, 17/2636
stairs, laying out and building, 18/2776
stairs, tightened with turnbuckle, 4/501
stairwalls, 2/202
stairwell, prefab, installing, 2/206
stone walls, replacing mortar, 11/1760
sumps, closed or open?, 6/847
tile floor, flooded, 16/2533
wall, concrete, patching, 6/844
walls, pivoting or sliding, 8/1186
walls, repairing crumbling concrete, 3/429
water seepage, preventing, 5/649
waterproofing, 2/210
window sashes, removing for painting, 18/2809
windows, burglar proofing, 3/460
windows, louvered, dummy frames, 8/1186
workshops, how to heat, 16/2467
Basketball: yard lighting for game areas, 20/3149
Basketball hoops: for children, 14/2196
Baskets, bushel: *stores garden hose, 8/1192*
Baskets, laundry: *used for cat cage, 17/2697*
Baskets, ring: made from metal tubing, 19/2956
Bass fishing
baitfish lures, how to make, 11/1755
spoons, how to make, 11/1752
Bathrooms
bathtubs, caulking, 2/231
bathtubs, installing, 2/224
bathtubs, prefab, installing, 2/220
bathtubs, sunken, illusion of, 2/214
ceramic tile, installing on backup board, 20/3049
ceramic tile, on exterior wall, 12/1864
darkroom, roll-away, 6/908
drains, how to unclog, 7/1032
energy costs, cutting, 7/1093
ladder shelves, 2/230
lavatory, covering fine cracks, 17/2669
lavatory, odor from, 12/1864
linen closet, 5/779
loose ceramic tile, replacing, 10/1470
magazine rack, 16/2434
measurements guide, 12/1784
medicine cabinet, 2/216
planter, supports lavatory, 10/1464
plumbing repairs, 1/157
plumbing repairs, 14/2216
porcelain fixtures, refinishing, 16/2557
remodeling for easy care, 2/224
remodeling ideas, 2/216
scale swings into wall, 16/2434
shaving cabinets, wall-mounted, 17/2612
shaving console, early American, 17/2616
shower, plastic sheet under shower pan, 18/2752
shower, regrouting tile, 17/2669
shower, soap film on door, cleaning, 17/2600
shower floor, pitch for water drainage, 18/2752
tile, installing, 2/224
toilet, installing, 2/224
towel cabinet, 2/216
towel racks, wooden, 19/2906
vanity, installing, 2/224
vanity-hamper, 2/216
wall tile, installing, 18/2869
Bathtubs
bathroom plumbing repairs, 1/157
caulking, 2/231
caulking seams, 10/1470
chipped enamel, repairing, 5/709
drains, how to unclog, 7/1032
gurgling when drained, cause, 13/2017
installing, 2/224
magazine rack, 16/2434
prefab tubs, installing, 2/220
refinishing, 16/2557
sunken tub, illusion of, 2/214
Batteries, auto
basic auto tune-up, 19/2960
cables maintenance, 4/506
how they work, 10/1524
'maintenance-free' battery care, 1/126
prewinter maintenance, 20/3074
tester, 2/240
Batteries, dry-cell
guide to types, 2/233
tester-recharger, 2/237
Batteries, transistor-radio: *tester, 8/1164*
Beading: scratch stock is beading tool, 17/2670
Beams, ceiling
hand-hewn, making and installing, 4/624
paneling, 2/202
simulated, installing, 4/622
Bearing walls: removing, 2/242
Bearings: *silencing on metal lathe, 13/2069*
Bed tables
footboard, for twin beds, 5/672
table-buffet, 2/246
Bedroom furniture
bed swings into wall cabinet, 16/2434
bed table, footboard, 5/672
bed table-buffet, 2/246
beds, slats, held with eyescrews, 3/433
bunk bed, children's, built-in chest, 5/674
bunk bed-desk, children's, 5/668
bunk beds are room divider, 18/2794
platform beds, three, 2/252
sofa-bed, 18/2726
tambour table, 13/1974
under-bed hideaway for model train, 18/2794
Bedrooms
attic-dormer framing, 1/116
divider-wall, 16/2434
freestanding wall, how to build, 16/2464
Beds
bed swings into wall cabinet, 16/2434
bunk bed, children's, built-in chest, 5/674
bunk bed-desk, children's, 5/668
bunk beds are room divider, 18/2794
platform beds, three, 2/252
slats, held with eyescrews, 3/433
sofa-bed, 18/2726
under-bed hideaway for model train layout, 18/2794
Bee pull toy: 15/2355
Beeper: *for darkroom timer, 14/2116*
Bell shelves: colonial, 9/1356
Belt carriers: *for camera accessories, 14/2116*
Belt sanders
abrasives, selecting and using, 1/20
basics, 16/2498
how to use, 2/258
sanding techniques, 16/2503
Belts: *hung on curtain rod, 3/416*
Belts, auto: drive-belt maintenance, 2/262
Bench grinders: *ceramic-tile nibbler, 5/689*
Bench hooks: holds work and protects benchtop, 17/2670
Bench saws
basics, 16/2514
blades, selecting, 5/722
dolly, rolling, 18/2784
miter-gauge hold-down, 2/295
mitering wide boards, 17/2664
portable circular saw on bench, 5/717
push stick, 2/268
push stick, from pencil, 8/1185
push stick, simple, 16/2514
push stick, supersafe, 2/292
using, accessories, 2/268
wedges, cutting, 17/2660
work support, roller top, 2/294
Bench-rest shooting: rifle accuracy, 17/2652
Benches
bench planter, pine, 14/2170
deck benches, wood, 2/264
deck benches, wood, 6/914
exercise bench, fold-up, 6/854
for trestle table, 7/998
foyer bench for boot storage, 16/2434
gossip bench, early American, 9/1365
padded benches used for storage, 18/2794
pine and maple bench, 1/90
potting bench, 2/267
potting benches, for garden work, 9/1332
radial-arm saw bench-cabinet, 15/2378
weight bench, 8/1162
yard benches, made from chimney blocks, 14/2152
Benches, work: see Workbenches
Benders, metal tubing: how to make, 19/2956
Benders, plexiglass: strip heater, 14/2205
Benders, sheet metal: brake made of wood, 17/2629
Benders, wire: *used in vise for bending, 14/2240*
Bending: hardboard bending, 9/1398
Bending, wood
how to bend wood, 20/3088
on bench saw, 2/268
Bevels
handsaw bevel guide, 17/2664
made on jointer, 10/1582
Bevels, T: *from table-saw miter gauge, 5/656*
Bicycles
bicycle touring, 2/306
carrier, car-roof, 2/300
cart, two-wheeled, 2/302
choosing right bike for you, 2/304
minibike, modernize with motorcycle

engine, 12/1836
repairs, basic, 2/313
tandem bicycle, building, 2/296
tune-up, basic, 19/2974
Bifold doors
casing hides track, 16/2434
installing, 5/770
Billiards
bumper-pool table, 15/2264
cue-and-ball wall rack, 20/3062
pool table, full-size, 15/2256
Binoculars
choosing, using, 3/324
guide to small optics, 3/328
Bins
kitchen grocery-bin canister, 10/1594
storage bins for small parts, 19/2948
tip-out bin, for kitchen, 11/1607
under kitchen wall cabinets, 4/492
Bins, storage: for garden work center, 9/1332
Bird candleholders: for Christmas, 5/702
Birdhouse terrarium: Tiffany-style, 18/2858
Birds
birdhouse masts, from thinwall conduit, 12/1782
birdhouse plans, 3/334
calling wild game, 10/1512
carving lifelike birds, 3/340
carving sea gulls, 3/343
feeder, automatic, 3/332
feeder, four-station, 3/331
feeder, made from scraps, 13/2079
keeping birds out of gardens, 19/3038
outdoor photography tips, 13/2006
photographing, through-window, 3/339
Bister: *clogs stove flue, 12/1864*
Bits, boring: metal lathe boring-bar set, 12/1790
Bits, drill: *holder from toothbrush case, 12/1853*
Bits, turning: lathe toolpost for hefty bits, 12/1792
Black-light insect trap: 10/1538
Black-powder guns: muzzleloaders, choosing and using, 13/1950
Blackouts
coping with power failures, 3/344
outdoor gear aids, 7/1085
Blacktop driveways: patching and resurfacing, 1/112
Blades, bandsaw
different types, 2/164
sharpening jig, 2/168
Blades, bench saw: selecting, 5/722
Blades, circular saw
carbide-tipped, 3/349
deburring, 5/724
selecting, 5/722
use carbide-tip blade to cut hardboard, 19/2937
Blades, hacksaw: *blade handle for tight quarters, 17/2673*
Blades, jigsaw: *holder, 11/1703*
Blades, sabre saw: *stored on shower hook, 9/1397*
Blades, table saw
blade-height gauge block, 17/2660
sharpening on arbor, 3/433
Blanket chests: decorated with moldings, 5/662
Blanket-chest toybox: 3/430
Bleach bottles: *used to fill photo developing tank, 14/2116*
Blenders: small-appliance repair, 1/96
Blind nailing: instructions, 12/1904
Blizzards: surviving in car, 3/351
Block toys
airplane, 19/2921
cars and trucks, 19/2911
children's block cars, 9/1352
circus train with animals, 15/2348
freight train, 19/2914
Blockmobiles: toy cars and trucks, 19/2911
'Blooming' finish: *removing, 13/1947*
Boards
lumber guide, 11/1747
measurements guide, 12/1784
uncupping thin boards, 13/2017
Boards, cutting
for kitchen-cabinet drawer, 11/1612
glass-cutting board for shop wall, 12/1781
kitchen accessory, 10/1596
multipurpose, for shop and darkroom, 6/900
of plexiglass, 14/2205
Boat accessories
boathooks, of PVC pipe, 15/2360
chart storage tube, of PVC pipe, 15/2360
dock hanger lines, of PVC pipe, 15/2360
fish club, of PVC pipe, 15/2360
flagstaffs, of PVC pipe, 15/2360
ladders, dock, of PVC pipe, 15/2360
PVC pipe projects, 15/2360
space heater, tin-can, 4/543
Boat camping: by kayak, 3/353
Boat cartopping
boat booster, 4/594
tie-downs, easy to use, 4/595
Travelpod, camper-boat-luggage carrier, 4/526
Boat propellers: how to choose, 15/2345
Boat repair: fiberglass boats, repairing, 16/2442
Boat speed: computing planing speed, 14/2166
Boat storage: winter layup, 3/370
Boat testing: gas consumption, determining, 13/2004
Boat trailers
maintenance tips, 3/373
trailering a boat, 3/376
Boathooks: of PVC pipe, 15/2360
Boating
binoculars, choosing and using, 3/324
binoculars, small-optic, 3/328
camping, by kayak, 3/353
canoe trip, gear for, 4/581
drowning, hypothermia prevention, 1/24
emergencies, how to handle, 3/361
keychain cork won't sink in water, 10/1555
knots, how to tie, 11/1640
outboard motors, service manual, 13/1981
outboard motors, starting problems, 13/2002
photography tips, 3/356
planing speed, computing, 14/2166
sailboat from a pram, 16/2494
towing in emergencies, 3/365
trailer maintenance tips, 3/373
trailering a boat, 3/376
white-water boating, 3/381
winter layup of boats, 3/370
Boating safety: life preservers, choosing, 11/1716
Boats
fiberglass, repairing, 16/2442
kayak, made of plywood, 10/1588
outboard motors, service manual, 13/1981
outboard motors, starting problems, 13/2002
pontoon boat, with surrey top, 15/2252
sailboat from a pram, 16/2494
trailer maintenance tips, 3/373
trailering a boat, 3/376
Travelpod, camper-boat-luggage carrier, 4/526
white-water boating, 3/381
winter layup, 3/370
Bodies, auto
lubricating, 11/1740
rust, repairing, 16/2480
Body care, auto
dents, repairing, 1/130
maintenance, 3/384
waxing, 3/388
Boilers
cleaning out, 9/1430
multifuel, installing, 3/390
Bolts
cut without damaged threads, 4/501
enlarging nut threads, 9/1429
made into setscrews, 6/819
selecting, using, 3/393
toggle bolts anchor tall cabinets, 18/2820
Book storage
book shelves, 3/396
bookcase, built-in-wall, 3/400
bookcase, fake shelf hides valuables, 16/2558
bookcase, from stacked drawers, 19/2948
bookcase closet, 3/405
bookcase wall with dropped soffit, 18/2807
bookcase-divider, 8/1186
bookends, adjustable shelf posts, 19/2956
bookends, initial, 3/409
bookends, photographic, 3/406
bookrack, colonial, 3/410
bookrack, desk carousel, 3/412
bookrack, metal, for paperbacks, 3/414
bookrack, metal, for paperbacks, 15/2364
bookstand, colonial, 3/415
cabinet, Mediterranean design, 9/1378
closet becomes bookcase, 18/2794
cookbook caddy, 10/1597
cookbook holder, plexiglass, 14/2205
tall bookcase anchored with toggle bolts, 18/2820
Books: *musty odor, removing, 8/1147*
Booster, boat: cartopping system, 4/594
Booster amplifiers: for transistor radio, 1/74
Bootboxes: children's, with coat rack, 5/671
Bootjacks: Lincoln replica, 5/650
Boots
Santa's candy cane boot ornament, 5/690
storage cupboard with drip rack, 18/2794
stored in foyer bench, 16/2434
Borders: *painting, picture frames, 8/1192*
Borers, wood: *unlikely in firewood, 11/1727*
Boring: metal lathe boring-bar set, 12/1790
Boring-bar sets: for metal lathe, 12/1790
Bottles, baby: *make glue or paint-applicator bottles, 9/1297*
Bottles, glass
cleaning inside residue, 5/800
fancy glassware, 3/418
loosening stuck stopper, 13/2017
model houses inside, 3/422
Bottles, nursing: *make glue or paint-applicator bottles, 9/1297*
Bottles, plastic: *used to fill photo developing tank, 14/2116*
Bounce-flash photos: 3/425
Bowls: cut from bottles, 3/418
Bowls, salad: laminated wood, 11/1652
Box joints
cutting on table saw, 17/2660
how to make and fit, 10/1576
Box stools: coffee table with box stools, 6/804
Box wrenches: basics of using, 19/2903
Box-end wrenches: *held on loose-leaf*

rings, 9/1297
Boxes
compound angles, cutting, 1/76
cotter pins used as hinges, 13/1936
Boxes, comb: colonial wall box, 6/824
Boxes, jewelry
heart-shaped box, 9/1360
heirloom case, musical, 10/1562
jewel box and overnight caddy, 10/1567
miniature chest, three-drawer, 10/1567
veneer-covered, 20/3044
Boxes, storage: for chain-saw accessories, 3/428
Boxes, trinket
cloth-tape inlays, 10/1537
decorating with pin-striping tape, 6/819
sanding, protecting corners, 7/982
self-closing hinge for lid, 11/1678
treasure chest, 9/1352
turned from plastic on metal lathe, 12/1814
wood carving project, 4/604
Brackets: bell shelf, colonial, 9/1356
Brackets, shelf: made from metal tubing, 19/2956
Brads
magnetic holder for storing, 6/887
nails, selecting and using, 13/1954
nailset, from masonry nail, 11/1626
Brakes, auto
checking lubricant, 11/1740
checkout inspection and road test, 3/434
disc brakes, replacing pads, 3/446
drum brakes, overhauling, 3/440
four-wheel drive tune-up, 19/2970
noises, stopping, 13/1967
prewinter maintenance, 20/3074
troubleshooting, 3/438
Brakes, sheet metal: bender made of wood, 17/2629
Brass
how to tell brass from brass-plated, 15/2341
remove lacquer before polishing, 13/2017
Breadboards: laminated wood, 11/1652
Breakfronts: built from module, 12/1890
Bric-a-brac cabinets: etagere, 8/1154
Brick
cracked brick, cause and remedy, 5/709
fireplaces, removing smoke stains, 3/369
measurements guide, 12/1784
painting masonry, 12/1778
patio, brick-in-sand, 14/2090
patio firepit, 8/1222
retaining walls, how to build, 16/2446
sidewalk, possible bases, 17/2600
simulated, wall covering, 3/450
spalling, caused by moisture, 1/95
stains, removing, 18/2772
steps, how to build, 18/2790
Bridge (card game)
playing-card holder, 3/452
table, parsons, 3/453
Bridges: rock-garden bridge with planter boxes, 14/2178
Broomstick unipods: *for steadying cameras, 14/2116*
Brownouts: outdoor gear aids, 7/1085
Brushes, finishing: *label with previous use, 9/1429*
Brushes, lacquer: *made from old felt, 9/1322*
Brushes, paint: see Paintbrushes
Buckets
magazine holder made from nail keg, 11/1759
photo chemicals mixed in bucket, 4/513
wrench on handle aids in carrying, 2/291
Bucking trees: correct method, 19/2954
Bucksaws: how to build, 16/2517
Buffet tables: knockdown, 8/1186
Buffets
bed table-buffet, 2/246
dining room in-a-wall buffet, 16/2434
mobile cooking center, 12/1865
Bug traps: black-light trap, 10/1538
Building
adding new story over attached garage, 10/1484
adding new story to house, 10/1474
adding wing to house, 10/1476
attic-dormer framing, 1/116
bearing walls, removing, 2/242
cabana poolhouse, 3/476
ceiling height, lowering, 14/2204
concrete blocks, how to lay, 6/848
contractors, choosing, 6/860
decks, 14/2102
decks, two, for front and rear, 14/2098
decks, wooden, 6/920
decks, wooden, 6/914
decks, wooden, two-level, 6/924
energy-saving tips, 7/1090
freestanding wall, 16/2464
garage remodeled into family room, 9/1312
garage remodeled into guest house, 9/1316
garden shelters, 9/1330
garden work shelter, 9/1332
gazebo cookout center, 9/1346
gazebos and screen house, 18/2821
greenhouse addition to home, 1/30
lumber guide, 11/1747
measurements guide, 12/1784
nails, selecting and using, 13/1954
partition walls, framing, 2/200
patio fiberglass roofs, 14/2095
room additions, planning, 1/28
screened porch, 16/2528
sheathing, guide to types, 17/2620
shims, how to use, 17/2638
siding, selecting, 17/2680
stairs, laying out and building, 18/2776
tips on placing new house on lot, 16/2467
Built-ins
bookcase, built-in-wall, 3/400
dining room in-a-wall buffet, 16/2434
dishwasher, 11/1608
entertainment center, 8/1170
kitchen cabinets, 3/454
laundry center, 3/454
laundry center for kitchen, 10/1464
room airconditioners, building in, 1/43
sewing centers, built-in ideas, 17/2601
Built-up roofs: *repairing, 3/369*
Bulbs, Christmas tree: *stored in egg cartons, 3/449*
Bulldozer blades: tractor hydraulic lift, 19/2924
Bulletin boards: *pushpins, king-size, 18/2857*
Bumblebee pull toy: 15/2355
Bumper-pool table: how to build, 15/2264
Bumpers, auto: snowplow, how to make, 18/2724
Bumpers, door
for kitchen cabinets, how to make, 5/765
from toothpaste caps, 7/982
Bunk beds
bunk bed-desk, children's, 5/668
children's, built-in chest, 5/674
double-decker bunk is room divider, 18/2794
Burglar proofing
door locks, installing, 11/1732
home protection guide, 16/2547
low-cost security tips, 3/460
safe inside colonial cabinet, 3/456
timers, for lamps, 10/1464
valuables, hiding places for, 16/2558
Burnishers: *using router to burnish, 12/1835*
Burns: furniture, repairing, 9/1302
Burrs: removing, circular saw blades, 5/724
Bushel baskets: *stores garden hose, 8/1192*
Butcher block furniture: sofa, chair, coffee table, 3/463
Butcher blocks: kitchen chopping block, 3/468
Butler's tables: serving tray-table, 3/472
Butt joints
making tighter, 1/119
strengthening, 10/1571
Buying
cameras, 4/522
houses, 10/1500
ladders, 11/1645
used cameras, 19/3002
used cars, 19/3006

C

C-clamps
enlarged for gluing wide work, 10/1581
gluing plywood panels, 4/553
hold paint cans on ladder, 11/1731
holding tiny parts in vise, 15/2397
make file handles, 3/389
makes radial-arm saw fence stop, 2/291
making one do work of two, 1/119
mitered joints held while gluing, 17/2664
selecting and using, 5/738
used as bench vise, 16/2560
used in gluing right angles, 10/1499
Cabanas
children's playhouse, 14/2200
poolhouse, 3/476
poolhouse for year-round use, 15/2270
Cabinet furniture: modules from kitchen cabinets, 4/484
Cabinetmaker scrapers: how to use, 16/2526
Cabinets
bar in elegant cabinet, 2/194
breakfront, built from module, 12/1890
cabinet workbench for small shop, 20/3138
chess set, 5/658
china cupboard, colonial, 6/888
clothes-sorting cabinet for laundry, 18/2794
decorated with moldings, 5/662
desk, opens into work center, 6/935
dining room in-a-wall buffet, 16/2434
dishwasher hideaway, 13/1948
door bolt-latch, improvised, 10/1555
drawers, how to make, 7/1036
dry sink, colonial, 7/1050
etagere, 8/1154
furniture from kitchen cabinets, 4/484
garage overhead storage cabinets, 18/2794
grill, portable electric, 9/1370
gun cabinet, Mediterranean design, 9/1378
hi-fi stereo wall, 4/488
hinges, selecting, 10/1450
home theater, hideaway, 18/2862
kitchen and laundry built-ins, 3/454
kitchen cabinet, cutting board on drawer, 11/1612
kitchen cabinet, how to install, 11/1616
kitchen cabinet, island work center, 11/1604
kitchen cabinet, pan storage-drawer, 11/1612
kitchen cabinet, pantry-door shelves,

11/1612
kitchen cabinet, spice rack fits inside door, 11/1612
kitchen cabinet, tip-out bin, 11/1607
kitchen cabinets, making door bumpers, 5/765
kitchen cabinets, metal, spot-painting, 15/2381
kitchen storage-space, 4/492
loudspeaker enclosures, 4/488
lowboy, colonial, 11/1739
medicine cabinet, for bathroom, 2/216
modelmaker's cabinet workshop, 17/2656
picnic chest, for auto tailgates, 4/494
power-tool stands, 15/2316
power-tool stands, retractable casters, 15/2321
pulls, ring turning on metal lathe, 12/1800
radial-arm saw bench-cabinet, 15/2378
radial-arm saw cabinet with extension tables, 16/2518
radial-arm saw cabinet-stand, 15/2372
room divider with lighted planter, 14/2172
router converted to shaper, 17/2602
security safe inside, 3/456
server, early American, 17/2564
sewing cabinet, chairside, 17/2582
sewing cabinet, for spools, 17/2585
sewing center, island unit, 17/2586
sewing center, wall and floor units, 17/2586
shaving cabinets, wall-mounted, 17/2612
shaving console, early American, 17/2616
Spanish chest, mosaic top, 5/665
storage trays, swing-out, 19/2949
tall cabinets anchored with toggle bolts, 18/2820
towel cabinet, for bathroom, 2/216
wall cabinet, hangs above desk, 6/935
wall cabinet, hobby center, 10/1454
wall cabinet for workbench, 20/3126
wall fasteners, types and sizes, 8/1193

Cabins: hunting-lodge vacation home, 19/3016
Cabins, log: *how to chink logs, 19/3027*
Cable releases, camera: *restraint for cable, 14/2116*
Cables, auto: cables and wiring maintenance, 4/506
Cables, ignition: testing and replacing, 10/1528

Caddies
cookbook shelf with drawer, 10/1597
hand-tool caddy, 4/510
mobile cart for TV set, 18/2794
nail caddy with handle, 10/1581
pen-and-pencil caddy for desk, 13/2078
ring caddy, in shape of hand, 9/1360
silverware-and-napkin caddy, 10/1594
smoking pipes, from coffee can, 3/416
table-tennis ball and paddle caddy, 4/509

Cage planters: hanging planter, 14/2106
Cages: *cat cage from plastic laundry basket, 17/2697*
Calcimine: *calcimined ceiling, covering, 8/1147*
Calculator stands: for pocket calculator, 4/511

Calipers
choosing and using, 4/502
made from clothespins, 5/656
making, for wood lathe, 17/2670
used to 'enlarge' micrometer, 12/1828

Callers, wild game: using, 10/1512

Camera bags
film holder, 14/2116
guitar strap eases load, 14/2116
made from suitcases, attache cases, 4/514
notebook taped to bag, 14/2116
photo-accessory inventory card, 4/521
zipper tab, 14/2116

Cameras
accessories toted in belt carrier, 14/2116
bellows, repairing holes in, 4/513
buying guide, 4/522
cable release, restraint for, 14/2116
camera-strap hardware, non-chip, 4/513
camerapods for low-level close-ups, 14/2116
care and repair, 4/516
close-up adjustable extension tube, 14/2116
double exposures, taking on 35-mm, 14/2116
eyepiece covered for long exposures, 4/521
film cartridges, loading, 4/596
film data sheet kept handy, 14/2116
film-type reminder, 14/2116
filters improve photos, 8/1206
flash photos, how to take, 14/2142
flashgun, stand for, 14/2116
good pictures with simple cameras, 14/2136
gunstock, telephoto, 4/520
harness for camera, 4/512
hung from backpack frame, 4/513
lens hood, curing vignetting, 14/2116
lenses, small-optic, 3/328
matte box to frame movies, 14/2148
neckstrap cushions, 14/2116
night photography tips, 13/1963
nut glued to bottom for tripod, 4/521
outdoor photography tips, 13/2006
repairing, small-parts dish, 4/513
snorkel box, for over/underwater photos, 19/2986
special effects dramatize photos, 14/2144
supported with photo clamp, 4/521
telescope, made from camera lens, 18/2846
timer, water-drip, 14/2116
tripod, braced against wall, 4/513
tripod camera-case screw, removing, 14/2116
underwater-photos guide, 19/2980
unipod made from dowel, 14/2116
used cameras, how to buy, 19/3002
vacation-photo tips, 14/2139
vignetter, from cardboard tube, 14/2116

Campaign desks: military design, 7/964

Campers
camper shell, for pickup truck, 4/534
fitting out, 4/550
improving and modernizing, 16/2412
safe-driving tips, 16/2404
Travelpod, camper-boat-luggage carrier, 4/526
van camp/work conversion, 4/531
winter-storage tips, 16/2408

Camping
backpacks, selecting, 4/540
boat camping, by kayak, 3/353
canoe trip, gear for, 4/581
clothing, sew-your-own kits, 4/538
gear used for home emergencies, 7/1085
map reading, 12/1764
recreational vehicles, fitting out, 4/550
salt-and-pepper shakers, from film cans, 1/119
space heater, tin-can, 4/543
tent trailer, how to build, 19/2932
wilderness-area camping, 4/545

Can openers
grommets make it easier to use, 10/1499
small-appliance repair, 1/96

Candid photos: tips on, 4/565
Candle lanterns: made from tin cans, 18/2875

Candle stands
flamed wooden cube, 4/564
musical centerpiece, 4/628
wooden centerpiece, 4/562

Candleholders: made on wood lathe, 20/3106

Candles
Christmas candle pot centerpiece, 5/690
candle holders, from cut bottles, 3/418
candlestand, interlocking wood links, 20/3118
fancy candles from molds, 4/554
holder, candy cane, 5/702
holders, bird-shaped, for Christmas, 5/702
holders, star-shaped, for Christmas, 5/698
holders, tree, for Christmas, 5/702
holders, wood, for Christmas, 5/698
lighted with alligator-clip tool, 10/1555
snow candles, free-form, 4/560
tree of life candleholder, 5/702
wall sconce, for Christmas, 5/702
wax, removing from wood furniture, 9/1302

Candlestand lamps: colonial design, 11/1664

Candy canes
boots, Christmas ornament, 5/690
candleholder, for Christmas, 5/702

Caning
chair caning, 4/568
chair caning, prewoven cane, 4/572

Canisters: grocery-bin canister, 10/1594
Canned goods: shelves inside pantry doors, 11/1612
Cannon models: brass and wood replica, 4/574

Canoes
exercises to get in shape, 8/1158
life preservers, choosing, 11/1716
white-water boating, 3/381
wilderness trip, gear for, 4/581

Canopy gazebo: summer house, 18/2821
Capsizing, boat: emergency practices, 3/361
Car models: Stutz Bearcat made from tin cans, 18/2875
'Car pit' ramp: rocker ramp for auto repair, 15/2390
Carbide blades: for circular saws, 3/349

Carburetors, auto
chokes, automatic, maintenance, 5/680
troubleshooting, 4/585
tune-up zip kit, 4/590

Card tables
game table, circular, 9/1304
simple, for family room, 8/1186

Cardboard
corrugated, scoring for bending, 10/1515
cutting board, 6/900
cutting strips with shears, 9/1335
punching with paper punch, 12/1853

Cards, greeting: Christmas, from photos, 5/684
Cards, note: *made from photos, 14/2116*

Cards, playing
bridge table, 3/453
holder, 3/452

Carousel bookrack: desk accessory, 3/412
Carpenter ants: *found in firewood, 14/2186*

Carpeting
furniture indentations, raising nap, 19/2889
kitchen, remove carpet before installing sheet flooring, 14/2204
pad for workbench top, 17/2673
removing stuck backing from hardwood floor, 18/2752
splicing carpet saves money, 12/1839

Carpeting, outdoor: for patios or decks, 4/592
Carriage bolts: selecting, using, 3/393
Carriers
auto trail-bike carrier, 12/1915
bicycle, on car-roof, 2/300
Carriers, luggage: Travelpod, camper-boat-luggage carrier, 4/526
Cars: see Autos
Cartons: *marked with ink-filled glue bottle, 16/2543*
Cartopping, boat
boat booster, 4/594
tie-downs, easy to use, 4/595
Travelpod, camper-boat-luggage carrier, 4/526
Cartridges, film: 35-mm, loading, 4/596
Carts
bar with running water, 12/1865
bicycle cart, two-wheeled, 2/302
built-in appliance cart, 3/454
cooking center, 12/1865
hi-fi music center, 12/1865
mobile cart for TV set, 18/2794
serving cart, with electric food warmer, 17/2570
Carts, leaf: *made from old screens, 10/1515*
Carving
birds, carving from wood, 3/340
birds, carving sea gulls, 3/343
candle stand, flamed, 4/564
carving with clear plastics, 10/1546
chisels, basics of using, 19/2904
interlocking wood links, 20/3118
jewelry carved from wood and plastic, 10/1556
musical creche, 9/1356
wood carving projects, 4, 4/604
Casa light box: 'stained' glass project, 18/2759
Casement windows: *latch used as planing stop, 8/1157*
Cassette recorders
in musical centerpieces, 4/628
repairing, 4/598
tape rewinder, 11/1678
Cassette tapes: snarled and broken, repairing, 4/602
Casters: retractable casters for power-tool stands, 15/2321
Casting, fly
fly-fishing instructions, 8/1254
popper plugs, making, 4/609
spoons, how to make, 11/1752
Casting, metal: 'lost wax' casting, 12/1786
Catalytic converters, auto: servicing, 4/610
Cats
cage made from laundry basket, 17/2697
wood carving project, 4/604
Caul bending: how to bend wood, 20/3088
Caulking
bathtub seams, 10/1470
bathtubs, caulking, 2/231
between shingles and foundation wall, 17/2720
cartridge cap, 11/1644
caulk, selecting and using, 4/614
energy costs, cutting, 7/1093
stopping home heat loss, 20/3078
CB radio
antenna light, 5/737
mounting in car, 5/730
on vacation trips, 5/734
TV interference, stopping, 10/1542
Cedar chests: decorated with moldings, 5/662
Cedar shakes: *used to replace shingles, 10/1570*
Cedar shingles
installing on roof, 16/2454
wood vs. asphalt shingles, 1/45
Ceiling tile
acoustical tile, cleaning, 15/2381
acoustical tile, painting, 4/573
installing, 4/616
replacing, 10/1470
Ceilings
acoustical tile, cleaning, 15/2381
acoustical tile, painting, 4/573
basements, beams, paneling, 2/202
beams, hand-hewn, making and installing, 4/624
beams, simulated, installing, 4/622
calcimined ceiling, covering, 8/1147
cracks in radiant-heated ceiling, 17/2720
drywall crack, repairing, 17/2600
lower ceiling height, advantages, 14/2204
nail dimples, spackling, 17/2669
patching plaster at ceiling-wall junction, 1/65
plaster patch, shows through paint, 5/649
plasterboard, how to install, 14/2180
tile, installing, 4/616
tiles, replacing, 10/1470
Cement: see Concrete
Centerpieces
candle stand, holiday, 4/562
Christmas candle pot, 5/690
lazy Susan table server, 11/1704
minitree for Christmas, 5/702
musical, for Christmas, 4/628
tree candleholders, for Christmas, 5/702
Ceramic tile
bathroom, installing, 2/224
bathroom, tile on exterior wall, 12/1864
facing for prefab fireplace, 10/1468
installing on backup board, 20/3049
loose tile, replacing, 10/1470
nibbler, wire-brush, 5/689
used in cheese tray, 9/1352
wall tile, installing, 18/2869
Chain: *used to make spade lugs, 13/2012*
Chain saws
box for accessories, 3/428
cutting down trees and limbs, 4/634
engines, servicing, 8/1128
firewood, how to cut, 8/1229
how to fell, buck, and limb a tree, 19/2954
logs, cutting and stacking, 11/1736
selecting, using, repairing, 4/632
Chains, tire: selecting and using, 4/638
Chairs
armchair, colonial, 1/102
butcher block design, 3/463
caning, 4/568
caning, prewoven cane, 4/572
glued joints, loosening, 18/2752
how to bend slats and rounds, 20/3088
hutch table, early American, 10/1516
lawn chairs, plastic webbing kept from tearing, 9/1297
legs, how to attach, 11/1710
Lincoln splint-seat chair, 5/650
outdoor, aluminum-and-canvas, 5/644
painting, jar lids under legs, 19/2931
patio aluminum chairs, stopping oxide coating, 15/2381
rocking chairs, Christmas ornaments, 5/690
rocking chairs, Christmas tree ornaments, 5/702
rolltop desk and chair, children's, 5/676
rung, loose, gluing, 12/1920
spindles, tool to scrape off finish, 11/1621
swivel, for dining set, 7/992
upholstered chairs, how to 'respring', 19/2998
upholstery, basic techniques, 19/2990
wobbly, tightening, 10/1470
Chalk: *makes scribed lines visible, 8/1259*
Chamfers: cut on bench saw, 16/2514
Chamfers, stopped: made on jointer, 10/1582
Chart storage tubes: of PVC pipe, 15/2360
Checkers: checkerboard cube-stools, 8/1186
Checkers, grounded-outlet: 5/657
Cheese trays: recessed ceramic tile, 9/1352
Chemicals, photo
depletion chart, 4/521
mixed in plastic bucket, 4/513
Chess: backgammon and chess table, 1/146
Chess sets: chessmen and cabinet, 5/658
Chests
cedar chest, decorated with moldings, 5/662
cutlery cupboard, colonial, 10/1600
desk, opens into work center, 6/935
drawers, repairing worn runners, 7/1023
drawers, tacks make them slide easily, 16/2467
drawers, won't open all the way, 11/1727
drawers stacked to make bookcase, 19/2948
dry sink, colonial, 7/1050
jewel box and overnight caddy, 10/1567
jewelry box, three-drawer, 10/1567
legs, how to attach, 11/1710
miniature treasure chest, 9/1352
picnic chest, for auto tailgates, 4/494
Spanish cabinet, mosaic top, 5/665
valet, dresser-top, 9/1352
Children's bicycle cart: 2/302
Children's boat: sailboat from a pram, 16/2494
Children's bootboxes: with coat rack, 5/671
Children's clothes tree: giraffe coat tree, 19/2914
Children's coat rack: freestanding, non-tip, 5/671
Children's furniture
bed table, footboard, 5/672
bookcase, from stacked drawers, 19/2948
bunk bed, built-in chest, 5/674
bunk bed-desk, 5/668
coat rack, freestanding, 5/671
desk, wall-hung, 5/672
rolltop desk and chair, 5/676
under-bed hideaway for model train layout, 18/2794
Children's games
bumper-pool table, 15/2264
checkerboard cube-stools, 8/1186
pool, cue-and-ball wall rack, 20/3062
shuffleboard table, 17/2678
'Swiss-cheese' mountain game, 20/3062
table tennis, playback for solo practice, 8/1157
table tennis ball and paddle caddy, 4/509
tabletop hockey, 1/58
yard lighting for game areas, 20/3149
Children's light-switch extension: *5/721*
Children's playground equipment
A-frame swing set, 1/41
basketball hoop, 14/2196
jungle-gym tree house, 14/2188
merry-go-round swing, 14/2189
roller coaster, 14/2190
sandbox, with roof, 14/2192
seesaw, rotating, 14/2194
stilt-house slide, 14/2187

stilts, 14/2196
swing, with guard rails, 14/2196
teeter board, bouncing, 14/2189
tetherball, 14/2196
water hoop, 14/2191
Children's playhouses
indoor two-sided playhouse, 14/2203
outdoor playhouse, 14/2200
Children's study centers: wall-hung learning center, 18/2818
Children's toyboxes
circus-wagon toybox, 19/2914
4 styles from 1 plan, 3/430
Children's toys
block cars, 9/1352
block toy, airplane, 19/2921
block toys, cars and trucks, 19/2911
bumblebee pull-toy, 15/2355
Christmas tree ornaments and gifts, 5/702
circus train pull-toy, 15/2348
coat tree, giraffe, 19/2914
crayon holder, 9/1360
dollhouse, 12/1830
dollhouse, English farmhouse, 19/2914
ducks and dachshund pull-toys, 15/2352
dump truck, wooden, 7/1059
kiddie car, 3-wheel, 9/1351
kitchen appliances—refrigerator, sink, stove, 19/2908
kites, how to build, 11/1627
pull toy, Hale the whale, 19/2914
racetrack for plastic cars, 19/2922
scooter, uses roller-skate wheels, 19/2907
sleds, preventing rust on runners, 17/2673
slide whistle, 19/2956
stilts, 14/2196
'Swiss-cheese' mountain game, 20/3062
train, wood-block, 19/2914
train engine, puffs 'smoke', 19/2914
Chimes, door: wiring, 10/1464
Chimney blocks: used to make picnic table, 14/2152
Chimneys
cleaning, 9/1430
cracked brick, cause and remedy, 5/709
fake, for hiding valuables, 16/2558
fireplace flue, cleaning smoke shelf, 15/2269
fireplace flue, how to clean, 11/1685
flashing leak, repairing, 12/1864
flue clogged by bister, 12/1864
frost-clogged chimney, preventing, 11/1735
water drips from gas-log fire, 11/1727
China cabinets
in Mediterranean design, 9/1378
lowboy, colonial, 11/1739
China cupboards
built from module, 12/1890
colonial display cabinet, 6/888
dining room in-a-wall buffet, 16/2434
Chisels
edge protected by pill bottle, 14/2155
handles, making, 17/2670
sharpening, 17/2608
wood chisels, basics of using, 19/2904
wood-lathe chisels, guide to, 20/3106
Chocolate stains: *removing from fabric, 12/1821*
Chokes, auto
automatic, maintenance, 5/680
troubleshooting, 4/585
Chopping blocks
butcher block, 3/468
top of island work center for kitchen, 11/1604
Christmas
acrylic plastic decorations, 5/698
balloon ornaments, 5/702
candle pot centerpiece, 5/690
candle stand, holiday, 4/562
candle wall sconce, 5/702
candleholders, bird-shaped, 5/702
candleholders, candy canes, 5/702
candleholders, star-shaped, 5/698
candleholders, tree centerpiece, 5/702
candleholders, tree of life, 5/702
candleholders, wood, 5/698
centerpieces, musical, 4/628
cookie cutter ornaments, 5/702
creche, musical, 9/1356
decorations, flashcubes on tree, 3/389
decorations, for table and tree, 5/702
decorations, for tree and home, 5/690
decorations, old-fashioned, 5/698
gifts to make—pipe rack and humidor, cheese tray, block cars, treasure chest, dresser-top valet, 9/1352
gifts to make—rustic planters, colonial bell shelf, musical creche, 9/1356
gifts to make—toy box, coat tree, whale pull toy, wood-block train, dollhouse, train engine, 19/2914
gifts to make—toy kiddie car, 9/1351
gingerbread ornaments, 5/690
glittering ornaments, 5/698
greeting cards, from photos, 5/684
horse ornaments, 5/690
macrame Christmas-tree wall-hanging, 5/698
minitree centerpiece, 5/702
mobile, rainbow, 5/690
plastic tree decorations, 5/702
punch-out ornaments, 5/690
reindeer table decorations, 5/690
rocking chair ornaments, 5/690
rocking chair tree ornaments, 5/702
Santa Claus doorpiece, 5/690
Santa Claus window hanging, 5/702
Santa's candy cane boot ornament, 5/690
'stained glass' window hangings, 5/698
tinsel art tree ornaments, 5/690
toys for tree ornaments, 5/702
train garland, 5/690
tree bulbs, stored in egg cartons, 3/449
tree stand, musical, 4/628
trees, flashcube decorations, 3/389
veneer ornaments for tree, 5/702
wreath window hanging, 5/702
Chrome: *removing water spots on faucets, 5/697*
Chuck keys: *substitutes for, 2/232*
Chucks, setscrew: for metal lathes, 12/1796
Cider presses: how to make, 5/710
Circles
ring turning on metal lathe, 12/1800
scriber compass, 5/716
Circles, wood
cutting on drill press, 7/1040
how to cut with router, 16/2468
jigsaw cutting-guide, 14/2240
made on bandsaw and sander, 7/1001
Circuit interrupters: electrical-shock preventers, 20/3082
Circuits, printed: *soldering guide, 8/1164*
Circular saws
blades, carbide-tipped, 3/349
blades, deburring, 5/724
blades, selecting, 5/722
hardboard cut with carbide-tip blade, 19/2937
maintenance, 15/2310
plywood cutoff jig, 14/2236
portable, bench for, 5/717
portable, selecting and using, 5/726
portable, used as cutoff machine, 6/894
Circus-train pull toy: 15/2348
Circus-wagon toybox: 19/2914
Citizens Band radio
antenna light, 5/737
mounting in car, 5/730
on vacation trips, 5/734
TV interference, stopping, 10/1542
Clamps
adhesives, selecting and using, 1/35
bar clamps, lengthening, 16/2523
bar clamps, making, 5/744
C-clamp holds tiny parts in vise, 15/2397
C-clamp makes radial-arm saw fence stop, 2/291
C-clamp used as bench vise, 16/2560
C-clamps, enlarged for gluing wide work, 10/1581
C-clamps, hold paint can on ladder, 11/1731
C-clamps, used in gluing right angles, 10/1499
double, for photo lamp, 14/2116
file handles, from C-clamps, 3/389
from thread spools, 3/433
gluing plywood panels, 4/553
hose clamp, king-size, 7/1009
hose clamp held open with tape, 16/2560
hose clamps, reinstalling, 11/1644
machine-vise clamp, making, 5/742
made from clothespins, 8/1185
made from wire solder, 9/1322
making one do work of two, 1/119
miter joints clamped with masking tape, 18/2783
mitered joints held while gluing, 17/2664
photo clamp supports camera, 4/521
photolamp clamps, hold moldings in miterbox, 13/2012
selecting and using, 5/738
spring clamps, hold hot tools, 13/2078
tabletop boards held for gluing, 17/2664
Claw hammers: how to use, 5/745
Clay pottery: without potter's wheel, 5/746
Cleats: *for storing appliance cords, clotheslines, 1/119*
Climbers: children's hand-over-hand climber, 1/41
Climbing: exercises to get in shape, 8/1158
Clipboards: *fuse clip holds pencil, 11/1703*
Clocks
grandfather clock, warped access door, 10/1570
grandmother hall clock, 5/754
oiling electric motor, 18/2820
old shelf clock, using alarm, 19/2979
shelf clock, Connecticut, 5/750
soiled dial, cleaning, 16/2523
wall clock, 'heirloom', 5/766
wall clock, plywood face, 5/768
Close-up photos
camerapods for low-level shots, 14/2116
extension tube, adjustable, 14/2116
macro images, 5/785
Closets
belt and necktie holder, 3/416
bookcase closet, 3/405
condensation, preventing, 11/1657
doors, bifold, installing, 5/770
floor 'vault,' for hiding valuables, 16/2558
garage closet for storage, 16/2434
home office built in closet, 18/2794
sewing center, built-in, 17/2601
shoe drawer, roll-out, 17/2651
single closet becomes bookcase, 18/2794
storage, adding to room, 5/774
storage for outdoor equipment, 18/2794
using wasted space, 5/779

vanity built into closet, 18/2794
Cloth tape: inlays for trinket boxes, 10/1537
Clothes dryers
electric, repairing, 5/788
gas, repairing, 5/794
laundry center for kitchen, 10/1464
Clothes trees: giraffe coat tree for children, 19/2914
Clothes washers: see Washing machines
Clotheslines
cleats for storing, 1/119
covering used as tubing, 9/1322
how to tighten, 2/232
tightener stick, 11/1626
Clothespins
calipers, improvised, 5/656
hold darkroom thermometers, 14/2116
hold photo thermometers in bottles, 4/521
marking gauges, 2/232
scoring cardboard for bending, 10/1515
used as clamps, 8/1185
used as memo holders, 3/416
Clothing: stains, removing, 18/2772
Clubs, fish: of PVC pipe, 15/2360
Clutches, auto: noise, diagnosing, 15/2324
Coat closets: stereo-closet room divider, 5/779
Coat hangers: *heavy-duty, 5/748*
Coat racks
children's, freestanding, 5/671
hat shelf and coat rack, of plexiglass, 14/2205
Coat trees: giraffe coat tree for children, 19/2914
Cobbler's bench table lamp: 11/1668
Coffee cans: *used to make small-parts bins, 19/2948*
Coffee jars: *instant coffee spout opening, 5/748*
Coffee percolators: repairing, 5/782
Coffee tables
butcher block design, 3/463
butler's table, 3/472
coffee-table aquarium, 6/810
coffee table-slide viewer, 6/806
for patio, with stools, 6/816
lattice strips decorate, 10/1462
made of plexiglass, 14/2205
nesting tables, four Sheraton replicas, 13/1958
stool table with box stools, 6/804
table matches barbecue bar, 2/171
yard tables, made from chimney blocks, 14/2152
Cold frames: cold frame-hotbed, 6/820
Cold water: hypothermia prevention, 1/24
Colonial design
armchair, cherry wood, 1/102
bell shelf, 9/1356
bookrack, 3/410
bookstand, 3/415
cabinet holds security safe, 3/456
china cupboard, 6/888
clock, shelf, Connecticut, 5/750
comb box, 6/824
cutlery cupboard, 10/1600
desk, trestle, 6/951
dry sink, 7/1050
gossip bench, 9/1365
house number on keymaker's sign, 20/3066
hutch table, 10/1516
lamp, candlestand, 11/1664
letter rack, 11/1712
lowboy, 11/1739
red paint, how to mix, 14/2186
server, 17/2564
serving cart, 17/2570
shaving console, 17/2616
stool, rustic slab, 18/2793
table lamp, cobbler's bench, 11/1668
trestle table with benches, 7/998
weather station, 20/3060
Comb boxes: colonial wall box, 6/824
Combination squares: how to use, 6/825
Combs: *used to space lines in drawing, 16/2502*
Common nails: *countersinking, 10/1495*
Compass dividers
made from scissors, 12/1853
points protected by tubing, 3/480
Compasses, circle-scribing: 5/716
Compound angles: wood, cutting, 1/76
Compressors, air: how to build, 6/826
Computers: TV interference, stopping, 10/1542
Concrete
basement floor, how to paint, 18/2809
basement floor, paint instead of cleaning, 11/1685
basement wall, boring holes, 3/338
basement wall, patching air-bubble holes, 11/1685
basement wall, repairing crumbling concrete, 3/429
coloring, 6/840
driveways, sealing, 19/2889
floor, slippery when wet, correcting, 17/2600
floors, hardboard eliminates cold, 19/2889
form boards cut in chisel shape, 20/3087
foundation walls, cause of paint peeling, 12/1839
foundation walls, preventing efflorescence, 11/1760
fuel-oil stain, removing, 1/65
garden paths and sidewalks, 14/2084
leveling with patches, 5/800
nails, selecting and using, 13/1954
paint spills, removing, 12/1839
painting, 6/840
painting masonry, 12/1778
patching, driveways and sidewalks, 6/844
patching concrete steps, 18/2809
patching with tape, 18/2842
patio-floor cracks, repairing, 16/2533
porch floor, slant for water runoff, 12/1839
powdery surface, cause of, 5/697
retaining walls, how to build, 16/2446
rust stains, removing, 15/2269
sidewalk, patching, 8/1280
slabs, casting, 6/838
slabs, laying out and pouring, 6/834
staining, 6/840
stains, removing, 18/2772
steps, how to build, 18/2790
steps, painting, 4/573
stucco foundation walls, patching cracks, 1/125
varnish, removing spill, 20/3137
working with concrete, 6/830
Concrete blocks
chimney blocks used to make picnic table, 14/2152
how to lay, 6/848
measurements guide, 12/1784
retaining walls, how to build, 16/2446
walls, waterproofing, 3/369
Condensation
aluminum window sashes, remedy, 12/1920
attic skylights, wetness from, 11/1621
attic vents, open in winter, 17/2720
attics, condensation inside roof, 3/338
attics, moisture cause and cure, 19/2937
basements, waterproofing, 2/210
caused by too much insulation, 18/2845
closet moisture, preventing, 11/1657
garage-floor moisture, preventing, 11/1735
moisture on basement floor, 11/1621
preventing moisture in home, 20/3137
preventing on patio door, 12/1821
preventing on storm windows, 15/2381
preventing on windows, 5/697
showers, venting, 5/800
Conditioning, physical
exercises to get in shape, 8/1158
home gym, 6/854
weight bench, 8/1162
Condominiums: *soundproofing, draperies keep out sound, 11/1727*
Conduit, thinwall: used for TV antenna masts, 12/1782
Confetti: *cutting confetti-size paper rectangles, 9/1397*
Connecticut shelf clock: 5/750
Connectors, crimp-on: splicing wires, 7/1072
Connectors, wire: *from copper tubing, 11/1678*
Consoles, shaving: early American cabinet, 17/2616
Constitution, U.S.: cannon model, 4/574
Construction
adding new story over attached garage, 10/1484
adding new story to house, 10/1474
adding wing to house, 10/1476
attic-dormer framing, 1/116
bearing walls, removing, 2/242
cabana poolhouse, 3/476
ceiling height, lowering, 14/2204
concrete blocks, how to lay, 6/848
contractors, choosing, 6/860
decks, 14/2102
decks, two, for front and rear, 14/2098
decks, wooden, 6/920
decks, wooden, 6/914
decks, wooden, two-level, 6/924
energy-saving tips, 7/1090
freestanding wall, 16/2464
garage remodeled into family room, 9/1312
garage remodeled into guest house, 9/1316
garden shelters, 9/1330
garden work shelter, 9/1332
gazebo cookout center, 9/1346
gazebos and screen house, 18/2821
greenhouse addition to home, 1/30
lumber guide, 11/1747
measurements guide, 12/1784
nails, selecting and using, 13/1954
partition walls, framing, 2/200
patio fiberglass roofs, 14/2095
room additions, planning, 1/28
screened porch, 16/2528
sheathing, guide to types, 17/2620
shims, how to use, 17/2638
siding, selecting, 17/2680
stairs, laying out and building, 18/2776
tips on placing new house on lot, 16/2467
Contact-print proofer: *picture-frame easel, 14/2116*
Continuity testers
in screwdriver, 18/2860
testing doorbells, 7/1018
Contour gauges: *copies molding profile, 1/119*
Contoured surfaces: *sanding block, 3/480*
Contractors, home improvement: choosing, 6/860
Control-line airplane models: 12/1886

Converters: photo-slide illuminator, 10/1535
Cookbook caddies: with recipe drawer, 10/1597
Cookbook holders: made of plexiglass, 14/2205
Cookie cutter ornaments: for Christmas, 5/702
Cooking center: mobile barbecue, 12/1865
Cookout bars: on tiled patio, 6/862
Cookout gazebos: backyard entertainment center, 9/1346
Coolant, auto: recovery system, 6/872
Cooling systems, auto
airconditioners, troubleshooting, 1/56
basic auto tune-up, 19/2960
coolant recovery system, 6/872
engine-overheating causes, 6/867
maintenance, 6/868
prewinter maintenance, 20/3074
Copiers: photo-slide illuminator, 10/1535
Copper pipe: working with plumbing pipe, 14/2232
Copper tubing: *used as wire connectors, 11/1678*
Copy frames, photo: *made from enlarging easel, 14/2116*
Copy photography: guide to, 6/874
Copy stands, photo:
holds hand grinder, 8/1259
improvised stand, 14/2116
Cord: *preventing ravelled ends, 6/847*
Cords, appliance
cleats for storing, 1/119
stored in tube, 2/251
Cords, extension
connections, reinforcing, 10/1555
reel, windup, 8/1165
Corner joints: how to make and fit, 10/1576
Corner lounges: for family room, 8/1174
Corrosion: see Rust
Corrugated aluminum roofing: *cutting, 13/2069*
Corrugated cardboard: *scoring for bending, 10/1515*
Cosmic-habitat design: painting unfinished furniture, 13/2039
Cottages: garage remodeled into guest house, 9/1316
Cotter pins: *used as hinges, 13/1936*
Couches: sofa-bed, 18/2726
Counters
laundry splashboard, 5/748
sewing center, 17/2601
wall counter is work-study area, 18/2794
Counters, snack: for family room, 8/1178
Countersinking: *common nails, 10/1495*
Countertops
how to install, 11/1616
island work center for kitchen, 11/1604
plastic laminates, how to apply, 11/1658
plastic laminates, replacing, 1/125
plastic laminates, replacing linoleum, 13/2017
sink, replacing, 11/1608
Cove moldings
cutting on bench saw, 2/268
guide to molding shapes, 12/1901
making on table saw, 17/2664
Cracks
bathtub seams, caulking, 10/1470
concrete patio floor, repairing, 16/2533
concrete sidewalks and driveways, patching, 6/844
cracks between floorboards, how to fill, 5/649
drywall ceiling, repairing, 17/2600
foundation walls, repairing, 2/210
patching radiant-heat-ceiling cracks, 17/2720
plaster cracks, sealing, 18/2845
stucco foundation walls, repairing, 1/125
wall cracks, patching, 10/1470
wall cracks, patching and painting, 13/2046
Cradles, garbage-can: for garden work center, 9/1332
Crafts
bottle cutting, 3/418
candles, from fancy molds, 4/554
candles, molded in snow, 4/560
crucible furnace, making, 6/884
cutting confetti-size paper rectangles, 9/1397
imitation 'stained' glass projects, 18/2759
internal carving with clear plastics, 10/1546
jewelry carving, 10/1556
lapidary, rock polisher, 11/1682
lapidary, rock sorter, 11/1686
marquetry, inlaid-veneer pictures, 12/1772
metal casting, 12/1786
potter's wheel, how to make and use, 15/2302
pottery without potter's wheel, 5/746
stained glass, making, 18/2766
tin-can projects, 18/2875
wood laminating, 11/1652
Crates: *marked with ink-filled glue bottle, 16/2543*
Crawl spaces
ductwork, insulating, 1/95
insulation, how to install, 10/1539
insulation, roofing paper, 13/1947
vents, leave open in winter, 15/2341
Crayons: holder, heart-shaped, 9/1360
Creches: musical Nativity scene, 9/1356
Creosote: *stains on wood-burning stove hearth, 18/2845*
Cribbage: board, pocket, 6/877
Crimp-on connectors: splicing wires, 7/1072
Croquet: yard lighting for game areas, 20/3149
Crosscut saws
cutting firewood, 6/878
handsaw basics, 9/1396
Crosscutting
duplicate pieces, on table saw, 17/2664
wide boards, on table saw, 17/2664
Crown moldings: guide to molding shapes, 12/1901
Crucible furnaces: how to make, 6/884
Cruets: *loosening stuck stopper, 13/2017*
Cube candle stands: wooden, 4/564
Cube stools: for family room, 8/1186
Cube tables: of plexiglass, 14/2205
Cue-and-ball wall rack: 20/3062
Cuff links: carved from wood and plastic, 10/1556
Cupboards
boot cupboard with drip rack, 18/2794
breakfront, built from module, 12/1890
cutlery cupboard, colonial, 10/1600
kitchen storage ideas, 18/2794
Cupboards, china: colonial display cabinet, 6/888
Curio cabinets: etagere, 8/1154
Curtain rods
traverse rods, hanging, 7/1034
used to hang belts, neckties, 3/416
Curves: *drawing irregular curves, 12/1781*
Cutlery
silverware cupboard, colonial, 10/1600
silverware tray, 10/1598
silverware-and-napkin caddy, 10/1594
Cutoff jigs
for bandsaws, 17/2660
for plywood sheets, 14/2236
Cutoff machines
how to make, 6/892
made from portable circular saw, 6/894
Cutoff saws
how to make, 6/892
made from portable circular saw, 6/894
Cutters: sheet-metal cutter, 6/899
Cutters, molding: storage holder, 12/1900
Cutters, paper: *paper held with wood rule, 11/1703*
Cutting boards
for kitchen-cabinet drawer, 11/1612
glass-cutting board for shop wall, 12/1781
kitchen accessory, 10/1596
multipurpose, for shop and darkroom, 6/900
of plexiglass, 14/2205
Cutting torches: propane-torch stand, 19/2905
Cylinders
banding round objects, 6/934
large drum supported by roller skates, 18/2783

D

Dachshund pull toy: 15/2352
Dado joints: making and using, 10/1571
Dadoes
duplicating, on table saw, 17/2664
how to cut with router, 16/2468
sawing on bench saw, 2/268
Dams, ice: preventing on roofs, 17/2717
Danny Dachshund pull toy: 15/2352
Darkrooms
chemicals mixed in plastic bucket, 4/513
coaster for developer beaker, 14/2116
developing goofs, avoiding, 7/970
developing tray, rod for rocking, 4/521
dishpans used for print processing, 4/513
enlarging-lens storage rack, 14/2116
hands dried with hair dryer, 4/521
knee switch, for print-inspection light, 14/2116
photo-chemical depletion chart, 4/521
portable, for apartments, 6/904
portable, in a suitcase, 6/910
roll-away, for bathrooms, 6/908
safelight, on pull-down reel, 14/2116
shelf fits laundry tub, 14/2116
thermometer held by clothespin, 14/2116
thermometer held in bottles with clothespin, 4/521
thermometer holder, 14/2116
toolholder, 4/513
weatherstripping used as door light seal, 14/2116
Dashed lines: *drawn with notebook cover, 13/2028*
Deburring: blades, circular saws, 5/724
Decals: *removing decal residue, 16/2523*
Deck boats: pontoon boat with surrey top, 15/2252
Decks
accessories and structures to build, 14/2110
benches, wood, 2/264
carpeting, outdoor, 4/592
coffee table, with stools, 6/816
diving deck, for above-ground swimming pool, 18/2832
fence, louvered, 15/2336
how to build, 14/2102
insect trap, black-light, 10/1538
masonry, painting, 12/1778
multilevel platforms, 6/920
planters and wine rack, 14/2106

privacy screens, 15/2334
roof leak, pinpointing, 12/1821
rooftop patio, 14/2094
rotted wood, repairing, 15/2269
swimming-pool deck and privacy wall, 15/2280
two decks, for front and rear, 14/2098
wood platforms, how to build, 6/920
wood platforms, how to build, 6/914
wood platforms, two-level, 6/924

Decorations, Christmas
for table and tree, 5/702
for tree and home, 5/690
trimmings, old-fashioned, 5/698

Decorative edges: how to cut with router, 16/2468

Deer: keeping out of gardens, 19/3038

Dents
furniture, repairing, 8/1208
furniture, repairing, 9/1302

Dents, auto body: repairing, 1/130

Design engraver: how to make, 16/2544

Desk accessories
bookrack, carousel, 3/412
calculator stand, 4/511
drill-bit holder, 6/932
mail organizer, 20/3062
pen and pencil holder, 6/932
pen-and-pencil caddy, 13/2078
stamp and pencil holder, 6/931

Desks
bunk bed-desk, children's, 5/668
campaign desk, 7/964
chest, opens into work center, 6/935
desk-hobby bench, built from module, 12/1890
drawers, how to make, 7/1036
hinged, folds against wall, 6/935
home office built in closet, 18/2794
leather top, cleaning and finishing, 3/369
modules from kitchen cabinets, 4/484
rolltop, 6/954
rolltop desk and chair, children's, 5/676
study center, wall-hung, 18/2818
suspended from storage wall, 18/2794
trestle desk, colonial, 6/951
two-level, with secretary return, 6/935
wall-hung, for children, 5/672

Detectors, smoke: choosing, 1/66

De-thatching machines: using on lawns, 11/1698

Developing, photo
chemicals mixed in plastic bucket, 4/513
coaster for developer beaker, 14/2116
color prints, plastic 'ferrotype', 14/2116
darkroom goofs, avoiding, 7/970
darkroom-timer beeper, 14/2116
darkrooms, in a suitcase, 6/910
darkrooms, portable, 6/904
darkrooms, roll-away, for bathrooms, 6/908
developing tray, rod for rocking, 4/521
dishpans used for print processing, 4/513
knee switch, for print-inspection light, 14/2116
mini-reel, for small film, 14/2116
muddy prints, curing, 15/2330
photo dryers, using hair dryers, 14/2116
photo-chemical depletion chart, 4/521
plastic bottle used to fill developing tank, 14/2116
print dryer, heated, 7/1056
shelf fits laundry tub, 14/2116
tape marks loaded film tank, 14/2116
thermometer grip made from eraser, 14/2116
thermometer held by clothespin, 14/2116
thermometer held in bottles with clothespin, 4/521
thermometer holder, 14/2116
timer-knob grip made from eraser, 14/2116
toolholder for darkroom, 4/513

Dieseling, auto
causes, 13/1971
how to stop, 7/974

Differentials, auto
noise, diagnosing, 15/2324
troubleshooting, 7/978

Diffusion: special effects dramatize photos, 14/2144

Dimmers, light
dimmer switch, installing, 10/1464
for photo enlarger, 14/2116

Dining room furniture
breakfront, built from module, 12/1890
china cupboard, colonial, 6/888
dining table, gateleg, 7/983
dining table, oaken, 7/987
dining table, trestle, with benches, 7/998
dining table, trestle, with swivel chairs, 7/992
hutch table, 10/1516
lowboy, colonial, 11/1739

Dining rooms: *buffet cabinet built in wall, 16/2434*

Dining tables
gateleg, folding, 7/983
hutch table, early American, 10/1516
oaken, pedestal, 7/987
trestle, colonial, with benches, 7/998
trestle table with swivel chairs, 7/992

Dinner-bell shelves: colonial, 9/1356

Disc brakes
replacing pads, 3/446
troubleshooting, 3/438

Disc sanders
abrasives, selecting and using, 1/20
cleaning clogged discs, 12/1835
discs cut with dividers, 2/251
how to build, 16/2500
used to make wood discs, 7/1001

Discs, wood
cutting on bandsaws, 1/154
cutting on drill press, 7/1040
drilling holes in circumference, 17/2664
how to cut with router, 16/2468
jigsaw cutting-guide, 14/2240
made on bandsaw and sander, 7/1001
rabbeting on table saw, 17/2664
saucer cavity, cut on table saw, 17/2660

Dishes
cut from bottles, 3/418
wood saucer, cutting on table saw, 17/2660

Dishes, snack: wood carving project, 4/604

Dishpans: *used for photo-print processing, 4/513*

Dishwashers
at counter level, 3/454
built-in, 11/1608
cabinet, 13/1948
repairing, 7/1002

Dispensers, stamp: for desk, 6/931

Displays, photo
montages, how to make, 12/1910
mountings, photo-print, 13/1930
mountings, 3-D, 13/1934

Disposers, garbage
installing, 9/1323
installing, 11/1608
repairing, 9/1326

Distress signals: boating emergencies, 3/365

Distributors, auto
basic auto tune-up, 19/2960
how they work, 10/1524
ignition cables, testing and replacing, 10/1528
maintenance, 7/1010
prewinter maintenance, 20/3074
servicing, 10/1525

Dividers
made from scissors, 12/1853
points protected by tubing, 3/480

Dividers, drawer: *diagonal, 6/887*

Dividers, room
archway, translucent panels, 8/1148
bedroom divider-wall, 16/2434
bookcase closet, 3/405
built from module, 12/1890
cabinet with lighted planter, 14/2172
closet, peninsula unit, 5/779
divider-storage walls, 16/2459
double-decker bunk beds, 18/2794
folding screen for photo displays, 14/2116
for family room, 8/1186
freestanding wall, how to build, 16/2464
freestanding wall, light fixture, 16/2462
modules from kitchen cabinets, 4/484
multipurpose storage wall, 18/2794
shelves at foot of stairs, 18/2794
zodiac panel, hanging, 18/2759

Dividers, view
grille fence, 15/2334
louvered fence, 15/2336
louvered screen, 15/2334
privacy wall with storage, 18/2794
redwood privacy screen, 14/2110

Diving, skin
basic techniques, 17/2692
underwater-photos guide, 19/2980

Diving decks: for above-ground swimming pool, 18/2832

Dock hanger lines: of PVC pipe, 15/2360

Dock ladders: of PVC pipe, 15/2360

Dog pull toy: 15/2352

Dogs
doghouse, low-radiant heat, 15/2269
obedience training, 7/1014

Dollhouses
English farmhouse, 19/2914
miniature house, 12/1830

Dollies
for bench saw, 18/2784
for shop vacuum cleaners, 19/3032

Doodling engravers: scriber, how to make, 16/2544

Door chimes: wiring, 10/1464

Doorbells
changing to chimes, 10/1464
testing and repairing, 7/1018

Doors
autos, wind noise and water leaks, stopping, 11/1706
bifold, installing, 5/770
bifold doors, casing hides track, 16/2434
bolt latch, improvised, 10/1555
bumpers, from toothpaste caps, 7/982
burglar proofing tips, 3/460
casing miters, stopping shrinkage and expansion, 15/2341
darkroom door light seal, 14/2116
finish, for exterior door, 3/429
frames, how to set, 7/1022
framing with drip-cap molding, 16/2434
hinges, selecting, 10/1450
hinges, tightening, 7/1024
how to hang, 7/1022
interior, types of, 7/1022
kitchen cabinets, making door bumpers, 5/765
locks, burglar proofing your home, 16/2547
lockset, installing, 11/1732
lubrication guide, 11/1744
mail-slot awning, 17/2697
measurements guide, 12/1784

moldings, decorating ideas, 12/1904
patio door, preventing moisture inside, 12/1821
piggyback door shelves, 4/492
pulls, made from metal tubing, 19/2956
restyling with translucent panels, 8/1148
screen doors, aluminum, repairing, 18/2810
screen doors, spring corrects sagging, 11/1626
shrinking and swelling, stopping, 12/1864
sliding glass doors, adding, 16/2430
sliding glass doors, installing, 17/2706
sticking, how to trim and plane, 7/1024
sticking doors, fixing, 10/1470
storm doors, aluminum, repairing, 18/2810
storm doors, repairing split in wood, 15/2341
storm doors, stopping heat loss, 20/3078
trimming bottom with handsaw, 17/2664
water marks from flood, eliminating, 6/847
weatherstrip, preventing noise from wind, 5/765
won't swing when hinge pins are bent, 17/2697

Dormers: attic dormers, framing, 1/116
Dotted lines: *drawn with notebook cover, 13/2028*
Double exposures: *taking on 35-mm cameras, 14/2116*
Dovetail joints
drawers, how to make, 7/1036
how to cut with router, 16/2468
how to make, 7/1026
Dowel joints: how to make, 10/1572
Dowels
cutting into pins, 5/656
dowel joints, how to make, 10/1572
drilling, on drill press, 7/1040
end-drilling in lathe, 12/1835
fitting tightly in holes, 3/433
glue dowels, with spiral kerfs, 17/2660
guide for drilling holes, 17/2673
storage racks, 5/778
used as inside-curve sanders, 14/2155
used to make camera unipod, 14/2116
Downspouts
cleaning, repairing, maintenance, 9/1390
drainage pipe from cinder blocks, 10/1495
drainage system, underground, 7/1030
installing, 9/1384
snow-melting systems, 17/2717
splash block, reversed, 1/150
splash blocks, installing, 9/1390
water runoff ideas, 2/210
Drafting instruments: *holder for templates and triangles, 14/2240*
Dragonfly mirror: 'stained' glass project, 18/2759
Drainage: *drain pipe from cinder blocks, 10/1495*
Drainage systems: for downspouts, underground, 7/1030
Drains
frozen, thawing, 7/1032
how to unclog, 7/1032
plumbing repairs, 14/2216
Draperies: *shutters cloth-covered to match draperies, 16/2434*
Drapery hooks: selecting, 7/1034
Drapery rods: traverse rods, hanging, 7/1034
Drawers
cutting board on kitchen-cabinet drawer, 11/1612
divider, diagonal, 6/887
false bottom hides valuables, 16/2558
how to make, 7/1036
joints, how to make and fit, 10/1576
joints, rabbet and dado, 10/1571
kitchen-knife storage, 11/1612
kitchen-pan storage, 11/1612
knobs, held with sandpaper 'washer', 3/449
lubrication guide, 11/1744
pulls, from paper fasteners, 3/416
pulls, made from metal tubing, 19/2956
pulls, painting, 8/1259
pulls, turning rings on metal lathe, 12/1800
razor blades stored safely, 11/1626
shoe drawer, roll-out, 17/2651
stacked to make bookcase, 19/2948
stick when part way open, 11/1727
storage, dust-free, for shop parts, 5/689
tacks make drawers slide easily, 16/2467
worn runner, repairing, 7/1023
Drawing
circle scriber, 5/716
comb used to space lines, 16/2502
combination square, using, 6/825
curve, using laminate strip, 12/1781
dotted lines with notebook cover, 13/2028
ellipses, 2/251
lines scribed with combination square, 18/2783
parallel lines, with taped ballpoint refills, 9/1322
pattern transfers, using newspapers, 6/887
Drawing boards: foldaway hobby center, 10/1454
Drawing tables: lightbox built in table, 11/1723
Dresser-top valets
jewel box and overnight caddy, 10/1567
overnight organizer, 9/1352
Drill bits: holder, for workshop, 6/932
Drill presses
angled holes, 1/78
angled holes, drilling, 7/1040
bar stock, drilling, 7/1040
cabinet-stand, 15/2316
clamp, machine-vise, making, 5/742
column stop for table, 4/584
depth gauge, making easy to read, 13/2028
discs and holes, cutting, 7/1040
dowel used as inside-curve sander, 14/2155
dowels, drilling, 7/1040
holes, boring edgewise through board, 17/2660
holes, drilling equally spaced, 7/1040
holes punched in paper, 5/778
maintenance, 15/2310
miniature, from copy stand, 8/1259
rods, marking centers, 7/1040
routing on drill press, 7/1040
sanding drum, using, 7/1040
screw plugs, cutting, 7/1040
screw pockets for tabletops, 17/2664
table, leveling, 4/584
table lifter, 11/1719
techniques for using, 7/1040
V-block, making, 17/2670
wood discs, drilling in circumference, 17/2664
work kept from spinning, 2/251
Drilling
angled holes, 1/78
angled holes, with doweling jig, 10/1515
centered hole through rod, 3/480
cup catches overhead-drilling dust, 3/480
dowel holes, 17/2673
mortises, drilling a row, 2/179
rivets, removing, 1/34
techniques on drill press, 7/1040
Drills
boring holes from both sides, 17/2664
cup catches overhead-drilling dust, 3/480
turned by chuck and faucet handle, 9/1335
Drills, portable electric
accessories, 15/2291
angled holes, 1/78
basics, 7/1045
bits and attachments, 15/2292
cotton swab for delicate polishing, 17/2639
dowel used as inside-curve sander, 14/2155
drill stand, rolling, 15/2322
drill-bit holder, 12/1853
hanging for storage, 9/1322
maintenance, 15/2310
using with accessories, 7/1046
Drills, twist
how to sharpen, 19/2976
stored in jar, 2/251
Drip-cap molding: *used to frame door, 16/2434*
Drive belts, auto: maintenance, 2/262
Drive trains, auto: differentials, troubleshooting, 7/978
Drivers, stud: *improvised from matching nut, 18/2738*
Driveways
asphalt, patching and resurfacing, 1/112
concrete, coloring, 6/840
concrete, patching, 6/844
concrete slabs, laying out and pouring, 6/834
form boards cut in chisel shape, 20/3087
sealing, 19/2889
snow-melting systems, 17/2717
snowblowers, using properly, 17/2712
snowplow, for auto bumper, 18/2724
working with concrete, 6/830
Driving, auto
blizzards, surviving in car, 3/351
CB radio, on vacation trips, 5/734
gas mileage, improving, 1/134
tire chains, selecting and using, 4/638
Driving, recreational vehicles: safe-driving tips, 16/2404
Drop-leaf tables: cutting joints with router, 16/2468
Drowning: hypothermia prevention, 1/24
Drum brakes
checkout inspection and road test, 3/434
overhauling, 3/440
troubleshooting, 3/438
Drum sanders
contouring furniture legs, 17/2664
how to build, 16/2500
Drums: *supported by roller skates, 18/2783*
Dry irons: how to repair, 10/1548
Dry rot: *preventing in damp basements, 11/1735*
Dry sinks: colonial chest, 7/1050
Dry-cell batteries
guide to types, 2/233
tester-recharger, 2/237
Dryers, clothes
electric, repairing, 5/788
gas, repairing, 5/794
laundry center for kitchen, 10/1464
Dryers, food: how to make, 7/1054
Dryers, lumber: solar kiln, 10/1593
Dryers, photo
print dryer, heated, 7/1056
using hair dryers, 14/2116

Drywall
crack in ceiling, repairing, 17/2600
holes, patching, 7/1058
nails, selecting and using, 13/1954
repairing with tape, 18/2842
Drywells: *removing excess yard water, 3/429*
Duck, of laminated wood: 11/1652
Duck pull toys: 15/2352
Ducks: calling wild game, 10/1512
Dump trucks, toy: wooden, 7/1059
Dust covers: *for photo enlarger, 14/2116*

E

Early American design
armchair, cherry wood, 1/102
bell shelf, 9/1356
bookrack, 3/410
bookstand, 3/415
cabinet holds security safe, 3/456
china cupboard, 6/888
clock, shelf, Connecticut, 5/750
comb box, 6/824
cutlery cupboard, 10/1600
desk, trestle, 6/951
dry sink, 7/1050
gossip bench, 9/1365
house number on keymaker's sign, 20/3066
hutch table, 10/1516
lamp, candlestand, 11/1664
letter rack, 11/1712
lowboy, 11/1739
red paint, how to mix, 14/2186
server, 17/2564
serving cart, 17/2570
shaving console, 17/2616
stool, rustic slab, 18/2793
table lamp, cobbler's bench, 11/1668
trestle table, 7/998
weather station, 20/3060
Earrings: carved from wood and plastic, 10/1556
Easels
enlarger, for big enlargements, 14/2116
enlarger, used as copy frame, 14/2116
enlarging easel, wall storage, 14/2116
miniature easels, 12/1889
proofer, photo, 14/2116
Eavestroughs
aluminum gutters, soldering, 1/125
cleaning, repairing, maintenance, 9/1390
drainage system, for downspouts, 7/1030
installing, 9/1384
snow-melting systems, 17/2717
Edge joints: how to make and fit, 10/1576
Edges, decorative: how to cut with router, 16/2468
Edges, plywood: how to hide, 14/2238
Efflorescence: *preventing on foundation walls, 11/1760*
Egg cartons: *used as toolboxes, 11/1703*
'Eggs,' plastic: used for small-parts storage, 17/2709
EGR systems, auto
servicing, 4/610
valve servicing, 7/1088
Electric appliances: see Appliances
Electric clothes dryers: repairing, 5/788
Electric irons: how to repair, 10/1548
Electric motors
guide to shop motors, 13/1924
metal lathes, silencing pulley bearing, 13/2069
repairing shop motors, 13/1926
speed reducer, 13/1929
Electric tools: see Tools, portable electric; Tools, power
Electric water heaters: maintenance and repair, 9/1410
Electrical equipment: *vacuum-cleaner tube for hard-to-reach places, 10/1499*
Electrical outlets
dummy, for hiding valuables, 16/2558
ground-fault circuit interrupters, 20/3082
grounded-outlet checker, 5/657
instant, in BX cable, 4/553
Electrical power
blackouts, coping with, 3/344
home emergencies, outdoor gear aids, 7/1085
Electrical switches
dimmer switch, installing, 10/1464
light switches, replacing, 10/1470
Electrical systems, auto
alternators, repair, 1/70
batteries, tester, 2/240
how they work, 10/1524
ignition cables, testing and replacing, 10/1528
Electrical wiring
basics of home wiring, 7/1060
checking in old house, 3/369
connectors, from copper tubing, 11/1678
continuity tester, in screwdriver, 18/2860
dimmer switch, installing, 10/1464
doorbells, testing and repairing, 7/1018
door chimes, wiring, 10/1464
dust catcher for sawing holes in walls, 2/179
extension cords, windup reel, 8/1165
fluorescent lamps, troubleshooting, 8/1250
ground-fault circuit interrupters, 20/3082
grounded-outlet checker, 5/657
house numbers, how to illuminate, 10/1487
kitchen light fixtures, installing, 11/1728
light switches, replacing, 10/1470
night lighting beautifies yard, 20/3144
outlet box, instant, 4/553
post lamp, installing and wiring, 15/2296
post lamp, installing and wiring, 10/1464
post lamp, mercury vapor, 15/2298
soldering tips, 18/2743
spade lugs made from chain, 13/2012
wire insulation, how to peel off, 1/150
wires, crimp-on connectors, 7/1072
yard lighting for game areas, 20/3149
Electrical-shock preventers: ground-fault circuit interrupters, 20/3082
Electronic ignition systems, auto
servicing, 10/1532
troubleshooting, 7/1075
Electronics
amplifier for transistor radios, 1/74
antennas, repair and maintenance, 18/2848
antennas, TV, putting up, 1/86
audio mixers, choosing and using, 12/1856
burglar proofing your home, 16/2547
cassette recorders, repairing, 4/598
cassette tapes, repairing, 4/602
CB radio, antenna light, 5/737
CB radio, mounting in car, 5/730
CB radio, on vacation trips, 5/734
hi-fi center, swiveling, 10/1444
hi-fi open rack, 10/1448
hi-fi stereo wall, 4/488
mobile hi-fi cart, 12/1865
speakers, auto, installing, 18/2753
stereo cables, identification tags, 5/778
television antennas, choosing, 1/82
television interference, stopping, 10/1542
wiring, how to solder, 18/2743
Ellipses: *drawing, 2/251*
Emergencies
blackouts, coping with, 3/344
blizzards, surviving in car, 3/351
boating, how to handle, 3/361
boating, towing practices, 3/365
fire extinguishers, selecting and using, 8/1218
home disasters, outdoor gear aids, 7/1085
Emissions controls, auto
basic auto tune-up, 19/2960
servicing, 4/610
servicing, 7/1088
End grain: planed on jointer, 10/1582
End tables
from kitchen cabinets, 4/484
lamp table, with lighted planter, 14/2172
nesting party tables, 13/2070
pedestal table, 13/1978
sewing cabinet, chairside, 17/2582
tambour table, French Provincial, 13/1974
trisected table of plexiglass, 14/2205
Energy
cutting home energy costs, 7/1093
energy-saving when building, 7/1090
fireplace cover saves energy, 12/1820
heat pumps, how they work, 9/1404
lower ceiling height, advantages, 14/2204
roof color, black or white?, 15/2269
solar hot-water heaters, 9/1416
Engines, auto
basic tune-up procedure, 19/2960
dieseling, causes, 13/1971
dieseling, how to stop, 7/974
hesitation problems, solving, 7/1100
lubricating, 11/1740
misfiring, troubleshooting, 12/1846
missing engine, curing, 7/1112
noise, diagnosing, 15/2324
noises, diagnosing, 13/1971
noises, stopping, 13/1967
oil consumption, diagnosing, 12/1912
overhauling engine, 8/1124
stalling problems, solving, 7/1100
stalls, stopping, 18/2780
starting problems, solving, 7/1100
surging, curing, 7/1112
Engines, gasoline: small, servicing, 8/1128
Engines, small
mowers, preparing for mowing season, 13/1937
mowers, repair and maintenance, 13/1944
servicing, 8/1128
Engines, toy train: puffs 'smoke', 19/2914
English-farmhouse dollhouse: 19/2914
Engravers, doodling: scriber, how to make, 16/2544
Enlarging, photo
easel for big enlargements, 14/2116
easel used as copy frame, 14/2116
enlarger dust cover, 14/2116
enlarging easel, wall storage, 14/2116
enlarging-lens storage rack, 14/2116
hands dried with hair dryer, 4/521
light dimmer, 14/2116
negatives, covering scratches, 4/521
test strips, kept in box lid, 14/2116
Entertainment centers
family room built-in, 8/1170
hi-fi center, swiveling, 10/1444
hi-fi open rack, 10/1448
mobile hi-fi cart, 12/1865
Entertainment wall: modules from kitchen cabinets, 4/484
Entryways
archway, translucent panels, 8/1148
bench for boot storage, 16/2434
entry revamping with landscaping, 8/1140
pier set, filigree, 14/2162
quarry tile, installing, 15/2362
room divider-storage wall, 16/2459
window decorated with leaf-grille,

16/2434
Erasers
grip for photo thermometers, 14/2116
grip for photo-timer knobs, 14/2116
polisher for metal lathe, 8/1164
Erasing shields: *made from film, 1/61*
Etageres
curio cabinet, 8/1154
hi-fi open rack, 10/1448
Evergreen lights: low yard lamp, 15/2301
Evergreens
choosing trees for your yard, 19/2952
how to transplant, 19/2942
landscaping techniques, 11/1679
Exercising
exercises to get in shape, 8/1158
hand mowers keep you in shape, 9/1394
home gym, 6/854
weight bench, 8/1162
Exhaust systems, auto
catalytic converters, servicing, 4/610
replacing, 8/1166
Expandable vacation home: built in three stages, 19/3016
Expansion bolts: fasteners, types and sizes, 8/1193
Exposure meters: night photography tips, 13/1963
Extension cords
connections, reinforcing, 10/1555
reel, windup, 8/1165
Extension ladders
choosing, 11/1645
hook holds paint can, 11/1731
using safely, 11/1650
Extension-spring overhead garage doors: maintenance, 9/1308
Exterminating: *do-it-yourself devices, 18/2845*
Extinguishers, fire: selecting and using, 8/1218
Eye droppers: *used to plant seeds, 19/2989*
Eyeglasses
case holds gardening tools, 13/2028
case used to store small tools, 16/2502

F

F-15: airplane model, 12/1886
F-105: airplane model, 12/1886
Fabrics: stains, removing, 18/2772
Faceplate lathes: how to make wood lathe, 20/3100
Faceplates: wood-lathe turning basics, 20/3106
Faceting: on bench saw, 2/268
Family photos: tips on candid photos, 4/565
Family rooms
bar, 'antiqued', 2/188
bar, mobile, with running water, 12/1865
bar, under basement heat pipes, 2/185
barbecue bar, 2/171
basement remodeling ideas, 8/1182
basements, remodeling, 8/1186
cooking center, mobile, 12/1865
decorating ideas, five, 8/1178
decorating ideas, four, 8/1174
game table, circular, 9/1304
grill, portable electric, 9/1370
hi-fi music center, mobile, 12/1865
mini projection booth, 18/2794
remodeled from garage, 9/1312
remodeled from sun porch, 8/1170
remodeling and adding to old house, 16/2421
remodeling ideas, 2/198
Fans
attics, how to cool, 1/120
attics, using, 1/46
Farmhouse dollhouse: 19/2914
Fast-set door locks: installing, 11/1732
Fasteners
bolts, selecting and using, 3/393
bolts and nails, cut without damage, 4/501
nails, blind nailing, 12/1904
nails, caddy with carrying handle, 10/1581
nails, countersinking, 10/1495
nails, headless, how to pull, 2/179
nails, overhead, starting, 2/179
nails, selecting and using, 13/1954
nailset, from masonry nail, 11/1626
nuts, use Allen hex-wrench in tight quarters, 11/1644
Pop rivets, banding round objects, 6/934
Pop-rivet stems, used as headless nails, 4/640
scaffold nails, from Pop rivets, 8/1192
screw anchors, removing from wall, 17/2600
screws, choosing the right one, 16/2540
screws, cutting plugs on drill press, 7/1040
screws, dowels help to hold, 3/480
screws, pilot hole made by scaffold nail, 13/1936
screws, starting in tight spots, 8/1164
setscrews, made from bolts, 6/819
setscrews, tightened by file tang, 13/2079
staple guns, raised with blocks, 8/1164
staplers, inch marks on side, 5/656
tabletop fastener, concealed, 4/553
tacks, holder for driving, 2/291
toggle bolts anchor tall cabinets, 18/2820
traverse rods, hanging, 7/1034
wall fasteners, types and sizes, 8/1193
Faucets
bathroom plumbing repairs, 1/157
buzzing noise, cause of, 14/2105
compression faucet, how to reassemble, 5/697
dripping faucets, repair, 10/1470
handle turns taps or drills, 9/1335
leaky single-lever faucet, repairing, 11/1657
plumbing repairs, 14/2216
washer seats, resurfacing, 13/1947
water spots on chrome, removing, 5/697
Feeders, bird
automatic feeder, 3/332
bird photos, through-window, 3/339
four-station feeder, 3/331
made from scraps, 13/2079
Felling trees: correct method, 19/2954
Felt
used for pads, washers, gaskets, 13/2078
used to make lacquer applicator, 9/1322
Fenceposts: how to set, 8/1202
Fences
eight designs, how to build, 8/1202
fence niche planter, 14/2178
fiberglass fences, building, 14/2095
gates, how to build, 15/2336
gates, latch, windproof, 5/778
gates, self-closing, 3/416
grille fence, 14/2110
grille privacy screen, 15/2334
hiding fences with climbing plants, 16/2533
louvered fence, 15/2336
louvered screen, 15/2334
with built-in toolhouse, 8/1199
Ferrotypes: *plastic 'ferrotype' for color prints, 14/2116*
Fertilizers: lawn improvement, 11/1688
Fiberboard: *walls, how to paint, 15/2341*
Fiberglass
boats, repairing, 16/2442
panels, sealing surface, 12/1864
panels solve window problem, 16/2434
patio roof, building, 14/2095
repairing with tape, 18/2842
shingles, vs. wood or asphalt, 1/45
Fieldstone walls: how to build, 16/2446
Filament tape: *aids in gluing, 11/1678*
Files
filing on a lathe, 12/1804
handles, improvised, 3/389
handles, making, 17/2670
metal finishes for lathe projects, 12/1808
sharpening, 17/2608
tang enlarges sheet-metal holes, 9/1297
tang tightens setscrews, 13/2079
Filigree archways: entryway, restyling, 8/1148
Filigree pier set: 14/2162
Fillers, wood: using, 8/1208
Film
cartridges, 35-mm, loading, 4/596
data sheet kept in camera case, 14/2116
developing goofs, avoiding, 7/970
film holder for gadget bag, 14/2116
film-type reminder for camera, 14/2116
kept cool in insulated jug, 14/2116
mini-reel, for developing small film, 14/2116
negatives, storing in envelopes, 14/2116
stencils made from film, 1/61
tape marks loaded developing tank, 14/2116
Filters, auto: oil filters, changing, 11/1740
Filters, furnace: cleaning, 9/1430
Filters, photo: improving photos, 8/1206
Filters, swimming pool: above-ground pool filter, 18/2831
Finger joints: cutting on table saw, 17/2660
Finishes, wood
abrasives, selecting and using, 1/20
applicator made from felt, 9/1322
'blooming' finish, removing, 13/1947
dark finish, lightening, 11/1657
doors, eliminating water marks from flood, 6/847
doors, exterior, weather-proof finish, 3/429
furniture, repairing scratches, 9/1302
furniture refinishing, 8/1208
guide to wood finishing, 20/3094
new wood, finishing to look old, 8/1280
piano, refinishing, 8/1280
picture frames, how to make, 8/1264
plywood finishing, 15/2244
red paint, for colonial furnishings, 14/2186
remover needs time to 'work', 14/2186
sanding techniques, 16/2503
scrapers, how to use, 16/2526
scratches, hiding, 10/1470
shoe-polish finish, 9/1397
spindles, tool to scrape off finish, 11/1621
staining, basic techniques, 18/2770
varnish, can shouldn't be shaken, 12/1839
varnish, how to use, 19/3033
varnish, preventing bubbles, 8/1280
varnish, stir don't shake, 13/1947
veneer patches, matching old finish, 4/544
wood-grain finish, simulating, 8/1208
wood-lathe application, 20/3106
working properties of common woods, 20/3122
Finishing, metal
filing on a lathe, 12/1804
finishing lathe projects, 12/1808
Finishing nails: *nailset, from masonry nail, 11/1626*

Finishing sanders
choosing and using, 13/2020
sanding techniques, 16/2503
stand for mounting sander, 13/2024
Fire alarms
home protection guide, 16/2547
smoke detectors, choosing, 1/66
Fire extinguishers: selecting and using, 8/1218
Fireman's pole: children's A-frame swing set, 1/41
Firepits: circular brick firepit, 8/1222
Fireplaces
chimney flue, how to clean, 11/1685
cover, how to build, 12/1820
dampers, proper length, 16/2523
energy costs, cutting, 7/1093
fires, smokeless, 8/1224
firewood, how to cut, 8/1229
firewood, insects in, 14/2186
firewood, wood borers in, 11/1727
flue, cleaning smoke shelf, 15/2269
gas logs cause moisture in flue, 11/1727
heater-furnace, 9/1430
how to use, 8/1229
inserts, 9/1419
jamb hook holds fire tools, 14/2186
log bin, 8/1178
mantel, correcting warping, 5/709
prefab, enclosing, 8/1226
prefab, faced with ceramic tile, 10/1468
prefab, selecting, 9/1419
raised hearth, 8/1178
smoke stains on brick, removing, 3/369
stopping home heat loss, 20/3078
woodbox next to fireplace, 8/1228
Fires: *valuables protected in refrigerator, 9/1397*
Firewood
bucksaw, how to build, 16/2517
chain saws, using and repairing, 4/632
cutting and stacking, 11/1736
how to cut, 8/1229
how to stack fireplace logs, 19/2954
insects hide in firewood, 14/2186
log bin, for fireplace, 8/1178
logs held inside tires for splitting, 19/2989
sawbuck, how to make, 11/1736
sawbuck handles long logs, 16/2509
using crosscut saws, 6/878
wood borers unlikely in wood, 11/1727
woodbox next to fireplace, 8/1228
Fish clubs: of PVC pipe, 15/2360
Fish pond bridge: with planter boxes, 14/2178
Fisheye photos: special effects for pictures, 14/2144
Fishing
bait can, double-ended, 6/819
club, fish, of PVC pipe, 15/2360
drowning, hypothermia prevention, 1/24
fly-casting instructions, 8/1254
fly-fishing poppers, making, 4/609
ice fishing, horn blows when fish strikes, 10/1521
ice fishing, rod, 10/1521
keychain cork won't sink in water, 10/1555
knots, how to tie, 11/1640
map reading, 12/1764
Fishing tackle
baitfish lures, how to make, 11/1755
choosing gear, 8/1232
fly-fishing poppers, making, 4/609
hooks carried in matchbook, 18/2820
horn blows when fish strikes, ice fishing, 10/1521
rod, fits suitcase, 8/1234
rod, ice-fishing, 10/1521
spoons, how to make, 11/1752
Flagstaffs: of PVC pipe, 15/2360
Flagstone walls: how to build, 16/2446
Flagstones: *sealing, 16/2557*
Flamed candle stands: wooden cubes, 4/564
Flash photos
bounce-flash photos, 3/425
filter for electronic flash, 14/2116
flashgun, stand for, 14/2116
taking good flash pictures, 14/2142
Flashband: aluminum-faced tape repairs, 18/2842
Flashcubes: *decorate Christmas tree, 3/389*
Flashing: *leak, repairing, 12/1864*
Flashlights: *rubber ball protects lens, 8/1192*
Flat iron: *twisting without bends, 17/2639*
Flat roofs: *tar roof, applying new roof, 18/2752*
Flatpod: *camerapod for low-level close-ups, 14/2116*
Floater frames: making picture frames, 8/1277
Floods: outdoor gear aids, 7/1085
Floor lamps: candlestand lamp, 11/1664
Floor tile
applying over old wide boards, 5/765
basement, needs waterproof adhesive, 15/2341
basement floor, flooded, 16/2533
how to install, 18/2866
mud-set tile, laying, 8/1245
resetting, 10/1470
stains, removing, 18/2772
underlayment, how to install, 8/1237
varnish spill, not removable, 14/2105
Floors
basement, how to paint, 18/2809
basement, installing sheet flooring over tile, 4/544
basement, tile needs waterproof adhesive, 15/2341
basement concrete floor, paint instead of cleaning, 11/1685
basement tile floor, flooded, 16/2533
basements, removing fuel-oil stain, 1/65
carpeting, remove before installing sheet flooring, 14/2204
carpeting, removing stuck backing from hardwood floor, 18/2752
concrete, hardboard eliminates cold, 19/2889
concrete, slippery when wet, correcting, 17/2600
concrete floor, leveling with patches, 5/800
cracks between boards, how to fill, 5/649
floorboards contract and expand, 13/1947
garage-floor condensation, preventing, 11/1735
hardwood floors, how to lay, 8/1240
joist bracing, replacing, 5/800
mud-set tile, laying, 8/1245
nails, selecting and using, 13/1954
oak floor, darkened with age, 1/95
painting graphics, for family room, 8/1178
painting graphics, for family room, 8/1174
porch floor, slant for water runoff, 12/1839
sheet flooring, patching holes, 8/1248
slate floor, removing stain, 8/1147
squeaks, plywood sub-floor, 17/2720
squeaks, stopping, 16/2467
stains, removing, 18/2772
tile, applying over old wide boards, 5/765
tile, how to install, 18/2866
tile, quarry, installing, 15/2362
tile, resetting, 10/1470
tongue-and-groove flooring, hammer protector, 16/2543
underlayment, how to install, 8/1237
varnish spill, removing, 20/3137
varnish spilled on asphalt tile, 14/2105
'vault,' for hiding valuables, 16/2558
vibration above furnace, 1/45
Flotation devices: choosing, 11/1716
Flower gardens: cold frame-hotbed, 6/820
Fluorescent lighting
kitchen fixtures, installing, 11/1728
troubleshooting, 8/1250
Fly-fishing
instructions, 8/1254
popper plugs, making, 4/609
spoons, how to make, 11/1752
FM radio: TV interference, stopping, 10/1542
Focusing tube: *for close-up photos, 14/2116*
Foldaway hobby center: 10/1454
Folding screens
for family room, 8/1186
for photo displays, 14/2116
Folding trays: snack server, 19/2944
Food: vegetable garden grown in small plot, 9/1336
Food dryers: how to make, 7/1054
Food freezers: repairing, 9/1286
Food mixers
how to repair, 12/1858
portable, how to repair, 8/1260
small-appliance repair, 1/96
Food processors
how to repair, 8/1262
parts rack, 1/99
small-appliance repair, 1/96
Food-waste disposers
installing, 9/1323
repairing, 9/1326
Footboard bed table: 5/672
Footstools
coffee table for patio, with stools, 6/816
coffee table with box stools, 6/804
holes for legs, drilling, 7/1040
outdoor, aluminum-and-canvas, 5/644
rustic slab stool, 18/2793
Forge: how to build, 12/1819
Forks, plastic: *spread glues, 2/232*
Forms, concrete: *stakes cut in chisel shape, 20/3087*
Foundation walls
adding under porch, 4/573
caulking between wall and shingles, 17/2720
cracks, repairing, 2/210
efflorescence, preventing, 11/1760
paint peeling, cause, 12/1839
stucco cracks, repairing, 1/125
Four-wheel drive, auto: tune-up, 19/2970
Foyers
archway, translucent panels, 8/1148
bench for boot storage, 16/2434
pier set, filigree, 14/2162
quarry tile, installing, 15/2362
room divider-storage wall, 16/2459
window decorated with leaf-grille, 16/2434
Frames, art
barn-siding frames, 9/1284
fancy overlays, repairing, 8/1278
floater frames, making, 8/1277
prints, mounting and framing, 8/1264
Frames, door: how to set, 7/1022
Frames, picture
barn-siding frames, 9/1284
clamped with masking tape for gluing, 18/2783
cutting board for mats, 6/900

decorating with pin-striping tape, 6/819
fancy overlays, repairing, 8/1278
fasteners, types and sizes, 8/1193
floater frames, making, 8/1277
gluing right angles, 10/1499
new wood, finishing to look old, 8/1280
painting borders, 8/1192
prints, mounting and framing, 8/1264
quick photo mounting, 14/2116
Framing
adding wing to house, 10/1476
attic dormers, 1/116
garage remodeled into family room, 9/1312
garage storage platform, 9/1321
greenhouse addition to home, 1/30
lumber guide, 11/1747
partition walls, basement, 2/200
shims, how to use, 17/2638
Framing movies: using matte box, 14/2148
Framing squares: *resquaring, 1/61*
Freestanding walls
how to build, 16/2464
light fixture, 16/2462
sewing center, 17/2586
Freezers: repairing, 9/1286
Freight trains, toy: wood-block train, 19/2914
French Provincial design: tambour table, 13/1974
Friction calipers: for wood lathe, 17/2670
Front-end alignment, auto: servicing, 18/2786
Fruit dryers: how to make, 7/1054
Fry pans: small-appliance repair, 1/96
Fuel consumption, boats: determining, 13/2004
Fuel pumps, auto: gaskets, replacing, 9/1342
Fuel systems, auto
basic auto tune-up, 19/2960
care and repair, 9/1292
gas mileage, improving, 1/134
Fuel systems, outboard motors: servicing, 13/1981
Fuel tanks: screen hides basement tank, 8/1186
Fuel-oil stains: *removing from concrete, 1/65*
Funnels: *used as twine dispenser, 11/1731*
Furnaces
blower, noisy, 13/2017
boilers, cleaning out, 9/1430
causes vibration of floor above, 1/45
chimneys, cleaning, 9/1430
crawl-space ductwork, insulating, 1/95
duct/pipe insulation, 20/3078
exterior unit, covering, 1/125
fireplace heater, 9/1430
flue-pipe retrofits, 20/3078
frost-clogged chimney, preventing, 11/1735
fuel-oil stain on concrete, removing, 1/65
heat pipes, reclaim flue-gas heat, 9/1430
heat pumps, how they work, 9/1404
heating pipes, insulating, 9/1430
humidifiers, installing, 10/1508
increasing efficiency, 9/1430
keeping water seepage out, 20/3137
multifuel boilers, installing, 3/390
radiator cover, 15/2386
radiators, cleaning valves, 9/1430
radiators, increasing efficiency, 9/1430
register vanes, tightening, 16/2467
repairing, 9/1298
screen hides furnace, 8/1186
smoke from heating ducts, cause, 13/1947
stack pipe, cleaning, 9/1430
stack pipe, saving heat, 9/1430
steam heat, noises in system, 16/2523
stopping home heat loss, 20/3078
thermostat controls, 20/3078
thermostat relocation may aid in heating home, 19/2979
thermostats, day-and-night, 9/1430
wood-burning stove, venting, 5/709
zoned heating, 9/1430
Furnaces, crucible: how to make, 6/884
Furniture
abrasives, selecting and using, 1/20
adhesives, selecting and using, 1/35
armchair, colonial, 1/102
bar, built from module, 12/1890
bar, from whiskey barrel, 2/190
bar, mobile, with running water, 12/1865
bar, under basement heat pipes, 2/185
bar in elegant cabinet, 2/194
bed, swings into wall cabinet, 16/2434
bed table, footboard, 5/672
bed table-buffet, 2/246
beds, slats, held with eyescrews, 3/433
bench, pine and maple, 1/90
'blooming' finish, removing, 13/1947
bookcase, from stacked drawers, 19/2948
bookcase-divider, 8/1186
bookstand, colonial, 3/415
breakfront, built from module, 12/1890
buffet table, knockdown, 8/1186
bunk bed, children's, built-in chest, 5/674
bunk bed-desk, children's, 5/668
bunk beds are room divider, 18/2794
butcher block, 3/468
butcher block designs, 3/463
butler's table, 3/472
cabinet, holds security safe, 3/456
card tables, simple, for family room, 8/1186
care and repair of finishes, 9/1302
chair, Lincoln, splint-seat, 5/650
chairs, caning, 4/568
chairs, caning, prewoven cane, 4/572
chairs, how to 'respring', 19/2998
chairs, how to bend slats and rounds, 20/3088
chairs, rungs, gluing when loose, 12/1920
chairs, swivel, for dining set, 7/992
chairs, tightening when wobbly, 10/1470
chairs, tool to scrape spindles, 11/1621
chest, Spanish, 5/665
chests, decorated with moldings, 5/662
china cupboard, colonial, 6/888
coat rack, children's, 5/671
coffee table, aquarium, 6/810
coffee table, for patio, with stools, 6/816
coffee table, lattice strips decorate, 10/1462
coffee table, matches barbecue bar, 2/171
coffee table, of plexiglass, 14/2205
coffee table, slide viewer, 6/806
coffee table, with box stools, 6/804
cooking center, mobile, 12/1865
corner lounge, for family room, 8/1174
dark wood finish, lightening, 11/1657
dents and scratches, repairing, 8/1208
desk, campaign, 7/964
desk, hinged, folds against wall, 6/935
desk, rolltop, 6/954
desk, trestle, 6/951
desk, two-level, with secretary return, 6/935
desk, wall-hung, children's, 5/672
desk-chest, opens into work center, 6/935
desk-hobby bench, built from module, 12/1890
dining table, gateleg, 7/983
dining table, oaken, pedestal, 7/987
dining table, trestle, with benches, 7/998
dining table, trestle, with swivel chairs, 7/992
dishwasher cabinet, 13/1948
dowel joints, how to make, 10/1572
drawers, how to make, 7/1036
drawers, repairing worn runners, 7/1023
drawers, stick when part way open, 11/1727
drawers, tacks make them slide easily, 16/2467
dry sink, colonial, 7/1050
etagere, 8/1154
game table, circular, 9/1304
glued joints, loosening, 18/2752
gossip bench, early American, 9/1365
gun cabinet, Mediterranean design, 9/1378
hi-fi center, swiveling, 10/1444
hi-fi music center, mobile, 12/1865
hi-fi open rack, 10/1448
hutch table, early American, 10/1516
joints, how to make and fit, 10/1576
joints, rabbet and dado, 10/1571
lamp table, with lighted planter, 14/2172
lawn furniture, washers keep webbing from tearing, 9/1297
lawn furniture, webbing cut with soldering iron, 12/1853
legs, how to attach, 11/1710
lowboy, colonial, 11/1739
lubrication guide, 11/1744
made from kitchen cabinets, 4/484
marble top table, attaching top, 16/2533
mudroom shelves, 13/1948
nesting tables, four Sheraton replicas, 13/1958
outdoor, aluminum-and-canvas, 5/644
painting, jar lids under legs, 19/2931
painting fittings, 8/1259
painting unfinished furniture, 13/2039
party tables, nesting, 13/2070
party tables, stacking, 13/2074
pedestal table, 13/1978
plastic-laminate tops, tips on applying, 6/847
platform beds, three, 2/252
portable electric grill, indoor, 9/1370
refinishing, 8/1208
rolltop desk and chair, children's, 5/676
room divider, built from module, 12/1890
room divider with lighted planter, 14/2172
scratches, hiding, 10/1470
server, early American, 17/2564
serving cart, 17/2570
sewing cabinet, chairside, 17/2582
sewing cabinet, for spools, 17/2585
sewing center, built from module, 12/1890
sewing center, island unit, 17/2586
snack tables, folding, 17/2710
sofa, wrap-around, for family room, 8/1178
sofa-bed, 18/2726
sponge tape protects fine wood, 18/2842
staining, basic techniques, 18/2770
stains, removing, 18/2772
stool, rustic slab, 18/2793
table, backgammon and chess, 1/146
tables, parsons bridge, 3/453
tables, tabletop fastener, 4/553
tambour table, French Provincial, 13/1974
telephone stand, of plexiglass, 14/2205
tray, folding, 19/2944
trisected table of plexiglass, 14/2205
upholstery, basic techniques, 19/2990

vanity center, built from module, 12/1890
varnish, how to use, 19/3033
veneer, applied on curved pieces, 17/2669
veneer, gluing when loose, 10/1570
veneer, re-cementing loose pieces, 14/2105
veneer, repairing ripples, 13/1947
veneer patches, matching old finish, 4/544
whitewood, definition of, 11/1727
wood-finishing techniques, 20/3094

Furring strips
insulation between strips, 13/2017
locating under softboard, 19/2979

G

Gadget bags, camera
film holder, 14/2116
guitar strap eases load, 14/2116
notebook taped to bag, 14/2116
photo-accessory inventory card, 4/521
two custom bags, 4/514
zipper tab, 14/2116

Game, wild: calling, 10/1512

Game tables
circular card table, 9/1304
coffee table with box stools, 6/804

Games
backgammon and chess table, 1/146
backgammon board, veneer-covered, 20/3044
bridge table, 3/453
bumper-pool table, 15/2264
checkerboard cube-stools, 8/1186
chess set and cabinet, 5/658
cribbage board, pocket, 6/877
game dividers, for basement family room, 8/1186
game table, circular, 9/1304
playing-card holder, 3/452
pool, cue-and-ball wall rack, 20/3062
pool table, full-size, 15/2256
shuffleboard table, how to build, 17/2678
'Swiss-cheese' mountain game, 20/3062
table tennis, playback for solo practice, 8/1157
table tennis ball and paddle caddy, 4/509
tabletop hockey, 1/58
yard lighting for game areas, 20/3149

Garage doors
burglar proofing tips, 3/460
lubrication guide, 11/1744
overhead-type, maintenance, 9/1308
weatherstrip, attaching, 4/573

Garages
adding new story over attached garage, 10/1484
floor, slippery when wet, correcting, 17/2600
floor condensation, preventing, 11/1735
floor rust stains, removing, 15/2269
garage door, attaching weatherstrip, 4/573
garage doors, maintenance, 9/1308
garage remodeled into family room, 9/1312
garage remodeled into guest house, 9/1316
garden-hose storage, 8/1192
overhead storage cabinets, 18/2794
screened garage, 16/2534
shelves, installing, 17/2630
shelves, sliding doors for, 17/2636
storage platform, 9/1321
storage racks, for pipe, molding, dowels, 5/778
storage unit hangs over car hood, 18/2794
storage wall with workbench, 18/2794
wide step at end curbs car, 16/2434

Garbage cans
can cradle, for garden work center, 9/1332
lid used to hold soaker hose, 17/2697

Garbage disposers
installing, 9/1323
installing, 11/1608
repairing, 9/1326

Garden bridge: with planter boxes, 14/2178

Garden fences: eight designs, how to build, 8/1202

Garden hoses
hand-tool holders, 2/291
stored in hanging basket, 8/1192

Garden ornaments: polar sundial, 18/2826

Garden paths
how to build, 14/2084
stepping stones, raising and leveling, 18/2789

Garden shelters
gardening work center, 9/1332
gazebo cookout center, 9/1346
gazebos and screen house, 18/2821
shaded yard shelters, 9/1330

Garden tractors
hydraulic lift for bulldozer blade, 19/2924
utility trailer, 19/2928

Gardening
cold frame-hotbed, 6/820
food dryer, how to make, 7/1054
greenhouse addition to home, 1/30
hiding fences with climbing plants, 16/2533
hotbed, for vegetable garden, 19/3034
indoor-garden arrangements, 10/1496
indoor gardens, tips on growing, 10/1496
keeping varmints out, 19/3038
lighting beautifies garden at night, 20/3144
melons, grown atop glass jars, 11/1644
mock orange, when to prune, 19/3027
potting bench, 2/267
seeds planted with eye dropper, 19/2989
shears, choosing and caring for, 17/2618
strawberry barrels, 18/2816
tools carried in eyeglass case, 13/2028
tools kept in egg cartons, 11/1703
tractor, hydraulic lift for bulldozer blade, 19/2924
tractor, utility trailer, 19/2928
transplanting, 19/2942
vegetable garden in small plot, 9/1336
window greenhouse, 10/1492
work center, 9/1332

Garlands, train: for Christmas, 5/690

Gas clothes dryers: repairing, 5/794

Gas furnaces: furnace repair, 9/1298

Gas leaks: *finding with shaving cream, 18/2820*

Gas mileage, auto: improving, 1/134

Gas water heaters: maintenance and repair, 9/1410

Gas-fired barbecue: 2/176

Gaskets
made from old felt hat, 13/2078
punch made from shafting, 9/1429

Gaskets, auto: replacing, 9/1342

Gasoline
auto gas mileage, improving, 1/134
for mowers, straining, 7/982

Gasoline consumption, boats: determining, 13/2004

Gasoline engines: small, servicing, 8/1128

Gateleg dining tables: folding, 7/983

Gates
how to build, 15/2336
latch, windproof, 5/778
self-closing, ball-and-chain, 3/416

Gauges
contour, copies molding profile, 1/119
marking, from screen wire, 5/656
marking, made from clothespins, 2/232
outboard motor fuel consumption, 13/2004
tire pressure, rack-holder, 7/1009
tire pressure, stored in glovebox, 6/887
weather gauges, colonial plaques, 20/3060
wire-cutting, for pliers, 18/2857

Gazebos
backyard cookout center, 9/1346
patio storage building, 14/2110
screen house and gazebos, 18/2821

Gemstones
rock polisher, 11/1682
rock sorter, 11/1686

Generators
blackouts, coping with, 3/344
home emergencies, outdoor gear aids, 7/1085

Gifts
bell shelf, colonial, 9/1356
bookends, initial, 3/409
bookends, photographic, 3/406
bumblebee pull-toy, 15/2355
candle stand, flamed cube, 4/564
candle stand, holiday, 4/562
candles, from fancy molds, 4/554
candles, molded in snow, 4/560
centerpieces, musical, 4/628
cheese tray, 9/1352
children's block cars, 9/1352
children's toys and tree ornaments, 5/702
circus-train pull toy, 15/2348
crayon holder, 9/1360
creche, musical, 9/1356
cutting board for kitchen, 10/1596
dollhouse, 12/1830
ducks and dachshund pull-toys, 15/2352
jewel box and overnight caddy, 10/1567
jewelry, from 'lost wax' casting, 12/1786
jewelry box, heart-shaped, 9/1360
jewelry box, musical, 10/1562
jewelry box, three-drawer, 10/1567
jewelry carving, 10/1556
jewelry keeper for women, 20/3066
mirror, heart-shaped, 9/1360
pipe rack and humidor, 9/1352
planters, rustic, 9/1356
ring caddy, 9/1360
toy kiddie car, 9/1351
toy kitchen appliances—refrigerator, sink, stove, 19/2908
toys to make—toy box, coat tree, whale pull toy, wood-block train, dollhouse, train engine, 19/2914
treasure chest, 9/1352
valet, dresser-top, 9/1352

Gingerbread ornaments: for Christmas, 5/690

Giraffe clothes tree: 19/2914

Glass
broken window panes, replacing, 20/3068
cutting board for shop wall, 12/1781
leaded-glass windows, stopping water leaks, 6/847
sheet glass, how to cut, 9/1363

Glass, fiber: see Fiberglass

Glass, stained
guide to making stained glass windows, 18/2766
imitation 'stained' glass projects, 18/2759

Glass bottles
cleaning inside residue, 5/800

fancy glassware, 3/418
loosening stuck stopper, 13/2017
model houses inside, 3/422
Glass cutting
cutting board, 6/900
instructions, 9/1363
Glass doors
adding to room, 16/2430
sliding doors, installing, 17/2706
Glass terrarium: Tiffany-style, 18/2858
Glasses, eye
case holds gardening tools, 13/2028
case used to store small tools, 16/2502
Glasses, wine: stemware shelf, 2/188
Glassware: cut from bottles, 3/418
Glazier's hammers: *for window panes, 5/689*
Glittering ornaments: for Christmas, 5/698
Globes, world: *replacing light bulb inside, 19/3027*
Gloves
silicone improves grip, 13/2028
toolholders, used on belts, 3/416
Glue bottles: *used for ink markers, 16/2543*
Glues
gluing plywood panels, 4/553
selecting and using, 1/35
spread with plastic forks, 2/232
waterproof adhesive for basement floor tile, 15/2341
Gluing
adhesives, selecting and using, 1/35
bar clamps, how to lengthen, 16/2523
bottles, glue-applicator, 9/1297
chair rungs, loose, 12/1920
clamps, selecting and using, 5/738
filament tape holds joints, 11/1678
glue dowels, cutting spiral kerfs, 17/2660
joints, half-lapped, 8/1157
joints clamped with masking tape, 18/2783
marbles, on styrofoam jig, 7/982
mirrors, gluing to wall, 3/338
miter-joint gluing clamp, 17/2664
right-angle joints, 10/1499
tabletops, from random-width boards, 17/2664
tape masks glue joints, 18/2738
wide work glued with enlarged C-clamps, 10/1581
Gold paint: *how to apply to wood, 5/765*
Golf: putting greens, from artificial turf, 15/2356
Gophers: keeping out of gardens, 19/3038
Gossip benches: telephone bench, early American, 9/1365
Grandfather clocks: *warped access door, repairing, 10/1570*
Grandmother clocks: hall clock, 5/754
Grass
dethatching, 11/1698
fall lawn care, 9/1368
mowers, preparing for mowing season, 13/1937
planting and improving, 11/1688
riding mowers, choosing, 13/1940
Grass shears: choosing, 17/2618
Gravel: *on built-up roofs, 3/369*
Gravel paths: for garden and yard, 14/2084
Gravel sorters: for lapidary work, 11/1686
Grease guns: *drain cock prevents air locks, 9/1397*
Green ash trees: *root problem, 17/2600*
Greenhouses
addition to home, 1/30
cold frame-hotbed, 6/820
window greenhouse, 10/1492
Greens, putting: made from artificial turf, 15/2356
Greeting cards: Christmas, from photos, 5/684
Grille fences: with open latticework, 14/2110
Grills
barbecue bar for family room, 2/171
barbecues, gas-fired, 2/176
cookout bar, 6/862
firepit, brick, 8/1222
gazebo cookout center, 9/1346
indoor portable electric grill, 9/1370
mobile cooking center, 12/1865
shelter-house for grill, 9/1375
wraparound table, 2/174
Grinders
bench, ceramic-tile nibbler, 5/689
hand, adjustable stand made from hinge, 9/1429
hand, cotton swab for delicate polishing, 17/2639
hand, used as mini drill press, 8/1259
mount swings out of way, 13/2069
Grinding wheels
grinding metal-rod ends, 11/1678
rubber band protects when storing, 10/1515
sharpening hand tools, 17/2608
twist drills, how to sharpen, 19/2976
Grocery-bin canister: 10/1594
Grooves: how to cut with router, 16/2468
Ground squirrels: keeping out of gardens, 19/3038
Ground-fault circuit interrupters: shock preventers, 20/3082
Grounded-outlet checker: 5/657
Grounding, boat: emergency practices, 3/361
Grouting
between plastic tiles, 4/640
regrouting shower tile, 17/2669
Guest houses: remodeled from garage, 9/1316
Gun cabinets: in Mediterranean design, 9/1378
Gun models: cannon, brass and wood, 4/574
Gun racks: custom-fit rack, 9/1383
Guns
gun cabinet, Mediterranean design, 9/1378
gun rack, custom-fit, 9/1383
muzzleloaders, choosing and using, 13/1950
rifles, bench-rest shooting, 17/2652
shotguns, selecting, 17/2674
sighting-in guns, 12/1768
target box, 12/1771
Gunstocks: telephoto camera stock, 4/520
Gutters
aluminum gutters, soldering, 1/125
cleaning, repairing, maintenance, 9/1390
drainage system, for downspouts, 7/1030
installing, 9/1384
snow-melting systems, 17/2717
Gyms: home gym plans, 6/854

H

Hacksaws
blade handle for tight quarters, 17/2673
blade used upside down, 16/2502
cutting angle iron, 17/2639
cutting metal tubing, 18/2820
cutting small-diameter tubing, 16/2543
overhead cutting, blade reversed, 5/748
power hacksaw, how to make, 15/2306
storage rack, 5/689
Hair dryers: *used to dry photo prints, 14/2116*
Hale the whale pull toy: 19/2914
Half-lapped joints: *gluing, 8/1157*
Half-round moldings: guide to molding shapes, 12/1901
Hall clocks: grandmother clock, 5/754
Hammers
belt holster, 19/2989
claw hammers, how to use, 5/745
glazier's hammer, for window panes, 5/689
holster for belt, 6/934
increasing leverage for drawing nails, 6/934
shield when nailing tongue-and-groove flooring, 16/2543
step block for pulling nails, 18/2738
Hampers: bathroom vanity-hamper, 2/216
Hand grinders
adjustable stand made from hinge, 9/1429
cotton swab for delicate polishing, 17/2639
used as mini drill press, 8/1259
Hand tools
adzes, making and using, 4/624
augers, screw-point protector, 3/389
calipers, choosing and using, 4/502
calipers, for wood lathe, 17/2670
chisels, edge protected by pill bottle, 14/2155
claw hammers, how to use, 5/745
combination square, using, 6/825
cutter, sheet-metal, 6/899
files, handles improvised, 3/389
files, tang tightens setscrews, 13/2079
framing squares, resquaring, 1/61
hacksaws, blade handle for tight quarters, 17/2673
hacksaws, blade used upside down, 16/2502
hacksaws, cutting angle iron, 17/2639
hacksaws, overhead cutting tip, 5/748
hacksaws, storage rack, 5/689
hammers, belt holster, 19/2989
hammers, holster for belt, 6/934
hammers, increasing leverage for drawing nails, 6/934
handles made from metal tubing, 19/2956
handles, making, 17/2670
handsaw basics, 9/1396
handsaws, bevel guide, 17/2664
handsaws, keeping vertical, 17/2664
handsaws, stored on door, 3/416
handsaws, straightening bent blade, 19/2979
handsaws, trimming door bottom, 17/2664
holders from garden hose, 2/291
keyhole saws, hose on blade protects work, 8/1157
levels, suction cups protect glass, 13/2079
micrometers, 'enlarging', 12/1828
oilstone, self-lubricating, 17/2610
pipe wrenches, improvised with pliers, 18/2857
planes, shooting board, 17/2670
pliers, basics of using, 19/2902
pliers, used as hand punch, 13/1936
pliers, wire-cutting gauge, 18/2857
punches, leather, improvised, 2/232
punches, rivet hole-sizer, 2/179
rasps, made from threaded rod, 11/1703
rust, removing, 5/697
safety in the shop, 16/2490
sawhorse tool-brackets, 13/2069
scrapers, how to use, 16/2526
scratch stock, for beading, 17/2670
screwdrivers, alligator clip on end, 10/1555

screwdrivers, continuity tester, 18/2860
screwdrivers, screw held to head, 8/1164
screwdrivers, spiral ratchet, avoiding pinched fingers, 13/2069
screwdrivers, using properly, 16/2538
scribers, chalk makes lines visible, 8/1259
scribers, tubing gives smooth grip, 8/1185
selecting basic tools, 19/2899
sharpening, 17/2608
spatulas, how to make, 14/2155
tool caddy, 4/510
toolbox, contemporary, 19/2896
whetstone, truing flattened surface, 11/1735
wood chisels, basics of using, 19/2904
wrenches, basics of using, 19/2903
wrenches, box-end, held on loose-leaf rings, 9/1297
wrenches, emergency, 17/2639
wrenches, ratcheting movement, 13/1936
wrenches, T-handle for Allen wrench, 16/2502

Hand-hewn ceiling beams: making and installing, 4/624
Handguns: sighting-in guns, 12/1768
Handles, hunting-knife: customizing, 11/1634
Handles, tool
for files and chisels, 17/2670
made from metal tubing, 19/2956
Handrails
made of wood, 15/2387
stair handrails, building, 18/2776
wrought-iron railings, installing, 15/2388
Handsaws
bent blade, straightening, 19/2979
bevel guide, 17/2664
block keeps saw vertical, 17/2664
guide made from angle bracket, 10/1499
handsaw basics, 9/1396
sandpaper on saw shapens pencil, 2/179
stored on inside of door, 3/416
trimming door bottom, 17/2664
Handscrews: selecting and using, 5/738
Hangers, coat: *heavy-duty, 5/748*
Hanging lamps: for patio, 14/2110
Hanging shelves: installing, 17/2630
Hardboard
paneling, painting, 3/338
paneling used to make wine rack, 20/3070
replacing damaged wall tile on paneling, 14/2105
saw with carbide-tip blade, 19/2937
selecting and using, 9/1398
siding, selecting, 17/2680
wall paneling, selecting and using, 13/2054
Hardware cloth: *storage drawer, 5/689*
Hardwood floors
how to lay, 8/1240
removing stuck carpet backing, 18/2752
Hardwood paneling: selecting and using, 13/2064
Hardwoods: solar kiln, dries lumber, 10/1593
Harness, camera: carries accessories, 4/512
Hat racks
fake, for hiding valuables, 16/2558
hat shelf and coat rack, of plexiglass, 14/2205
Hats: *felt hats used to make pads, washers, gaskets, 13/2078*
Hearth, raised: for fireplace, 8/1178
Heat pipes: reclaim flue-gas heat, 9/1430

Heat pumps
how they work, 9/1404
solar energy guide, 18/2730
Heat-treating: *clamps hold tools, 13/2078*
Heaters: fireplace furnace, 9/1430
Heaters, kerosene: getting more heat, 9/1425
Heaters, room
getting more heat, 9/1425
repairing, 9/1407
selecting, 9/1419
Heaters, solar: hot-water heating, 9/1416
Heaters, space
camping, from tin can, 4/543
getting more heat, 9/1425
repairing, 9/1407
selecting, 9/1419
Heaters, strip: for plexiglass, 14/2205
Heaters, water
energy costs, cutting, 7/1093
insulating, 20/3078
maintenance and repair, 9/1410
must be vented, 11/1760
noises, cause and cure, 1/95
plastic pipe connections, 14/2182
solar heaters, 9/1416
solar system, installing, 18/2739
Heaters, zone
getting more heat, 9/1425
repairing, 9/1407
selecting, 9/1419
Heating, metal: forge, how to build, 12/1819
Heating systems, home
boilers, cleaning out, 9/1430
chimneys, cleaning, 9/1430
crawl-space ductwork, insulating, 1/95
cutting energy costs, 7/1093
duct/pipe insulation, 20/3078
exterior unit, covering, 1/125
fireplace heater, 9/1430
frost-clogged chimney, preventing, 11/1735
fuel-oil stain on concrete, removing, 1/65
furnace, keeping water seepage out, 20/3137
furnace blower, noisy, 13/2017
furnace causes vibration of floor above, 1/45
furnace flue-pipe retrofits, 20/3078
furnace repair, 9/1298
heat pipes, reclaim flue-gas heat, 9/1430
heat pumps, how they work, 9/1404
heating pipes, insulating, 9/1430
humidifiers, installing, 10/1508
humidity, too high in winter, 17/2720
increasing efficiency, 9/1430
multifuel boilers, installing, 3/390
radiant heat, cracks in ceiling, 17/2720
radiator cover, 15/2386
radiators, cleaning valves, 9/1430
radiators, increasing efficiency, 9/1430
register vanes, tightening, 16/2467
smoke from heating ducts, cause, 13/1947
solar collector, passive, 9/1440
solar energy, sources of information, 18/2737
solar energy systems, guide to, 18/2730
stack pipe, cleaning, 9/1430
stack pipe, saving heat, 9/1430
steam heat, noises in system, 16/2523
stopping home heat loss, 20/3078
thermostat controls, 20/3078
thermostat relocation may aid in heating home, 19/2979
thermostats, day-and-night, 9/1430
wood-burning stove, venting, 5/709
wood-burning stoves, installing, 18/2812
zoned heating, 9/1430

Heating systems, solar: passive collector for home, 9/1440
Heating tape: water pipes kept from freezing, 18/2842
Hedge shears: choosing, 17/2618
Hedge trimmers: *using rotary mower, 12/1835*
Hedges: landscaping techniques, 11/1679
Hesitation, auto: troubleshooting, 7/1100
Hex-wrenches, Allen: *used on nuts in tight quarters, 11/1644*
Hexagon picnic table: 14/2159
Hideaway furniture
dishwasher cabinet, 13/1948
mudroom shelf unit, 13/1948
Hiding places: for valuables in the home, 16/2558
High fidelity
amplifier for transistor radios, 1/74
audio mixers, choosing and using, 12/1856
cassette recorders, repairing, 4/598
cassette tape rewinder, 11/1678
cassette tapes, repairing, 4/602
entertainment center, built-in, 8/1170
hi-fi center, multipurpose storage wall, 18/2794
hi-fi center, swiveling, 10/1444
hi-fi open rack, 10/1448
loudspeaker enclosures, 4/488
mobile music center, 12/1865
record care and cleaning, 15/2398
speakers, auto, installing, 18/2753
stereo cables, identification tags, 5/778
stereo wall, 4/488
stereo-closet room divider, 5/779
Hiking
backpacks, selecting, 4/540
camera, hung from backpack frame, 4/513
clothing, sew-your-own kits, 4/538
exercises to get in shape, 8/1158
map reading, 12/1764
new gear, 1/151
wilderness-area camping, 4/545
Hinges
cotter pins used as hinges, 13/1936
door, tightening, 7/1024
door won't swing when hinge pins are bent, 17/2697
holders for punches, nailsets, 8/1185
lubrication guide, 11/1744
selecting, 10/1450
self-closing, for box lid, 11/1678
used to make hand-grinder stand, 9/1429
Hobbies
airplane models, control-line, 12/1886
airplane models, radio-controlled, 1/62
aquarium, coffee-table, 6/810
aquarium, wall-mounted, 6/810
birds, carving from wood, 3/340
birds, carving sea gulls, 3/343
cannon model, 4/574
cider press, how to make, 5/710
hobby bench, built from module, 12/1890
hobby bench with swing-up top, 18/2794
hobby center, drop-down table, 18/2794
hobby center, foldaway, 10/1454
internal carving with clear plastics, 10/1546
jewelry carving, 10/1556
lapidary, rock polisher, 11/1682
lapidary, rock sorter, 11/1686
lathe, tabletop, 20/3103
marquetry, inlaid-veneer pictures, 12/1772
model houses inside bottles, 3/422
model train layout hides under bed, 18/2794
modelmaker's cabinet workshop, 17/2656

modelmaking, ships from original plans, 17/2642
plastic models, building tips, 12/1883
potter's wheel, how to make and use, 15/2302
telescope, made from camera lens, 18/2846
wood carving, 4 projects, 4/604

Hobby centers
foldaway workbench, 10/1454
hobby bench, built from module, 12/1890
modelmaker's cabinet workshop, 17/2656

Hockey game, tabletop: 1/58

Holes
angled, drilling, 1/78
angled, drilling on drill press, 7/1040
boring edgewise through board, 17/2660
boring from both sides, 17/2664
concrete walls, boring holes, 3/338
cutting on drill press, 7/1040
dowel holes, drilling guide, 17/2673
drilling equally spaced, on drill press, 7/1040
drilling with doweling jig, 10/1515
drywall, patching, 7/1058
end-drilling dowels, 12/1835
metal lathe boring-bar set, 12/1790
mortises, drilling a row, 2/179
nail holes, filling with toothpicks, 19/3027
patching in sheet flooring, 8/1248
punched in paper by drill press, 5/778
sheet metal, enlarged by file tang, 9/1297
wall holes, patching with spackling, 15/2329
wood discs, drilling in circumference, 17/2664

Holiday candle stands: of wood, 4/562

Holiday centerpieces: musical, 4/628

Hollow walls: fasteners, types and sizes, 8/1193

Home improvement
adding windows and sliding glass doors, 16/2430
asphalt shingles, installing, 16/2450
attic dormers, framing, 1/116
barbecue bar for family room, 2/171
bathroom scale swings into wall, 16/2434
bathtubs, caulking, 2/231
bed swings into wall cabinet, 16/2434
bedroom divider-wall, 16/2434
bifold doors, casing hides track, 16/2434
bookcase wall with dropped soffit, 18/2807
ceramic tile, installing on backup board, 20/3049
closet, storage, adding to room, 5/774
closets, using wasted space, 5/779
contractors, choosing, 6/860
dining room in-a-wall buffet, 16/2434
door framed with drip-cap molding, 16/2434
doors, bifold, installing, 5/770
exterior facelifting ideas, 16/2426
family room decorating ideas, 8/1174
family room decorating ideas, 8/1178
family room from sun porch, 8/1170
family room in basement, 8/1186
family room in basement, 8/1182
fiberglass panels solve window problem, 16/2434
fireplace, faced with tile, 10/1468
fireplaces, prefab, enclosing, 8/1226
floor tile, installing, 18/2866
floors, hardwood, how to lay, 8/1240
floors, underlayment, how to install, 8/1237
foyer bench for boot storage, 16/2434
foyer window decorated with leaf-grille, 16/2434
freestanding wall, how to build, 16/2464
freestanding wall, light fixture, 16/2462
garage step curbs car, 16/2434
garage turned into family room, 9/1312
greenhouse addition, 1/30
gutters and downspouts, installing, 9/1384
insulation, installing, 10/1539
kitchen dishwasher, built-in, 11/1608
kitchen storage-space adders, 4/492
lattice, on walls and furniture, 10/1462
magazine rack in bathroom, 16/2434
moldings, decorating ideas, 12/1904
paneling, hardboard, selecting and using, 13/2054
paneling, hardwood, selecting and using, 13/2064
paneling, plywood, selecting and using, 13/2056
re-siding, instructions, 17/2685
remodeling and adding to old house, 16/2421
revamping house fronts, 8/1140
room addition, planning, 1/28
room divider-storage walls, 16/2459
shutters cloth-covered to match draperies, 16/2434
siding, selecting, 17/2680
6 low-cost improvements, 10/1464
skylights, installing, 10/1458
sliding glass doors, installing, 17/2706
steps, brick and masonry, how to build, 18/2790
storage-space ideas, 18/2794
summer home remodeled inside and out, 16/2416
termites, detecting and preventing, 18/2854
tile, mud-set, laying, 8/1245
12 common fixups, 10/1470
wall shelves, how to build, 17/2632
wall tile, installing, 18/2869
wallpaper, how to hang, 20/3052
windows, narrow, how to decorate, 19/3027
wood shakes and shingles, installing, 16/2454

Home lubrication: general guide, 11/1744

Home offices
desks and work centers, three, 6/935
office built into closet, 18/2794
storage trays, swing-out, 19/2949

Home security
burglar proofing tips, 3/460
door locks, installing, 11/1732
home protection guide, 16/2547
safe inside colonial cabinet, 3/456
valuables, hiding places for, 16/2558

Home winterizing
caulking, selecting and using, 4/614
doors, noisy weatherstrip, 5/765
energy costs, cutting, 7/1093
insulation, installing, 10/1539
stopping heat loss, 10 ways, 20/3078
summer home, plumbing system care, 4/573
vacation homes, closing down for the winter, 19/3022

Homes
buying tips, 10/1500
cutting home energy costs, 7/1093
energy-saving when building, 7/1090
entry revamping with landscaping, 8/1140
summer home, plumbing system care, 4/573
tips on placing new house on lot, 16/2467
vacation home, built around motor home, 19/3024
vacation homes, closing down for the winter, 19/3022
vacation homes, plans for five, 19/3016
vacation homes, plans for four, 19/3010

Honing
oilstone, self-lubricating, 17/2610
sharpening hand tools, 17/2608

Hoods, oven: for wall oven over range, 13/2018

Hooks, drapery: selecting, 7/1034

Hooks, fishing: *carried in matchbook, 18/2820*

Hooks, jamb: *hold fireplace tools, 14/2186*

Hoop, basketball: for children, 14/2196

Hoop, water: children's summer toy, 14/2191

Horn, ice-fishing: blows when fish strikes, 10/1521

Horse ornaments: for Christmas, 5/690

Horseshoes: yard lighting for game areas, 20/3149

Hose clamps
held open with tape, 16/2560
king-size, made from two small clamps, 7/1009
reinstalling, 11/1644

Hoses, garden
hand-tool holders, 2/291
stored in hanging basket, 8/1192

Hoses, soaker: *coiled in garbage-can lid, 17/2697*

Hotbeds
cold frame-hotbed, 6/820
for vegetable garden, 19/3034

Hothouses: window greenhouse, 10/1492

House additions
adding new story, 10/1474
adding new story over attached garage, 10/1484
adding wing to house, 10/1476
garage remodeled into family room, 9/1312
greenhouse addition, 1/30
measurements guide, 12/1784
planning your addition, 1/28
remodeling and adding to old house, 16/2421

House models: inside bottles, 3/422

House numbers
displayed on keymaker's sign, 20/3066
how to illuminate, 10/1487
lighted, 1/34

House painting
aluminum siding, painting, 19/2889
aluminum siding, repainting, 5/800
fiberboard walls, how to paint, 15/2341
foundation walls, cause of paint peeling, 12/1839
hook holds paint can on ladder, 11/1731
how to paint house exteriors, 13/2034
latex paint over oil paint, 5/649
paint fails from sun exposure, 12/1839
painting basics and regional colors, 10/1488
peeling paint, removing and repainting, 4/544
scaffold, mobile, how to build, 16/2524
siding, how to paint, 10/1488
siding, painted or weathered without paint?, 11/1735
using paint rollers, 13/2029
windows, painting, 10/1488

House plants
dry sink, used as planter, 7/1050
greenhouse addition to home, 1/30
indoor gardens, 10/1496
lighted planter, in lamp table, 14/2172
potting bench, 2/267
room divider with lighted planter, 14/2172
stepladder plant stand, of plexiglass, 14/2205
terrarium, made of plexiglass, 14/2205
terrarium, Tiffany-style, 18/2858

tips on growing, 10/1496
welded support for tall plants, 12/1889
window greenhouse, 10/1492
Houses
buying tips, 10/1500
cutting home energy costs, 7/1093
energy-saving when building, 7/1090
entry revamping with landscaping, 8/1140
summer home, plumbing system care, 4/573
tips on placing new home on lot, 16/2467
vacation home, built around motor home, 19/3024
vacation homes, closing down for the winter, 19/3022
vacation homes, plans for five, 19/3016
vacation homes, plans for four, 19/3010
Houses, guest: remodeled from garage, 9/1316
Houses, summer: gazebos and screen house, 18/2821
Hulls, boat: fiberglass, repairing, 16/2442
Humidifiers
attic vapor barrier needed, 16/2557
selecting, installing, 10/1508
Humidity: *too high in winter, 17/2720*
Humidity gauge: colonial weather station, 20/3060
Humidors: pipe rack and humidor, 9/1352
Hunting
drowning, hypothermia prevention, 1/24
knives, customized handles, 11/1634
knives, customized sheaths, 11/1637
map reading, 12/1764
rifles, bench-rest shooting, 17/2652
shotguns, selecting, 17/2674
sighting-in guns, 12/1768
wild game, calling, 10/1512
Hunting lodge: vacation home, 19/3016
Hutch tables: early American chair-table, 10/1516
Hutches
appliance center and snack bar, 18/2794
breakfront, built from module, 12/1890
room divider with lighted planter, 14/2172
Hydraulic lifts: for tractor bulldozer blade, 19/2924
Hygrometers: banjo barometer, 2/182
Hypothermia: lifesaving techniques, 1/24

I

Ice dams: preventing on roofs, 17/2717
Ice fishing
horn blows when fish strikes, 10/1521
rod, made from spinning rod, 10/1521
Ice skates: sharpening jig, 10/1522
Ice-cube trays: *storage for small parts, 10/1495*
ID photos: how to take, 10/1523
Identification tags: *for stereo cables, 5/778*
Ignition systems, auto
basic auto tune-up, 19/2960
battery care, 'maintenance-free', 1/126
cables and wiring maintenance, 4/506
dieseling, how to stop, 7/974
distributors, maintenance, 7/1010
electronic, troubleshooting, 7/1075
electronic ignition, servicing, 10/1532
how they work, 10/1524
ignition cables, testing and replacing, 10/1528
servicing, 10/1525
sparkplugs, guide to, 18/2746
Ignition systems, outboard motors: servicing, 13/1981
Illuminators: photo-slide copy-box, 10/1535
In-and-out box: mail organizer for desk, 20/3062
Indexing: metal-lathe attachment, 12/1795
Indoor gardening
indoor-garden arrangements, 10/1496
stepladder plant stand, of plexiglass, 14/2205
tips on growing house plants, 10/1496
window greenhouses, 10/1492
Indoor-outdoor carpeting: for patios or decks, 4/592
Initial bookends: 3/409
Ink markers: *made from glue bottles, 16/2543*
Inlays
cloth-tape inlays, 10/1537
decorating colored tape, 13/2079
marquetry, inlaid-veneer pictures, 12/1772
Insect traps: black-light trap, 10/1538
Insects
exterminating, do-it-yourself, 18/2845
found hidden in firewood, 14/2186
termites, detecting and preventing, 18/2854
termites, how to check for, 14/2186
unlikely in firewood, 11/1727
Inside calipers: *made from clothespins, 5/656*
Inside curves: *sanded by dowels, 14/2155*
Inspection lights: *knee switch, for photo light, 14/2116*
Instant coffee jars: *spout opening, 5/748*
Insulation
attic insulation needed for central airconditioning, 16/2523
attics, adding batts to blown-in, 8/1280
attics, vapor barrier needed for house humidifier, 16/2557
crawl-space ductwork, insulating, 1/95
energy costs, cutting, 7/1093
gouges in planks, how to fill, 11/1621
heating pipes, insulating, 9/1430
how to install, 10/1539
humidity caused by too much insulation, 18/2845
stopping home heat loss, 10 ways, 20/3078
walls, between furring strips, 13/2017
Interference, TV: stopping, 10/1542
Interior doors: types of, 7/1022
Interlocking links: wood sculpture, 20/3118
Internal carving: clear-plastic carving, 10/1546
Interrupters, ground-fault circuit: shock preventers, 20/3082
Investment casting: metal casting, 12/1786
Iron, angle: *cutting with hacksaw, 17/2639*
Iron, flat: *twisting without bends, 17/2639*
Irons: how to repair, 10/1548
Island work centers: for kitchen, 11/1604
Isometric exercises: getting in shape, 8/1158
Isotonic exercises: getting in shape, 8/1158

J

Jacks, leveling: for radial-arm saw table, 15/2383
Jamb hooks: *hold fireplace tools, 14/2186*
Jars: *instant coffee spout opening, 5/748*
Jeweler's saws
used to cut plastic tile, 13/2078
using, 10/1552
Jewelry
carving from wood and plastic, 10/1556
hiding places in the home, 16/2558
metal casting, 12/1786
ring turning on metal lathe, 12/1800
storing in refrigerator on vacations, 9/1397
Jewelry boxes
heart-shaped box, 9/1360
heirloom case, musical, 10/1562
jewel box and overnight caddy, 10/1567
miniature chest, three-drawer, 10/1567
veneer-covered, 20/3044
Jewelry keepers: woman's jewelry 'tree', 20/3066
Jigsaws
blade holder, 11/1703
cabinet-stand, 15/2316
disc-cutting guide, 14/2240
Joinery
box or finger joints, cutting on table saw, 17/2660
butt joints, making tighter, 1/119
compound angles, cutting, 1/76
dadoes, duplicating on table saw, 17/2664
door-casing miters, stopping shrinkage and expansion, 15/2341
dovetail joints, how to make, 7/1026
dowel joints, how to make, 10/1572
dowels, fitting tightly in holes, 3/433
drawers, how to make, 7/1036
floater frames, making, 8/1277
furniture legs, how to attach, 11/1710
glued joints on chair, loosening, 18/2752
gluing, filament tape aids, 11/1678
gluing half-lapped joints, 8/1157
gluing right angles, 10/1499
how to make and fit joints, 10/1576
miter board, for radial-arm saw, 12/1850
miter board, for table saw, 12/1850
miter jig, for table saw, 17/2664
miter joints, angle blocks for table saw, 12/1854
miter joints, clamped with tape when gluing, 18/2783
miter joints, gluing clamp, 17/2664
mitering wide boards on bench saw, 17/2664
moldings, joining, 12/1904
mortises, boring tip, 2/179
picture frames, how to make, 8/1264
plywood edges, how to hide, 14/2238
rabbet and dado joints, 10/1571
rabbet joints, made on jointer, 10/1582
routers, how to use, 16/2468
screws, dowels help to hold, 3/480
tape masks glue joints, 18/2738
tenoning jig, 10/1576
tenons, cut on table saw, 17/2660
tenons, shouldered, made on jointer, 10/1582
Jointers
cabinet-stand, 15/2316
push block, 10/1582
stand, mobile, 10/1586
used on 13 tricky jobs, 10/1582
Joist bracing: *replacing below floor, 5/800*
Jugs: *insulated jug keeps film cool, 14/2116*
Jumping hoop: children's water hoop, 14/2191
Jungle gyms: combination gym and tree house, 14/2188

K

Kayaks
boat camping, 3/353
life preservers, choosing, 11/1716
plywood kayak, how to build, 10/1588
white-water boating, 3/381
Kegs, nail: made into magazine holder,

11/1759
Kerf bending: how to bend wood, 20/3088
Kerfing: on bench saw, 2/268
Kerosene heaters: getting more heat, 9/1425
Key chains: turned from plastic, 12/1814
Keyhole saws: *hose on blade protects work, 8/1157*
Keymaker's sign with house numbers: 20/3066
Keys: *keychain cork won't sink in water, 10/1555*
Keys, chuck: *substitutes for, 2/232*
Kiddie cars: 'you-haul' pickup, 9/1351
Kilns: solar, for drying lumber, 10/1593
Kitchen accessories
breadboard, laminated wood, 11/1652
butcher block, 3/468
can openers, grommets make handle easier to use, 10/1499
canister, grocery-bin, 10/1594
comb box, 6/824
cookbook caddy, 10/1597
cookbook holder, 14/2205
cutlery cupboard, colonial, 10/1600
cutting board, plexiglass, 14/2205
cutting board, turned-handle, 10/1596
dinner-bell shelf, 9/1356
lazy Susan table server, 11/1704
rolling pin, laminated wood, 11/1652
salad bowls, laminated wood, 11/1652
salad scoops, laminated wood, 11/1652
silverware tray, 10/1598
silverware-and-napkin caddy, 10/1594
towel racks, wooden, 19/2906
Kitchen-cabinet furniture: cabinet modules, 4/484
Kitchens
bin, tip-out, between stove and counter, 11/1607
built-in cabinets, 3/454
cabinet drawers, how to make, 7/1036
cabinets, how to install, 11/1616
carpet, remove before installing sheet flooring, 14/2204
countertop laminate, replacing, 1/125
countertops, replacing linoleum with laminate, 13/2017
cupboard storage ideas, 18/2794
cutting board for cabinet drawer, 11/1612
dishwasher, built-in, 11/1608
dishwashers, cabinet, 13/1948
dishwashers, repairing, 7/1002
drains, how to unclog, 7/1032
energy costs, cutting, 7/1093
food mixers, how to repair, 12/1858
food mixers, portable, how to repair, 8/1260
food processors, how to repair, 8/1262
food-processor-parts rack, 1/99
freezers, repairing, 9/1286
garbage disposer, installing, 11/1608
hood for wall oven over range, 13/2018
island work center, 11/1604
kitchen cabinets, making door bumpers, 5/765
kitchen cabinets, metal, spot-painting, 15/2381
knife storage-drawer, 11/1612
laundry center, built-in, 10/1464
lighting fixures, installing, 11/1728
measurements guide, 12/1784
pan storage-drawer, 11/1612
pantry shelves for cabinet doors, 11/1612
plastic laminates, how to apply, 11/1658
plumbing repairs, 14/2216
refrigerator tune-up, 1/100
remodeling and adding to old house, 16/2421
sink, replacing, 11/1608
small-appliance repair, 1/96
snack counter, 8/1178
spice rack, for inside of cabinet door, 11/1612
storage-space adders, 4/492
wall tile, installing, 18/2869
Kitchens, toy: appliances for children, 19/2908
Kites: how to build, 11/1627
Kits, plastic models: building tips, 12/1883
Knee switch: *for photo-print inspection light, 14/2116*
Knives
electric knives, repairing, 1/96
hunting knives, customized handles, 11/1634
hunting knives, customized sheaths, 11/1637
kitchen knife storage-drawer, 11/1612
sharpening, 17/2608
Knives, putty: *used to trim wallpaper, 19/2948*
Knobs
held with sandpaper 'washer', 3/449
painting, 8/1259
spray-painting, 4/640
Knockdown buffet tables: for family room, 8/1186
Knots: how to tie, 11/1640

L

Labels: *three labels on jar for easy identification, 12/1853*
Lacquer: *applicator made from felt, 9/1322*
Ladder shelves: for bathroom, 2/230
Ladders
choosing, 11/1645
dock, of PVC pipe, 15/2360
hook holds paint can on ladder, 11/1731
scaffold, mobile, how to build, 16/2524
stepladder, inner tube holds tools, 3/389
stepladder plant stand, of plexiglass, 14/2205
stepladders, choosing, 11/1645
stepladders, paint can held on shelf, 8/1157
stepladders, paintbrush holder, 13/2028
stepladders, platform for extra foot space, 10/1581
stepladders, shelf locked with hooks, 15/2329
stepladders, shelf parts-holder, 10/1581
stepladders, storage idea, 5/748
stepladders, using safely, 11/1650
using safely, 11/1650
Laminates, plastic
care of, 9/1302
countertop, replacing, 1/125
countertop, replacing linoleum, 13/2017
how to apply, 11/1658
how to cut with router, 16/2468
tips on applying to furniture, 6/847
Laminating, wood: six projects, 11/1652
Lamp tables: lighted-planter table, 14/2172
Lamps
candlestand lamp, 11/1664
hanging lamp for patio, 14/2110
post lamp, for shrubbery, 15/2301
post lamp, installing and wiring, 10/1464
post lamp, installing and wiring, 15/2296
post lamp, mercury vapor, 15/2298
post lamp, wooden, for patio, 14/2110
spoonholder rack for table lamp, 11/1670
table lamp, cobbler's bench, 11/1668
table lamp, Spanish-style, 11/1662
table lamp, wood, six-in-one, 11/1672
timers, using, 10/1464
Lamps, photo: *double clamps, 14/2116*
Landscaping
choosing trees, 19/2952
revamping house fronts, 8/1140
shrubbery, growing, 11/1679
techniques, 11/1675
trees, sugar maple best for shade, 10/1570
trees, young trees braced with soaker hose, 15/2329
Lanterns: candle lantern, made from tin cans, 18/2875
Lap joints: how to make and fit, 10/1576
Lapidary
rock polisher, 11/1682
rock sorter, 11/1686
Latches
door bolt-latch, improvised, 10/1555
gate, windproof, 5/778
Latches, casement window: *used as planing stop, 8/1157*
Lathes, faceplate: how to make wood lathe, 20/3100
Lathes, metal
boring-bar set, 12/1790
chuck jaws, operating quickly, 8/1259
chuck key, substitute for, 2/232
end-drilling dowels, 12/1835
eraser used as polisher, 8/1164
filing on a lathe, 12/1804
finishing lathe projects, 12/1808
increasing speed, 6/819
indexing attachment, 12/1795
lock pliers stops chuck slippage, 10/1499
plastic turning, 12/1814
pulley bearing, silencing, 13/2069
ring turning, 12/1800
setscrew chucks, 12/1796
swing toolholder, 12/1799
tailstock center, spring-loaded, 4/501
tailstock oiler, automatic, 18/2738
toolpost for hefty turning bits, 12/1792
Lathes, wood
basic lathe techniques, 20/3106
calipers, how to make, 17/2670
chisels, guide to, 20/3106
faceplate lathe, how to make, 20/3100
maintenance, 15/2310
scraping tool, 17/2670
tabletop hobby lathe, 20/3103
wood-finish application, 20/3106
Lattice: on walls and furniture, 10/1462
Latticework fences: has open grillework, 14/2110
Laundry
built-in cabinets, 3/454
center for washer, dryer, shelves, 10/1464
clothes dryers, electric, repairing, 5/788
clothes dryers, gas, repairing, 5/794
clothes-sorting cabinet, 18/2794
counter splashboard, 5/748
darkroom shelf fits laundry tub, 14/2116
energy costs, cutting, 7/1093
home laundry center, 18/2794
mudroom shelves, 13/1948
screen hides basement laundry, 8/1186
sewing center, built-in, 17/2601
washing machines, how to repair, 20/3056
Laundry baskets: *used for cat cage, 17/2697*
Lavatories
bathroom plumbing repairs, 1/157
covering fine cracks, 17/2669
drain pipes, flexible, 14/2204
drains, how to unclog, 7/1032
gurgling when drained, cause, 13/2017
odor of sewer gas, stopping, 12/1864
refinishing, 16/2557

Lawn furniture
plastic webbing cut with soldering iron, 12/1853
washers keep webbing from tearing, 9/1297
Lawn tractors
hydraulic lift for bulldozer blade, 19/2924
utility trailer, 19/2928
Lawns
accessories and structures to build, 14/2110
choosing trees, 19/2952
de-thatching, 11/1698
deep-watering penetrator pipe, 5/748
drainage pipe from cinder blocks, 10/1495
drywell removes excess water, 3/429
fall lawn care, 9/1368
garden paths and sidewalks, 14/2084
hand mowers, maintenance, 9/1394
landscaping techniques, 11/1675
leaf cart, made from old screens, 10/1515
mowers, preparing for mowing season, 13/1937
mowers, repair and maintenance, 13/1944
mowers, two-cycle, do they harm grass?, 5/649
planting and improving, 11/1688
putting greens from artificial turf, 15/2356
reel mower, sharpening, 20/3137
retaining walls, how to build, 16/2446
riding mowers, choosing, 13/1940
rough bumps under trees, 16/2533
seeding existing lawns, 15/2381
seeding lawn after tree removal, 1/65
shears, choosing and caring for, 17/2618
shrubbery, growing, 11/1679
snow mold, ridding lawn of, 1/65
sprinklers, children's water hoop, 14/2191
stepping stones, raising and leveling, 18/2789
transplanting guidelines, 19/2942
tree stumps, tips on burning out, 14/2105
trees, sugar maple best for shade, 10/1570
trees, young trees braced with soaker hose, 15/2329
yard swing, two-seater, 18/2836
Layering, wood: six projects, 11/1652
Lazy Susans
bookrack, desk accessory, 3/412
table server-centerpiece, 11/1704
Leaded glass: *stopping water leaks in windows, 6/847*
Leaders
cleaning, repairing, maintenance, 9/1390
drainage pipe from cinder blocks, 10/1495
installing, 9/1384
snow-melting systems, 17/2717
splash block, reversed, 1/150
splash blocks, installing, 9/1390
Leaf carts: *made from old screens, 10/1515*
Leaks, auto
body leaks, 3/384
wind noise and water leaks, stopping, 11/1706
Leaks, gas: *finding with shaving cream, 18/2820*
Leather
cleaning and finishing desktop, 3/369
sheaths, hunting-knife, 11/1637
Leather punches
improvised, 2/232
used to countersink common nails, 10/1495
Legs, furniture
contouring with sanding drum, 17/2664
holes for legs, drilling, 7/1040
how to attach, 11/1710
painting, jar lids under legs, 19/2931
rung, loose, gluing, 12/1920
Lenses, photo
camera care and repair, 4/516
close-up adjustable extension tube, 14/2116
close-up macro images, 5/785
enlarging-lens storage rack, 14/2116
lens hood, curing vignetting, 14/2116
small-optic lenses, 3/328
telescope, made from camera lens, 18/2846
Letter racks: two mail organizers, 11/1712
Letter scales: *improvised, 4/584*
Leveling jacks: for radial-arm saw table, 15/2383
Levels: *suction cups protect glass, 13/2079*
Lids, box
cotter pins used as hinges, 13/1936
self-closing hinge, 11/1678
Life preservers: choosing, 11/1716
Lifters: drill-press table, 11/1719
Lifts, hydraulic: for tractor bulldozer blade, 19/2924
Light box: 'stained' glass project, 18/2759
Light dimmers
dimmer switch, installing, 10/1464
for photo enlarger, 14/2116
Light fixtures
for freestanding wall, 16/2462
kitchen lights, installing, 11/1728
pull-chain grips, 14/2155
Light meters, photo: *worn on belt, 4/513*
Light switches: *extension for children, 5/721*
Lightboxes
coffee table-slide viewer, 6/806
drawing table with built-in lightbox, 11/1723
Lighting
basics of home wiring, 7/1060
dimmer switch, installing, 10/1464
energy costs, cutting, 7/1093
fixture for freestanding wall, 16/2462
fluorescent lamps, troubleshooting, 8/1250
hanging lamp for patio, 14/2110
house numbers, how to illuminate, 10/1487
house numbers, lighted, 1/34
kitchen light fixtures, installing, 11/1728
lamp, candlestand, 11/1664
light switches, replacing, 10/1470
post lamp, for shrubbery, 15/2301
post lamp, installing and wiring, 10/1464
post lamp, installing and wiring, 15/2296
post lamp, mercury vapor, 15/2298
post lamp, wooden, for patio, 14/2110
pull-chain grips for light fixtures, 14/2155
switch extension for children, 5/721
table lamp, cobbler's bench, 11/1668
table lamp, spoonholder rack, 11/1670
table lamp, Spanish-style, 11/1662
table lamp, wood, six-in-one, 11/1672
timers, using, 10/1464
workbench ceiling fixture, 20/3126
yard lighting beautifies grounds, 20/3144
yard lighting for game areas, 20/3149
Lights, antenna: for CB radio, 5/737
Lights, photo-print inspection: *knee switch, 14/2116*
Limbing trees: correct method, 19/2954
Lincoln, Abraham
bench, pine and maple, 1/90
bootjack, 5/650
chair, splint-seat, 5/650
mirror reproductions, two, 12/1840
Lincoln, Mary: vanity mirror reproduction, 12/1840
Linen buffets: *dining room in-a-wall buffet, 16/2434*
Linen cabinets: for bathroom, 2/216
Lines: *drawing with combination square, 18/2783*
Lines, dotted: *drawn with notebook cover, 13/2028*
Lines, parallel: *drawing with taped ballpoint refills, 9/1322*
Links, interlocking: wood sculpture, 20/3118
Linoleum: patching holes, 8/1248
Living picture aquarium: 6/810
Living walls: indoor-garden arrangements, 10/1496
Locaters, letter: two mail organizers, 11/1712
Lock joints: how to make and fit, 10/1576
Lock pliers: *stops lathe chuck slippage, 10/1499*
Locks
burglar proofing tips, 3/460
burglar proofing your home, 16/2547
door lockset, installing, 11/1732
lubrication guide, 11/1744
Lodge, hunting: vacation home, 19/3016
Log cabins: *how to chink logs, 19/3027*
Log cradles: log-cutting aid, 11/1736
Logs
bucksaw, how to build, 16/2517
cutting and stacking, 11/1736
firewood, how to cut, 8/1229
held upright inside tires for splitting, 19/2989
how to stack firewood, 19/2954
log bin, for fireplace, 8/1178
sawbuck, how to make, 11/1736
sawbuck handles long logs, 16/2509
using crosscut saws, 6/878
woodbox next to fireplace, 8/1228
Loose-leaf rings: *hold box-end wrenches, 9/1297*
Lopping shears: choosing, 17/2618
'Lost wax' casting: metal casting, 12/1786
Loudspeakers
amplifier for transistor radios, 1/74
auto stereo speakers, installing, 18/2753
cabinet enclosures, 4/488
Lounges: corner lounge, for family room, 8/1174
Louver windows: basements, dummy frames, 8/1186
Lowboys: china cabinet, colonial, 11/1739
Lower units, outboard motors: servicing, 13/1981
Lubrication, auto
four-wheel drive tune-up, 19/2970
how to lubricate, 11/1740
oil consumption, diagnosing, 12/1912
prewinter maintenance, 20/3074
Lubrication, home: general guide, 11/1744
Luggage carriers: Travelpod, camper-boat-luggage carrier, 4/526
Lugs, spade: *made from brass chain, 13/2012*
Lumber
dry lumber, avoiding splitting when nailing, 1/45
guide for the craftsman, 11/1747
measurements guide, 12/1784
solar kiln, dries lumber, 10/1593

uncupping thin boards, 13/2017
walnut planks, air-curing, 19/2937
Lures, fishing
baitfish lures, how to make, 11/1755
fly-fishing poppers, making, 4/609
spoons, how to make, 11/1752

M

Machine bolts: selecting, using, 3/393
Machine screws: selecting, using, 3/393
Machine-vise clamps: making, 5/742
Machining: metal lathe boring-bar set, 12/1790
Macrame: Christmas-tree wall-hanging, 5/698
Macrophotography
camerapods for low-level close-ups, 14/2116
close-up photos, 5/785
Magazine holders
bathroom magazine rack, 16/2434
bucket made from nail keg, 11/1759
tree-holder for rolled papers and magazines, 11/1758
Magazines: *rolled, writing mailing address, 2/291*
Magnetic holder: *for small parts, 6/887*
Magnets
hold parts for soldering, 1/61
holds toaster plug, 2/291
Magnified photos: close-ups, macro images, 5/785
Mail organizers
desk accessory, 20/3062
two letter racks, 11/1712
Mail slots, door: *awning for slot, 17/2697*
Mailing addresses: *writing on rolled magazine, 2/291*
Manger scenes: musical creche, 9/1356
Manifold vacuum gauges, auto: gas mileage, improving, 1/134
Mantels, fireplace: *correcting warping, 5/709*
Map reading: guide for outdoorsmen, 12/1764
Maple trees: *sugar maple best for shade, 10/1570*
Marble
attaching marble top to table, 16/2533
cleaning and polishing, 4/573
stains, removing, 18/2772
Marbles: *gluing, on styrofoam jig, 7/982*
Marine photography
snorkel box, for over/underwater photos, 19/2986
tips on, 3/356
underwater-photos guide, 19/2980
Markers, ink: *made from glue bottles, 16/2543*
Marking gauges
from screen wire, 5/656
made from clothespins, 2/232
Marking pens
how to soften tip, 19/2989
substitute for layout dye, 12/1889
Marksmanship
sighting-in guns, 12/1768
target box, 12/1771
Marquetry: inlaid-veneer pictures, 12/1772
Martin birdhouses: masts, from thinwall conduit, 12/1782
Masking tape
clamps miter joints when gluing, 18/2783
repair jobs around the house, 18/2842
Masonry
concrete blocks, how to lay, 6/848
measurements guide, 12/1784
nails, selecting and using, 13/1954
painting masonry, 12/1778
retaining walls, how to build, 16/2446
stains, removing, 18/2772
steps, how to build, 18/2790
Masonry walls: fasteners, types and sizes, 8/1193
Masts: from thinwall conduit, 12/1782
Matchbooks: *used to carry fishhooks, 18/2820*
Mats
cutting board, 6/900
how to mat a picture, 8/1264
photo-print mountings, 13/1930
Matte boxes: framing movies, 14/2148
Mattock-adzes: making and using, 4/624
Measurements
calipers, choosing and using, 4/502
calipers, for wood lathe, 17/2670
calipers, inside, improvised, 5/656
combination square, using, 6/825
guide to basic measurements, 12/1784
metric system, guide to, 12/1822
micrometer, 'enlarge' to read larger spans, 12/1828
Measuring tapes: *wall holder for tape, 7/1009*
Medicine cabinets: bathroom wall cabinet, 2/216
Mediterranean design
chest, mosaic top, 5/665
chests, decorated with moldings, 5/662
gun cabinet, 9/1378
table lamp, 11/1662
Melons: *grown atop glass jars, 11/1644*
Melting furnace, metal: how to make, 6/884
Memo holders: *made from clothespins, 3/416*
Mercury vapor lamps: installing and wiring, 15/2298
Merry-go-round swing: for children, 14/2189
Metal casting: 'lost wax' casting, 12/1786
Metal cutting
cutting angle iron with hacksaws, 17/2639
miterbox kerfed to hold metal moldings, 7/1009
power hacksaw, how to make, 15/2306
propane-torch stand, 19/2905
sabre saws, how to use, 16/2482
sheet metal, cutting, 17/2623
sheet-metal cutter, 6/899
Metal finishing
filing on a lathe, 12/1804
finishing lathe projects, 12/1808
Metal lathes
boring-bar set, 12/1790
chuck jaws, operating quickly, 8/1259
chuck key, substitute for, 2/232
end-drilling dowels, 12/1835
eraser used as polisher, 8/1164
filing on a lathe, 12/1804
finishing lathe projects, 12/1808
increasing speed, 6/819
indexing attachment, 12/1795
lock pliers stops chuck slippage, 10/1499
plastic turning, 12/1814
pulley bearing, silencing, 13/2069
ring turning, 12/1800
setscrew chucks, 12/1796
swing toolholder, 12/1799
tailstock center, spring-loaded, 4/501
tailstock oiler, automatic, 18/2738
toolpost for hefty turning bits, 12/1792
Metal scribers: doodling engraver, how to make, 16/2544
Metal tile: wall tile, installing, 18/2869
Metal tubing
cutting thin tubing with hacksaw, 16/2543
cutting without scratching, 13/2012
hacksawing in a vise, 18/2820
made into useful objects, 19/2956
protecting thinwall tubing in vise, 15/2397
ring turning on metal lathe, 12/1800
thin-wall, held in vise, 5/721
Metal turning
finishing turned projects, 12/1808
lathe toolpost for hefty bits, 12/1792
ring turning on a lathe, 12/1800
Metal, sheet: see Sheet metal
Metalworking
abrasive cutoff machine, how to make, 6/892
abrasive cutoff machine, made from portable circular saw, 6/894
bookrack, for paperbacks, 3/414
bookrack, for paperbacks, 15/2364
calipers, choosing and using, 4/502
crucible furnace, making, 6/884
drilling on drill press, 7/1040
file tang enlarges sheet-metal holes, 9/1297
fireplace cover, how to build, 12/1820
forge, how to build, 12/1819
grinding metal-rod ends, 11/1678
layout-dye substitute, for scribing, 12/1889
metal casting, 12/1786
power hacksaw, how to make, 15/2306
propane-torch stand, 19/2905
sheet metal, working, 17/2623
sheet metal bending brake, made of wood, 17/2629
tin-can crafts, 18/2875
tubing, cutting without scratching, 13/2012
Metric system: learning to use, 12/1822
Micrometers: 'enlarge' to read larger spans, 12/1828
Microphones: audio mixers, choosing and using, 12/1856
Mildew: *on interior walls, how to remove and prevent, 5/709*
Military campaign desks: 7/964
Mineral siding: re-siding, instructions, 17/2685
Mini carving: from wood and plastic, 10/1556
Mini offices: desks and work centers, three, 6/935
Mini-maxi gateleg table: 7/983
Miniature houses: dollhouse, 12/1830
Miniature tabletop lathe: for hobby work, 20/3103
Miniatures: *painting tiny items, 9/1335*
Minibikes: modernizing with motorcycle engine, 12/1836
Minnow lures: how to make, 11/1755
Mirror clocks: Connecticut shelf clock, 5/750
Mirrors
comb box, colonial, 6/824
fasteners, types and sizes, 8/1193
gluing to wall, 3/338
heart-shaped mirror, 9/1360
partridge mirror, wood carving project, 4/604
pier set, filigree, 14/2162
shaving mirror, Lincoln's, 12/1840
'stained' glass design, 18/2759
vanity mirror, Lincoln's, 12/1840
Misfiring, auto: troubleshooting, 12/1846
Miter boards
radial-arm-saw jig, 12/1850
table-saw jig, 12/1850
Miter gauges
compound angles, cutting, 1/76
hold-down, for bench saw, 2/295
Miter joints
angle blocks for table saw, 12/1854

clamped with masking tape when gluing, 18/2783
gluing clamp, 17/2664
mitering wide boards on bench saw, 17/2664
table saws, miter jig, 17/2664
Miterboxes
how to miter and cope moldings, 12/1904
in bench vise, held steady, 5/721
kerfed to hold metal moldings, 7/1009
moldings held by clamps, 13/2012
used to hold sabre-saw work, 15/2397
Mitering: *window-screen molding corners, 1/119*
Mixers, audio: choosing and using, 12/1856
Mixers, food
how to repair, 12/1858
portable, how to repair, 8/1260
small-appliance repair, 1/96
Mobile darkrooms: for bathrooms, 6/908
Mobile furniture
bar with running water, 12/1865
cart for TV set, 18/2794
cooking center, 12/1865
electric grill, indoor, 9/1370
hi-fi music center, 12/1865
serving cart, 17/2570
Mobile scaffold: how to build, 16/2524
Mobiles: rainbow mobile, for Christmas decor, 5/690
Mock orange shrubs: *when to prune, 19/3027*
Modelmaking
airplane models, control-line, 12/1886
airplane models, radio-controlled, 1/62
cabinet workshop for modelmakers, 17/2656
cannon model, 4/574
hobby bench with swing-up top, 18/2794
jeweler's saws, using, 10/1552
metal casting, 12/1786
model houses inside bottles, 3/422
model train layout hides under bed, 18/2794
paint-applicator bottles, 9/1297
plastic kits, building tips, 12/1883
ship models, from original plans, 17/2642
Stutz Bearcat, made from tin cans, 18/2875
tabletop lathe, for hobby work, 20/3103
Modular furniture
bar, built from module, 12/1890
breakfront hutch, 12/1890
desk-hobby bench, built from module, 12/1890
from kitchen cabinets, 4/484
hi-fi center, swiveling, 10/1444
room divider, 12/1890
sewing center, 12/1890
vanity center, built from module, 12/1890
Moisture
aluminum window sashes, remedy, 12/1920
attics, condensation cause and cure, 19/2937
basement, moisture caused by outside landfill, 11/1760
caused by too much insulation, 18/2845
causes brick spalling, 1/95
closet condensation, preventing, 11/1657
condensation on basement floor, 11/1621
condensation on patio door, 12/1821
dry rot, preventing in basements, 11/1735
preventing condensation in home, 20/3137
preventing on basement walls, 12/1821
preventing on windows, 5/697
Molding cutters: storage holder, 12/1900
Moldings
contour gauge copies profile, 1/119
cove molding, making on table saw, 17/2664
cutting on bench saw, 2/268
decorating chests and cabinets, 5/662
decorating with moldings, 12/1904
door framed with drip-cap molding, 16/2434
framing art prints, 8/1264
guide to molding shapes, 12/1901
held in miterbox by clamps, 13/2012
how to miter and cope, 12/1904
joining at right angles, 12/1904
laundry counter splashboard, 5/748
metal moldings held in miterbox, 7/1009
molding-cutter storage holder, 12/1900
novelty molding, made on jointer, 10/1582
plywood edges, how to hide, 14/2238
storage racks, 5/778
window screens, mitering, 1/119
Moles: keeping out of gardens, 19/3038
Monkey bars: children's stilt-house slide, 14/2187
Monkey wrenches: *used as table-saw stop, 3/433*
Monoculars: guide to small optics, 3/328
Monopods
camerapod for low-level close-ups, 14/2116
pod made from dowel, 14/2116
Montages, photo: how to make, 12/1910
Mortise-and-tenon joints: how to make and fit, 10/1576
Mortises: *boring a row, 2/179*
Mosaic tile: Spanish chest, mosaic top, 5/665
Mosquitoes: insect trap, 10/1538
Motor homes
fitting out, 4/550
improving and modernizing, 16/2412
safe-driving tips, 16/2404
vacation home built around motor home, 19/3024
winter-storage tips, 16/2408
Motor oil
consumption, diagnosing, 12/1912
selecting and changing, 11/1740
Motorcycles
minibike, modernize with motorcycle engine, 12/1836
safe-cycling tips, 12/1916
trail-bike carrier for auto, 12/1915
Motors, electric
guide to shop motors, 13/1924
metal lathes, silencing pulley bearing, 13/2069
repairing shop motors, 13/1926
speed reducer, 13/1929
Motors, outboard: see Outboard motors
Mountain game: ball scales 'Swiss-cheese' mountain, 20/3062
Mountings
art prints, mounting and framing, 8/1264
photo montages, how to make, 12/1910
photo prints, 3-D, 13/1934
photo-print, 13/1930
quick picture mounting, 14/2116
Mousetraps: *hold parts for soldering, 2/251*
Movies
home theater, hideaway, 18/2862
matte box to frame movies, 14/2148
mini projection booth, 18/2794
projector stand, roll-away, 15/2342
underwater-photos guide, 19/2980
Mowers
engines, servicing, 8/1128
gasoline, straining, 7/982
hand mowers, maintenance, 9/1394
leaf cart, made from old screens, 10/1515
mower used to trim hedge, 12/1835
preparing for mowing season, 13/1937
reel mower, sharpening, 20/3137
repair and maintenance, 13/1944
riding mowers, choosing, 13/1940
rotary mowers, two-cycle, do they harm grass?, 5/649
Mud-set floor tile: laying, 8/1245
Muddy photo prints: how to cure, 15/2330
Mudrooms: shelf unit, 13/1948
Mufflers, auto: replacing, 8/1166
Multifuel boilers: installing, 3/390
Multiple lines: *drawing with taped ballpoint refills, 9/1322*
Multiple-image photos: special effects for pictures, 14/2144
Murphy beds: *bed swings into wall cabinet, 16/2434*
Music boxes: built into jewelry box, 10/1562
Music centers: mobile hi-fi cart, 12/1865
Musical centerpieces: for Christmas, 4/628
Musical creche: for Christmas, 9/1356
Musty odors
on books, removing, 8/1147
removing from basement, 12/1920
Muzzleloading: choosing and using muzzleloaders, 13/1950

N

Nail kegs: made into magazine holder, 11/1759
Nails
blind nailing, 12/1904
caddy with carrying handle, 10/1581
claw hammers, how to use, 5/745
countersinking common nails, 10/1495
cut without damaged heads, 4/501
dimples, spackling, 17/2669
drawing with hammer, increasing leverage, 6/934
dry lumber, avoiding splitting when nailing, 1/45
headless, from Pop-rivet stems, 4/640
headless nail, how to pull, 2/179
nailset, from masonry nail, 11/1626
overhead nails, starting, 2/179
scaffold nail makes screw pilot-hole, 13/1936
scaffold nails, from Pop rivets, 8/1192
selecting and using, 13/1954
step block for pulling nails, 18/2738
Nailsets
holder made from hinge, 8/1185
made from masonry nail, 11/1626
Nameplates: *miniature easels, 12/1889*
Napkins: silverware-and-napkin caddy, 10/1594
Nativity scenes: musical creche, 9/1356
Neckties: *hung on curtain rod, 3/416*
Needles
sewing, for heavy fabric, 5/748
stored in ballpoint-pen cap, 13/2012
Negatives, film
covering scratches for enlarging, 4/521
developing goofs, avoiding, 7/970
storing in envelopes, 14/2116
Nesting tables
fit within end table, 13/2070
four Sheraton replicas, 13/1958
Newspaper holders: tree-holder for rolled papers and magazines, 11/1758
Newspapers
make pattern transfers, 6/887
rolled, writing mailing address, 2/291

Nibblers: *ceramic tile, 5/689*
Nicks: furniture, repairing, 9/1302
Night photography
outdoor photo tips, 13/2006
shooting tips, 13/1963
special effects dramatize photos, 14/2144
Night tables: from kitchen cabinets, 4/484
Noises, auto
engine noises, diagnosing, 13/1971
power-train noise, diagnosing, 15/2324
rattles, stopping, 3/384
ten noises, stopping, 13/1967
wind noise, stopping, 11/1706
Noises, furnace: *steam heat, noises in system, 16/2523*
Noises, plumbing
cause and cure, 19/3027
faucets, buzzing noise, 14/2105
gurgling drains, cause, 13/2017
silencing hammer noises in pipes, 12/1920
water-pipe noise, quieting, 5/800
Nomograph: boat speed, computing, 14/2166
Note cards: *made from photos, 14/2116*
Notebook binders: *hold paintbrushes, 13/2028*
Notebooks: *photo notebook taped to gadget bag, 14/2116*
Numbers, house
displayed on keymaker's sign, 20/3066
how to illuminate, 10/1487
lighted, 1/34
Nursing bottles: *make glue or paint-applicator bottles, 9/1297*
Nuts
enlarging thread, 9/1429
use Allen hex-wrench in tight quarters, 11/1644

O

Oak floors: *darkened with age, 1/95*
Oaken pedestal dining table: 7/987
Occasional tables
nesting party tables, 13/2070
pedestal table, 13/1978
sewing cabinet, chairside, 17/2582
tambour table, French Provincial, 13/1974
Octagon picnic table: 14/2159
Octagon planters: for patio, 14/2110
Octagonal house: vacation-home plans, 19/3010
Offices, home
desks and work centers, three, 6/935
office built into closet, 18/2794
storage trays, swing-out, 19/2949
Oil, motor
consumption, diagnosing, 12/1912
selecting and changing, 11/1740
Oil burners: furnace repair, 9/1298
Oil filters, auto
changing, 11/1740
gaskets, replacing, 9/1342
Oil finish, wood: wood-finishing techniques, 20/3094
Oil pans, auto: gaskets, replacing, 9/1342
Oil tank: *buried, filling with sand, 19/2889*
Oiling: see Lubrication
Oilstones: self-lubricating stone, 17/2610
Old houses: home-buying tips, 10/1500
Old Ironsides: cannon model, 4/574
Open-end wrenches
basics of using, 19/2903
ratcheting movement, 13/1936
used as tire spreaders, 8/1192
Open-grained wood: filling, 8/1208
Opossums: keeping out of gardens, 19/3038
Orbital sanders: *abrasive paper, strengthening, 9/1297*
Organizers
dresser-top valet, 9/1352
jewel box and overnight caddy, 10/1567
mail organizer for desk, 20/3062
two letter racks, 11/1712
workshop 'drawers', 17/2659
Oriental design: painting unfinished furniture, 13/2039
Ornamental iron: railings, installing, 15/2388
Ornaments, yard: polar sundial, 18/2826
Outboard motors
gas consumption, determining, 13/2004
propellers, how to choose, 15/2345
service manual, 13/1981
starting problems, troubleshooting, 13/2002
Outdoor carpeting: for patios or decks, 4/592
Outdoor cooking: see Barbecues
Outdoor living
backpacking, new gear, 1/151
backpacks, selecting, 4/540
bicycle touring, 2/306
binoculars, choosing and using, 3/324
binoculars, small-optic, 3/328
boat camping, by kayak, 3/353
boating, white-water, 3/381
camper shell, for pickup truck, 4/534
canoe trip, gear for, 4/581
clothing, sew-your-own kits, 4/538
exercises to get in shape, 8/1158
gear used for home emergencies, 7/1085
map reading, 12/1764
recreational vehicles, fitting out, 4/550
space heater, tin-can, 4/543
Travelpod, camper-boat-luggage carrier, 4/526
van camp/work conversion, 4/531
wild game, calling, 10/1512
wilderness-area camping, 4/545
Outdoor photography
bird photos, through-window, 3/339
boat photos, 3/356
camerapods for low-level close-ups, 14/2116
good pictures with simple cameras, 14/2136
how to take good outdoor pictures, 13/2006
night photography tips, 13/1963
panorama photos, 13/2066
vacation-photo tips, 14/2139
Outdoor sports
badminton, restringing rackets, 18/2851
binoculars, choosing and using, 3/324
binoculars, small-optic, 3/328
golf, putting greens, 15/2356
skin and scuba diving, basic techniques, 17/2692
snow skis, maintenance, 17/2698
tennis, restringing rackets, 18/2851
water skiing, acrobatic, 18/2756
yard lighting for game areas, 20/3149
Outdoor tables: picnic tables, stowaway, 13/2013
Outlets, electrical
dummy, for hiding valuables, 16/2558
ground-fault circuit interrupters, 20/3082
grounded-outlet checker, 5/657
instant, in BX cable, 4/553
Oven, toy: kitchen appliances for children, 19/2908
Ovens
electric ranges, repairing, 15/2391
hood for wall oven over range, 13/2018
Overhead garage doors: maintenance, 9/1308

P

Packages: how to tie packages, 11/1640
Pad sanders
abrasives, selecting and using, 1/20
choosing and using, 13/2020
sanding techniques, 16/2503
stand for mounting sander, 13/2024
Pads: *made from old felt hat, 13/2078*
Pads, paint: selecting and using, 13/2048
Pails
used to make pool-skimmer strainer basket, 11/1731
wrench on handle aids in carrying, 2/291
Paint
exact color shown by dabbing blotter, 19/2931
house paint, selecting, 13/2034
latex paint over oil paint, 5/649
painting a room, 13/2045
preserving finish on yard shed, 18/2752
preventing 'skin' on leftovers, 15/2381
red paint, for colonial furnishings, 14/2186
removers, using outdoors, 18/2809
spills on concrete, removing, 12/1839
Paint cans
brush held in can's wire bail, 19/2948
can rim, keeping free of paint, 3/433
foil keeps rim clean, 16/2560
held on stepladder shelf, 8/1157
hook holds paint can on ladder, 11/1731
preventing 'skin' on leftovers, 15/2381
wire screen in can strains lumps, 19/2931
wrench on handle aids in carrying, 2/291
Paint pads: selecting and using, 13/2048
Paint removers
apply with roller, 4/544
using outdoors, 18/2809
Paint rollers
painting a room, 13/2045
selecting, 13/2032
selecting and using, 13/2048
using on house exteriors, 13/2029
Paintbrushes
cleaning, in turpentine, 3/389
hanger for soaking, 8/1185
hardened brushes, making usable, 11/1657
held in wire bail of can, 19/2948
hung on notebook binder, 13/2028
keeping soft without cleaning, 18/2820
label with previous use, 9/1429
paint-hardened, cleaning, 6/934
selecting and using, 13/2048
Painting
basement concrete floor, how to paint, 18/2809
basement concrete floor, paint instead of cleaning, 11/1685
basement window sashes, removing for painting, 18/2809
borders, straight, 8/1192
bottles, paint-applicator, 9/1297
brush held in wire bail of can, 19/2948
concrete steps, 4/573
exact color shown by dabbing blotter, 19/2931
fiberboard walls, how to paint, 15/2341
furniture, unfinished, 13/2039
furniture fittings, 8/1259
furniture legs, jar lids underneath, 19/2931
gear kept in box cover, 19/2931
gold paint, applying to wood, 5/765
hardboard paneling, painting, 3/338
hook holds paint can on ladder, 11/1731
kitchen cabinets, metal, spot-painting, 15/2381

miniature items, 9/1335
paint rollers, selecting, 13/2032
paintbrushes, cleaning in turpentine, 3/389
paintbrushes, hardened, making usable, 11/1657
painting over old wallpaper paste, 1/45
plaster, delay painting until plaster dries, 16/2523
plaster patch, let dry before painting, 10/1570
red paint, for colonial furnishings, 14/2186
tile, acoustical, 4/573
tools, selecting and using, 13/2048
wire screen in paint can strains lumps, 19/2931

Painting, exterior
aluminum siding, painting, 19/2889
aluminum siding, repainting, 5/800
concrete, coloring, 6/840
concrete steps, painting, 4/573
fiberboard walls, how to paint, 15/2341
foundation walls, cause of paint peeling, 12/1839
hook holds paint can on ladder, 11/1731
how to paint house exteriors, 13/2034
latex paint over oil paint, 5/649
masonry, painting, 12/1778
paint fails from sun exposure, 12/1839
painting basics and regional colors, 10/1488
peeling paint, removing and repainting, 4/544
scaffold, mobile, how to build, 16/2524
siding, how to paint, 10/1488
siding, painted or weathered without paint?, 11/1735
using paint rollers, 13/2029
windows, painting, 10/1488

Painting, interior
concrete, coloring, 6/840
cracks, patching and painting, 13/2046
hardboard paneling, painting, 3/338
painting a room, 13/2045
painting over old wallpaper paste, 1/45
plaster, delay painting until plaster dries, 16/2523
plaster patch, let dry before painting, 10/1570
plaster patch, shows through paint, 5/649

Painting, spray-can
aerosol valves, cleaning, 1/34
gold paint, applying to wood, 5/765
how to paint with spray cans, 13/2052
small parts, knobs, 4/640
small parts, painting, 1/61
small-parts holder, 12/1781

Paintings: *miniature easels, 12/1889*

Paneling
basement ceiling panels, 2/202
fiberglass, sealing surface, 12/1864
fiberglass panels for patio roofs, 14/2095
hardboard, replacing damaged wall tile, 14/2105
hardboard, selecting and using, 9/1398
hardboard wall paneling, painting, 3/338
hardboard wall paneling, selecting and using, 13/2054
hardwood wall paneling, selecting and using, 13/2064
insulation, between furring strips, 13/2017
insulation planks, how to fill gouges, 11/1621
plasterboard, how to install, 14/2180
plasterboard, preparing for wallpaper, 12/1920
plywood, framed with moldings, 12/1904
plywood edges, gluing together, 4/553
plywood edges, smoothing, 8/1259
plywood wall paneling, selecting and using, 13/2056
plywood wall paneling, working with and finishing, 15/2244
saw hardboard with carbide-tip blade, 19/2937
used to make wine rack, 20/3070

Panels, raised: making on bench saw, 2/268

Panorama photos: splicing small prints, 13/2066

Pans, kitchen: storage drawer, 11/1612

Pantries: shelves for cabinet doors, 11/1612

Paper
cutting a piece from a roll, 15/2329
cutting confetti-size rectangles, 9/1397
held with wood rule when cut, 11/1703
holes punched by drill press, 5/778

Paper, roll: cutting board, 6/900

Paper cutters: *paper held with wood rule, 11/1703*

Paper punches: *using for heavier materials, 12/1853*

Parallel lines: *drawing with taped ballpoint refills, 9/1322*

Parquet flooring: hardwood floors, how to lay, 8/1240

Parsons tables: bridge table, 3/453

Partition walls: basement, framing, 2/200

Partitions: basement, pivoting or sliding, 8/1186

Partridge mirror: wood carving project, 4/604

Party centers: hi-fi entertainment center, swiveling, 10/1444

Party tables
coffee table with box stools, 6/804
nesting serving tables, 13/2070
stacking TV tables, 13/2074

Passports: ID photos, how to take, 10/1523

Patching
asphalt driveways, 1/112
ceiling patch, shows through paint, 5/649
concrete basement wall, air-bubble holes, 11/1685
concrete floor, leveling with patches, 5/800
concrete patio floor cracks, 16/2533
concrete sidewalk, 8/1280
concrete steps, patching corners, 18/2809
driveways and sidewalks, concrete, 6/844
drywall holes, 7/1058
flat-roof blister-leak, repairing, 7/1023
holes in sheet flooring, 8/1248
insulation planks, how to fill gouges, 11/1621
plaster, let dry before painting, 10/1570
plaster patching at ceiling-wall junction, 1/65
plaster walls and ceilings, 18/2845
stucco, repairing loose blisters, 19/2937
stucco foundation-wall cracks, 1/125
wall cracks, 10/1470
wall cracks, patching and painting, 13/2046
wall holes, patching with spackling, 15/2329

Paths
garden paths and sidewalks, 14/2084
stepping stones, raising and leveling, 18/2789

Patios
accessories and structures to build, 14/2110
aluminum chairs, stopping oxide coating, 15/2381
appliance center, 11/1622
bar, mobile, with running water, 12/1865
barbecue table, wraparound, 2/174
barbecues, gas-fired, 2/176
benches, wood, 2/264
brick-in-sand patio, 14/2090
carpeting, outdoor, 4/592
chairs, aluminum-and-canvas, 5/644
coffee table, with stools, 6/816
concrete, coloring, 6/840
concrete floor, repairing cracks, 16/2533
concrete slabs, casting, 6/838
concrete slabs, laying out and pouring, 6/834
cooking center, mobile, 12/1865
cookout bar, 6/862
decks, how to build, 14/2102
decks, two, for front and rear, 14/2098
fence, louvered, 15/2336
fiberglass roof, building, 14/2095
firepit, brick, 8/1222
flagstones, sealing, 16/2557
furniture, washers keep webbing from tearing, 9/1297
furniture, webbing cut with soldering iron, 12/1853
garden shelters, 9/1330
gazebo cookout center, 9/1346
grill weatherproof shelter-house, 9/1375
hi-fi music center, mobile, 12/1865
insect trap, black-light, 10/1538
masonry, painting, 12/1778
night lighting beautifies yard, 20/3144
picnic table, folds flat for storage, 14/2150
picnic table, hexagon shape, 14/2159
picnic table, made from chimney blocks, 14/2152
picnic table, octagon shape, 14/2159
picnic table, rejuvenating weathered redwood, 11/1685
picnic table-and-benches, folds up, 14/2156
planter, bench-type, 14/2170
planter, hanging cubed redwood, 14/2170
planters, from whiskey barrels, 14/2168
planters, wheelbarrow, 14/2179
planters and wine rack, 14/2106
privacy screens, 15/2334
privacy wall with storage cabinets, 18/2794
rooftop patio, 14/2094
screened garage, 16/2534
screened porch, building, 16/2528
sliding doors, burglar proofing, 3/460
sliding glass doors, installing, 17/2706
stowaway tables, two, 13/2013
strawberry barrels, 18/2816
tiled patio, building, 6/862
working with concrete, 6/830

Pattern sawing
on bench saw, 2/268
on table saw, 17/2664

Patterns: *transfers, using newspapers, 6/887*

PCV systems, auto: servicing, 7/1088

Pedestal dining table: oaken, 7/987

Pedestal tables: contemporary design, 13/1978

Pencil marks: *removing from hardwood, 5/765*

Pencil sharpeners: *how to sharpen, 2/232*

Pencils
held on clipboard by fuse clip, 11/1703
pen and pencil holder, for desk, 6/932
pencil-and-pen caddy for desk, 13/2078
sharpening, sandpaper on saw, 2/179
stamp and pencil holder, for desk, 6/931
used as bench-saw push stick, 8/1185

Pendants: carved from wood and plastic, 10/1556
Pennsylvania Dutch blanket-chest toy-box: 3/430
Pennsylvania Dutch design: painting unfinished furniture, 13/2039
Pens
ballpoint pens cut into washers and spacers, 16/2543
ballpoint refills used to draw parallel lines, 9/1322
ballpoint-pen cap stores needles, 13/2012
marking pen, softening tip, 19/2989
marking pens substitute for layout dye, 12/1889
pen and pencil holder, for desk, 6/932
pen-and-pencil caddy for desk, 13/2078
stamp and pen holder, for desk, 6/931
Percolators, coffee: repairing, 5/782
Personal flotation devices: choosing, 11/1716
PFDs: choosing, 11/1716
Photo dryers: print dryer, heated, 7/1056
Photographic bookends: 3/406
Photography
beeper for darkroom timer, 14/2116
belt carrier for camera accessories, 14/2116
bird photos, through-window, 3/339
boat photos, tips on, 3/356
bookends, photographic, 3/406
bounce-flash photos, 3/425
cable release, restraint for, 14/2116
camera, hung from backpack frame, 4/513
camera, nut glued to bottom for tripod, 4/521
camera bag zipper-tab, 14/2116
camera bags, 2, 4/514
camera bags, straps for, 14/2116
camera bellows, repairing holes, 4/513
camera eyepiece covered for long exposures, 4/521
camera film-type reminder, 14/2116
camera gunstock, for telephotos, 4/520
camera harness, 4/512
camera neckstrap cushions, 14/2116
camera repair, small-parts dish, 4/513
camera supported with photo clamp, 4/521
camera-strap hardware, non-chip, 4/513
camerapods for low-level close-ups, 14/2116
cameras, buying guide, 4/522
cameras, care and repair, 4/516
candid photos, tips on, 4/565
chemicals mixed in plastic bucket, 4/513
close-up adjustable extension tube, 14/2116
close-up photos, macro images, 5/785
coaster for developer beaker, 14/2116
color prints, plastic 'ferrotype', 14/2116
copy frame from enlarging easel, 14/2116
copy photography, 6/874
copy stand, holds hand grinder, 8/1259
copy stand, improvised, 14/2116
cutting board, photo mats, 6/900
darkroom door, weatherstripping light seal, 14/2116
darkroom shelf for laundry tub, 14/2116
darkrooms, in a suitcase, 6/910
darkrooms, portable, 6/904
darkrooms, roll-away, for bathrooms, 6/908
developing goofs, avoiding, 7/970
developing tray, rod for rocking, 4/521
dishpans used for print processing, 4/513
double exposures, taking on 35-mm, 14/2116
easel, for big enlargements, 14/2116
enlarger dust cover, 14/2116
enlarger light dimmer, 14/2116
enlarging easel, wall storage, 14/2116
enlarging-lens storage rack, 14/2116
film cartridges, loading, 4/596
film data sheet kept handy, 14/2116
film holder for gadget bag, 14/2116
film kept cool in insulated jug, 14/2116
film used as stencils, 1/61
filter for electronic flash, 14/2116
filters improve photos, 8/1206
flash pictures, how to take, 14/2142
flashgun, stand for, 14/2116
folding screen displays photos, 14/2116
good pictures with simple cameras, 14/2136
greeting cards, from photos, 5/684
hands dried with hair dryer in darkroom, 4/521
home theater, hideaway, 18/2862
ID photos, how to take, 10/1523
illuminator, slide-copy, 10/1535
knee switch, for print-inspection light, 14/2116
lens hood, curing vignetting, 14/2116
lenses, small-optic, 3/328
light meter, worn on belt, 4/513
lightbox built in drawing table, 11/1723
map reading, 12/1764
matte box to frame movies, 14/2148
mini-reel, for developing small film, 14/2116
montages, photo, how to make, 12/1910
mounting picture frame, 14/2116
mountings, photo-print, 13/1930
mountings, 3-D display, 13/1934
muddy prints, curing, 15/2330
negatives, covering scratches for enlarging, 4/521
negatives, storing in envelopes, 14/2116
night photography tips, 13/1963
note cards from photos, 14/2116
notebook taped to gadget bag, 14/2116
outdoor photography tips, 13/2006
panorama photos, 13/2066
photo dryers, using hair dryers, 14/2116
photo-accessory inventory card, 4/521
photo-chemical depletion chart, 4/521
photo-lamp double-clamp, 14/2116
plastic bottle aids developing-tank filling, 14/2116
print dryer, heated, 7/1056
print-spotting tips, 14/2116
projection booth, mini, 18/2794
projector stand, roll-away, 15/2342
proofer, photo, 14/2116
safelight, on pull-down reel, 14/2116
slide shows, improving, 17/2702
slide viewer-coffee table, 6/806
snorkel box, for over/underwater photos, 19/2986
special effects dramatize photos, 14/2144
tape marks loaded film tank, 14/2116
telescope, made from camera lens, 18/2846
test strips, kept in box lid, 14/2116
thermometer grip from eraser, 14/2116
thermometer held by clothespin, 14/2116
thermometer held in bottles with clothespin, 4/521
thermometer holder, 14/2116
timer, water-drip, for cameras, 14/2116
timer knob grip made from eraser, 14/2116
toolholder for darkroom, 4/513
tripod, braced against wall, 4/513
tripod camera-case screw, removing, 14/2116
tripods, adjusting legs to same length, 14/2116
underwater photos, guide to, 19/2980
unipod made from dowel, 14/2116
used cameras, how to buy, 19/3002
vacation-photo tips, 14/2139
vignetter, from cardboard tube, 14/2116
Photolamp clamps: *hold moldings in miterbox, 13/2012*
Physical conditioning
exercises to get in shape, 8/1158
home gym, 6/854
weight bench, 8/1162
Pianos: *refinishing, 8/1280*
Pickup campers: see Campers
Pickup trucks: camper shell, 4/534
Pickup trucks, toy: 'you-haul' kiddie car, 9/1351
Picnic chests: for auto tailgates, 4/494
Picnic tables
hexagon redwood table, 14/2159
octagon redwood table, 14/2159
stowaway tables, two, 13/2013
table folds flat for storage, 14/2150
table made from chimney blocks, 14/2152
table-and-benches, folds up, 14/2156
weathered redwood, rejuvenating, 11/1685
Picnics: *salt-and-pepper shakers, from film cans, 1/119*
Picture frames
barn-siding frames, 9/1284
clamped with masking tape for gluing, 18/2783
cutting board for mats, 6/900
decorating with pin-striping tape, 6/819
fancy overlays, repairing, 8/1278
fasteners, types and sizes, 8/1193
floater frames, making, 8/1277
gluing right angles, 10/1499
new wood, finishing to look old, 8/1280
painting borders, 8/1192
prints, mounting and framing, 8/1264
quick photo mounting, 14/2116
Pictures
marquetry, inlaid-veneer pictures, 12/1772
toothpicks inserted in hook holes when wallpapering, 19/2931
Pier sets: filigree mirror and table, 14/2162
Piercing saws: using, 10/1552
Pin-striping tape: *decorating boxes, 6/819*
Ping pong
ball and paddle caddy, 4/509
false wall hides table, 18/2794
playback for solo practice, 8/1157
Pins: *king-size pushpins for bulletin boards, 18/2857*
Pins, wooden: *cutting from dowels, 5/656*
Pipe
anvil, small, from pipe fitting, 5/689
ring turning on metal lathe, 12/1800
sheet metal, drilling on drill press, 7/1040
storage racks, 5/778
Pipe, PVC
boat accessories, 15/2360
turning plastic on metal lathe, 12/1814
Pipe, copper: working with plumbing pipe, 14/2232
Pipe, plastic: working with plumbing pipe, 14/2182
Pipe, plumbing
plumbing repairs, 14/2216
working with copper pipe, 14/2232
working with plastic pipe, 14/2182
Pipe straps: *made from metal banding, 20/3087*
Pipe wrenches: *improvised wrench using pliers, 18/2857*
Pipes, heating: insulating, 9/1430
Pipes, smoking
caddy, from coffee can, 3/416

pipe rack and humidor, 9/1352
Pipes, water
leak, finding, 3/429
leak, temporary repair, 2/179
leaks, how to stop, 19/2937
noises, quieting, 5/800
tape keeps from freezing, 18/2842
tape seals pipe joints, 18/2842
Pirate's chest toybox: 3/430
Pistols
muzzleloaders, choosing and using, 13/1950
target box, 12/1771
Pivoting walls: for basement family room, 8/1186
Planes: shooting board, 17/2670
Planing
doors, when they stick, 7/1024
stop made from window latch, 8/1157
Planing speed, boat: computing, 14/2166
Plank flooring: hardwood floors, how to lay, 8/1240
Planks, wood: *walnut planks, air-curing, 19/2937*
Plans
house additions, planning, 1/28
project-a-plans for unfinished furniture painting designs, 13/2080
Plant stands: indoor-garden arrangements, 10/1496
Planters
bench planter, pine, 14/2170
dry sink, for house plants, 7/1050
fence niche planter, 14/2178
floor planter for patio, 14/2106
for wood decks, 6/924
for wood decks, 6/920
hanging cage planter, 14/2106
hanging cubed planter, redwood, 14/2170
indoor, for bathroom, 10/1464
indoor, for family room, 8/1174
lamp table with lighted planter, 14/2172
patio and deck accessories, 14/2110
rock-garden bridge, 14/2178
room divider with lighted planter, 14/2172
rustic planters, 9/1356
strawberry barrels, 18/2816
trellis planter for vines, 14/2106
wheelbarrow planter, 14/2179
whiskey-barrel tubs, 14/2168
Plants: how to transplant, 19/2942
Plants, house
dry sink, used as planter, 7/1050
greenhouse addition to home, 1/30
indoor gardens, 10/1496
lighted planter, in lamp table, 14/2172
potting bench, 2/267
room divider with lighted planter, 14/2172
stepladder plant stand, of plexiglass, 14/2205
terrarium, made of plexiglass, 14/2205
terrarium, Tiffany-style, 18/2858
tips on growing, 10/1496
welded support for tall plants, 12/1889
window greenhouse, 10/1492
Plaques: sculpunch designs, made from tin cans, 18/2875
Plaster
ceiling patch, shows through paint, 5/649
dust catcher for sawing holes in walls, 2/179
mildew on plaster walls, how to remove and prevent, 5/709
painting, delay until plaster dries, 16/2523
patch, let dry before painting, 10/1570
patching at ceiling-wall junction, 1/65
patching wall-and-ceiling cracks, 18/2845
wall cracks, patching and painting, 13/2046
wall holes, patching with spackling, 15/2329
Plasterboard
how to install, 14/2180
preparing for wallpaper, 12/1920
wall cracks, patching and painting, 13/2046
Plastic bottles: *used to fill photo developing tank, 14/2116*
Plastic carving
internal carving, 10/1546
jewelry, 10/1556
Plastic ceiling beams: installing, 4/622
Plastic decorations
for Christmas, 5/698
for Christmas tree, 5/702
Plastic laminates
care of, 9/1302
countertop, replacing, 1/125
countertop, replacing linoleum, 13/2017
how to apply, 11/1658
how to cut with router, 16/2468
tips on applying to furniture, 6/847
Plastic model kits: building tips, 12/1883
Plastic panels: restyling entryway, 8/1148
Plastic pipe: working with plumbing pipe, 14/2182
Plastic tile
cut with jeweler's saw, 13/2078
grouting tip, 4/640
wall tile, installing, 18/2869
Plastic tubing: *clothesline covering, 9/1322*
Plastic turning: on metal lathe, 12/1814
Plastic webbing
cut with soldering iron, 12/1853
washers keep from tearing, 9/1297
Plastics
plexiglass projects and working instructions, 14/2205
plexiglass strip heater, 14/2205
plexiglass wine rack, 20/3070
Plate glass: how to cut, 9/1363
Platform beds: three to build, 2/252
Playgrounds
A-frame swing set, 1/41
basketball hoop, 14/2196
jungle-gym tree house, 14/2188
merry-go-round swing, 14/2189
roller coaster, 14/2190
sandbox, with roof, 14/2192
seesaw, rotating, 14/2194
stilt-house slide, 14/2187
stilts, 14/2196
swing with guard rail, 14/2196
teeter board, bouncing, 14/2189
tetherball, 14/2196
water hoop, 14/2191
Playhouses
indoor two-sided playhouse, 14/2203
outdoor playhouse, 14/2200
Playing cards
bridge table, 3/453
holder, 3/452
Plexiglass
jewelry carving, 10/1556
projects and working instructions, 14/2205
strip heater for bending, 14/2205
wine rack, tabletop, 20/3070
Pliers
basics of using, 19/2902
lock pliers stops lathe chuck slippage, 10/1499
used as hand punch, 13/1936
wire-cutting gauge, 18/2857
Plugs, popper: making, 4/609
Plugs, screw: cutting on drill press, 7/1040
Plumb bobs
eye made from Pop rivet, 4/640
made from toy top, 7/1009
tape-spool carrying case, 3/449
Plumbing
access panels, basement walls, 2/202
bathrooms, plumbing repairs, 1/157
bathtubs, installing, 2/224
bathtubs, prefab, installing, 2/220
bathtubs, sunken, illusion of, 2/214
copper pipe, working with, 14/2232
drain pipes, flexible, 14/2204
drains, frozen, thawing, 7/1032
drains, how to unclog, 7/1032
faucets, cause of buzzing noise, 14/2105
faucets, dripping, repair, 10/1470
faucets, how to reassemble compression faucet, 5/697
faucets, removing water spots on chrome, 5/697
faucets, resurfacing washer seats, 13/1947
faucets, single-lever, repairing leaks, 11/1657
garbage disposers, installing, 11/1608
garbage disposers, installing, 9/1323
gurgling noises, cause, 13/2017
high water-meter reading indicates leak, 3/429
home plumbing repairs, 14/2216
lavatory, odor from, 12/1864
noises, cause and cure, 19/3027
noises, quieting water pipes, 5/800
noises from sink pipes, 12/1920
pipe joints, sealed with tape, 18/2842
plastic pipe, working with, 14/2182
septic systems, installation, maintenance, cleaning, 17/2575
septic systems, odor from, 5/800
septic tanks, tips on using, 11/1727
sinks, replacing, 11/1608
sumps, closed or open?, 6/847
toilet, installing, 2/224
toilet-tank leak, preventing, 20/3137
toilets, bubbles from bottom, cause and cure, 1/125
toilets, how to unclog, 7/1032
toilets, trickling water, stopping, 10/1470
water pipes kept from freezing, 18/2842
water-pipe leak, temporary repair, 2/179
water-pipe leaks, stopping, 19/2937
winterizing summer home, 4/573
Plywood
applying wood tape to edges, 20/3087
cutoff jig, 14/2236
edges, how to hide, 14/2238
edges, smoothing, 8/1259
how to bend plywood, 20/3088
panels, gluing together, 4/553
selecting, working with, finishing, 15/2244
siding, selecting, 17/2680
wall paneling, selecting and using, 13/2056
Pocket cribbage board: 6/877
Poker tables: circular game table, 9/1304
Polar sundial: 18/2826
Polishers
cotton swab in drill or grinder, 17/2639
eraser used on metal lathe, 8/1164
pot cleaners substitute for steel wool, 13/2079
rock-gemstone polisher, 11/1682
steel-wool holder, from crutch tip, 9/1335
Polishing: metal finishes for lathe projects, 12/1808
Polygraph machine: doodling engraver, how to make, 16/2544
Polyvinyl chloride
boat accessories, 15/2360
turning plastic on metal lathe, 12/1814
Pontoon boats: deck boat with surrey top, 15/2252

Pool tables
bumper-pool table, 15/2264
cue-and-ball wall rack, 20/3062
full-size pool table, 15/2256
Poolhouses
cabana, 3/476
cabana for year-round use, 15/2270
children's playhouse, 14/2200
Pools, swimming
cabana poolhouse, 3/476
carpeting, outdoor, 4/592
decks and privacy wall, 15/2280
diving deck, for above-ground pool, 18/2832
drownproofing, 1/24
filter, for above-ground pool, 18/2831
ground-fault circuit interrupters, 20/3082
installing tips, 15/2274
pool maintenance, 18/2828
poolhouse for year-round use, 15/2270
pre-summer maintenance, 15/2278
skimmer strainer basket made from pail, 11/1731
yard lighting for game areas, 20/3149
Pop rivets
banding round objects, 6/934
stems, used as headless nails, 4/640
used as scaffold nails, 8/1192
used as studs in metal, 4/640
Poppers, fly-fishing: making, 4/609
Porcelain
bathroom fixtures, refinishing, 16/2557
chipped bathtub, repairing, 5/709
Porch swings: hangs on A-frame, 15/2285
Porches
brick and masonry steps, how to build, 18/2790
concrete floor, slant for water runoff, 12/1839
foundation, adding under porch, 4/573
handrail, wooden, 15/2387
remodeled into family room, 8/1170
screened garage, 16/2534
screened porch, building, 16/2528
stairs, laying out and building, 18/2776
wrought-iron railings, installing, 15/2388
Portable darkrooms
for apartments, 6/904
in a suitcase, 6/910
Portable electric drills
accessories, 15/2291
angled holes, 1/78
basics, 7/1045
bits and attachments, 15/2292
cotton swab for delicate polishing, 17/2639
dowel used as inside-curve sander, 14/2155
drill stand, rolling, 15/2322
drill-bit holder, 12/1853
hanging for storage, 9/1322
maintenance, 15/2310
using with accessories, 7/1046
Portable electric grills: indoor cooker, 9/1370
Portable electric tools
abrasives, selecting and using, 1/20
basic tools for home shop, 7/1023
belt sanders, basics, 16/2498
belt sanders, how to use, 2/258
circular saws, bench for, 5/717
circular saws, blades, selecting, 5/722
circular saws, plywood cutoff jig, 14/2236
circular saws, selecting and using, 5/726
circular saws, used as cutoff machine, 6/894
disc sanders, discs cut with dividers, 2/251
drilling angled holes, 1/78
drills, accessories, 15/2291
drills, basics, 7/1045
drills, bit holder, 12/1853
drills, bits and attachments, 15/2292
drills, hanging for storage, 9/1322
drills, rolling stand, 15/2322
drills, using with accessories, 7/1046
ground-fault circuit interrupters, 20/3082
hand grinders, adjustable stand, 9/1429
maintenance, 15/2310
motors, guide to, 13/1924
motors, repairing, 13/1926
motors, speed reducer, 13/1929
orbital sanders, strengthening abrasive paper, 9/1297
pad sanders, choosing and using, 13/2020
pad sanders, stand for mounting, 13/2024
routers, converted to shaper, 17/2602
routers, how to use, 16/2468
routers, rolling stand, 15/2322
sabre saws, how to use, 16/2482
sabre saws, making a table for saw, 16/2486
sabre saws, penlight taped to front, 9/1335
sabre saws, work supported on miterbox, 15/2397
sanders, marking grade of abrasive paper, 13/2078
sanders, protecting corners from overcutting, 7/982
sanders, sanding techniques, 16/2503
Portable humidifiers: selecting, 10/1508
Portable room heaters
repairing, 9/1407
selecting, 9/1419
Portrait photography
bounce-flash photos, 3/425
good pictures with simple cameras, 14/2136
ID photos, how to take, 10/1523
special effects dramatize photos, 14/2144
Post lamps
installing and wiring, 15/2296
installing, wiring, 10/1464
mercury vapor lamp, installing, 15/2298
shrubbery light, 15/2301
wooden, for patio, 14/2110
Postage scales: *improvised, 4/584*
Postage stamps: stamp and pencil holder, for desk, 6/931
Postcard paintings: *miniature easels, 12/1889*
Pot cleaners: *used as steel-wool substitute, 13/2079*
Potter's wheels: how to make and use, 15/2302
Pottery: made without potter's wheel, 5/746
Potting benches
for gardening work, 2/267
for garden work, 9/1332
Power, electrical
blackouts, coping with, 3/344
home emergencies, outdoor gear aids, 7/1085
Power hacksaws: how to make, 15/2306
Power roof ventilators: 1/120
Power tools
abrasive cutoff machine, how to make, 6/892
abrasive cutoff machine, made from portable circular saw, 6/894
Allen screws, permanent handles for, 14/2240
bandsaws, basics of using, 2/164
bandsaws, blades, sharpening, 2/168
bandsaws, cutoff jig, 17/2660
bandsaws, cutting spiral kerfs on glue dowels, 17/2660
bandsaws, king-size table, 2/170
bandsaws, rip fence, 2/167
bandsaws, using, 8 tricks, 1/154
bench grinders, ceramic-tile nibbler, 5/689
bench saws, basics, 16/2514
bench saws, cutting wedges, 17/2660
bench saws, miter-gauge hold-down, 2/295
bench saws, mitering wide boards, 17/2664
bench saws, pencil push stick, 8/1185
bench saws, push stick, supersafe, 2/292
bench saws, rolling dolly, 18/2784
bench saws, using, accessories, 2/268
bench saws, work support, roller top, 2/294
cabinet-stands, retractable casters, 15/2321
cabinet-stands for power tools, 15/2316
chain saws, accessory box, 3/428
chain saws, cutting and stacking logs, 11/1736
chain saws, cutting down trees and limbs, 4/634
chain saws, using and repairing, 4/632
circular saws, blades, carbide-tipped, 3/349
circular saws, blades, deburring, 5/724
circular saws, blades, selecting, 5/722
disc and drum sander, how to build, 16/2500
disc sanders, cleaning clogged discs, 12/1835
drill presses, boring holes edgewise through boards, 17/2660
drill presses, column stop, 4/584
drill presses, holes punched in paper, 5/778
drill presses, making screw pockets, 17/2664
drill presses, mini, from copy stand, 8/1259
drill presses, table, leveling, 4/584
drill presses, table lifter, 11/1719
drill presses, techniques for using, 7/1040
drill presses, V-block, 17/2670
drill presses, wood discs, drilling in circumference, 17/2664
drill presses, work kept from spinning, 2/251
electric motors, guide to, 13/1924
electric motors, repairing, 13/1926
electric motors, speed reducer, 13/1929
jigsaws, disc-cutting guide, 14/2240
jointers, 13 tricky jobs, 10/1582
maintenance, 15/2310
power hacksaw, how to make, 15/2306
radial-arm saw cabinet with extension tables, 16/2518
radial-arm saws, avoiding sawdust buildup, 15/2397
radial-arm saws, bench-cabinet, 15/2378
radial-arm saws, cabinet-stand, 15/2372
radial-arm saws, dovetail joints, making, 7/1026
radial-arm saws, fence stop, 2/291
radial-arm saws, how to use, 15/2365
radial-arm saws, leveling jacks for table, 15/2383
radial-arm saws, miter board, 12/1850
radial-arm saws, molding-cutter storage holder, 12/1900
radial-arm saws, molding-head fence, 15/2382
radial-arm saws, sharpening tools, 15/2384
radial-arm saws, table extensions, 15/2377
radial-arm saws, tool stand, 20/3138
routers, dovetail joints, making, 7/1026

sabre saws, blade cuts cardboard, 1/150
sabre saws, pointer guide, 4/553
safety in the shop, 16/2490
shaper, converted from router, 17/2602
table saws, angle blocks for miter joints, 12/1854
table saws, blade-height gauge block, 17/2660
table saws, crosscutting duplicate pieces, 17/2664
table saws, crosscutting wide boards, 17/2664
table saws, cutting box or finger joints, 17/2660
table saws, cutting compound angles, 1/76
table saws, cutting dowels into pins, 5/656
table saws, dovetail joints, making, 7/1026
table saws, duplicating dadoes, 17/2664
table saws, extensions for long boards, 18/2841
table saws, jig for same-size cuts, 18/2783
table saws, lining up blade and work, 17/2664
table saws, making cove molding, 17/2664
table saws, miter board, 12/1850
table saws, miter jig, 17/2664
table saws, molding-cutter storage holder, 12/1900
table saws, pattern sawing, 17/2664
table saws, push stick made from coat hanger, 17/2660
table saws, rabbeting wood discs, 17/2664
table saws, ripping tapers, 17/2664
table saws, sandpaper stops workpiece creeping, 17/2664
table saws, saucer cavity in wood disc, 17/2660
table saws, sharpening blade on arbor, 3/433
table saws, spring board, 17/2660
table saws, squaring board, 17/2664
table saws, stop, from monkey wrench, 3/433
table saws, T-bevel, 5/656
table saws, tenoner, 17/2660
wood discs, made on bandsaw and sander, 7/1001
workbench and power-tool stand, 20/3132
workshops, how to lay out, 20/3142

Power trains, auto: noise, diagnosing, 15/2324

Power-tool stands
bandsaw stand, 15/2316
casters, retractable, 15/2321
combination workbench and tool stand, 20/3132
drill-press stand, 15/2316
jigsaw stand, 15/2316
jointer, mobile stand, 10/1586
jointer-and-saw stand, 15/2316
pad-sander stand, 13/2024
portable-electric-drill stand, 15/2322
radial-arm saw cabinet with extension tables, 16/2518
radial-arm saw cabinet-stand, 15/2372
radial-arm saw stand, 20/3138
radial-arm saws, bench-cabinet, 15/2378
router stand, 15/2322

Powerheads, outboard motors: servicing, 13/1981

Prams: sailboat from a pram, 16/2494

Prefab basements stairwells: installing, 2/206

Prefab bathtubs: installing, 2/220

Prefab fireplaces
enclosures, 8/1226
faced with ceramic tile, 10/1468
selecting, 9/1419

Preservers, life: choosing, 11/1716

Presses, cider: how to make, 5/710

Pressure gauges, tire
rack-holder, 7/1009
stored in glovebox, 6/887

Printed circuits: *soldering guide, 8/1164*

Prints, art
floater frames, making, 8/1277
mounting and framing, 8/1264

Prints, photo
color prints, plastic 'ferrotype', 14/2116
copy frame from enlarging easel, 14/2116
darkroom-timer beeper, 14/2116
dishpans used for print processing, 4/513
dried with hair dryers, 14/2116
how to mount, 13/1930
knee switch, for print-inspection light, 14/2116
made into note cards, 14/2116
montages, how to make, 12/1910
muddy prints, curing, 15/2330
panorama photos, 13/2066
print dryer, heated, 7/1056
print-spotting tips, 14/2116
quick photo mounting, 14/2116
3-D displays, 13/1934

Privacy screens
grille fence, 15/2334
louvered fence, 15/2336
louvered screen, 15/2334
privacy wall with storage cabinets, 18/2794
redwood view divider, 14/2110

Processors, food
how to repair, 8/1262
parts rack, 1/99
small-appliance repair, 1/96

Project-a-plans: unfinished furniture painting designs, 13/2080

Projection booths
home theater, hideaway, 18/2862
mini home theater, 18/2794

Projectors
home theater, hideaway, 18/2862
mini projection booth, 18/2794
roll-away stand, 15/2342
slide shows, improving, 17/2702

Proofers, photo: *easel made from picture frame, 14/2116*

Propane torches: stand for torch, 19/2905

Propellers, boat: how to choose, 15/2345

Pruning shears: choosing, 17/2618

Puff puff engine: toy puffs 'smoke', 19/2914

Pull chains: *light-fixture-chain grips, 14/2155*

Pull toys
bumblebee, 15/2355
circus train, 15/2348
ducks and dachshund, 15/2352
Hale the whale, 19/2914

Pulls, drawer
from paper fasteners, 3/416
made from metal tubing, 19/2956
painting, 8/1259
ring turning on metal lathe, 12/1800

Pulls, window-shade: turned from plastic, 12/1814

Punch-out ornaments: for Christmas, 5/690

Punches
drill press punches holes in paper, 5/778
gasket punch, made from shafting, 9/1429
hand punch made from pliers, 13/1936
holder made from hinge, 8/1185
leather punch, improvised, 2/232
rivets, hole-sizer, 2/179
used to countersink common nails, 10/1495
using paper punch for heavier materials, 12/1853

Purchasing, house: buying tips, 10/1500

Push blocks: for jointer, 10/1582

Push sticks
for bench saw, 2/268
for bench saw, supersafe, 2/292
for table saws, made from wooden coat hanger, 17/2660
pencil used on bench saw, 8/1185
simple, for bench saw, 16/2514

Pushpins: *king-size, for bulletin boards, 18/2857*

Putting greens: made from artificial turf, 15/2356

Putty
windows, substitute for putty, 11/1621
windows, why putty loosens, 11/1621

Putty knives: *used to trim wallpaper, 19/2948*

Puzzles: rubber-band-and-dowel trick, 20/3066

PVC
boat accessories, 15/2360
turning plastic on metal lathe, 12/1814

Q

Quarry tile
installing, 15/2362
mud-set tile, laying, 8/1245

Quartetto tables: Sheraton replicas, 13/1958

R

Rabbet joints
made on jointer, 10/1582
making and using, 10/1571

Rabbeting
on bench saw, 2/268
wood discs on a table saw, 17/2664

Rabbits
keeping out of gardens, 19/3038
trap, how to build, 19/3038

Raccoons: keeping out of gardens, 19/3038

Racetrack, toy: for plastic cars, 19/2922

Rackets, tennis: how to restring, 18/2851

Racks
cue-and-ball wall rack, 20/3062
food-processor-parts rack, 1/99
gun rack, custom-fit, 9/1383
hi-fi open rack, 10/1448
ice-cube-tray rack holds small parts, 10/1495
letter racks, 11/1712
magazine rack in bathroom, 16/2434
pipe rack and humidor, 9/1352
spice racks, fit inside of cabinet doors, 11/1612
spoonholder rack, for table lamp, 11/1670
towel racks, wooden, 19/2906
wine racks, three to make, 20/3070

Radial-arm saws
bench-cabinet, 15/2378
cabinet with extension tables, 16/2518
cabinet-stand, 15/2372
dovetail joints, making, 7/1026
fence stop, from C-clamp, 2/291
how to use, 15/2365
leveling jacks for table, 15/2383
maintenance, 15/2310
miter board, 12/1850
molding-cutter storage holder, 12/1900
molding-head fence, 15/2382
sawdust, avoiding buildup, 15/2397

sharpening tools, 15/2384
table extensions, 15/2377
tool stand with storage, 20/3138
Radiators, auto
coolant recovery system, 6/872
maintenance, 6/868
Radiators, home
cover, hardboard, 15/2386
increasing efficiency, 9/1430
steam heat, noises in system, 16/2523
valves, cleaning and repairing, 9/1430
Radio
antennas, repair and maintenance, 18/2848
auto radios, interference, 3/384
auto stereo speakers, installing, 18/2753
CB, antenna light, 5/737
CB, mounting in car, 5/730
CB, on vacation trips, 5/734
transistor, amplifier, 1/74
transistor radios, battery tester, 8/1164
TV interference, stopping, 10/1542
Radio-controlled airplane models: 1/62
Raft boats: pontoon boat with surrey top, 15/2252
Rafts: white-water boating, 3/381
Railings
for decks, wooden, 6/924
for decks, wooden, 6/920
for decks, wooden, 6/914
for elevated deck, 14/2098
handrail, wooden, 15/2387
measurements guide, 12/1784
stairs, laying out and building, 18/2776
wrought-iron, installing, 15/2388
Railroad ties
borders for patios, 14/2090
cribbing with railroad ties, 16/2446
retaining walls, how to build, 16/2446
Rain drainage systems: for downspouts, 7/1030
Rain leaks, auto: stopping, 11/1706
Rainbow mobiles: Christmas ornaments, 5/690
Raised panels: making on bench saw, 2/268
Rakes: *used to straighten wire, 18/2857*
Ramps, auto: folding, how to build, 1/142
Ramps, auto repair: rocker 'car pit', 15/2390
Range, toy: kitchen appliances for children, 19/2908
Ranges
electric ranges, repairing, 15/2391
hood for wall oven over range, 13/2018
Rasps
emergency rasp from threaded rod, 11/1703
smoothing plywood edges, 8/1259
Razor blades: *stored safely in drawer, 11/1626*
Re-siding: instructions, 17/2685
Rechargers: dry-cell batteries, 2/237
Recipes: cookbook caddy with recipe drawer, 10/1597
Recorders, cassette
in musical centerpieces, 4/628
repairing, 4/598
tape rewinder, 11/1678
Recorders, tape
audio mixers, choosing and using, 12/1856
cassette recorders, repairing, 4/598
cassette tape rewinder, 11/1678
Records, hi-fi: care and cleaning, 15/2398
Recreation rooms: see Family rooms
Recreational vehicles
camper shell, for pickup truck, 4/534
fitting out, 4/550
improving and modernizing, 16/2412
safe-driving tips, 16/2404
space heater, tin-can, 4/543
tent trailer, how to build, 19/2932
Travelpod, camper-boat-luggage carrier, 4/526
vacation home built around motor home, 19/3024
van camp/work conversion, 4/531
winter-storage tips, 16/2408
Red paint: *for colonial furnishings, 14/2186*
Red-cedar shingles
installing on roof, 16/2454
wood vs. asphalt shingles, 1/45
Reducers, speed: for electric shop-motors, 13/1929
Redwood: *rejuvenating weathered redwood, 11/1685*
Reels, developing: *mini-reel, for small film, 14/2116*
Reels, extension cords: windup reel, 8/1165
Reels, fishing: choosing fishing tackle, 8/1232
Refinishing: furniture, 8/1208
Refrigerator, toy: kitchen appliances for children, 19/2908
Refrigerators
built into cabinet bar, 2/194
part of mobile cooking center, 12/1865
storing valuables in fireproof refrigerator, 9/1397
tune-up cuts costs, 1/100
Registers, heating: *tightening vanes, 16/2467*
Reindeer table decorations: for Christmas, 5/690
Remodeling
adding new story over attached garage, 10/1484
adding new story to house, 10/1474
adding windows and sliding glass doors, 16/2430
adding wing to house, 10/1476
attic dormers, framing, 1/116
bar, under basement heat pipes, 2/185
bars, 'antiqued' family room, 2/188
basements, finish details, 2/202
basements, ideas, 2/198
basements, partition walls, framing, 2/200
basements, stairwell, prefab, 2/206
bathroom scale swings into wall, 16/2434
bathrooms, for easy care, 2/224
bathrooms, ideas, 2/216
bathtubs, prefab, installing, 2/220
bathtubs, sunken, illusion of, 2/214
bearing walls, removing, 2/242
bed swings into wall cabinet, 16/2434
bedroom divider-wall, 16/2434
bifold doors, casing hides track, 16/2434
bookcase wall with dropped soffit, 18/2807
ceiling beams, hand-hewn, making and installing, 4/624
ceiling beams, simulated, installing, 4/622
ceiling tile, installing, 4/616
contractors, choosing, 6/860
dining room in-a-wall buffet, 16/2434
door framed with drip-cap molding, 16/2434
entryways, with translucent panels, 8/1148
exterior facelifting ideas, 16/2426
family room decorating ideas, 8/1178
family room decorating ideas, 8/1174
family room from sun porch, 8/1170
family room in basement, 8/1186
family room, in basement, 8/1182
fiberglass panels solve window problem, 16/2434
foyer bench for boot storage, 16/2434
foyer window decorated with leaf-grille, 16/2434
freestanding wall, how to build, 16/2464
freestanding wall, light fixture, 16/2462
garage remodeled into family room, 9/1312
garage remodeled into guest house, 9/1316
garage step curbs car, 16/2434
greenhouse addition, 1/30
hardboard, selecting and using, 9/1398
insulation, how to install, 10/1539
magazine rack in bathroom, 16/2434
measurements guide, 12/1784
paneling, hardboard, selecting and using, 13/2054
paneling, hardwood, selecting and using, 13/2064
paneling, plywood, selecting and using, 13/2056
re-siding, instructions, 17/2685
remodeling and adding to old house, 16/2421
revamping house fronts, 8/1140
room addition, planning, 1/28
room divider-storage walls, 16/2459
scaffold, mobile, how to build, 16/2524
shutters cloth-covered to match draperies, 16/2434
siding, selecting, 17/2680
sliding glass doors, installing, 17/2706
storage-space ideas, 18/2794
summer home remodeled inside and out, 16/2416
wall tile, installing, 18/2869
Resawing: on a bench saw, 16/2514
Restringing tennis rackets: 18/2851
Retaining walls: how to build, 16/2446
Return, secretary: part of two-level desk, 6/935
Reupholstering
basic techniques, 19/2990
how to 'respring', 19/2998
Revolvers: muzzleloaders, choosing and using, 13/1950
Rewinders: *for cassette tape, 11/1678*
Riding mowers: choosing, 13/1940
Rifles
bench-rest shooting, 17/2652
gun cabinet, 9/1378
gun rack, custom-fit, 9/1383
muzzleloaders, choosing and using, 13/1950
sighting-in guns, 12/1768
Ring baskets: made from metal tubing, 19/2956
Ring caddy: in shape of hand, 9/1360
Ring turning: on metal lathe, 12/1800
Rip fences: for bandsaws, 2/167
Rip saws: handsaw basics, 9/1396
Riveting: *punches, hole-sizer, 2/179*
Rivets: *removal, by drilling, 1/34*
Rivets, Pop
banding round objects, 6/934
stems, used as headless nails, 4/640
used as scaffold nails, 8/1192
used as studs in metal, 4/640
Rock garden bridge: with planter boxes, 14/2178
Rock polishers: how to make, 11/1682
Rock sorters: for lapidary work, 11/1686
Rocker arm covers, auto: gaskets, replacing, 9/1342
Rocker 'car pit' ramp: for auto repair, 15/2390

Rocking chairs
Christmas ornaments, 5/690
Christmas tree ornaments, 5/702
Rods
cutting small-diameter rods with hacksaw, 16/2543
grinding metal-rod ends, 11/1678
marking center on drill press, 7/1040
threaded, used as rasp, 11/1703
Rods, drapery: traverse rods, hanging, 7/1034
Rods, fishing
choosing fishing tackle, 8/1232
custom-made for suitcase, 8/1234
ice-fishing rod, 10/1521
Rods, traverse: hanging, 7/1034
Roll paper: cutting board, 6/900
Roll-away darkrooms: for bathrooms, 6/908
Roller coasters: children's backyard coaster, 14/2190
Roller skates: *support large drum or cylinder, 18/2783*
Rollers, paint
painting a room, 13/2045
selecting, 13/2032
selecting and using, 13/2048
using on house exteriors, 13/2029
Rolling pins: laminated wood, 11/1652
Rolling stands: for bench saw, 18/2784
Rolls, paper: *cutting a piece from a roll, 15/2329*
Rolltop desks
children's, with chair, 5/676
made of cherry wood, 6/954
Roofs
adding new story to house, 10/1474
adding wing to house, 10/1476
asphalt shingles, installing, 16/2450
attic, stopping condensation inside roof, 3/338
attic vents, open in winter, 17/2720
attic-dormer framing, 1/116
blister-leak on flat roof, repairing, 7/1023
built-up roofs, repairing, 3/369
cedar shakes, replacing shingles, 10/1570
color choice, black or white?, 15/2269
corrugated aluminum, cutting, 13/2069
damaged roofs, repairing, 17/2640
flashing leak, repairing, 12/1864
flat tar roof, applying new roof, 18/2752
gutters and downspouts, cleaning, repairing, maintenance, 9/1390
gutters and downspouts, installing, 9/1384
leak, locating, 14/2204
leak in shingles, pinpointing, 12/1821
nails, selecting and using, 13/1954
patio on the roof, 14/2094
patio roofs of fiberglass, 14/2095
repairing with tape, 18/2842
reroofing, safe weight-margin, 4/544
reroofing over original roof, 17/2669
shed roof, vacation-home plans, 19/3010
shingles, asphalt vs. red-cedar, 1/45
shingles, loose coating is common, 5/649
shingles, meaning of shingle number, 18/2809
shingles, removing rust stains, 1/125
skylights, installing, 10/1458
snow-melting systems, 17/2717
stacks, waterproofing, 16/2450
wood shakes and shingles, installing, 16/2454
Roofs, auto: bicycle carrier, 2/300
Room additions
adding new story, 10/1474
adding new story over attached garage, 10/1484
adding wing to house, 10/1476
garage remodeled into family room, 9/1312
greenhouse addition, 1/30
measurements guide, 12/1784
planning your addition, 1/28
remodeling and adding to old house, 16/2421
Room airconditioners
building in, 1/43
choosing, using, 1/46
repair, servicing, 1/50
Room dividers
archway, translucent panels, 8/1148
bedroom divider-wall, 16/2434
bookcase closet, 3/405
built from module, 12/1890
cabinet with lighted planter, 14/2172
closet, peninsula unit, 5/779
divider-storage walls, 16/2459
double-decker bunk beds, 18/2794
folding screen for photo displays, 14/2116
for family room, 8/1186
freestanding wall, how to build, 16/2464
freestanding wall, light fixture, 16/2462
modules from kitchen cabinets, 4/484
multipurpose storage wall, 18/2794
shelves at foot of stairs, 18/2794
zodiac panel, hanging, 18/2759
Room heaters
getting more heat, 9/1425
repairing, 9/1407
selecting, 9/1419
Room humidifiers: selecting, 10/1508
Rooms: painting a room, 13/2045
Ropes
cord, preventing ravelled ends, 6/847
knots, how to tie, 11/1640
splicing, 11/1640
Rot, wood: *preventing in damp basements, 11/1735*
Routers
converted to wood shaper, 17/2602
dovetail joints, making, 7/1026
how to use, 16/2468
maintenance, 15/2310
mini, made from hand grinder, 8/1259
routing on drill press, 7/1040
stand, rolling, 15/2322
used as burnisher, 12/1835
Rowboats: sailboat from a pram, 16/2494
Rubber stamps: *cushion for stamping, 4/584*
Rubber-band-and-dowel puzzle: 20/3066
Rugs
furniture indentations, raising nap, 19/2889
splicing carpet saves money, 12/1839
Rungs, chair: *gluing when loose, 12/1920*
Runners, sled: *preventing rust, 17/2673*
Rust
on garage floor, removing, 15/2269
on sled runners, preventing, 17/2673
on white roof shingles, removing, 1/125
removing from old tools, 5/697
Rust, auto
removing, 3/384
repairing, 16/2480
Rustic planters: made of redwood and moldings, 9/1356
Rustic stools: slab stool, rough-hewn, 18/2793

S

Sabre saws
blade cuts cardboard, cloth, 1/150
blades, stored on shower hook, 9/1397
how to use, 16/2482
maintenance, 15/2310
making a sabre-saw table, 16/2486
penlight taped to front, 9/1335
pointer guide aids following lines, 4/553
work supported on miterbox, 15/2397
Safelights, photo: *on pull-down reel, 14/2116*
Safes: safe inside colonial cabinet, 3/456
Safety
blizzards, surviving in car, 3/351
boats, emergency drills, 3/361
boats, towing practices, 3/365
drowning, hypothermia prevention, 1/24
fire extinguishers, selecting and using, 8/1218
fireplaces, how to use, 8/1229
ground-fault circuit interrupters, 20/3082
ladders, choosing, 11/1645
ladders, using safely, 11/1650
life preservers, choosing, 11/1716
motorcycle safe-cycling tips, 12/1916
razor blades stored in drawer, 11/1626
recreational vehicles, driving tips, 16/2404
skin diving, basic techniques, 17/2692
smoke alarms, choosing, 1/66
tire chains, selecting and using, 4/638
workshop safety, 16/2490
Sailboats
kayak, made of plywood, 10/1588
sailboat from a pram, 16/2494
Salad bowls: laminated wood, 11/1652
Salad scoops: laminated wood, 11/1652
Salt-and-pepper shakers: *from film cans, 1/119*
Sandboxes: deluxe sandbox, with roof, 14/2192
Sanders
abrasive paper, marking grade, 13/2078
abrasives, selecting and using, 1/20
corners protected from overcutting, 7/982
dowels sand inside curves, 14/2155
maintenance, 15/2310
Sanders, belt
basics, 16/2498
how to use, 2/258
sanding techniques, 16/2503
Sanders, disc
cleaning clogged discs, 12/1835
discs cut with dividers, 2/251
how to build, 16/2500
used to make wood discs, 7/1001
Sanders, drum
contouring furniture legs, 17/2664
how to build, 16/2500
Sanders, finishing
choosing and using, 13/2020
sanding techniques, 16/2503
stand for mounting sander, 13/2024
Sanders, orbital: *abrasive paper, strengthening, 9/1297*
Sanders, pad
choosing and using, 13/2020
sanding techniques, 16/2503
stand for mounting sander, 13/2024
Sanding
abrasives, selecting and using, 1/20
air compressor, how to build, 6/826
belt sander basics, 16/2498
belt sanders, how to use, 2/258
corners protected from overcutting, 7/982
disc and drum sander, how to build, 16/2500
discs cut with dividers, 2/251
furniture refinishing, 8/1208
on drill press, 7/1040
sanding blocks, for contoured surfaces, 3/480
wood-sanding techniques, 16/2503

working properties of common woods, 20/3122
Sanding blocks
abrasive paper clamped in vise, 20/3087
for contoured surfaces, 3/480
two-faced, 17/2670
Sandpaper
grades of sandpaper, 8/1208
on saw, sharpens pencil, 2/179
selecting and using, 1/20
stops table-saw workpiece creeping, 17/2664
using and cleaning, 16/2503
wall holder, from ring clamp, 5/656
'washer' holds wood knobs, 3/449
working properties of common woods, 20/3122
Santa Claus
candy cane boot ornament, 5/690
doorpiece decor, 5/690
window hanging, of plastic, 5/702
Sash cords, window: *replacing on upper sash, 12/1821*
Saucers: saucer cavity, cut in wood disc, 17/2660
Sawbucks
handles long logs, how to build, 16/2509
how to make, 11/1736
Sawdust: *avoiding buildup on radial-arm saw, 15/2397*
Sawhorses
brackets hold hand tools, 13/2069
gusset-reinforced, for cider press, 5/710
sawhorse, how to build, 16/2510
shelf for tools, paint cans, 5/748
workbench-sawhorse, 16/2512
Saws, band
basics of using, 2/164
blades, sharpening jig, 2/168
cabinet-stand, 15/2316
cutoff jig, 17/2660
glue dowels, cutting spiral kerfs, 17/2660
maintenance, 15/2310
rip fence, 2/167
table, king-size, 2/170
used to make wood discs, 7/1001
using, 8 tricks, 1/154
Saws, bench
basics, 16/2514
blades, selecting, 5/722
dolly, rolling, 18/2784
miter-gauge hold-down, 2/295
mitering wide boards, 17/2664
portable circular saw on bench, 5/717
push stick, 2/268
push stick, from pencil, 8/1185
push stick, simple, 16/2514
push stick, supersafe, 2/292
using, accessories, 2/268
wedges, cutting, 17/2660
work support, roller top, 2/294
Saws, buck: how to build, 16/2517
Saws, chain
box for accessories, 3/428
cutting down trees and limbs, 4/634
engines, servicing, 8/1128
firewood, how to cut, 8/1229
how to fell, buck, and limb a tree, 19/2954
logs, cutting and stacking, 11/1736
selecting, using, repairing, 4/632
Saws, circular
blades, carbide-tipped, 3/349
blades, deburring, 5/724
blades, selecting, 5/722
hardboard cut with carbide-tip blade, 19/2937
maintenance, 15/2310
plywood cutoff jig, 14/2236
portable, bench for, 5/717
portable, selecting and using, 5/726
portable, used as cutoff machine, 6/894
Saws, crosscut
cutting firewood, 6/878
handsaw basics, 9/1396
Saws, cutoff
how to make, 6/892
made from portable circular saw, 6/894
Saws, hack
blade handle for tight quarters, 17/2673
blade used upside down, 16/2502
cutting angle iron, 17/2639
cutting metal tubing, 18/2820
cutting small-diameter tubing, 16/2543
overhead cutting, blade reversed, 5/748
power hacksaw, how to make, 15/2306
storage rack, 5/689
Saws, hand
bent blade, straightening, 19/2979
bevel guide, 17/2664
block keeps saw vertical, 17/2664
guide made from angle bracket, 10/1499
handsaw basics, 9/1396
sandpaper on saw sharpens pencil, 2/179
stored on inside of door, 3/416
trimming door bottom, 17/2664
Saws, jeweler's
used to cut plastic tile, 13/2078
using, 10/1552
Saws, jig
blade holder, 11/1703
cabinet-stand, 15/2316
disc-cutting guide, 14/2240
Saws, keyhole: *hose on blade protects work, 8/1157*
Saws, piercing: using, 10/1552
Saws, radial-arm
bench-cabinet, 15/2378
cabinet with extension tables, 16/2518
cabinet-stand, 15/2372
dovetail joints, making, 7/1026
fence stop, from C-clamp, 2/291
how to use, 15/2365
leveling jacks for table, 15/2383
maintenance, 15/2310
miter board, 12/1850
molding-cutter storage holder, 12/1900
molding-head fence, 15/2382
sawdust, avoiding buildup, 15/2397
sharpening tools, 15/2384
table extensions, 15/2377
tool stand with storage, 20/3138
Saws, rip: handsaw basics, 9/1396
Saws, sabre
blade cuts cardboard, cloth, 1/150
blades, stored on shower hook, 9/1397
how to use, 16/2482
maintenance, 15/2310
making a sabre-saw table, 16/2486
penlight taped to front, 9/1335
pointer guide aids following lines, 4/553
work supported on miterbox, 15/2397
Saws, table
angle blocks for miter joints, 12/1854
blade-height gauge block, 17/2660
blades, sharpening on arbor, 3/433
box or finger joints, cutting, 17/2660
cabinet-stand, 15/2316
compound angles, cutting, 1/76
cove molding, how to make, 17/2664
crosscutting duplicate pieces, 17/2664
crosscutting wide boards, 17/2664
dadoes, duplicating, 17/2664
dovetail joints, how to make, 7/1026
dowels, cutting into pins, 5/656
extensions for long boards, 18/2841
jig for same-size cuts, 18/2783
lining up blade and work, 17/2664
maintenance, 15/2310
miter board, 12/1850
miter jig, 17/2664
molding-cutter storage holder, 12/1900
pattern sawing, 17/2664
push stick, made from coat hanger, 17/2660
sandpaper stops workpiece creeping, 17/2664
spring board, 17/2660
squaring board, 17/2664
stop, made from monkey wrench, 3/433
tapers, ripping, 17/2664
T-bevel, from miter gauge, 5/656
tenoner, 17/2660
wood disc saucer cavity, 17/2660
wood discs, rabbeting, 17/2664
Scaffold nails
from Pop rivets, 8/1192
make screw pilot-holes, 13/1936
Scaffolding: mobile scaffold, building, 16/2524
Scales: *bathroom scale swings into wall, 16/2434*
Scales, postage: *improvised, 4/584*
Scatterguns: see Shotguns
Scissors
cutting cardboard strips, 9/1335
sharpening, 17/2608
used as compass divider, 12/1853
Sconces: candle wall sconce, 5/702
Scoops, salad: laminated wood, 11/1652
Scooters: wooden scooter, uses roller-skate wheels, 19/2907
Scrapers: how to use, 16/2526
Scraping tool: for wood lathe, 17/2670
Scratch stock: beading tool, 17/2670
Scratches
furniture, hiding scratches, 10/1470
furniture, repairing, 9/1302
furniture, repairing, 8/1208
Screen doors
aluminum doors, repairing, 18/2810
hinges, selecting, 10/1450
spring corrects sagging, 11/1626
Screen houses: gazebos and screen house, 18/2821
Screen wire: *marking gauge, 5/656*
Screened summer rooms
screened garage, 16/2534
screened porch, building, 16/2528
Screens: hide furnace, laundry, fuel-tank, 8/1186
Screens, folding
for family room, 8/1186
for photo displays, 14/2116
Screens, privacy
grille fence, 15/2334
louvered fence, 15/2336
louvered screen, 15/2334
privacy wall with storage, 18/2794
redwood view divider, 14/2110
Screens, window
aluminum screens, repairing, 18/2810
combination screens, lubricating, 15/2341
moldings, mitering corners, 1/119
screen wire, how to stretch, 16/2536
Screw anchors
fasteners, types and sizes, 8/1193
removing from wall, 17/2600
Screw pockets: for tabletops, 17/2664
Screwdrivers
continuity tester, 18/2860
how to use properly, 16/2538
made from washers, 13/1936
screw held to head, 8/1164
spiral ratchet driver, avoiding pinched fingers, 13/2069
Screws
Allen screws, permanent handles for, 14/2240
choosing the right screw, 16/2540

dowels help to hold, 3/480
machine screws, selecting and using, 3/393
pilot hole made by scaffold nail, 13/1936
plugs, cutting on drill press, 7/1040
setscrews, made from bolts, 6/819
setscrews, tightened by file tang, 13/2079
starting in tight spots, 8/1164
Scribers
chalk makes lines visible, 8/1259
circle-scribing compass, 5/716
doodling engraver, how to make, 16/2544
tubing gives smooth grip, 8/1185
Scribing, metal: *layout-dye substitute, 12/1889*
Scrolls: *router burnishes scroll workpieces, 12/1835*
Scuba diving
basic techniques, 17/2692
underwater-photos guide, 19/2980
Sculpture: interlocking wood links, 20/3118
Sculpunch designs: plaques, made from tin cans, 18/2875
Sea gulls: carving from wood, 3/343
Seals, auto: replacing, 9/1342
Seats, auto: *foil keeps seats cool, 4/584*
Seats, chair
caning, 4/568
caning, prewoven cane, 4/572
splint chair seat, 5/650
Secretary return: part of two-level desk, 6/935
Security, home
burglar proofing tips, 3/460
door locks, installing, 11/1732
home protection guide, 16/2547
safe inside colonial cabinet, 3/456
valuables, hiding places for, 16/2558
Seed, grass: *seeding existing lawns, 15/2381*
Seeds: *planted with eye dropper, 19/2989*
Seesaws
bouncing teeter board, 14/2189
rotating teeter board, 14/2194
Septic systems
installation, maintenance, cleaning, 17/2575
odor from roof vents, 5/800
tips on using, 11/1727
Servers
early American server, 17/2564
folding snack server, 19/2944
lazy Susan table server, 11/1704
mobile cooking center, 12/1865
mobile food server, 15/2342
Serving carts: with electric food warmer, 17/2570
Serving tables
nesting party tables, 13/2070
stacking party tables, 13/2074
Serving trays
butler's table, 3/472
laminated wood, 11/1652
lifts off wine rack, 3/424
veneer-covered, 20/3044
Setscrews
made from bolts, 6/819
permanent handles for Allen screws, 14/2240
setscrew chucks for metal lathes, 12/1796
tightened by file tang, 13/2079
Settees: bench, pine and maple, 1/90
Sewage systems: septic tanks, installation, maintenance, cleaning, 17/2575
Sewing
basket made from nail keg, 11/1759
camping gear, sew-your-own kits, 4/538
needle for heavy fabric, from can opener, 5/748
sewing cabinet, chairside, 17/2582
sewing center, built from module, 12/1890
sewing center, drop-down table, 18/2794
sewing center, freestanding wall, 17/2586
sewing center, island unit, 17/2586
sewing center, retracts against wall, 17/2586
sewing center, wall and floor units, 17/2586
sewing centers, built-in ideas, 17/2601
sewing machine, how to oil bearings, 11/1657
spool cabinet, wall-hung, 17/2585
Shades, window
how to tighten ratchets, 10/1570
pulls, turned from plastic, 12/1814
Shakers, salt-and-pepper: *from film cans, 1/119*
Shakes
siding, selecting, 17/2680
wood shakes and shingles, installing, 16/2454
Shakes, cedar: *used to replace shingles, 10/1570*
Shapers, wood
made from inverted router in cabinet, 17/2602
radial-arm saw with molding-head fence, 15/2382
Sharpeners, pencil: *how to sharpen, 2/232*
Sharpening, ice skates: sharpening jig, 10/1522
Sharpening, tool
bandsaws, blades, 2/168
circular saws, blades, 5/724
keeping cutting edges sharp, 17/2608
oilstone, self-lubricating, 17/2610
table-saw blades, on arbor, 3/433
twist drills, 19/2976
using radial-arm saw to sharpen tools, 15/2384
whetstone, truing flattened surface, 11/1735
wood-lathe turning tools, 20/3106
Shaving cabinets
early American console, 17/2616
wall-mounted cabinets, 17/2612
Shaving mirrors: reproduction of Lincoln's, 12/1840
Shears
cutting cardboard strips, 9/1335
garden shears, choosing and caring for, 17/2618
Sheathing: guide to types, 17/2620
Sheaths, hunting-knife: customizing, 11/1637
Shed roof: vacation-home plans, 19/3010
Sheds: *metal sheds, preserving paint, 18/2752*
Sheet flooring
installing over tile in basement, 4/544
patching holes, 8/1248
remove carpet before installing, 14/2204
underlayment, how to install, 8/1237
Sheet glass: how to cut, 9/1363
Sheet metal
bending brake, made of wood, 17/2629
cutter, hand, 6/899
holes enlarged by file tang, 9/1297
pipe, drilling on drill press, 7/1040
working sheet metal, 17/2623
Shelf clocks: Connecticut, 5/750
Shelf post-bookends: made from metal tubing, 19/2956
Shellac: guide to wood finishing, 20/3094
Shelters: shelter-house for grill, 9/1375
Shelters, garden
gardening work center, 9/1332
gazebo cookout center, 9/1346
gazebo and screen house, 18/2821
shaded yard shelters, 9/1330
Shelves
bathroom ladder-shelves, 2/230
bell shelf, colonial, 9/1356
book shelves, 3/396
bookcase, built-in-wall, 3/400
bookcase wall with dropped soffit, 18/2807
brackets, made from metal tubing, 19/2956
built inside pantry doors, 11/1612
closet, storage, adding to room, 5/774
closet, using wasted space, 5/779
darkroom shelf fits laundry tub, 14/2116
door shelves, piggyback, 4/492
etagere, 8/1154
fasteners, types and sizes, 8/1193
garage storage platform, 9/1321
gun rack, custom-fit, 9/1383
hanging shelves, installing, 17/2630
hat shelf and coat rack, of plexiglass, 14/2205
hi-fi open rack, 10/1448
laundry center for kitchen, 10/1464
mudroom shelf unit, 13/1948
shelves at foot of stairs, 18/2794
small-parts shelf from plastic 'eggs', 17/2709
stemware shelf, for wine glasses, 2/188
storage shelves and suspended desk, 18/2794
trays, swing-out, under shelves, 2/232
utility shelves, sliding doors for, 17/2636
wall shelf, for family room, 8/1174
wall shelf, valuables hidden behind, 16/2558
wall shelves, how to build, 17/2632
wall shelves, installing, 17/2630
Sheraton nesting tables: 13/1958
Shields, erasing: *made from film, 1/61*
Shims
cutting on bench saw, 17/2660
how to use, 17/2638
Shingles
asbestos shingles, re-siding over, 16/2557
asphalt shingles, installing, 16/2450
asphalt vs. red-cedar shingles, 1/45
caulking between shingles and foundation wall, 17/2720
damaged roofs, repairing, 17/2640
loose coating is common, 5/649
painted shingles can't be stained, 11/1685
re-siding, instructions, 17/2685
re-siding over original shingles, 17/2669
replacing shingles with cedar shakes, 10/1570
reroofing, safe weight-margin, 4/544
roof leak, locating, 14/2204
roof leak, pinpointing, 12/1821
rust stains on white shingles, removing, 1/125
shingle number, meaning of, 18/2809
wood shakes and shingles, installing, 16/2454
Ship models: fine models from original plans, 17/2642
Shipping crates: *marked with ink-filled glue bottle, 16/2543*
Shock absorbers, auto
checking, selecting, and replacing, 17/2647
servicing, 18/2786
Shock preventers: ground-fault circuit interrupters, 20/3082
Shoe polish: *used as wood finish, 9/1397*
Shoes: roll-out shoe drawer for closet, 17/2651

Shooting
bench-rest shooting, rifles, 17/2652
gun cabinet, 9/1378
gun rack, custom-fit, 9/1383
muzzleloaders, choosing and using, 13/1950
shotguns, selecting, 17/2674
sighting-in guns, 12/1768
target box, 12/1771
Shooting board: tool squares edge of board, 17/2670
Short-bar clamps: selecting and using, 5/738
Shortwave radio: TV interference, stopping, 10/1542
Shotguns
gun cabinet, 9/1378
gun rack, custom-fit, 9/1383
muzzleloaders, choosing and using, 13/1950
selecting, 17/2674
sighting-in guns, 12/1768
Showcase cabinets: for guns, trophies, china, books, 9/1378
Showers
bathroom plumbing repairs, 1/157
bathtubs, prefab, installing, 2/220
condensation, adding vent fan, 5/800
floor, pitch for water drainage, 18/2752
plastic sheet under shower pan, 18/2752
regrouting tile, 17/2669
soap film on door, cleaning, 17/2600
Shows, photo-slide: improving slides, 17/2702
Shrubbery
deep-watering penetrator pipe, 5/748
how to transplant, 19/2942
landscaping techniques, 11/1679
mock orange, when to prune, 19/3027
Shrubbery lights: low yard lamp, 15/2301
Shuffleboard: yard lighting for game areas, 20/3149
Shuffleboard tables: how to build, 17/2678
Shutters
cloth-covered to match draperies, 16/2434
louvered, in dummy frames, 8/1186
Sidewalks
brick, possible bases, 17/2600
broken by tree roots, 8/1147
concrete, coloring, 6/840
concrete, patching, 6/844
concrete, patching, 8/1280
concrete slabs, laying and pouring, 6/834
flagstones, sealing, 16/2557
form boards cut in chisel shape, 20/3087
garden paths and sidewalks, 14/2084
powdery surface, cause of, 5/697
snow-melting systems, 17/2717
snowblowers, using properly, 17/2712
working with concrete, 6/830
Siding
aluminum or vinyl, choosing, 4/544
aluminum siding, painting, 19/2889
aluminum siding, repainting, 5/800
aluminum siding, won't make house cold, 18/2809
barn-siding picture frames, 9/1284
caulking between shingles and foundation wall, 17/2720
lumber guide, 11/1747
nails, selecting and using, 13/1954
narrow siding gives house longer look, 11/1685
painted or weathered without paint?, 11/1735
painting, 10/1488
re-siding, instructions, 17/2685
re-siding, over asbestos shingles, 16/2557
re-siding over original shingles, 17/2669
scaffold, mobile, how to build, 16/2524
selecting, 17/2680
sheathing, guide to types, 17/2620
Signals, distress: boating emergencies, 3/365
Signs: *stencils made from wire screen, 13/2012*
Silicone: *improves workglove grip, 13/2028*
Silverware
cutlery cupboard, colonial, 10/1600
cutlery tray, 10/1598
cutlery-and-napkin caddy, 10/1594
Simulated brick: wall covering, 3/450
Sink, toy: kitchen appliances for children, 19/2908
Sinks
built into cabinet bar, 2/194
built into mobile bar, 12/1865
drain pipes, flexible, 14/2204
drains, how to unclog, 7/1032
installing sink fronts, 11/1616
kitchen, replacing, 11/1608
plumbing repairs, 14/2216
refinishing, 16/2557
Sinks, dry: colonial chest, 7/1050
Siphons: made from metal tubing, 19/2956
Six-in-one wood table lamp: 11/1672
Skates, ice: sharpening jig, 10/1522
Skates, roller: *support large drum or cylinder, 18/2783*
Skeet shooting: shotguns, selecting, 17/2674
Skimmers, pool: *strainer basket made from pail, 11/1731*
Skin diving
basic techniques, 17/2692
underwater-photos guide, 19/2980
Skis, snow: maintenance, 17/2698
Skylights
condensation drips on attic floor, 11/1621
installing, 10/1458
Slabs, concrete
casting, 6/838
garden paths and sidewalks, 14/2084
laying out and pouring, 6/834
Slate floors: *removing stain, 8/1147*
Slats, bed: *held with eyescrews, 3/433*
Sleds: *preventing rust on runners, 17/2673*
Sleeping bags: sew-your-own kits, 4/538
Slide whistles: made from metal tubing, 19/2956
Slides, children's
A-frame swing set, 1/41
stilt-house slide, 14/2187
Slides, photo
coffee table-slide viewer, 6/806
illuminator, slide-copy, 10/1535
lightbox built in drawing table, 11/1723
projector stand, roll-away, 15/2342
slide shows, improving, 17/2702
Sliding doors
adding to room, 16/2430
burglar proofing, 3/460
for utility shelves, 17/2636
glass doors, installing, 17/2706
Sliding partitions: for basement family room, 8/1186
Sliding walls: panels hide storage space, 18/2794
Slip-joint pliers: basics of using, 19/2902
Slots, mail: *awning protects door mail-slot, 17/2697*
Small engines: servicing, 8/1128
Small parts
holder for spray-painting, 12/1781
magnetic holder, 6/887
paint spraying, 1/61
spray-painting, 4/640
storage bins from coffee cans, 19/2948
storage shelf from plastic 'eggs', 17/2709
stored in ice-cube trays, 10/1495
three labels on jar for identification, 12/1853
tongs to pick up small parts, 7/1009
workshop organizer 'drawers', 17/2659
Smoke alarms: choosing, 1/66
Smokeless fireplaces: 8/1224
Smoking pipes
caddy, from coffee can, 3/416
pipe rack and humidor, 9/1352
Smoking stands: made from nail keg, 11/1759
Snack bars: appliance center and snack bar, 18/2794
Snack counters: for family room, 8/1178
Snack dishes: wood carving project, 4/604
Snack servers: folding tray, 19/2944
Snack tables: folding, 17/2710
Snapshots: tips on candid photos, 4/565
Snorkel boxes: for over/underwater photos, 19/2986
Snow candles: free-form, molded in snow, 4/560
Snow mold: *removing from lawn, 1/65*
Snow removal
engines, servicing, 8/1128
snow-melting systems, 17/2717
snowblowers, using properly, 17/2712
snowplow, for auto bumper, 18/2724
Snow skis: maintenance, 17/2698
Snow-melting systems: for roofs and walks, 17/2717
Snowblowers: using properly, 17/2712
Snowplows: homemade plow for auto bumper, 18/2724
Snowstorms
surviving in car, 3/351
tire chains, selecting and using, 4/638
Soaker hoses: *coiled in garbage-can lid, 17/2697*
Socket wrenches
Allen wrench T-handle, 16/2502
extensions for cramped areas, 16/2560
Socket-head wrenches: *handle, 4/501*
Sofa-beds: couch doubles as bed, 18/2726
Sofas
butcher block design, 3/463
corner lounge, for family room, 8/1174
upholstered sofas, how to 'respring', 19/2998
upholstery, basic techniques, 19/2990
wrap-around, for family room, 8/1178
Soffits: storage over kitchen cabinets, 4/492
Soft-focus photos: special effects dramatize pictures, 14/2144
Solar energy
guide to heating systems, 18/2730
sources of information, 18/2737
water heater, installing, 18/2739
Solar heaters: hot-water heating, 9/1416
Solar heating systems: passive collector for home, 9/1440
Solar kilns: for drying lumber, 10/1593
Solder: *clamps made from wire solder, 9/1322*
Soldering
adjustable stand made from hinge, 9/1429
aluminum gutters, soldering, 1/125
copper plumbing-pipe soldering tips, 14/2232
magnets hold parts, 1/61
mousetrap holds parts, 2/251
printed circuits, tape guide, 8/1164

soldering-iron support, 1/34
wires held with alligator-clip tool, 10/1555
wiring, how to solder, 18/2743
Solvents: stains, removing, 18/2772
Sorters: rock sorter for lapidary work, 11/1686
Soundproofing
adding insulation to walls, 1/95
draperies keep out sound, 11/1727
Space heaters
camping, from tin can, 4/543
getting more heat, 9/1425
repairing, 9/1407
selecting, 9/1419
Space-habitat design: painting unfinished furniture, 13/2039
Spacers
cut from ballpoint pens, 16/2543
made from metal tubing, 19/2956
Spackling
filling nail dimples, 17/2669
patching wall holes, 15/2329
***Spade lugs:** made from brass chain, 13/2012*
Spanish design
chest, mosaic top, 5/665
chests, decorated with moldings, 5/662
gun cabinet, 9/1378
table lamp, 11/1662
Sparkplugs, auto
basic auto tune-up, 19/2960
cables maintenance, 4/506
complete guide to plugs, 18/2746
replacing, 7/1112
***Spatulas:** for shop, made from steel strapping, 14/2155*
Speakers
amplifier for transistor radios, 1/74
auto stereo speakers, installing, 18/2753
cabinet enclosures, 4/488
Special effects
dramatizing photos, 14/2144
framing movies with matte box, 14/2148
Speed, boat: computing planing speed, 14/2166
Speed reducers: for electric shop-motors, 13/1929
Speedway, toy: racetrack for plastic cars, 19/2922
Spice racks: fit inside of kitchen cabinet doors, 11/1612
***Spikepod:** camerapod for low-level close-ups, 14/2116*
Spindles: turning on wood lathe, 20/3106
***Spindles, chair:** tool to scrape off finish, 11/1621*
***Spiral ratchet screwdrivers:** avoiding pinched fingers, 13/2069*
Splash blocks: for downspouts, installing, 9/1390
***Splashboards:** for laundry counter, 5/748*
Splicing
electrical wires, with crimp-on connectors, 7/1072
how to splice ropes, 11/1640
Splint-seat chair: Lincoln replica, 5/650
Sponge tape: protects furniture, 18/2842
Spool cabinet: wall-hung, 17/2585
***Spools, thread:** clamps made from, 3/433*
Spoonholder racks: for table lamps, 11/1670
Spoons, fishing: how to make, 11/1752
Spoons, salad: laminated wood, 11/1652
Sports
badminton, restringing rackets, 18/2851
binoculars, choosing and using, 3/324
binoculars, small-optic, 3/328
drowning, hypothermia prevention, 1/24
exercises to get in shape, 8/1158
golf, putting greens, 15/2356
ice skates, sharpening jig, 10/1522
skin diving, basic techniques, 17/2692
skin diving, underwater-photos guide, 19/2980
sleds, preventing rust on runners, 17/2673
snow skis, maintenance, 17/2698
storage for outdoor equipment, 18/2794
tennis, restringing rackets, 18/2851
water skiing, acrobatic, 18/2756
yard lighting for game areas, 20/3149
***Spotting, photo-print:** tips on spotting, 14/2116*
Spray cans
aerosol valves, cleaning, 1/34
how to paint with spray cans, 13/2052
Spray-painting
gold paint, applying to wood, 5/765
holder for small parts, 12/1781
how to paint with spray cans, 13/2052
small parts, 1/61
small parts, knobs, 4/640
Sprayers: air compressor, how to build, 6/826
Spring boards: for table saws, 17/2660
***Spring clamps:** hold tools for heat-treating, 13/2078*
***Springs:** screen doors, spring corrects sagging, 11/1626*
Sprinklers, lawn
children's water hoop, 14/2191
deep-watering penetrator pipe, 5/748
Squares, combination: how to use, 6/825
***Squares, framing:** resquaring, 1/61*
Squaring board: for table saw, 17/2664
Squeaks, floor
squeaking plywood sub-floor, 17/2720
stopping squeaks, 16/2467
Squirrels: keeping out of gardens, 19/3038
Stack, roof: how to waterproof, 16/2450
Stack pipes
cleaning out, 9/1430
heat pipes, reclaim flue-gas heat, 9/1430
saving furnace heat, 9/1430
Stacking party tables: store in serving table, 13/2074
Stagecoach-trunk toybox: 3/430
Stained glass
guide to making stained glass windows, 18/2766
imitation 'stained' glass projects, 18/2759
'Stained glass': Christmas window hangings, 5/698
Staining, concrete: coloring concrete, 6/840
Staining, wood
basic techniques, 18/2770
furniture refinishing, 8/1208
painted shingles can't be stained, 11/1685
red 'paint,' for colonial furnishings, 14/2186
working properties of common woods, 20/3122
Stains, removing
chocolate stains on fabric, 12/1821
common solvents and their use, 18/2772
creosote stains on stove hearth, 18/2845
fireplace, smoke stains on brick, 3/369
fuel-oil stain on concrete, 1/65
furniture repair, 9/1302
paint spills on concrete, 12/1839
pencil marks on hardwood, 5/765
rust on concrete, 15/2269
rust stains on white shingles, 1/125
slate floor, yellow stain, 8/1147
varnish, removing from floor, 20/3137
varnish on asphalt tile, 14/2105
Stairs
basement, prefab, installing, 2/206
basement, tightened with turnbuckle, 4/501
basement stairwall, 2/202
brick and masonry, how to build, 18/2790
concrete steps, painting, 4/573
concrete steps, patching, 18/2809
for decks, laying out, 14/2102
for two-level deck, 6/924
handrail, wooden, 15/2387
laying out and building, 18/2776
measurements guide, 12/1784
shelves at foot of stairs, 18/2794
snow-melting systems, 17/2717
wrought-iron railings, installing, 15/2388
Stairwalls: basement, 2/202
Stairwells: basement, prefab, installing, 2/206
***Stakes, concrete-form:** cut in chisel shape, 20/3087*
Stalling, auto
stopping stalls, 18/2780
troubleshooting, 7/1100
Stamps, postage: stamp and pencil holder, for desk, 6/931
***Stamps, rubber:** cushion for stamping, 4/584*
Stands, calculators: for pocket calculator, 4/511
Stands, power-tool
bandsaw stand, 15/2316
casters, retractable, 15/2321
combination workbench and tool stand, 20/3132
drill-press stand, 15/2316
jigsaw stand, 15/2316
jointer, mobile stand, 10/1586
jointer-and-saw stand, 15/2316
pad-sander stand, 13/2024
portable-electric-drill stand, 15/2322
radial-arm saw cabinet with extension tables, 16/2518
radial-arm saw cabinet-stand, 15/2372
radial-arm saw stand, 20/3138
radial-arm saws, bench-cabinet, 15/2378
router stand, 15/2322
Stands, projector: roll-away stand, 15/2342
Stands, rolling: for bench saw, 18/2784
***Staple guns:** raised with blocks, 8/1164*
***Staplers:** inch marks on side, 5/656*
Star effects: special effects dramatize photos, 14/2144
Starters, auto: how they work, 10/1524
Starting systems, outboard motors
servicing, 13/1981
starting problems, troubleshooting, 13/2002
Starting, hard, auto: troubleshooting, 7/1100
Station wagons: tailgate picnic chest, 4/494
Station-wagon workbench: mounted on tailgate, 20/3131
Steam bending: how to bend wood, 20/3088
Steam irons: how to repair, 10/1548
Steel siding: selecting, 17/2680
Steel wool
holder from crutch tip, 9/1335
pot cleaners substitute for, 13/2079
Steering, auto: servicing steering system, 18/2786
Stemware shelves: with wine rack, 2/188
***Stencils:** made from wire screen, 13/2012*
***Step blocks:** for pulling nails, 18/2738*
Stepladders
choosing, 11/1645
inner tube holds tools, 3/389
paint can held on shelf, 8/1157
paintbrush holder, 13/2028

plant stand, of plexiglass, 14/2205
platform for extra foot space, 10/1581
shelf locked with hooks, 15/2329
shelf parts-holder, 10/1581
storage idea, 5/748
using safely, 11/1650

Stepping stones: raising and leveling, 18/2789

Steps
brick and masonry, how to build, 18/2790
concrete, how to patch, 18/2809
concrete, painting, 4/573
for decks, laying out, 14/2102
for two-level deck, 6/924
handrail, wooden, 15/2387
laying out and building, 18/2776
measurements guide, 12/1784
snow-melting systems, 17/2717
working with concrete, 6/830
wrought-iron railings, installing, 15/2388

Stereo
audio mixers, choosing and using, 12/1856
auto speakers, installing, 18/2753
cables, identification tags, 5/778
entertainment center, built-in, 8/1170
hi-fi stereo wall, 4/488
mobile music center, 12/1865
record care and cleaning, 15/2398

Sticking doors: how to trim and plane, 7/1024

Stilt house: combined slide and stilt house, 14/2187

Stilts: children's toys, 14/2196

Stone paths: for garden and yard, 14/2084

Stone walls
how to build, 16/2446
replacing mortar, 11/1760

Stones, stepping: raising and leveling, 18/2789

Stools
coffee table for patio, with stools, 6/816
coffee table with box stools, 6/804
for family-room seating, 8/1186
holes for legs, drilling, 7/1040
outdoor, aluminum-and-canvas, 5/644
rustic slab stool, 18/2793

Stopped chamfers: made on jointer, 10/1582

Stoppers, cruet: *loosening stuck stopper, 13/2017*

Storage, boat: winter layup, 3/370

Storage bins
for garden work center, 9/1332
under kitchen wall cabinets, 4/492

Storage boxes: for chain-saw accessories, 3/428

Storage buildings
children's playhouse, 14/2200
fence with built-in toolhouse, 8/1199
garden work shelter, 9/1332
grill shelter-house, 9/1375
metal sheds, preserving paint, 18/2752
patio gazebo, 14/2110
poolhouse for year-round use, 15/2270

Storage closets
adding to room, 5/774
using wasted space, 5/779

Storage drawers
dust-free, for shop parts, 5/689
workshop organizer, 17/2659

Storage ideas: finding extra storage space, 18/2794

Storage racks: *for pipe, molding, dowels, 5/778*

Storage shelves
for bathroom, 2/230
garage storage platform, 9/1321
installing, 17/2630
kitchen-door shelves, 4/492
made from plastic 'eggs', 17/2709
sliding doors cover utility shelves, 17/2636

Storage trays: swing-out stacked trays, 19/2949

Storage walls
bookcase wall with dropped soffit, 18/2807
built under attic eaves, 18/2794
false wall hides Ping-Pong table, 18/2794
garage storage wall with workbench, 18/2794
modules from kitchen cabinets, 4/484
multipurpose room divider, 18/2794
room divider-walls, 16/2459
shelves and suspended desk, 18/2794
shutters hide under-eaves attic storage, 18/2794
sliding panels hide storage space, 18/2794
storage for outdoor equipment, 18/2794
study center, wall-hung, 18/2818
units slide in and out, 18/2794

Storm doors
aluminum doors, repairing, 18/2810
hinges, selecting, 10/1450
repairing split in wood, 15/2341
stopping heat loss, 20/3078

Storm windows
aluminum windows, repairing, 18/2810
preventing condensation, 15/2381
stopping heat loss, 20/3078

Stove, toy: kitchen appliances for children, 19/2908

Stove bolts: selecting, using, 3/393

Stoves
electric ranges, repairing, 15/2391
hood for wall oven over range, 13/2018

Stoves, wood-burning
creosote stains on hearth, 18/2845
flue clogged by bister, 12/1864
getting more heat, 9/1425
installing, 18/2812
selecting, 9/1419
venting tip, 5/709

Stowaway tables: picnic tables, two, 13/2013

Strainer baskets: *for swimming pool, 11/1731*

Straps, pipe: *made from metal banding, 20/3087*

Strawberry barrels: how to make, 18/2816

String dispensers: *made from funnels, 11/1731*

Stringing tennis rackets: 18/2851

Strip flooring: hardwood floors, how to lay, 8/1240

Strip heaters: for plexiglass, 14/2205

Stucco
patching foundation walls, 1/125
patching loose blisters, 19/2937

Stud drivers: *improvised from matching nut, 18/2738*

Studs: *installing in metal, 4/640*

Study centers
bunk bed-desk, children's, 5/668
modules from kitchen cabinets, 4/484
rolltop desk and chair, children's, 5/676
wall counter is work-study area, 18/2794
wall-hung study center, 18/2818

Stumps
how to remove, 19/2954
tips on burning out, 14/2105

Stutz Bearcat: model car from tin cans, 18/2875

Styrofoam: *marble-gluing jig, 7/982*

Styrofoam Christmas tree: musical centerpiece, 4/628

Suitcase darkrooms: portable, 6/910

Suitcases: made into camera bag, 4/514

Summer houses: gazebos and screen house, 18/2821

Summer rooms, screened
screened garage, 16/2534
screened porch, building, 16/2528

Sump pumps: *sumps, closed or open?, 6/847*

Sun porches: remodeled into family room, 8/1170

Sundials: polar sundial, 18/2826

Sunken bathtubs: illusion of, 2/214

Super camp: plans for vacation home, 19/3010

Surging, auto: curing, 7/1112

Survival: blizzards, surviving in car, 3/351

Suspension, auto
servicing suspension system, 18/2786
shock absorbers, checking, selecting, and replacing, 17/2647

Swimming pools
cabana poolhouse, 3/476
carpeting, outdoor, 4/592
decks and privacy wall, 15/2280
diving deck, for above-ground pool, 18/2832
drownproofing, 1/24
filter, for above-ground pool, 18/2831
ground-fault circuit interrupters, 20/3082
installing tips, 15/2274
pool maintenance, 18/2828
poolhouse for year-round use, 15/2270
pre-summer maintenance, 15/2278
skimmer strainer basket made from pail, 11/1731
yard lighting for game areas, 20/3149

Swing-out trays: *under workshop shelves, 2/232*

Swings
A-frame swing set, 1/41
children's merry-go-round swing, 14/2189
children's swing with guard rail, 14/2196
porch swing, on A-frame, 15/2285
yard swing, two-seater, 18/2836

'Swiss-cheese' mountain game: 20/3062

Switch, knee: *for photo-print inspection light, 14/2116*

Switches, electrical
dimmer switch, installing, 10/1464
light switches, replacing, 10/1470

Switches, light: *extension for children, 5/721*

Swivel chairs: for dining set, 7/992

Swiveling hi-fi center: 10/1444

Synthetic turf: used for putting greens, 15/2356

T

T-bevels: *from table-saw miter gauge, 5/656*

Table lamps
cobbler's bench lamp, 11/1668
spoonholder rack, 11/1670
Spanish style, 11/1662
wood, six-in-one, 11/1672

Table saws
angle blocks for miter joints, 12/1854
blade-height gauge block, 17/2660
blades, sharpening on arbor, 3/433
box or finger joints, cutting, 17/2660
cabinet-stand, 15/2316
compound angles, cutting, 1/76
cove molding, how to make, 17/2664
crosscutting duplicate pieces, 17/2664
crosscutting wide boards, 17/2664
dadoes, duplicating, 17/2664

dovetail joints, how to make, 7/1026
dowels, cutting into pins, 5/656
extensions for long boards, 18/2841
jig for same-size cuts, 18/2783
lining up blade and work, 17/2664
maintenance, 15/2310
miter board, 12/1850
miter jig, 17/2664
molding-cutter storage holder, 12/1900
pattern sawing, 17/2664
push stick, made from coat hanger, 17/2660
sandpaper stops workpiece creeping, 17/2664
spring board, 17/2660
squaring board, 17/2664
stop, made from monkey wrench, 3/433
tapers, ripping, 17/2664
T-bevel, from miter gauge, 5/656
tenoner, 17/2660
wood disc saucer cavity, 17/2660
wood discs, rabbeting, 17/2664

Table servers: lazy Susan centerpiece, 11/1704
Table shuffleboard: how to build, 17/2678
Table tennis
ball and paddle caddy, 4/509
false wall hides table, 18/2794
playback for solo practice, 8/1157
Tables
backgammon and chess table, 1/146
barbecue table, wraparound, 2/174
bed table, footboard, 5/672
bed table-buffet, 2/246
buffet table, knockdown, 8/1186
butcher block, 3/468
butler's table, 3/472
card tables, simple, for family room, 8/1186
coffee table, aquarium, 6/810
coffee table, butcher block, 3/463
coffee table, for patio, with stools, 6/816
coffee table, lattice strips decorate, 10/1462
coffee table, made from chimney blocks, 14/2152
coffee table, matches barbecue bar, 2/171
coffee table, plexiglass, 14/2205
coffee table, slide viewer, 6/806
coffee table, with box stools, 6/804
dining table, gateleg, 7/983
dining table, oaken, pedestal, 7/987
dining table, trestle, with benches, 7/998
dining table, trestle, with swivel chairs, 7/992
dowel joints, how to make, 10/1572
drawing table, with built-in lightbox, 11/1723
drop-leaf table joints, cutting with router, 16/2468
end tables, from kitchen cabinets, 4/484
game table, circular, 9/1304
hutch table, early American, 10/1516
joints, how to make and fit, 10/1576
lamp table, with lighted planter, 14/2172
legs, how to attach, 11/1710
marble top, attaching to table, 16/2533
nesting tables, four Sheraton replicas, 13/1958
night tables, from kitchen cabinets, 4/484
outdoor tables, stowaway, 13/2013
painting, jar lids under legs, 19/2931
parsons bridge table, 3/453
party tables, nesting, 13/2070
party tables, stacking, 13/2074
pedestal table, 13/1978
picnic table, folds flat for storage, 14/2150
picnic table, hexagon shape, 14/2159
picnic table, made from chimney blocks, 14/2152
picnic table, octagon shape, 14/2159
picnic table, rejuvenating weathered redwood, 11/1685
picnic table-and-benches, folds up, 14/2156
pool table, bumper-pool, 15/2264
pool table, full-size, 15/2256
sewing cabinet, chairside, 17/2582
snack tables, folding, 17/2710
tabletop fastener, concealed, 4/553
tambour table, French Provincial, 13/1974
telephone stand, of plexiglass, 14/2205
trisected table of plexiglass, 14/2205
wall-hung table, for pier set, 14/2162

Tables, bandsaw: king-size table, 2/170
Tabletop hockey game: 1/58
Tabletop lathes: miniature, for hobby work, 20/3103
Tabletops
gluing random-width boards, 17/2664
screw pockets, making on drill press, 17/2664
Tackle boxes, fishing: choosing fishing gear, 8/1232
Tacks: *holder for driving tacks, 2/291*
Tags, identification: *for stereo cables, 5/778*
Tailgate workbench: for station wagons, 20/3131
Tailgates, auto: picnic chest, 4/494
Tailpipes, auto: replacing, 8/1166
Tambour tables: French Provincial design, 13/1974
Tampers: for patio sand-bed, how to make, 14/2090
Tandem bicycles: building, 2/296
Tangs, file
enlarging sheet-metal holes, 9/1297
tightening setscrews, 13/2079
Tape
cloth-tape inlays for trinket boxes, 10/1537
filament tape aids in gluing, 11/1678
inlays decorate tape, 13/2079
masking tape clamps joints when gluing, 18/2783
solving home repair problems, 18/2842
used to mask glue joints, 18/2738
wood tape, applying to plywood edges, 20/3087
Tape, pin-striping: *decorating boxes, 6/819*
Tape decks: auto stereo speakers, installing, 18/2753
Tape recorders
audio mixers, choosing and using, 12/1856
cassette recorders, repairing, 4/598
cassette tape rewinder, 11/1678
Tapers: ripping on table saw, 17/2664
Tapes, cassette: snarled and broken, repairing, 4/602
Tapes, measuring: *wall holder for tape, 7/1009*
Taps
enlarging nut threads, 9/1429
slip-on extension, 10/1495
turned by chuck and faucet handle, 9/1335
Tar roofs: *applying new roof, 18/2752*
Targets
sighting-in guns, 12/1768
target box, 12/1771
Teeter boards
children's bouncing seesaw, 14/2189
children's rotating seesaw, 14/2194
Telephone benches: gossip bench, early American, 9/1365
Telephones: telephone stand, of plexiglass, 14/2205
Telephotos
camera gunstock, 4/520
panorama photos, 13/2066
small-optic lenses, 3/328
telescope, made from camera lens, 18/2846
Telescopes: scope made from camera lens, 18/2846
Television
antenna masts, from thinwall conduit, 12/1782
antennas, choosing the right one, 1/82
antennas, putting up, 1/86
antennas, repair and maintenance, 18/2848
entertainment center, swiveling, 10/1444
interference, stopping, 10/1542
mobile cart for TV set, 18/2794
Tennis
restringing rackets, 18/2851
yard lighting for game areas, 20/3149
Tenons
jig to make tenons, 10/1576
shouldered, made on jointer, 10/1582
table-saw tenoner, 17/2660
Tent trailers: how to build, 19/2932
Tents
sew-your-own kits, 4/538
space heater, tin-can, 4/543
Termites
detecting, treating, preventing, 18/2854
how to check for termites, 14/2186
Terraces: terracing with retaining walls, 16/2446
Terrariums
made of plexiglass, 14/2205
Tiffany-style terrarium, 18/2858
Test strips, photo: *kept in enlarging box lid, 14/2116*
Testers
auto batteries, 2/240
batteries, transistor-radio, 8/1164
continuity, testing doorbells, 7/1018
continuity tester, in screwdriver, 18/2860
doorbells, 7/1018
dry-cell batteries, 2/237
grounded-outlet checker, 5/657
Tetherball: children's game, 14/2196
Thatch: lawn de-thatching, 11/1698
Theaters, home
hideaway theater, 18/2862
mini projection booth, 18/2794
Thermometers
banjo barometer, 2/182
colonial weather station, 20/3060
darkroom thermometer held by clothespin, 14/2116
darkroom thermometer holder, 14/2116
eraser used as grip, 14/2116
held in photo bottles with clothespin, 4/521
Thermostats
day-and-night thermostats, 9/1430
furnace thermostat-controls, 20/3078
zoned heating for the home, 9/1430
Thermostats, auto: gaskets, replacing, 9/1342
Thinwall conduit: used for TV antenna masts, 12/1782
Thinwall tubing: *held in vise for slitting, 5/721*
Thread spools: *clamps made from, 3/433*
Threading: metal lathe swing toolholder, 12/1799
Three-dimensional photo-print displays: 13/1934

Tie wire: *cut to uniform length, 3/449*
Tie-downs, boat: cartopping system, 4/595
Tie-tacks: carved from wood and plastic, 10/1556
Tier cabinets: etagere, 8/1154
Tiffany-style terrarium: 18/2858
Tile, ceiling
acoustical tile, cleaning, 15/2381
acoustical tile, painting, 4/573
installing, 4/616
replacing, 10/1470
Tile, ceramic
bathroom, installing, 2/224
bathroom, tile on exterior wall, 12/1864
facing for prefab fireplace, 10/1468
installing on backup board, 20/3049
loose tile, replacing, 10/1470
nibbler, wire-brush, 5/689
used in cheese tray, 9/1352
wall tile, installing, 18/2869
Tile, floor
applying over old wide boards, 5/765
basement, needs waterproof adhesive, 15/2341
basement floor, flooded, 16/2533
how to install, 18/2866
mud-set tile, laying, 8/1245
quarry tile, installing, 15/2362
resetting, 10/1470
stains, removing, 18/2772
underlayment, how to install, 8/1237
varnish spill, not removable, 14/2105
Tile, metal: wall tile, installing, 18/2869
Tile, mosaic: Spanish chest, mosaic top, 5/665
Tile, patio: installing, 6/862
Tile, plastic
cut with jeweler's saw, 13/2078
grouting tip, 4/640
wall tile, installing, 18/2869
Tile, quarry: installing on floor, 15/2362
Tile, wall
bathroom, installing, 2/224
bathroom, tile on exterior wall, 12/1864
ceramic tile, installing on backup board, 20/3049
grouting tip, 4/640
installing, 18/2869
loose ceramic tile, replacing, 10/1470
replacing damaged tile on hardboard, 14/2105
shower, regrouting tile, 17/2669
Time exposures: night photography tips, 13/1963
Timepieces
clock, grandmother, 5/754
clock, shelf, Connecticut, 5/750
clock, using alarm on old shelf clock, 19/2979
clock, wall, 'heirloom', 5/766
clocks, cleaning soiled dial, 16/2523
clocks, oiling electric motor, 18/2820
clocks, wall, plywood face, 5/768
grandfather clock, repairing warped access door, 10/1570
Timers
camera timer, water-drip, 14/2116
darkroom-timer beeper, 14/2116
for house lamps, 10/1464
photo, eraser grip for knobs, 14/2116
thermostats, day-and-night, 9/1430
Tin cans: craft projects from tin cans, 18/2875
Tinsel art Christmas tree: Christmas ornaments, 5/690
Tip-out bins: for kitchen, 11/1607
Tires, auto
care and maintenance, 19/2886
chains, selecting and using, 4/638
'fork' aids in removal, 1/150
labels, how to read, 19/2884
noises, stopping, 13/1967
pressure gauge, stored in glovebox, 6/887
pressure-gauge rack, 7/1009
prewinter maintenance, 20/3074
rotation patterns, 19/2886
spreader made from open-end wrench, 8/1192
steering and suspension, servicing, 18/2786
Toasters
how to repair, 19/2890
magnet holds plug to toaster, 2/291
small-appliance repair, 1/96
Toboggans: how to bend slats, 20/3088
Toggle bolts
anchoring tall cabinets, 18/2820
fasteners, types and sizes, 8/1193
Toilets
bathroom plumbing repairs, 1/157
bubbles from bottom, cause and cure, 1/125
how to unclog, 7/1032
installing, 2/224
toilet-tank leak, preventing, 20/3137
trickling water, stopping, 10/1470
Tongs: *made to pick up small parts, 7/1009*
Tongue-and-groove flooring: *hammer protector, 16/2543*
Tool caddy: for hand tools, 4/510
Toolboards: valuables hidden behind, 16/2558
Toolboxes
contemporary 'portable workshop', 19/2896
handle from wrecking bar, 3/449
made from egg cartons, 11/1703
Toolholders
darkroom tool storage, 4/513
glove, slipped onto belt, 3/416
Toolholders, swing: for metal lathes, 12/1799
Toolhouses: built into fence, 8/1199
Toolposts: lathe toolpost for hefty turning bits, 12/1792
Tools
bar clamps, making, 5/744
carried in eyeglass case, 13/2028
clamp, machine-vise, making, 5/742
clamps, selecting and using, 5/738
clamps hold tools for heat-treating, 13/2078
electric motors, guide to, 13/1924
electric motors, repairing, 13/1926
electric motors, speed reducer, 13/1929
painting tools, selecting and using, 13/2048
propane-torch stand, 19/2905
sharpening, on radial-arm saw, 15/2384
small tools stored in eyeglass case, 16/2502
small tools stored in ice-cube trays, 10/1495
stored in photo-gear cases, 5/721
twist drills, how to sharpen, 19/2976
woodworking tools to make, eight, 17/2670
Tools, hand
adzes, making and using, 4/624
augers, screw-point protector, 3/389
calipers, choosing and using, 4/502
calipers, for wood lathe, 17/2670
chisels, edge protected by pill bottle, 14/2155
claw hammers, how to use, 5/745
combination square, using, 6/825
cutter, sheet-metal, 6/899
files, handles improvised, 3/389
files, tang tightens setscrews, 13/2079
framing squares, resquaring, 1/61
hacksaws, blade handle for tight quarters, 17/2673
hacksaws, blade used upside down, 16/2502
hacksaws, cutting angle iron, 17/2639
hacksaws, overhead cutting tip, 5/748
hacksaws, storage rack, 5/689
hammers, belt holster, 19/2989
hammers, holster for belt, 6/934
hammers, increasing leverage for drawing nails, 6/934
handles made from metal tubing, 19/2956
handles, making, 17/2670
handsaw basics, 9/1396
handsaws, bevel guide, 17/2664
handsaws, keeping vertical, 17/2664
handsaws, stored on door, 3/416
handsaws, straightening bent blade, 19/2979
handsaws, trimming door bottom, 17/2664
holders from garden hose, 2/291
keyhole saws, hose on blade protects work, 8/1157
levels, suction cups protect glass, 13/2079
micrometers, 'enlarging', 12/1828
oilstone, self-lubricating, 17/2610
pipe wrenches, improvised with pliers, 18/2857
planes, shooting board, 17/2670
pliers, basics of using, 19/2902
pliers, used as hand punch, 13/1936
pliers, wire-cutting gauge, 18/2857
punches, leather, improvised, 2/232
punches, rivet hole-sizer, 2/179
rasps, made from threaded rod, 11/1703
rust, removing, 5/697
safety in the shop, 16/2490
sawhorse tool-brackets, 13/2069
scrapers, how to use, 16/2526
scratch stock, for beading, 17/2670
screwdrivers, alligator clip on end, 10/1555
screwdrivers, continuity tester, 18/2860
screwdrivers, screw held to head, 8/1164
screwdrivers, spiral ratchet, avoiding pinched fingers, 13/2069
screwdrivers, using properly, 16/2538
scribers, chalk makes lines visible, 8/1259
scribers, tubing gives smooth grip, 8/1185
selecting basic tools, 19/2899
sharpening, 17/2608
spatulas, how to make, 14/2155
tool caddy, 4/510
toolbox, contemporary, 19/2896
whetstone, truing flattened surface, 11/1735
wood chisels, basics of using, 19/2904
wrenches, basics of using, 19/2903
wrenches, box-end, held on loose-leaf rings, 9/1297
wrenches, emergency, 17/2639
wrenches, ratcheting movement, 13/1936
wrenches, T-handle for Allen wrench, 16/2502
Tools, portable electric
abrasives, selecting and using, 1/20
basic tools for home shop, 7/1023
belt sanders, basics, 16/2498
belt sanders, how to use, 2/258
circular saws, bench for, 5/717
circular saws, blades, selecting, 5/722
circular saws, plywood cutoff jig,

improving and modernizing, 16/2412
safe-driving tips, 16/2404
space heater, tin-can, 4/543
tent trailer, how to build, 19/2932
utility trailer, for garden tractor, 19/2928
winter-storage tips, 16/2408
Trailers, boat
maintenance tips, 3/373
trailering a boat, 3/376
Train, circus: pull toy, 15/2348
Train engine, toy: puffs 'smoke', 19/2914
Train garlands: for Christmas, 5/690
Train models: layout hides under bed, 18/2794
Trains, toy: wood-block freight train, 19/2914
Transfers: *patterns, using newspapers, 6/887*
Transistor radios
amplifier, 1/74
battery tester, 8/1164
Translucent panels: restyling entryway, 8/1148
Transmissions, auto
automatic-transmission fluid, changing, 19/2938
checking lubricant, 11/1740
differentials, troubleshooting, 7/978
four-wheel drive tune-up, 19/2970
noise, diagnosing, 15/2324
noises, stopping, 13/1967
Transplanting: moving plants, trees, shrubbery, 19/2942
Trap shooting: shotguns, selecting, 17/2674
Traps: rabbit trap, how to build, 19/3038
Traps, insect: black-light trap, 10/1538
Trash cans: can cradle, for garden work center, 9/1332
Travel photos: vacation-photo tips, 14/2139
Travelpod: camper-boat-luggage carrier, 4/526
Traverse rods: hanging, 7/1034
Tray tables: stack in serving table, 13/2074
Trays: *workshops, under shelves, 2/232*
Trays, cheese: recessed ceramic tile, 9/1352
Trays, folding: snack server, 19/2944
Trays, ring: made from metal tubing, 19/2956
Trays, serving
butler's table, 3/472
laminated wood, 11/1652
lifts off wine rack, 3/424
veneer-covered, 20/3044
Trays, silverware: wood cutlery holder, 10/1598
Trays, storage: swing-out stacked trays, 19/2949
Treasure chests: trinket box, 9/1352
Tree houses: combination jungle gym and tree house, 14/2188
Tree of life candleholders: for Christmas, 5/702
Tree-holders: for magazines and newspapers, 11/1758
Trees
chain saws, cutting down trees and limbs, 4/634
chain saws, using and repairing, 4/632
choosing trees for your yard, 19/2952
cutting with crosscut saws, 6/878
deep-watering penetrator pipe, 5/748
how to fell, buck, and limb, 19/2954
how to transplant, 19/2942
landscaping techniques, 11/1675
roots, green ash tree, 17/2600
roots break up sidewalk, 8/1147
rough lawn bumps under trees, 16/2533
seeding lawn after tree removal, 1/65
stumps, how to remove, 19/2954
stumps, tips on burning out, 14/2105
sugar maple is best shade tree, 10/1570
young trees braced with soaker hose, 15/2329
Trellises: trellis planter for vines, 14/2106
Trestle desks
campaign desk, 7/964
colonial design, 6/951
Trestle tables
dining table with benches, 7/998
dining table with swivel chairs, 7/992
hutch table, early American, 10/1516
Tricks: rubber-band-and-dowel puzzle, 20/3066
Trimmers, hedge: *using rotary mower, 12/1835*
Trinket boxes
cloth-tape inlays, 10/1537
decorating with pin-striping tape, 6/819
sanding, protecting corners, 7/982
self-closing hinge for lid, 11/1678
treasure chest, 9/1352
turned from plastic on metal lathe, 12/1814
wood carving project, 4/604
Trinket chests: treasure chest, 9/1352
Tripods
adusting legs to same length, 14/2116
braced against wall, 4/513
camera-case screw, removing, 14/2116
camerapods for low-level close-ups, 14/2116
nut glued to camera bottom for tripod, 4/521
unipod made from dowel, 14/2116
Trisected tables: of plexiglass, 14/2205
Trivets: dadoes cut on bench saw, 2/268
Trophy cabinets: in Mediterranean design, 9/1378
Trucks, pickup: camper shell, 4/534
Trucks, toy
dump truck, wooden, 7/1059
kiddie car, 'you-haul' pickup, 9/1351
Trundle beds: sofa-bed, 18/2726
Trunk toybox: 3/430
Trunks, auto: water leaks, stopping, 11/1706
Trunks, storage: *freshening stale odor, 8/1147*
Tubing, copper: *used as wire connectors, 11/1678*
Tubing, metal
cutting thin tubing with hacksaw, 16/2543
cutting without scratching, 13/2012
hacksawing in a vise, 18/2820
made into useful objects, 19/2956
protecting thinwall tubing in vise, 15/2397
ring turning on metal lathe, 12/1800
thin-wall, held in vise, 5/721
Tubing, plastic: *clothesline covering, 9/1322*
Tubs, planter: made of whiskey barrels, 14/2168
Tune-up, auto
basic tune-up procedure, 19/2960
carburetor zip kit, 4/590
electronic ignition systems, servicing, 10/1532
four-wheel drive tune-up, 19/2970
ignition systems, servicing, 10/1525
Tung oil: guide to wood finishing, 20/3094
Turbine ventilators: attics, cooling, 1/120
Turf, artificial: used for putting greens, 15/2356
Turnbuckles: *hose clamps, reinstalling, 11/1644*
Turning, metal
finishing turned projects, 12/1808
lathe toolpost for hefty bits, 12/1792
ring turning on a lathe, 12/1800
Turning, plastic: on metal lathe, 12/1814
Turning, wood
basic lathe techniques, 20/3106
faceplate lathe, how to make, 20/3100
tabletop hobby lathe, 20/3103
Turpentine: *paintbrushes, cleaning, 3/389*
Turtles: keeping out of gardens, 19/3038
TV: see Television
TV tables: stack in serving table, 13/2074
Twine dispensers: *made from funnels, 11/1731*
Twist drills
how to sharpen, 19/2976
stored in jar, 2/251

U

Underground drainage systems: for downspouts, 7/1030
Underlayment: nails, selecting and using, 13/1954
Underlayment, floor: how to install, 8/1237
Underwater
photography, guide to, 19/2980
skin diving, basic techniques, 17/2692
snorkel box, for over/underwater photos, 19/2986
Unfinished furniture
painting, 13/2039
whitewood, definition of, 11/1727
Unipods
camerapod for low-level close-ups, 14/2116
pod made from dowel, 14/2116
Universal joints, auto
noise, diagnosing, 15/2324
noises, stopping, 13/1967
Upholstery
basic techniques, 19/2990
chairs, how to 'respring', 19/2998
nails, selecting and using, 13/1954
Used cameras: how to buy, 19/3002
Used cars: 20 buying tips, 19/3006
Utility trailers: for garden tractor, 19/2928

V

V-belts: *how to stretch, 3/416*
V-blocks: for drill presses, 17/2670
Vacation homes
built around motor home, 19/3024
closing down for the winter, 19/3022
log cabin, how to chink logs, 19/3027
plans for five hideaway homes, 19/3016
plans for four vacation cabins, 19/3010
plumbing winterizing, 4/573
Vacations
CB radio, on vacation trips, 5/734
storing valuables in refrigerator, 9/1397
trailering a boat, 3/376
vacation-photo tips, 14/2139
Vacuum cleaners
dollies for shop vacuums, 19/3032
how to repair, 19/3028
tube for hard-to-reach places, 10/1499
Vacuum gauges, auto: gas mileage, improving, 1/134
Valentine's Day: gifts to make—mirror, ring caddy, crayon holder, jewelry box, 9/1360
Valets
dresser-top organizer, 9/1352
jewel box and overnight caddy, 10/1567
Valuables
hiding places in the home, 16/2558
storing in refrigerator on vacations, 9/1397

Valves, aerosol: *cleaning, 1/34*
Vanities
bathroom vanity-hamper, 2/216
installing, 2/224
mirror, reproduction of Lincoln's, 12/1840
vanity built into closet, 18/2794
vanity center, built from module, 12/1890
Vans: camp/work conversion, 4/531
Vapor barriers
attics, stopping condensation, 3/338
needed in attic for house humidifier, 16/2557
too tight, causes humidity, 17/2720
Varnish
guide to wood finishing, 20/3094
how to use, 19/3033
preventing bubbles on surface, 8/1280
using outdoors, 18/2809
removing spill from floor, 20/3137
spilled on asphalt tile, 14/2105
stir varnish, don't shake it, 13/1947
removers, using outdoors, 18/2809
why can shouldn't be shaken, 12/1839
Vases: cut from bottles, 3/418
Vegetable dryers: how to make, 7/1054
Vegetable gardens
cold frame-hotbed, 6/820
grown in small plot, 9/1336
hotbed, how to make, 19/3034
keeping varmints out, 19/3038
seeds planted with eye dropper, 19/2989
Veneering
backgammon and chess table, 1/146
Christmas tree ornaments, 5/702
curved pieces, applying veneer, 17/2669
gluing loose veneer, 10/1570
jewelry box, 10/1562
jewelry carving, 10/1556
loose veneer pieces, re-cementing, 14/2105
marquetry, inlaid-veneer pictures, 12/1772
patches, matching old finish, 4/544
ripples in veneer, repairing, 13/1947
three wood-covering projects, 20/3044
Ventilation
attic fans and ventilators, 1/120
attics, condensation cause and cure, 19/2937
attics, fans, using, 1/46
attics, vents open in winter, 17/2720
crawl space vents, leave open in winter, 15/2341
shower, fan stops condensation, 5/800
Vents: fake, for hiding valuables, 16/2558
Vernier calipers
choosing and using, 4/502
used to 'enlarge' micrometer, 12/1828
Vestibules
archway, translucent panels, 8/1148
bench for boot storage, 16/2434
pier set, filigree, 14/2162
quarry tile, installing, 15/2362
room divider-storage wall, 16/2459
window decorated with leaf-grille, 16/2434
View dividers
grille fence, 15/2334
louvered fence, 15/2336
louvered screen, 15/2334
privacy wall with storage, 18/2794
redwood privacy screen, 14/2110
Viewers, slide
coffee table-slide viewer, 6/806
lightbox built in drawing table, 11/1723
Vigilante III: airplane model, 12/1886
Vignetters: *made from cardboard tube, 14/2116*
Vignetting: special effects dramatize photos, 14/2144
Vinyl siding
re-siding over asbestos shingles, 16/2557
selecting, 17/2680
vinyl or aluminum, choosing, 4/544
Vinyl tubing: *clothesline covering, 9/1322*
Vises
bench vise made from C-clamp, 16/2560
C-clamp holds tiny parts in vise, 15/2397
clamp, machine-vise, making, 5/742
clamping abrasive paper to sanding block, 20/3087
cutting metal tubing, 18/2820
flat iron, twisting, 17/2639
grinder mount swings out of way, 13/2069
miterbox held steady, 5/721
protecting thinwall tubing in vise, 15/2397
tapered workpieces, clamping, 4/501
thin-wall tubing, held for slitting, 5/721
unfreezing stuck vise handle, 11/1731
wire bender gripped in vise, 14/2240
Volleyball: yard lighting for game areas, 20/3149

W

Wainscoting
installing, 10/1470
moldings, decorating ideas, 12/1904
Walks: see Sidewalks
Wall clocks
'heirloom' clock, 5/766
plywood face, 5/768
Wall coverings
brick, simulated, 3/450
self-adhesive, installing, 2/252
Wall desks
children's, 5/672
hinged, folds against wall, 6/935
Wall switches
dimmer switch, installing, 10/1464
replacing, 10/1470
Wall tables: hutch table, early American, 10/1516
Wall tile
bathroom, ceramic tile on exterior wall, 12/1864
bathroom, installing, 2/224
ceramic tile, installing on backup board, 20/3049
grouting tip, 4/640
installing, 18/2869
loose ceramic tile, replacing, 10/1470
replacing damaged tile on hardboard, 14/2105
shower, regrouting tile, 17/2669
Wall-mounted aquarium: 6/810
Wallpaper
framed with moldings, 12/1904
how to hang, 20/3052
how to remove, 19/2979
keep room measurements on back of picture, 19/2931
painting over old wallpaper paste, 1/45
papering over plasterboard, 12/1920
removing old paper, 20/3052
toothpicks inserted in picture-hook holes, 19/2931
trimmed with sharpened putty knife, 19/2948
Walls
basement, access panels, 2/202
basement, moisture caused by outside landfill, 11/1760
basement, partitions, framing, 2/200
basement, repairing crumbling concrete, 3/429
basement, waterproofing, 2/210
basement partitions, pivoting or sliding, 8/1186
basement walls, moisture prevention, 12/1821
basement water seepage, preventing, 5/649
bathroom, ceramic tile on exterior wall, 12/1864
bearing walls, removing, 2/242
book shelves, 3/396
bookcase, built-in-wall, 3/400
brick, simulated, 3/450
ceramic tile, installing on backup board, 20/3049
concrete basement wall, boring holes, 3/338
concrete basement wall, patching air-bubble holes, 11/1685
concrete blocks, how to lay, 6/848
concrete wall, basement, patching, 6/844
concrete-block walls, waterproofing, 3/369
covering, self-adhesive, installing, 2/252
cracks, patching, 10/1470
cracks, patching and painting, 13/2046
cracks in walls and ceiling, patching, 18/2845
drywall, repairing with tape, 18/2842
drywall holes, patching, 7/1058
dust catcher, when sawing holes, 2/179
fasteners, types and sizes, 8/1193
fiberboard walls, how to paint, 15/2341
foundation walls, adding under porch, 4/573
foundation walls, caulking between shingles and wall, 17/2720
foundation walls, preventing efflorescence, 11/1760
furring strips, locating under softboard, 19/2979
hardboard, selecting and using, 9/1398
holes, patching with spackling, 15/2329
insulation, between furring strips, 13/2017
insulation, how to install, 10/1539
insulation planks, how to fill gouges, 11/1621
lattice strips decorate, 10/1462
mildew, how to remove and prevent, 5/709
moldings, decorating ideas, 12/1904
painting a room, 13/2045
painting over old wallpaper paste, 1/45
paneling, hardboard, painting, 3/338
paneling, hardboard, selecting and using, 13/2054
paneling, hardwood, selecting and using, 13/2064
paneling, plywood, selecting and using, 13/2056
paneling, plywood, working with and finishing, 15/2244
patching plaster at ceiling-wall junction, 1/65
plasterboard, how to install, 14/2180
screw anchors, removing, 17/2600
sheathing, guide to types, 17/2620
shelves, how to build, 17/2632
shelves, installing, 17/2630
shelves, sliding doors for, 17/2636
soundproofing, adding insulation, 1/95
soundproofing, draperies keep out sound, 11/1727
stone walls, replacing mortar, 11/1760
stucco foundation walls, repairing cracks, 1/125
tile, damaged, replacing on hardboard, 14/2105
tile, installing, 18/2869
wainscoting, installing, 10/1470
wallpaper, how to hang, 20/3052
wallpaper, how to remove, 19/2979
wallpaper, keep room measurements on back of picture, 19/2931
wallpaper, papering over plasterboard,

2/1920
wallpaper, removing, 20/3052
wallpaper, toothpicks inserted in picture-hook holes, 19/2931
wallpaper, trimmed with putty knife, 19/2948
Walls, freestanding
how to build, 16/2464
light fixture, 16/2462
sewing center, 17/2586
Walls, retaining: how to build, 16/2446
Walls, storage
bookcase wall with dropped soffit, 18/2807
built under attic eaves, 18/2794
false wall hides Ping-Pong table, 18/2794
garage storage wall with workbench, 18/2794
multipurpose room divider, 18/2794
room divider-walls, 16/2459
shelves and suspended desk, 18/2794
shutters hide under-eaves attic storage, 18/2794
sliding panels hide storage space, 18/2794
storage for outdoor equipment, 18/2794
study center, wall-hung, 18/2818
units slide in and out, 18/2794
Walnut planks: *how to air-cure, 19/2937*
Washers
cut from ballpoint pens, 16/2543
keep plastic webbing from tearing, 9/1297
knob held by sandpaper 'washer', 3/449
made from old felt hat, 13/2078
turned from plastic on metal lathe, 12/1814
used as pocket screwdrivers, 13/1936
Washing machines
how to repair, 20/3056
laundry center for kitchen, 10/1464
Waste disposers
installing, 9/1323
repairing, 9/1326
Waste-disposal systems
installation, maintenance, cleaning, 17/2575
tips on using, 11/1727
Water barometers: 2/180
Water heaters
energy costs, cutting, 7/1093
insulating, 20/3078
maintenance and repair, 9/1410
must be vented, 11/1760
noises, cause and cure, 1/95
plastic pipe connections, 14/2182
solar heaters, 9/1416
solar system, installing, 18/2739
Water hoop: children's summer toy, 14/2191
Water leaks, auto: stopping, 11/1706
Water meters: *high reading indicates leak, 3/429*
Water pipes
leak, finding, 3/429
leak, temporary repair, 2/179
leaks, how to stop, 19/2937
noises, quieting, 5/800
tape keeps from freezing, 18/2842
tape seals pipe joints, 18/2842
Water skiing: acrobatic tricks, 18/2756
Water sports
drowning, hypothermia prevention, 1/24
skin diving, basic techniques, 17/2692
skin diving, underwater-photos guide, 19/2980
water skiing, acrobatic, 18/2756
Water-drip camera timer: *14/2116*
Waterproofing
basements, 2/210
bathtubs, caulking, 2/231
concrete-block basement walls, 3/369
Wax: removing from wood furniture, 9/1302
'Wax' casting: metal casting, 12/1786
Waxing, auto: when and how, 3/388
Weather instruments
barometer, replacing mercury tube, 7/1023
barometers, banjo, 2/182
barometers, water, 2/180
colonial weather station, 20/3060
Weatherstripping
auto wind noise and water leaks, stopping, 11/1706
caulking, selecting and using, 4/614
doors, preventing noise from wind, 5/765
energy costs, cutting, 7/1093
garage door, attaching, 4/573
stopping home heat loss, 20/3078
used as darkroom-door light seal, 14/2116
Webbing, plastic
cut with soldering iron, 12/1853
washers keep from tearing, 9/1297
Wedges
cutting on bench saw, 17/2660
how to use shims, 17/2638
Weeds: lawn improvement, 11/1688
Weekend homes
built around motor home, 19/3024
closing down for the winter, 19/3022
log cabin, how to chink logs, 19/3027
plans for five hideaway homes, 19/3016
plans for four vacation cabins, 19/3010
plumbing winterizing, 4/573
Weekend projects
cue-and-ball rack, 20/3062
house number on keymaker's sign, 20/3066
jewelry keeper, 20/3066
mail organizer for desk, 20/3062
puzzle, rubber-band-and-dowel, 20/3066
'Swiss-cheese' mountain game, 20/3062
Weight benches: how to build, 8/1162
Whale pull toy: 19/2914
Wheelbarrow planter: for patio, 14/2179
Wheels, auto
four-wheel drive tune-up, 19/2970
noises, stopping, 13/1967
seals, replacing, 9/1342
steering and suspension, servicing, 18/2786
wheel covers, stopping rattle, 1/34
Wheels, cutoff
how to make, 6/892
made from portable circular saw, 6/894
Whetstones: *truing flattened surface, 11/1735*
Whiskey barrels
bar, portable, 2/190
planter tubs, 14/2168
Whistles: slide whistle, made from metal tubing, 19/2956
White-water boating: 3/381
Whitewood: *definition of, 11/1727*
Wild game: calling, 10/1512
Wilderness areas
camping, 4/545
canoe trip, gear for, 4/581
Wildlife photography
bird photos, through-window, 3/339
outdoor photo tips, 13/2006
Williamsburg gates: *self-closing, 3/416*
Wind noise: stopping in autos, 11/1706
Wind-powered attic ventilators: 1/120
Window boxes: *held by storm-sash hangers, 3/449*
Window greenhouses: for house plants, 10/1492
Window shades
how to tighten ratchets, 10/1570
pulls, turned from plastic, 12/1814
Windows
adding windows to room, 16/2430
aluminum sashes, moisture on, 12/1920
basement, louvered, dummy frames, 8/1186
basement sashes, removing for painting, 18/2809
broken panes, replacing, 20/3068
burglar proofing, 16/2547
burglar proofing tips, 3/460
casing miters, stopping shrinkage and expansion, 15/2341
condensation, preventing, 5/697
condensation, preventing, 20/3137
fiberglass panels solve window problem, 16/2434
fixed sash, removing from frame, 7/1023
foyer window decorated with leaf-grille, 16/2434
glass, how to cut, 9/1363
glass-cutting board for shop wall, 12/1781
leaded glass, stopping water leaks, 6/847
lower sash pulls down upper sash, 1/95
lubrication guide, 11/1744
measurements guide, 12/1784
narrow windows, how to decorate, 19/3027
paint peels under window, cause and cure, 1/65
painting, 10/1488
panes, removing-installing tip, 5/689
putty, substitute for, 11/1621
putty, why it loosens, 11/1621
sash cords, replacing on upper sash, 12/1821
screens, aluminum, repairing, 18/2810
screens, combination, lubricating, 15/2341
screens, how to stretch screen wire, 16/2536
screens, moldings, mitering corners, 1/119
shutters cloth-covered to match draperies, 16/2434
skylights, installing, 10/1458
stained glass, making, 18/2766
storm windows, aluminum, repairing, 18/2810
storm windows, preventing condensation, 15/2381
storm windows, stopping heat loss, 20/3078
traverse rods, hanging, 7/1034
Windows, auto: wind noise and water leaks, stopping, 11/1706
Windshield wipers, auto: maintenance, 1/143
Windshields, auto
wind noise and water leaks, stopping, 11/1706
wiper maintenance, 1/143
Wine glasses: stemware shelf, 2/188
Wine racks
made of plexiglass, 14/2205
six-bottle rack for patio, 14/2106
three racks to make, 20/3070
with stemware shelf, 2/188
wood, with serving tray, 3/424
Winter driving
blizzards, surviving in car, 3/351
tire chains, selecting and using, 4/638
Winter mold: *removing from lawn, 1/65*
Winter sports
ice skates, sharpening jig, 10/1522
sleds, preventing rust on runners, 17/2673
snow skis, maintenance, 17/2698

Winter storage: boat layup, 3/370
Winterizing, auto: prewinter maintenance, 20/3074
Winterizing, home
caulking, selecting and using, 4/614
doors, noisy weatherstrip, 5/765
energy costs, cutting, 7/1093
insulation, installing, 10/1539
stopping heat loss, 10 ways, 20/3078
summer home, plumbing system care, 4/573
vacation homes, closing down for the winter, 19/3022
Winterizing, recreational vehicles: winter-storage tips, 16/2408
Wire
bender used in vise, 14/2240
gauge for wire-cutting pliers, 18/2857
insulation how to peel off, 1/150
kinked, straightening, 3/389
kinks removed using garden rake, 18/2857
soldering tips, 18/2743
splicing, with crimp-on connectors, 7/1072
tie wire, cut to uniform length, 3/449
Wire, screen
how to stretch, 16/2536
marking gauge, 5/656
Wire-cutting gauges: *for pliers, 18/2857*
Wiring, electrical
basics of home wiring, 7/1060
checking in old house, 3/369
connectors, from copper tubing, 11/1678
continuity tester, in screwdriver, 18/2860
dimmer switch, installing, 10/1464
door chimes, wiring, 10/1464
doorbells, testing and repairing, 7/1018
dust catcher for sawing holes in walls, 2/179
extension cords, windup reel, 8/1165
fluorescent lamps, troubleshooting, 8/1250
ground-fault circuit interrupters, 20/3082
grounded-outlet checker, 5/657
house numbers, how to illuminate, 10/1487
kitchen light fixtures, installing, 11/1728
light switches, replacing, 10/1470
night lighting beautifies yard, 20/3144
outlet box, instant, 4/553
post lamp, installing and wiring, 10/1464
post lamp, installing and wiring, 15/2296
post lamp, mercury vapor, 15/2298
soldering tips, 18/2743
spade lugs made from chain, 13/2012
wire insulation, how to peel off, 1/150
wires, crimp-on connectors, 7/1072
yard lighting for game areas, 20/3149
Wobbler minnow lures: how to make, 11/1755
Wood bending
hardboard bending, 9/1398
how to bend wood, 20/3088
on bench saw, 2/268
Wood borers: *unlikely in firewood, 11/1727*
Wood carving
birds, carving, 3/340
birds, carving sea gulls, 3/343
candle stand, flamed, 4/564
chisels, basics of using, 19/2904
4 projects, 4/604
interlocking-links sculpture, 20/3118
jewelry, 10/1556
musical creche, 9/1356
Wood chisels: basics of using, 19/2904
Wood discs
cutting on bandsaws, 1/154
cutting on drill press, 7/1040
drilling holes in circumference, 17/2664
how to cut with router, 16/2468
jigsaw cutting-guide, 14/2240
made on bandsaw and sander, 7/1001
rabbeting on table saw, 17/2664
saucer cavity, cut on table saw, 17/2660
Wood fillers: using, 8/1208
Wood finishes
abrasives, selecting and using, 1/20
applicator made from felt, 9/1322
'blooming' finish, removing, 13/1947
dark finish, lightening, 11/1657
doors, eliminating water marks from flood, 6/847
doors, exterior, weather-proof finish, 3/429
furniture, repairing scratches, 9/1302
furniture refinishing, 8/1208
guide to wood finishing, 20/3094
new wood, finishing to look old, 8/1280
piano, refinishing, 8/1280
picture frames, how to make, 8/1264
plywood finishing, 15/2244
red paint, for colonial furnishings, 14/2186
remover needs time to 'work', 14/2186
sanding techniques, 16/2503
scrapers, how to use, 16/2526
scratches, hiding, 10/1470
shoe-polish finish, 9/1397
spindles, tool to scrape off finish, 11/1621
staining, basic techniques, 18/2770
varnish, can shouldn't be shaken, 12/1839
varnish, how to use, 19/3033
varnish, preventing bubbles, 8/1280
varnish, stir don't shake, 13/1947
veneer patches, matching old finish, 4/544
wood-grain finish, simulating, 8/1208
wood-lathe application, 20/3106
working properties of common woods, 20/3122
Wood floors: how to lay, 8/1240
Wood jointers: used on 13 tricky jobs, 10/1582
Wood laminating: six projects, 11/1652
Wood lathes
basic lathe techniques, 20/3106
calipers, how to make, 17/2670
chisels, guide to, 20/3106
faceplate lathe, how to make, 20/3100
maintenance, 15/2310
scraping tool, 17/2670
tabletop hobby lathe, 20/3103
wood-finish application, 20/3106
Wood paneling: selecting and using, 13/2064
Wood planks: *walnut planks, air-curing, 19/2937*
Wood rot: *preventing in damp basements, 11/1735*
Wood scrapers: how to use, 16/2526
Wood screws: choosing the right screw, 16/2540
Wood sculpture: interlocking-links sculpture, 20/3118
Wood shakes
installing on roof, 16/2454
siding, selecting, 17/2680
Wood shapers
made from inverted router, 17/2602
radial-arm saw with molding-head fence, 15/2382
Wood shingles
installing on roof, 16/2454
red-cedar vs. asphalt shingles, 1/45
Wood siding: selecting, 17/2680
Wood staining
basic techniques, 18/2770
furniture refinishing, 8/1208
working properties of common woods, 20/3122
Wood-burning stoves
creosote stains on hearth, 18/2845
flue clogged by bister, 12/1864
getting more heat, 9/1425
installing, 18/2812
selecting, 9/1419
venting tip, 5/709
Wood-grain finishes: simulating, 8/1208
Woodboxes: dual-access box next to fireplace, 8/1228
Wooden pins: *cutting from dowels, 5/656*
Woods
firewood, how to cut, 8/1229
logs, cutting and stacking, 11/1736
lumber guide, 11/1747
properties of common woods, 20/3122
solar kiln, dries lumber, 10/1593
stains, removing, 18/2772
uncupping thin boards, 13/2017
walnut planks, air-curing, 19/2937
whitewood, definition of, 11/1727
Woodturning
basic lathe techniques, 20/3106
faceplate lathe, how to make, 20/3100
tabletop hobby lathe, 20/3103
Woodworking
abrasives, selecting and using, 1/20
adhesives, selecting and using, 1/35
bar clamps, making, 5/744
birdhouses, 3/334
book shelves, 3/396
calipers, choosing and using, 4/502
ceiling beams, making and installing, 4/624
circle scriber, 5/716
clamps, selecting and using, 5/738
claw hammers, how to use, 5/745
compound angles, cutting, 1/76
dovetail joints, how to make, 7/1026
dowel joints, how to make, 10/1572
drawers, how to make, 7/1036
furniture legs, how to attach, 11/1710
furniture refinishing, 8/1208
handsaw basics, 9/1396
hardboard, selecting and using, 9/1398
how to bend wood, 20/3088
jointers, used on 13 tricky jobs, 10/1582
joints, how to make and fit, 10/1576
joints, rabbet and dado, 10/1571
lumber guide, 11/1747
molding-cutter storage holder, 12/1900
moldings, decorating ideas, 12/1904
moldings, guide to shapes, 12/1901
nail holes, filling with toothpicks, 19/3027
nails, selecting and using, 13/1954
pencil marks, removing, 5/765
properties of common woods, 20/3122
routers, how to use, 16/2468
sabre saws, how to use, 16/2482
sanding techniques, 16/2503
sawhorse, how to build, 16/2510
sawhorse-workbench, 16/2512
scrapers, how to use, 16/2526
shaper, made from inverted router, 17/2602
shop techniques, ten, 17/2660
shop techniques, twenty-one, 17/2664
solar kiln, dries lumber, 10/1593
staining, basic techniques, 18/2770
tools to make, eight, 17/2670
veneering, three projects, 20/3044
Woodworking projects
armchair, colonial, 1/102
art prints, mounting and framing, 8/1264
backgammon and chess table, 1/146
backgammon board, veneer-covered, 20/3044
bar, built from module, 12/1890

bar, in elegant cabinet, 2/194
bar, under basement heat pipes, 2/185
bar, whiskey-barrel, 2/190
barn-siding picture frames, 9/1284
barometer, banjo, 2/182
bed table-buffet, 2/246
bell shelf, colonial, 9/1356
bench, pine and maple, 1/90
birds, carving from wood, 3/340
birds, carving sea gulls, 3/343
block toy, airplane, 19/2921
block toys, cars and trucks, 19/2911
bookends, initial, 3/409
bookends, photographic, 3/406
bookrack, colonial, 3/410
bookrack, desk carousel, 3/412
bookstand, colonial, 3/415
bootjack, Lincoln replica, 5/650
breakfront, built from module, 12/1890
bumblebee pull-toy, 15/2355
bunk bed, children's, built-in chest, 5/674
butcher block, 3/468
butler's table, 3/472
cabinet holds security safe, 3/456
candle stand, flamed cube, 4/564
candle stand, holiday, 4/562
candle stand, musical, 4/628
canister, grocery-bin, 10/1594
chair, Lincoln, splint-seat, 5/650
chairs, swivel, for dining set, 7/992
cheese tray, 9/1352
chess set and cabinet, 5/658
chest, Spanish, 5/665
chests, decorated with moldings, 5/662
children's block cars, 9/1352
china cupboard, 6/888
circus-train pull toy, 15/2348
clock, grandmother, 5/754
clock, shelf, Connecticut, 5/750
clock, wall, 'heirloom', 5/766
clock, wall, plywood face, 5/768
coat tree, giraffe, 19/2914
coffee table, for patio, with stools, 6/816
coffee table, lattice strips decorate, 10/1462
coffee table, with box stools, 6/804
comb box, colonial, 6/824
cookbook caddy, 10/1597
crayon holder, 9/1360
creche, musical, 9/1356
cutlery cupboard, colonial, 10/1600
cutting board for kitchen, 10/1596
desk, campaign, 7/964
desk, hinged, folds against wall, 6/935
desk, rolltop, 6/954
desk, trestle, 6/951
desk, two-level, with secretary return, 6/935
desk-chest, opens into work center, 6/935
desk-hobby bench, built from module, 12/1890
dining table, gateleg, 7/983
dining table, oaken, pedestal, 7/987
dining table, trestle, with benches, 7/998
dining table, trestle, with swivel chairs, 7/992
dollhouse, 12/1830
dollhouse, English farmhouse, 19/2914
dry sink, colonial, 7/1050
ducks and dachshund pull-toys, 15/2352
etagere, 8/1154
floater frames, making, 8/1277
gossip bench, early American, 9/1365
grill, portable electric, 9/1370
gun cabinet, 9/1378
hi-fi stereo wall, 4/488
house number on keymaker's sign, 20/3066
hutch table, early American, 10/1516
jewel box and overnight caddy, 10/1567
jewelry box, heart-shaped, 9/1360
jewelry box, musical, 10/1562
jewelry box, three-drawer, 10/1567
jewelry box, veneer-covered, 20/3044
jewelry keeper, 20/3066
laminating wood, 11/1652
lamp, candlestand, 11/1664
lamp table, with lighted planter, 14/2172
lazy Susan table server, 11/1704
letter rack, colonial, 11/1712
lowboy, 11/1739
mail organizer for desk, 20/3062
mirror, heart-shaped, 9/1360
mirror, shaving, Lincoln's, 12/1840
mirror, vanity, Lincoln's, 12/1840
nesting tables, four Sheraton replicas, 13/1958
party tables, nesting, 13/2070
party tables, stacking, 13/2074
pipe rack and humidor, 9/1352
planters, rustic, 9/1356
playing-card holder, 3/452
pool table, bumper-pool, 15/2264
pool table, full-size, 15/2256
pull toy, Hale the whale, 19/2914
puzzle, rubber-band-and-dowel, 20/3066
ring caddy, 9/1360
room divider, built from module, 12/1890
room divider with lighted planter, 14/2172
sculpture, interlocking links, 20/3118
server, early American, 17/2564
serving cart, 17/2570
sewing cabinet, chairside, 17/2582
sewing cabinet, for spools, 17/2585
sewing center, built from module, 12/1890
shaving console, early American, 17/2616
silverware tray, 10/1598
silverware-and-napkin caddy, 10/1594
snack tables, folding, 17/2710
stamp and pencil holder, for desk, 6/931
stool, rustic slab, 18/2793
storage trays, swing-out, 19/2949
'Swiss-cheese' mountain game, 20/3062
table lamp, cobbler's bench, 11/1668
table lamp, Spanish-style, 11/1662
table lamp, wood, six-in-one, 11/1672
tambour table, French Provincial, 13/1974
toolbox, contemporary, 19/2896
towel racks, 19/2906
toybox, circus-wagon, 19/2914
toyboxes, 4 styles from 1 plan, 3/430
toy dump truck, wooden, 7/1059
toy kiddie car, 9/1351
toy kitchen appliances—refrigerator, sink, stove, 19/2908
toy train, wood-block, 19/2914
train engine, puffs 'smoke', 19/2914
tray, folding, 19/2944
tray, veneer-covered, 20/3044
treasure chest, 9/1352
tree-holder for magazines and newspapers, 11/1758
valet, dresser-top, 9/1352
vanity center, built from module, 12/1890
weather station, colonial, 20/3060
wheelbarrow planter, 14/2179
wine rack, wall-hung, 20/3070
wood carving, 4 projects, 4/604

Work supports: for bench saws, roller top, 2/294

Workbenches
basic workbench, 20/3124
bench hook, how to make, 17/2670
cabinet bench for small shop, 20/3138
carpeting pads bench top, 17/2673
combination bench and power-tool stand, 20/3132
deluxe workbench and wall cabinet, 20/3126
foldaway hobby center, 10/1454
garage storage wall with benchtop, 18/2794
grinder mount swings out of way, 13/2069
how to lay out workshops, 20/3142
modelmaker's cabinet workshop, 17/2656
sawhorse-workbench, 16/2512
tailgate bench for station wagons, 20/3131

Workshops
basement shops, how to heat, 16/2467
combination workbench and power-tool stand, 20/3132
electric motors, guide to, 13/1924
electric motors, repairing, 13/1926
electric motors, speed reducer, 13/1929
hand tools, selecting, 19/2899
how to lay out shops, 20/3142
modelmaker's cabinet workshop, 17/2656
organizer 'drawers', 17/2659
safety in the shop, 16/2490
storage racks, for pipe, molding, dowels, 5/778
trays, swing-out, under shelves, 2/232

World globes: *replacing light bulb inside, 19/3027*

Wrap-around sofa: for family room, 8/1178

Wreath window hanging: for Christmas, 5/702

Wrecking bars
hose protects wood surface, 3/480
used as toolbox handles, 3/449

Wrenches
aid in carrying paint cans, 2/291
Allen hex-wrenches, used on nuts in tight quarters, 11/1644
Allen wrench, used as door bolt-latch, 10/1555
basics of using, 19/2903
box-end, held on loose-leaf rings, 9/1297
emergency wrench, from bolt and nuts, 17/2639
monkey, used as table-saw stop, 3/433
open-end, used as tire spreader, 8/1192
open-end wrench, ratcheting movement, 13/1936
pipe wrench, improvised with pliers, 18/2857
socket wrenches, Allen wrench T-handle, 16/2502
socket wrenches, extensions for cramped areas, 16/2560
socket-head wrench, handle for, 4/501

Wrought iron: railings, installing, 15/2388

Y

Yard benches: wood, 2/264

Yard buildings
cabana poolhouse, 3/476
children's playhouse, 14/2200
fence with built-in toolhouse, 8/1199
garden shelters, 9/1330
garden work shelter, 9/1332
gazebo cookout center, 9/1346
gazebos and screen house, 18/2821
grill shelter-house, 9/1375
metal sheds, preserving paint, 18/2752
patio storage gazebo, 14/2110
poolhouse for year-round use, 15/2270

Yard decks
accessories and structures to build, 14/2110
diving deck, for above-ground swimming pool, 18/2832
fence, louvered, 15/2336
how to build, 14/2102
painting masonry, 12/1778
privacy screens, 15/2334
swimming-pool deck and privacy wall, 15/2280
two decks, for front and rear, 14/2098
wood platforms, how to build, 6/914
wood platforms, how to build, 6/920
wood platforms, two-level, 6/924
Yard firepits: circular brick firepit, 8/1222
Yard furniture
chairs, aluminum-and-canvas, 5/644
washers keep webbing from tearing, 9/1297
Yard insect traps: black-light trap, 10/1538
Yard landscaping
choosing trees, 19/2952
shrubbery, growing, 11/1679
techniques, 11/1675
Yard lighting
hanging lamp for patio, 14/2110
lighting game areas, 20/3149
night lighting beautifies yard, 20/3144
post lamp, for shrubbery, 15/2301
post lamp, installing and wiring, 15/2296
post lamp, installing and wiring, 10/1464
post lamp, mercury vapor, 15/2298
post lamp, wooden, for patio, 14/2110
Yard machines
de-thatching machines, using, 11/1698
engines, servicing, 8/1128
hand mowers, maintenance, 9/1394
hedge trimmer, using rotary mower, 12/1835
leaf cart, made from old screens, 10/1515
mowers, gasoline, straining, 7/982
mowers, preparing for mowing season, 13/1937
mowers, reel, sharpening, 20/3137
mowers, repair and maintenance, 13/1944
mowers, two-cycle, do they harm grass?, 5/649
riding mowers, choosing, 13/1940
snowblowers, using properly, 17/2712
snowplow, for auto bumper, 18/2724
tractor hydraulic lift, for bulldozer blade, 19/2924
tractor utility trailer, 19/2928
tractors, ignition systems, testing, 13/1944
Yard ornaments: polar sundial, 18/2826
Yard paths
how to build, 14/2084
stepping stones, raising and leveling, 18/2789
Yard putting greens: made from artificial turf, 15/2356
Yard retaining walls: how to build, 16/2446
Yard swings
hangs on A-frame, 15/2285
two-seater swing, 18/2836
Yard tables
barbecue table, wraparound, 2/174
coffee table, with stools, 6/816
picnic table, folds flat for storage, 14/2150
picnic table, hexagon shape, 14/2159
picnic table, made from chimney blocks, 14/2152
picnic table, octagon shape, 14/2159
picnic table, rejuvenating weathered redwood, 11/1685
picnic table-and-benches, folds up, 14/2156
stowaway tables, two, 13/2013
'You-haul' kiddie car pickup: 9/1351

Z

Zip kits: auto carburetor tune-up, 4/590
Zippers: *camera bag zipper-tab, 14/2116*
Zizzers: Christmas tree ornament and gift, 5/702
Zodiac panel: hanging divider, 18/2759
Zone heaters
getting more heat, 9/1425
repairing, 9/1407
selecting, 9/1419
Zoned heating
choosing space heaters, 9/1419
saves home fuel bills, 9/1430

METRIC CONVERSION

Conversion factors can be carried so far they become impractical. In cases below where an entry is exact it is followed by an asterisk (*). Where considerable rounding off has taken place, the entry is followed by a + or a - sign.

CUSTOMARY TO METRIC

Linear Measure

inches	millimeters
1/16	1.5875*
1/8	3.2
3/16	4.8
1/4	6.35*
5/16	7.9
3/8	9.5
7/16	11.1
1/2	12.7*
9/16	14.3
5/8	15.9
11/16	17.5
3/4	19.05*
13/16	20.6
7/8	22.2
15/16	23.8
1	25.4*

inches	centimeters
1	2.54*
2	5.1
3	7.6
4	10.2
5	12.7*
6	15.2
7	17.8
8	20.3
9	22.9
10	25.4*
11	27.9
12	30.5

feet	centimeters	meters
1	30.48*	.3048*
2	61	.61
3	91	.91
4	122	1.22
5	152	1.52
6	183	1.83
7	213	2.13
8	244	2.44
9	274	2.74
10	305	3.05
50	1524*	15.24*
100	3048*	30.48*

1 yard =
.9144* meters
1 rod =
5.0292* meters
1 mile =
1.6 kilometers
1 nautical mile =
1.852* kilometers

Fluid Measure

(Milliliters [ml] and cubic centimeters [cc or cu cm] are equivalent, but it is customary to use milliliters for liquids.)

1 cu in = 16.39 ml
1 fl oz = 29.6 ml
1 cup = 237 ml
1 pint = 473 ml
1 quart = 946 ml
= .946 liters
1 gallon = 3785 ml
= 3.785 liters
Formula (exact):
fluid ounces × 29.573 529 562 5*
= milliliters

Weights

ounces	grams
1	28.3
2	56.7
3	85
4	113
5	142
6	170
7	198
8	227
9	255
10	283
11	312
12	340
13	369
14	397
15	425
16	454

Formula (exact):
ounces × 28.349 523 125* =
grams

pounds	kilograms
1	.45
2	.9
3	1.4
4	1.8
5	2.3
6	2.7
7	3.2
8	3.6
9	4.1
10	4.5

1 short ton (2000 lbs) =
907 kilograms (kg)
Formula (exact):
pounds × .453 592 37* =
kilograms

Volume

1 cu in = 16.39 cubic centimeters (cc)
1 cu ft = 28 316.7 cc
1 bushel = 35 239.1 cc
1 peck = 8 809.8 cc

Area

1 sq in = 6.45 sq cm
1 sq ft = 929 sq cm
= .093 sq meters
1 sq yd = .84 sq meters
1 acre = 4 046.9 sq meters
= .404 7 hectares
1 sq mile = 2 589 988 sq meters
= 259 hectares
= 2.589 9 sq kilometers

Kitchen Measure

1 teaspoon = 4.93 milliliters (ml)
1 Tablespoon = 14.79 milliliters (ml)

Miscellaneous

1 British thermal unit (Btu) (mean)
= 1 055.9 joules
1 calorie (mean) = 4.19 joules
1 horsepower = 745.7 watts
= .75 kilowatts
caliber (diameter of a firearm's bore in hundredths of an inch)
= .254 millimeters (mm)
1 atmosphere pressure = 101 325* pascals (newtons per sq meter)
1 pound per square inch (psi) = 6 895 pascals
1 pound per square foot = 47.9 pascals
1 knot = 1.85 kilometers per hour
25 miles per hour = 40.2 kilometers per hour
50 miles per hour = 80.5 kilometers per hour
75 miles per hour = 120.7 kilometers per hour